Dayspring

Dayspring

Daily Devotions from the Four Gospels

JOHN T. SEAMANDS

FRANCIS ASBURY PRESS
of Zondervan Publishing House

Grand Rapids, Michigan

DAYSPRING
Copyright © 1989 by John T. Seamands

Francis Asbury Press is an imprint of Zondervan Publishing House, 1415 Lake Drive, S.E., Grand Rapids, Michigan 49506.

Library of Congress Cataloging in Publication Data

Seamands, John T.
    Dayspring : daily devotions from the four Gospels / John T. Seamands.
      p.   cm.
    ISBN 0-310-51410-X
    1. Devotional calendars. I. Title.
BV4811.S375   1989
242'.2–dc20
                                          89-35769
                                            CIP

In many places the author has paraphrased Scripture. However, many Scripture quotations are from the Revised Standard Version of the Bible, Copyright © 1946, 1952, 1971, 1973 by the Division of Christian Education, National Council of Churches of Christ in the United States of America, and are used by permission.

Edited by Robert D. Wood

Printed in the United States of America

89 90 91 92 93 94 / AK / 10 9 8 7 6 5 4 3 2 1

PREFACE

Daily devotions, consisting of Bible study and prayer, constitute one of the most essential elements of the Christian life. Without a consistent, meaningful devotional program, one cannot maintain an effective relationship with Christ or grow in the grace and knowledge of our Lord. Nothing can take the place of the daily quiet time. Motivated by this conviction, I have written this book of daily devotions as a tool to help the Christian begin the day with God. Certain basic ideas have been kept in mind throughout the writing.

First, it is essential that a set of devotions be based upon the Word of God. It is God's Word that is authoritative and life-giving. Thus at the beginning of each devotion a particular Scripture passage is suggested. It is hoped that the reader will first open God's Word and carefully read the portion that is assigned before going on to read the comments. The devotion is not intended to be a commentary on the passage—many excellent commentaries are already available—but it is based on one particular thought inherent in the passage. Explanation of the verses is given only when needed to drive home the main thought.

Again, it is necessary to read the Word of God in some progressive fashion, rather than jumping around from one passage to another throughout the Bible. So I have chosen to write this set of devotions on the four New Testament Gospels in order to give plan and progress to the total study. The devotions on Matthew's gospel were previously published in 1976 by Abingdon Press under the title *Power for the Day*. Many readers who benefited from these meditations encouraged me to go on and do the same for the remaining three Gospels, making enough material for an entire year. This publication is the result.

The new devotions on Mark, Luke, and John's gospels have been added to the meditations on Matthew's gospel. It is hoped that by the time the reader has completed this study, he or she will have captured something of the spirit of the gospel writers and their different perspectives of the life and ministry of our Lord.

Furthermore, it is essential that a set of devotions stimulate the thinking of the readers and challenge them to greater surrender and service. It is my prayer that through these meditations those who do not know Christ as Savior will come to know Him in a personal way, and that those who already know Him will enter into a more intimate and dynamic relationship with our Lord. After reading each devotion, it will be helpful for the individual to apply the challenge to his or her own life and make it the central thought of a closing prayer. In cases where the book is being used for family devotions, I recommend that the members discuss the implications of the meditation and ways it may be implemented in their own lives.

God bless you as you make this exciting journey through the four Gospels with the guidance and help of the Holy Spirit.

John T. Seamands

The book of the genealogy of Jesus Christ (v. 1).

The genealogy of just any person does not provide inspiration for devotional reading. But there are significant factors in the genealogy of our Lord that require attention.

Matthew is writing to the Jews and so he traces the lineage of Christ back to Abraham, father of the Jewish nation. As Abraham was the source of blessing to many nations, so Christ would now be the center of universal blessing. With Abraham God had made the first covenant, and now through Christ God inaugurates the new covenant.

Matthew seeks to portray Jesus as the King of Israel, so he presents the birth roll of Jesus as the genealogy of a king. It is designed to show that Jesus was the lawful heir to the throne of David. Joseph is proved to be the descendant of David and because of his marriage to Mary, her Son becomes in all reality the "Son of David," the King.

Though rejected by His enemies, Christ will ultimately appear in power and glory as the King of kings and will establish His kingdom of righteousness forever.

Matthew also seeks to portray Jesus as *the Savior of the world*, so he does something very unusual for a Jewish genealogy. He includes the names of four women, namely, Tamar, Rahab, Ruth, and Bathsheba. Three of these were guilty of gross sin and two were members of hated, heathen races. If Matthew had ransacked the pages of the Old Testament, he could not have found four more improbable candidates as ancestors for Jesus Christ. But, surely, there is something most significant here. At the very beginning of his gospel, Matthew shows us in symbol that the King whom the Jews rejected was a Savior who identified himself with sinful humanity, who offered pardon and blessing to all penitent sinners, male and female, Jew and Gentile, king and harlot.

Thought for the day: *The Son of God became the Son of Man in order that the sons of men might become the sons of God.*

Matthew 1:18–25   JANUARY 2

You shall call his name Jesus ... his name shall be called Emmanuel (vv. 21, 23).

In every way the birth of Christ was unusual. All persons have two parents; Jesus had only one. He was "conceived by the Holy Spirit, born of the virgin Mary." Expectant parents often are not sure of the sex of their baby. Mary knew she was going to have a son, even from the time of His conception. Usually the parents pick out the name of their child, but God Himself chose the name of this Child.

Mary's baby was given two names. When the angel appeared to Joseph in a dream, he gave the explicit command, "You shall call his name *Jesus,* for he will save his people from their sins." "Jesus" is the Greek form of the Hebrew word "Joshua," which means "Jehovah is salvation." Other men had borne the same name before, notably the great deliverer, Joshua, who had won astonishing victories over the peoples of Canaan; and also Joshua, the high priest, who had aided in the restoration of Jerusalem. But now One was to appear who was to be the embodiment of all that the name implied; He was to save people from the guilt and power of sin. The name Jesus, therefore, clearly signifies that Christ is the Savior.

The second name was given to Christ centuries before His birth. Under the inspiration of the Holy Spirit, the prophet Isaiah predicted that God would grant deliverance to His people. A virgin would bring forth a son who would be called "Emmanuel," which means, "God with us." God could not deliver His people from a distance by divine decree. He had to leave His throne in glory, take upon Himself human form, and become personally involved in our human predicament. He had to completely identify Himself with our weakness, our temptations, our suffering, and our sin. Only thus could He become our Savior.

Thought for the day: *Jesus is the only One who ever fully lives up to His name.*

Matthew 2:1–12   JANUARY 3

Wise men from the East came to Jerusalem (v. 1).

The birth of Christ became the center of cosmic interest. The educational world was represented by the wise men; the peasants, by the shepherds; royalty, by King Herod. Nature was represented in their gifts—gold, frankincense, and myrrh—and by the star which led the way. The heavens were represented by the angelic choir; the lower creation, by the cattle around the manger.

When the wise men from the East came to Jerusalem, they asked King Herod, "Where is he who has been born king of the Jews?" This is the first question recorded in the New Testament. The first question recorded in the Old Testament was that put by God to Adam, when the latter had tasted of the forbidden fruit: "Adam, where are you?" Notice the change in emphasis in these two questions. "Where are you?" That was God in search of fallen humankind. "Where is he?" That was sinful humankind in search of the Savior. The twofold nature of salvation is hereby stressed. God always takes the initiative, but we must respond in obedience and faith. When the seeking Savior and the seeking sinner meet face to face, then there is salvation.

When the wise men found the baby Jesus in Bethlehem, they fell at His feet and worshiped Him. Then they opened their treasures and offered Him costly gifts. The result? "They departed to their own country by another way."

If we come to see Jesus and tarry to worship Him, we will always go back a different way than that by which we came. If we come by the road of hate, we will return by the road of love. If we come by the road of selfishness, we will go back by the road of self-denial. If we come by the road of sin, we will return by the road of righteousness. For no person can meet Christ and be the same. We will become new persons in Christ, and all things will become new.

Thought for the day: *It is not fools, but the wise, who seek Jesus.*

Matthew 2:13–23   JANUARY 4

Herod is about to search for the child, to destroy him (v. 13).

In the beautiful Christmas story much good and evil are mixed. From the East came devout men bringing princely gifts, with reverence in their hearts and adoration on their lips. Lurking in the shadows was the evil King Herod—cunning and treacherous, quick to lie, and savage to destroy. History and life are pictured here, with God's plan accepted by some and opposed by others, with love and hatred side by side in the presence of goodness and beauty.

When the wise men came inquiring, "Where is he who has been born king of the Jews?" and adding, *"We have come to worship him,"* Herod also sought to know the whereabouts of the child. He explained, *"I too [will] come and worship him."* His words were identical with those of the wise men, but the inner motive of his heart was completely different. The three from the East were devout men, looking for the coming of the Messiah and had come to pay sincere homage to Him. As for Herod, he had no intention of worshiping the child. He was determined to destroy Jesus because he felt that his kingship was threatened.

If people are determined to go their own way, if they see in Christ someone who is a threat to their lifestyle and selfish ambitions, then they will do their best to eliminate Him.

However, throughout the Christmas story, as in all of life, we see the marvelous providence of God, keeping watch over His own and working out His eternal plan. Before Herod gave the order for the slaughter of the children, God had already warned Joseph to "take the child and his mother, and flee to Egypt." Upon the death of Herod, God told Joseph to return to Israel, but when Archelaus was appointed ruler over Judea, God commanded Joseph to withdraw to the district of Galilee. There Jesus remained until He was ready to begin His public ministry.

Thought for the day: *Our plots cannot overthrow God's plans.*

Matthew 3:1–10   JANUARY 5

In those days came John the Baptist, preaching (v. 1).

In many ways John the Baptist was the ideal preacher. He was a man with a message for his generation.

John the Baptist was a *commissioned* preacher, "a man sent from God" (John 1:6). He came both as a herald to announce the advent of the King, and as a forerunner to prepare the way. In those days, when roads were few and poor, it was the practice to send an officer before the monarch to command the repair of the highways. So John, by his call to repentance, was preparing the people for the public ministry of Jesus. He knew his divinely appointed task, and he sought to fulfill it.

There is much aimlessness in the Christian ministry today. We need commissioned preachers who have a strong sense of divine impulsion and purpose.

John the Baptist was a *courageous* preacher. He fearlessly denounced evil wherever he found it—in the palace, in the temple, in the crowd. When Herod sinned by taking his brother's wife, John rebuked him. When the Sadducees and Pharisees tried to hide their sin beneath a mass of ritual and formalism, John uncovered their hypocrisy. When ordinary people were indifferent to the claims of God, John sought to arouse their conscience. He preached that all should repent, that is, turn away from their sin and toward God.

John was also a *consistent* preacher. His mode of life was in keeping with the solemn character of his office. He clothed himself in camel's skin, and ate locusts and wild honey. He did not advocate that people become ascetics, but he did call them from a life of self-indulgence and sin. So he himself set an example of self-denial and discipline. He embodied the message he preached. The man and the message were one.

May God grant us more preachers like John the Baptist in our pulpits today.

Thought for the day: *The best way to communicate an idea is to demonstrate it in person.*

Matthew 3:11—17   JANUARY 6

He will baptize you with the Holy Spirit and with fire (v. 11).

There are two baptisms mentioned in this passage: the baptism with water for repentance, and the baptism with the Holy Spirit and fire. In the first baptism, the agent is the minister of God, the subject is the penitent sinner, and the element is water. In the second baptism, the agent is Christ, the subject is the child of God, and the element is the Holy Spirit.

The key to the understanding of this baptism is in the word "fire." Fire is one of the many symbols of the Holy Spirit that are used in the Scriptures. In the Old Testament there is the symbol of *air* or *breath*. The Holy Spirit is the Breath of God within us, signifying the life-giving ministry of the Spirit. Then there is the symbol of *oil*, which signifies the anointing of the individual by the Holy Spirit for a particular task. In the New Testament we have the symbol of *water*, which portrays

12

the washing away of our sins. Finally, we have the symbol of *fire*, which is perhaps the most dramatic and picturesque of all the symbols. It describes the refining ministry of the Holy Spirit.

Sin is twofold in its nature. It resides in the *action* and also in the *attitude*. It is in the *outer conduct* as well as in the *inner character*. It is a matter of *transgression* as well as of *disposition*. There are the sins of the *flesh* and the sins of the *spirit*. Thus we need deliverance not only from outward sinful actions but also from our sinful disposition. Consequently, the ministry of the Holy Spirit is twofold. In *regeneration*, the Holy Spirit acts like *water*, cleansing away the guilt of our outer transgressions. In *sanctification*, He acts like *fire*, purging away our inner impurity and refining our dispositions. Both ministries are essential to our full redemption.

Thought for the day: *The baptism with the Holy Spirit is not a spiritual luxury, but a necessity for effective living.*

Matthew 4:1–11   JANUARY 7

Jesus was . . . tempted by the devil (v. 1).

Temptation is an experience common to all of us. Even the Son of God was not immune to it. "In every respect [He] has been tempted as we are" (Heb. 4:15).

We must not suppose that this was the only time that Jesus was tempted. Luke, in his gospel, makes it clear that after the conflict in the wilderness, "the devil . . . departed from him *until an opportune time.*" (4:13). Satan was certainly working through Peter when he tried to turn Christ away from the cross (Mark 8:33). He was present in the Garden of Gethsemane as Jesus faced the shame and the agony of the crucifixion.

The timing of Christ's temptation was significant. It took place immediately after His baptism, when the Spirit of God descended upon Him, and a voice from heaven declared,

"This is my beloved Son, with whom I am well pleased." Jesus had just been assured of His divine sonship and become conscious of His supernatural powers. We must be ever mindful that seasons of highest spiritual exaltation are often followed by our greatest trials and temptations. Every advancement in life, every increase in privilege is accompanied by some new danger to the soul.

The three temptations that came to Jesus are typical of all the attacks of Satan. There was the *temptation to enjoy*, the enticement to satisfy normal physical desires in the wrong way. There was the *temptation to do the spectacular thing*, to presume upon the providential care of God. And there was the *temptation to be somebody*, by satisfying one's personal ambitions on the devil's terms through compromise. All temptations are merely variations of these three basic approaches.

Jesus overcame temptation with the Word of God. Each time He answered the devil with the statement, "It is written." The Word of God is powerful, like a two-edged sword. It can break through the guard of the Enemy and disarm him.

Jesus overcame Satan so we can also overcome in His name.

Thought for the day: *Temptation is the proving ground of Christian character.*

Matthew 4:12–17   JANUARY 8

Repent, for the kingdom of heaven is at hand (v. 17).

True repentance consists of two basic elements. First, it involves *genuine sorrow for sin*. This is more than just a sense of remorse for the consequences of sin, or feeling sorrow that we have been caught. It means a whole new attitude toward sin. We begin to see that sin is not just a frailty of human nature, but is a transgression of divine law. To sin is to flout God's command and to trample on His love. Sin is so terrible that it sent the Son of God to a cross. When we realize this, we can no longer treat sin lightly. It is a moral tragedy.

Repentance also involves the *complete forsaking of all known sin* in our lives. It means being so sick and tired of sin that we resolve, by God's grace, to give it up.

The farmers of South India suffer severe losses from monkeys that swarm over their peanut crops. Their religion will not permit the farmers to kill the monkeys, so instead they try to discourage the animals. The farmer buries a small earthen pot in the ground and fills it with peanuts. When a monkey comes along, it tries to put its hand into the pot, but the opening is too small. So it makes its hand as small as possible, squeezes it into the pot, and grabs a handful of peanuts. But when it tries to pull its hand out, it is now too big, so it is caught. The farmer rushes out and gives the monkey a few hard hits with a cane. The monkey struggles and struggles, but it can't get free. Finally, it turns loose of the peanuts, makes its hand small once again, and pulls it out. At last the monkey is free.

Only when we are willing to let go of our sins and turn our backs on the old life can we find complete forgiveness and deliverance.

Thought for the day: *Sin is not a pimple on the chin; it is a cancer of the heart.*

Matthew 4:18–22   JANUARY 9

Follow me, and I will make you fishers of men (v. 19).

Here we have the account of Jesus calling His first disciples. They were two sets of brothers—Peter and Andrew, James and John. What a magnificent foursome they eventually turned out to be! Three of them became writers of the New Testament and leaders in the early church; the fourth,

Andrew, held a less conspicuous position but was an effective soul-winner for Christ.

We must not suppose that this was the first time these men met Jesus. According to John's account, at least some of them were already disciples of John the Baptist. No doubt they had all heard Jesus preach at some time and witnessed His miracles. They already believed that He was the Messiah. But now came the moment of decision. Jesus challenged them to follow Him and become His disciples.

It is interesting that Jesus called these men when they were hard at work. Our Lord did not go through the streets and gather the idle. He had a job to be done, a mission to fulfill. He needed people who were used to hard work, who were courageous and perseverant. So he chose four rugged fishermen, accustomed to toiling in the night hours and unafraid of the fury of the sea. These were qualifications needed to make them effective fishers of people and builders of the church.

The response of the four was immediate. Twice the account says that "immediately they . . . followed him." There was no delay on their part; no hint of "Now, Lord, give us until next week to think this over," or, "Master, we need to talk this over with the family first." When the call came, they responded at once. This, of course, involved considerable sacrifice on their part. They had to leave behind their nets, boats, and families. They had to give up their income and accept a life of faith. But to them partnership with Christ was worth everything.

Thought for the day: *Christ's* call *demands our* all.

Matthew 5:1−12   **JANUARY 10**

Blessed are those who. . . . (v. 4)

The word *blessed* describes the type of joy which is self-contained, which has its secret within itself. It is completely

16

independent of the chances and changes of life. Blessedness is not a recompense for goodness, but a natural consequence. It is the concept of a happiness that is true because our deepest needs are satisfied by the gracious gifts and provision of God. It is a state of contentment that is the result of the grace of God and a proper relationship to Him.

Blessed are "the poor in spirit," those who humbly recognize their spiritual poverty, their absolute inadequacy and helplessness, their complete dependence upon God. They shall enter the kingdom.

Blessed are "those who mourn" for their own sins and for the sufferings of others, for they shall be comforted.

Blessed are "the meek," those whose instincts, impulses, and energies are controlled or harnessed by God, for they shall be great among people.

Blessed are those who long for total righteousness as a starving person longs for food, and one perishing of thirst longs for water, for they will be truly satisfied—not with a snack but with a feast.

Blessed are "the merciful." They will receive mercy in return.

Blessed are those whose motives are unmixed, like unadulterated water or metal without alloy, for they shall see God.

Blessed are "the peacemakers," those who establish right relationships between persons, who bridge gulfs and heal breaches, for they are doing a God-like work.

Blessed are they who suffer for a righteous cause; they will receive a prophet-like reward.

Thought for the day: *Happiness depends upon happenings; joy comes from God.*

Matthew 5:13–16   JANUARY 11

You are ... salt ... you are ... light (vv. 13, 14).

17

In the Beatitudes Jesus tells us what we are to be *in ourselves*—"blessed are. . . ." Now He tells us what we are to be *to the world*—"you are." First, what we are *inwardly in character*; then what we are *outwardly in influence*. The Beatitudes begin with self-renunciation—"blessed are the poor in spirit." Then Jesus offers self-expression in world-encompassing terms. Self-expression that has self-renunciation at its center is safe, both for the individual and for the world.

Salt and light represent what every Christian should be—a *penetrating* and an *illuminating* influence; something to be *felt* and something to be *seen*.

In the ancient world, salt was the commonest of all preservatives. Salt saves from putrefaction, decay, corruption. Likewise, the Christian saves the world from moral putrefaction. Society holds together only because of the influence of God's people. Take God's people out of society and society decays and rots.

Salt also saves from *insipidity*. Food without salt is insipid and sickening. Salt brings seasoning to food; it lends flavor. The world has lost its savor; we go from thing to thing and from thrill to thrill to put seasoning back into dull, tasteless lives. Christians bring flavor and zest back into life. They make life worth living.

Christians are also "the light of the world." We must shine with the reflection of Christ's light. Light is meant to be seen; it exposes, it guides, it warns. Christianity is something to be seen; there can be no such thing as secret discipleship. The Christian must be an example to others; we must warn others of impending danger. The good deeds of the Christian are attractive, pointing to God.

The influence of Christian character is thus twofold: a silent, hidden, and pervasive thing reaching into the very fibre of our thoughts and outlook; and it is open, manifest, lighting the outer life of our affairs and the world.

18

Thought for the day: *What the soul is to the body, the Christian is to the world.*

Matthew 5:17—20

I have come [not] to abolish ... but to fulfill (v. 17).

Since the Exile, the Law had played an increasing role in the lives of the Jewish people. A new class of scribes had appeared whose task was to study and explain the Law, and to show its application to every possible situation in life. They made it their perennial business to reduce the great principles of the Law to literally thousands upon thousands of rules and regulations. The "Scribes and the Pharisees" regarded this man-made mass of regulations as possessing a sanctity and authority equal to that of the Mosaic Law itself.

Our Lord accepted without question the divine origin of the Mosaic Law, but at the same time He attacked Pharisaism. Its formalism destroyed the true meaning of the Law. Its legalism made a Jew's duty both too heavy and too light a burden, for it encumbered the good with a load of detail, but made the way easy for the formalist and the hypocrite to evade the spirit of the Law. Jesus kept the Mosaic Law perfectly, but He repeatedly broke the rules and regulations laid down by the scribes; and repeatedly He condemned them.

Jesus emphasized the permanent character of the Law in its basic principles. He declared that He had come not to amend or abrogate the Law but to fulfill it; that is, to complete the partial meaning, and to give us deeper understanding of the Law. The picture described here is that of filling a partly filled vessel to the brim.

Our regard for the Law, our righteousness, must be of a higher quality than that of the scribes and Pharisees. For them it was a matter of external observance, of form, of pretense. Christ insists that true righteousness is a matter of the heart, of motive, of desire as well as of external performance. The end of the Law is to know and to do God's will in every situation in life.

Thought for the day: *The spirit of the Law matters; the letter is often an escape.*

Matthew 5:21–26   JANUARY 13

It was said to men of old ... but I say to you (vv. 21, 22).

The contrast here is between a superficial interpretation and a profound interpretation of the Law. Jesus is not contrasting the Mosaic Law with His, but the scribal oral interpretation of the Law as over against His. Notice that each time Jesus begins with the words, "It is *said*," not "It is *written*."

The scribes and Pharisees were concerned only with external acts. Jesus traces every deed to the underlying motive and thought. Law, He insists, must be understood in internal or spiritual terms. Righteousness of the Law is righteousness of the spirit. Obedience to the Law has a dual character: the inner attitude or motive, the causative element of obedience; and the other, visible act, the effect of inner righteousness. The scribes considered only the outer aspect of righteousness. The Law demands right inner spirit as well as right external action. It always connects motive and act.

For his first illustration, Jesus refers to the law against murder. He goes beyond the outer act to the inner attitude. Anger, says Jesus, is equivalent to murder. The person who is angry with another, who insults another with words of contempt, who seek to destroy one's good name with malicious slander may never have committed a murder in action, but nevertheless is a murderer at heart.

Jesus also insists that the Law must be interpreted positively, not negatively. Don't simply avoid murder and hate—that is negative—but be positive and promote recon-

20

ciliation between yourself and another. And notice carefully that Jesus does not say, "Go to your brother *if you have something against him,* " but "Go to your brother if you remember that *he has something against you.*" This is the implementation of the Beatitudes. A correct human relationship is essential to genuine worship of God. God will not accept our gift at the altar, however costly it may be, until we have first been reconciled with others.

Thought for the day: *Don't hold on to a grudge—it's too heavy.*

Matthew 5:27—32   **JANUARY 14**

Every one who looks at a woman lustfully has already committed adultery (v. 28).

The Law says, "You shall not *commit* adultery." Jesus says, "You shall not *think* adultery." Just as He equates anger with murder, He equates lust with adultery. Adultery is an attitude as well as an act.

We must be careful that we do not misunderstand the words of Jesus. He is not speaking of the natural, normal desire for sex, which is part of human nature. This is God-given and beautiful and innocent in itself. The one who is condemned here is the one who looks at another with the deliberate intention of lusting after her or him; looking in such a way that passion is awakened and desire is intentionally stimulated. One can do this by undressing the person with one's eyes, by feasting upon pictures of nude women or men in pornographic magazines, or by gazing at obscene sexual acts in X-rated movies.

Jesus emphasizes what the modern psychologist is saying, namely that "ideas are motor." If you hold them within the mind long enough, they will brush past your will and become action, in spite of your protests. It is exactly as the oft-repeated adage warns us: Sow a thought and you reap an act;

sow an act and you reap a habit; sow a habit and you reap a character; sow a character and you reap a destiny.

Note that the thought has to be sown. It will bring forth no act if it is dismissed at once. The sin is not in the coming of the thought, but in the harboring of it. Thoughts of sin become sinful thoughts only when they are accepted and held. As one wise person has said, "You cannot help the birds flying over your head, but you can prevent them from building nests in your hair." You cannot help the vagrant thought flying through your mind, but you can help brooding over it, warming it, and thus hatching it into action.

Thought for the day: *The best antidote for lust is love.*

Matthew 5:33–37   JANUARY 15

Let what you say be simply "Yes" or "No" (v. 37).

Jesus taught that there must be absolute sincerity and honesty in compliance with the Law. The scribes and Pharisees were constantly endeavoring to manipulate or evade the Law by subtle means. This was especially true in regard to the taking of oaths.

In Jesus' day the Jews practiced what might be called "evasive swearing." They distinguished between oaths which were binding and those which were not. Any oath which contained the name of God was considered binding; any oath which somehow succeeded in evading the name of God was held to be nonbinding. Thus if one swore by the name of God in any form, he felt obliged to keep that oath; but if he swore by heaven, or earth, or Jerusalem, or by his own head, he felt quite free to break that oath. In this way, evasion was fashioned into a fine art. The slightest verbal change in an oath could relieve one from all moral obligation.

Jesus condemned all such chicanery and said, "Do not swear at all ... let your speech be simply 'Yes' or 'No.' " He knew that oaths were of no use—a good person would not need one, and an evil person would not heed one. Jesus brushed them aside, for He knew that nothing extraneous will produce truth if one is not inwardly truthful. The ideal is that one should never need an oath to buttress the truth of anything he may say. His character should make swearing unnecessary. His guarantee and his witness should lie in what he is himself.

Jesus insists that our speech should be simple. Evil is complicated—lies cover lies, intrigue follows intrigue. But the good is simple, straightforward, frank, and utterly truthful. Our motives, our thoughts, and our lives should be so sincere and so honest that a simple "yes" or "no" in our speech and dealings should suffice to satisfy others of the truthfulness of our statements.

Thought for the day: *A check is as good as the writer's signature.*

Matthew 5:38–48   JANUARY 16

Love your enemies and pray for [them] (v. 44).

The Christian must have a redemptive attitude toward Law. The Pharisees had a legal attitude—that of retaliation. Jesus says the purpose of the Law is not revenge or punishment, but reconciliation and redemption.

The Old Testament Law limited revenge to the exact equivalent—one eye for one eye and one tooth for one tooth. Before that it was unlimited so that if someone knocked out one tooth of yours, you were to knock out as many as you could of his. The Jewish law *limited* revenge; Jesus *abolished* it. He declares that the true child of God will never seek retaliation for any injustice or insult, however calculated and deadly it may be.

But Jesus doesn't stop there. "Love your enemies and pray for those who persecute you." That is a positive command. Thus Jesus raises the standard of human relationships to its highest level. First there was the law of the jungle—unlimited revenge. Then there was the Old Testament law—limited revenge. Now we have the law of Christ— unlimited love.

Jesus not only taught love; He practiced it. In Pilate's judgment hall when they scourged Him, mocked Him, and brought false accusations against Him, He never said a word; He never fought back. Then when He was hanging on the cross, He cried out in love, "Father, forgive them, for they know not what they do."

Jesus says to you that if you are a child of God, then be like God. He doesn't love only those who love Him; He loves even His enemies. He's the example of law. You must look at the God of the law and be like Him. If you're not like Him, you haven't obeyed the law, for love is the fulfillment of the law.

Thought for the day: *Law is retributive; love is redemptive.*

Matthew 6:1–6; 16–18   JANUARY 17

Beware of practicing your piety before men (v. 1).

Once again Jesus is emphasizing the significance of the inner motive. The underlying motive is important in acts demanded by the moral law; it is also important in the observance of religious duties.

Every act of piety has two aspects; the overt, visible aspect—what one does; and the inner, invisible aspect—why one does it. There are proper and improper motives for acts of piety. The improper motive is doing an act meant for God or for strengthening our relationship with Him, for theatrical purposes—"before men," "to be seen by men." This involves hypocrisy. The proper motive is to perform an act of piety for the sake of fellowship with God, to please Him!

Jesus illustrates His principle by applying it to the observance of certain Christian duties, namely, alms-giving, prayer, and fasting. These functions represent the basic relationships of life: alms, our relationship to *others*; prayer, our relationship to *God*; fasting, our relationship to *ourselves*. They also practically cover the field of religion: *receiving*— prayer; *giving*—alms; and *self-discipline*—fasting.

The value of these acts of piety lies in the actualization of their motives. You get what you seek. The reward is the extension of the motive. "Tell me your motive and I will tell you your reward." If a subtle desire to be seen by others runs through your observance of religious duties, then the deed dies with the moment; there is no lasting quality. You wanted the praise of others; you got it. That settles the account; there is no reward from your heavenly Father.

The great paradox of Christian reward is this. If you seek for reward and feel that it is your due, you will not receive it. But if your only motive is love and you are not concerned about the reward, you *will* receive it. The strange fact is that reward is both the *by-product* and the *ultimate end* of the Christian life.

Thought for the day: *God's approval is better than applause from others.*

Matthew 6:7—15   JANUARY 18

Our Father who art in heaven (v. 9).

The Lord's Prayer is indeed the model prayer. It is short and simple, yet deep and comprehensive. It consists of only sixty-seven words; it can be offered in twenty-five seconds. And yet it covers the entire range—from food to forgiveness. No one can sincerely offer this prayer and remain the same person.

The prayer contains six major petitions. The first three have to do with God and His glory—His name, His kingdom, and His will. The next three petitions represent our needs and our dependence upon God—for daily bread, for forgiveness, and for protection from moral evil. The prayer begins with

God—"Our Father"—and ends with God—"Thine is the glory." Only when He is given first place in our lives, can we expect our needs to be met.

The various relationships represented in the Lord's prayer make an interesting study:

"Our Father who art in heaven"—our relationship to God; a child speaking to his Father.

"Hallowed be thy name"—reverence of God; a worshiper speaking to his God.

"Thy kingdom come"—the reign of God on earth; a subject speaking to his King.

"Thy will be done"—the rulership of God in the human heart; a slave speaking to his Master.

"Give us this day our daily bread"—dependence on God; a beggar speaking to his Lord.

"Forgive us our debts"—the divine mercy of God; a sinner speaking to his Savior.

"Lead us not into temptation, but deliver us from evil"— deliverance by God; a traveler speaking to his Guide.

"For Thine is the kingdom and the power and the glory, for ever. Amen." The Doxology. (The RSV places this in the margin.)

Thought for the day: *In prayer we don't bend God's will to ours; we submit our wills to His.*

Matthew 6:19–24   JANUARY 19

Where your treasure is, there will your heart be also (v. 21).

A person's attitude toward material things can greatly affect his spiritual life. For this reason Jesus warns us against two dangers in regard to worldly possessions, namely, *avarice* and *anxiety*. The former is the special temptation of the rich—those who try to amass material things. The latter is the temptation of the poor—those who lack material goods.

To the affluent Jesus says, "Do not lay up for yourselves treasures on earth." To do so is foolish, for earthly treasure is perishable and temporary. Falling markets and depreciating stocks may consume, and dishonest directors may break through and steal. The prohibition is not against laying up treasure, but against laying up treasure "for yourselves." Material possessions can become an *evil* if they are sought in order to gain personal power and prestige or to satisfy one's love of comfort and display. But they may also become an *anvil*, upon which is wrought out the purposes of the kingdom of God. Riches invested in the lives of others and for kingdom business are like treasures stored up in heaven. There they will never perish, and no one can take them away from us.

The danger of material possessions is that they tend to turn the mind away from God, for where one's treasure lies, there will be his heart also. Furthermore, an inordinate desire for wealth can easily dull a person's moral sense. It can produce double vision, with one eye on God and one eye on material things. Jesus says, focus the eye on God alone. Love of the material can also result in making us slaves so that we no longer master our possessions but they possess us. Jesus says that you can't serve two masters. So make up your mind. Decide whether you will serve God or whether you will serve mammon. It will make a big difference which one is master in your life.

Thought for the day: *Can God bank on my character?*

Matthew 6:25–34 JANUARY 20

Do not be anxious about tomorrow (v. 34).

The poor can be just as materialistically-minded as the rich. The abundance of the rich can lead one to avarice, but the poverty of the common person can lead him to anxiety.

Thus to the poor Jesus says, "Do not be anxious about

your body, what you shall eat or drink, or what you shall put on." Privation can lead to over-concern and worry, and thus detract from concern for the kingdom. Jesus is not speaking against foresight and prudence. His thrust is against needless preoccupation with material things that transcends normal concern; against needless and ineffective worry.

Your anxiety-spot is focused all wrong, says Jesus. You are worried about paying the bills, about food and clothing, about putting the children through college, and a host of other legitimate things. That makes the body the master rather than the servant. Shift your anxiety-spot to the kingdom of God, and then the material world will fall into proper place. After you have done all that is needed and proper, then place your trust in the providence of God. He is concerned; He will provide. If He can provide for the birds and flowers, surely He can take care of you.

In 1963 I stood before the parliament buildings in Accra, Ghana, in Africa. The president was Kwame Nkruma, an exceedingly egotistical and selfish man. He erected a full-sized statue of himself at the entrance to the parliament, and underneath he put the inscription, "Seek ye first the political kingdom and all other things will be added unto you." But within a few years the people rose up against Nkruma, overthrew his administration, and forced him into exile. When I returned to Accra in 1969 the statue with its inscription was gone. The people had torn it down.

Thought for the day: *The only safe place to invest is in the kingdom of God.*

Matthew 7:1–6   JANUARY 21

Judge not, that you be not judged (v. 1).

Jesus is not speaking against making evaluative judgments. Later on in this same chapter He advises us to discriminate between true and false prophets by judging them

28

on the basis of their deeds. What He is denouncing is derogatory, censorious criticism without knowledge and love, the type of criticism that is meant to destroy.

Uncharitable judging of others is foolish. It acts like a boomerang. If we throw out criticism, it will come back to us with deadly aim, for the other person is doing the same thing to us. We get what we give. It is against our own best interest to be constantly criticizing others. We've started something that we wish we could turn off. Someone has suggested a test for sanity. Turn on the faucet until water starts overflowing on the floor. Call in a person and hand him a mop. If he starts mopping vigorously, he's crazy. If he turns off the faucet, he's sane. The wise person will turn off the faucet of criticism rather than stand around mopping up the mess he has created.

Jesus declared that unkind criticism is hypocrisy. He must have laughed inside when He pointed out how ridiculous it is for a person who has a log in his own eye to try and remove the sawdust speck from another's eye. You're making a fool of yourself, said Jesus. The log is sticking out so far from your eye that you can't even get close to the other fellow.

If we follow the example of Christ, we do not think it our business to condemn people for their shortcomings, but to try to deliver them from their shortcomings. Our first duty is not to find fault with others but to try to rescue them from their faults. Our task as Christians is to extricate others from their bonds; to convert them to better things.

Thought for the day: *The faults of others are like headlights on their automobiles; they always seem more glaring than our own.*

Matthew 7:7–14   JANUARY 22

... your Father who is in heaven [will] give good things to those who ask him! (v. 11)

29

In this brief discourse on prayer, Jesus emphasizes two important characteristics of the Christian's prayer life.

First, we must pray with *persistence*. Jesus said, "Ask . . . seek . . . knock." He chose His words carefully. There is a purposeful build-up of the intensity of our approach, beginning with a soft-spoken appeal and ending with a loud knock on the door. The force of the original text makes the command even more dramatic. " *Keep on* asking; *keep on* seeking; *keep on* knocking!" Prayer must be concentrated, not casual.

Then we must pray with *confidence*. We can do this when we remember the kind of God to whom we are appealing. He is a God who hears and answers prayer. He is a God who is more willing to give than we are to ask. He is a loving heavenly Father who wants to give good gifts to His children. He gives, not on the basis of our merits, but on the basis of our needs.

Though God hears every prayer, He does not always answer in the same way. Sometimes the answer is *direct*, for example, when the sinner prays for forgiveness or the tempted Christian prays for strength, God's grace is immediately imparted. There is not the slightest pause between petition and provision.

But sometimes the answer is *delayed*. This is especially true when we pray for the salvation of a loved one, and the individual's freedom of choice is involved.

Sometimes the petition is *denied*. "No" is just as much an answer to prayer as "yes." At times we ask for things that are really not in our best interest, so God has gently but firmly to deny our petitions. He knows what is best for us.

Then sometimes the answer is *different*. Paul prayed that his affliction might be removed; instead God gave him grace to bear the affliction victoriously and cheerfully. But in every case God does hear and give an answer.

Thought for the day: *Prayer is not seeking to overcome God's reluctance, but laying hold of His highest willingness.*

You will know them by their fruits (v. 20).

In a day when we are surrounded by false prophets and hypocrites, how up-to-date are these words of our Lord! Jesus declares that the prophet is to be judged, not by his appearance, but by his actions; not by the form of his dress, but by the fruit of his deeds. In outward appearance the person may look like a prophet. He dresses like a prophet; he claims to be a prophet; he talks like a prophet. Perhaps he is a seminary graduate, wears a clerical collar, and bears the title of Reverend before, and Doctor of Divinity after, his name. But still he may be a "wolf in sheep's clothing."

We must judge the prophet by the fruit of his deeds and the fruit of his doctrine. The true shepherd of the sheep cares more for the flock than for his own life; he sacrificially provides for their needs and guides them in the right paths. The false prophet, however, is motivated by self-interest. Like a wolf, he will even plunder the sheep to fulfill his own desires. The teaching of the true shepherd will tend to promote serious piety, humility, love, and holiness with other Christian graces. On the contrary, the doctrines of the false prophet have a manifest tendency to make people proud, worldly, contentious, divisive, and uncharitable.

From the preacher in the pulpit, Jesus now turns His attention to the disciple in the pew. If it is possible for the minister to be a wolf in sheep's clothing, the church member can be a goat in sheep's clothing. The disciple also must be judged, not by his words, but by his deeds; not by his profession, but by his practice. Obedience to the will of God is the supreme test. Jesus says, "Not everyone who says to me, 'Lord, Lord,' shall enter the kingdom of heaven, but he who does the will of my Father who is in heaven."

Thought for the day: *Do our actions complement or contradict what we say?*

... like a wise man who built his house upon the rock (v. 24).

Jesus concludes the Sermon on the Mount by emphasizing the responsibility of His listeners. It is not enough to hear His words, or understand, or remember, or repeat, or even dispute for them. We must *hear* and *do* His words. Obedience is the final test. The person who hears without doing is like a foolish person who builds his house on sand. The one who hears and obeys is like a wise person who builds his house on rock.

From India comes the story of a king and his favorite contractor. One day the king called for the contractor and told him that he was going on a long journey, and that during his absence he wanted the contractor to build a new house. "Spend as much money as you like" said the king. "I want this house to be special."

After the king left, a friend of the contractor came to him and said, "Here's a great chance to become rich. If you will use inferior materials you can save a lot of money and keep the difference for yourself. The king is not here to inspect your work." The contractor succumbed to this temptation and did exactly as was suggested.

Immediately upon his return, the king came to see the new house. He was pleased with its appearance and design. Then he turned to the contractor and said, "This house is my gift to you for all the hard work you have done. I want you and your family to move in tomorrow."

Then the monsoon rains came and beat upon the house, and because it was built of inferior materials, it crashed to the ground, killing all the inhabitants.

Each one of us is building a life, a character. The only sure foundation is Christ. He is the solid rock which can withstand all the storms, the disasters, and the temptations of life. Anyone else, anything else, is mere sand.

Thought for the day: *Jesus can put a new foundation under your life without tearing down the building.*

Great crowds followed him; and behold a leper came to him (vv. 1, 2).

During World War II a couple boarded a train of factory workers in Glasgow, Scotland, when suddenly the wife cried out to her husband, "Wait, we have forgotten our *non-entity* cards." Of course, she meant to say "our identity cards," but the phrase she used is very descriptive. With the population explosion around the world, the modern person has been losing his individuality; he feels a sense of insignificance in the world. The individual is asking himself, "Who am I in this vast world, anyhow? Do I count at all? Does anyone really care for me?"

The answers to these questions are found in chapters eight and nine of Matthew's gospel. Again and again we read something like this: "Great crowds followed him"; and immediately after that, ". . . a certain leper," or "a certain blind man," or "a certain demoniac came to Him." And then we read how Jesus stopped to heal or comfort or forgive. How often Jesus turned away from the crowd to minister to an individual in need. These two chapters alone describe how He stopped to heal a leper, then a sick servant, a sick wife, a couple of demoniacs, a paralytic, a ruler's daughter, and two blind men.

Even in the hour of His greatest suffering, Jesus stopped to minister to someone in need. In Gethsemane He stopped to restore the ear of a servant whom Peter had smitten with the sword. In the judgment hall of Pilate He stopped to look at Peter and win him back from his denial. Amidst the din and confusion of Calvary, He took time to make provision for His mother, and later to speak peace to a repentant thief.

The great message of the Gospels is this: You *are*

important. You *are* of tremendous value. There *is* Someone who cares for you!

Thought for the day: *God doesn't love humanity in general; he loves you!*

Matthew 8:5–17   JANUARY 26

Only say the word, and my servant will be healed (v. 8).

The healing of the centurion's servant is one of the most remarkable miracles that Jesus performed. In almost every other incident of healing, Jesus was actually present physically. There was bodily contact between Healer and patient. Jesus usually stretched forth His hand and touched the leper, or blind man, or paralytic, or whoever he was, and then spoke the word of healing. But in this case, Jesus was not present in person, there was no physical contact, and healing took place at a distance in a man whom Jesus had never seen. The whole affair seemed absolutely incredible.

Yet from another viewpoint, was there anything so unusual about this healing? There had been occasions when Jesus did not actually touch the supplicant, but merely spoke the word of healing. There was no physical contact when Jesus raised Lazarus from the tomb; He could not even see the body. But when He gave the command, Lazarus rose and came forth. After all, if Jesus really is the Son of God, if He is perfectly able to heal any disease by mere touch or word of mouth, then is it any more difficult for Him to heal at a distance?

The truth is that Jesus is Lord—not only over nature and human nature, but He is also Lord over time and space. This should not be hard for us to believe in an age when finite humans are conquering outer space. We are able to send a rocket toward the moon, and from a control tower on earth direct the speed and maneuvers of that rocket 240,000 miles

34

out in space. So is it not possible for the Lord of the universe who transcends time and space, to speak the word of healing or forgiveness or deliverance to any person anywhere in the world, and for a miracle to take place?

Thought for the day: *Christ is Lord of inner space as well as outer space.*

Matthew 8:18—27   **JANUARY 27**

... he was asleep ... then he rose and rebuked the winds and the sea (vv. 24, 26).

Here we have a beautiful illustration of the perfect humanity and deity of Jesus. He was fully man and fully God. As a human being, He was tired and fell asleep in the boat; as God, he arose and stilled the wind and the waves.

In like manner throughout the life of Christ, we observe the dual aspect of His nature. As a man, He was born in a manger; as God, He was worshiped by the wise men. As a man, He suffered the pangs of hunger; as God, He was able to spread a table for five thousand and have bread and fish to spare. As a man, He was thirsty and asked for water to drink; as God, he said, "Whoever drinks of the water that I shall give him will never thirst." As a man, He wept at the tomb of His friend, Lazarus; as God, he commanded, "Lazarus, come out." As a man, He was tempted in all points like we are; as God, he lived a sinless life. As a man, He was "crucified, dead and buried"; as God, He rose from the dead and lives forever more.

Thus there are two things in Jesus—one like me and one unlike me. He meets life as a human being, calls on no power that is not at the disposal of anyone. He is so much like me that I feel I can put my arms around Him and say, "My Brother." But the moment I am about to do that I am confronted with that something in Him which is unlike me. He confronts me with an offer of salvation that only God can

35

offer. So instead of putting my arm around Him, I am forced to kneel at His feet.

I need both the likeness and the unlikeness of Jesus. He is like me, therefore my Example; He is unlike me, therefore my Redeemer. He is the combination of both; He gives me what I need.

Thought for the day: *God became my elder brother in order to become my Redeemer.*

Matthew 8:28–34   JANUARY 28

The whole herd rushed down the steep bank into the sea, and perished in the waters (v. 32).

In the mountains of New Guinea live some of the most backward tribes in the world. The people are just now coming out of the stone age. Someone has described their culture as that of the "pig culture." Everyone raises pigs. The pig is used as part of the bride price when a young man desires to marry. The pig is used as a sacrifice to appease evil spirits. Pigs are killed and eaten by the score at the time of the annual "Sing-Sing" festivals. The people are so fond of pigs that they stroke them like their own children. It used to be common for a woman to nurse a little pig at her breast, if the pig's mother died suddenly.

A few years ago, a couple serving under Wycliffe Bible Translators worked on the translation of the Gospels into one of the tribal languages. When they had completed the translation of the story of the Gadarene demoniac, the missionaries gathered the people and read to them that story in their own mother tongue. The mountaineers listened in rapt silence. Then one of the men spoke up as he heard how Jesus ordered the demons to enter the herd of pigs and how the herd ran into the sea and was drowned. He exclaimed to the missionaries, "Two thousand pigs [the number is mentioned in Mark's Gospel]! That's a lot of pigs. Do you mean to say that Jesus thought more of *one person* than he did of two thousand pigs? In this area the value of a man is just about that of one pig!"

Primitive as these people might be, they had grasped the real significance of this narrative of healing. The man was exactly right. Jesus *does* care more for one person than for two thousand pigs. That person's welfare and redemption are worth the whole world to Him.

Thought for the day: *A delivered man is worth more than tons of deviled ham!*

Matthew 9:1–8   JANUARY 29

... he said to the paralytic ... your sins are forgiven (v. 2).

Jesus never divorced the physical from the spiritual. He dealt with a person as a unit. Before He said to the paralytic, "Rise, take up your bed," He said to him, "Take heart, my son, your sins are forgiven." After Jesus fed the hungry multitude in the wilderness, He followed with a spiritual discourse of the Bread of Life (John 6). After He healed the man who was blind from birth, He faced him with the question, "Do you believe in the Son of man?" (John 9). After He healed the sick man at the pool of Bethesda, Jesus said to him, "Sin no more, that nothing worse befall you" (John 5).

It used to be that we treated a person in separate parts. We handed the body over to the doctor, the mind over to the educator and psychologist, and the soul over to the minister. Now we have discovered that we can't do that. Each person is a unit. One part affects the other. Sometimes the body gets sick and passes disease on to the mind and soul. Sometimes the soul gets sick and passes illness on to the mind and body. The American Medical Association says that fifty percent of all medical cases are rooted in the body, and the other fifty percent in the spirit. The latter are passing on the sicknesses of the mind and soul to the body, and they will never be well until they change their attitudes.

Some people are ill because of deep emotional conflicts such as anxiety, stress, fear, resentment, frustration, and guilt. These people drain back into their bodies the diseased thoughts of their minds. For them physical healing is not enough. They need to experience the grace and forgiveness of God so that they will have a new attitude toward life and a new purpose in life. As one outstanding physician said, "Many of my ailing patients could be well if they would have a real experience with God."

Thought for the day: *The best pill of all is the Gos-pill.*

Matthew 9:9–17   JANUARY 30

Why does your teacher eat with tax collectors and sinners? (v. 11)

Christ's answer to this question was perfectly clear. He simply said that *He went to those who needed Him most.* Sick people need a doctor; sinners need a Savior. If a doctor wants to help people, he doesn't go to a health club; he goes to a hospital. Likewise, if a Savior wants to redeem people, he must go where sinners are. The Pharisees scrupulously avoided sinners. They were more concerned with the preservation of their own "holiness" than with the prevention of other people's sins. Jesus went among sinners; He ate with them in order to reach and redeem them. The only way to convert people is to contact them.

This is a lesson that the church needs to learn today. The church is not a club for saints, but a clinic for sinners. And the only way to influence sinners is to go directly to them.

I once saw a cartoon that pictured a fisherman in his boat, reclining on a plush cushion, sipping a soft drink, and reading a book. On the side of the boat he had placed a large sign: "Welcome, fish, jump in!" Everyone knows you can't catch fish that way. You have to throw in your line, hook a fish, and reel it in. The church cannot be content with a big sign, "Morning worship at 11:00 a.m. All are welcome." The church must go out into the homes, offices, factories, classrooms, and arenas and reach people where they are.

Jesus said that the Christian is the salt of the earth. Salt does no good if it is left on the shelf. It must be placed in contact with food—it must be rubbed in. In the same way, we Christians are useless if we withdraw from society and keep our faith to ourselves.

Thought for the day: *Don't use so much tact that you lose contact.*

Matthew 9:18–26   JANUARY 31

Jesus ... saw ... the crowd making a tumult (v. 23).

When Jesus arrived at the house of Jairus, He found the place in tumult. Jewish mourning customs were very vivid and detailed, designed to stress the desolation and final separation of death. Upon the death of an individual a loud wailing was set up so that all might know that death had struck. The mourners beat their breasts, tore their hair, and rent their garments, accompanied by the wail of many flutes.

The composure of Jesus presented a great contrast to this scene. Amidst the tumult He stood poised and serene. In the face of gloom He radiated confidence. In the place of despair He brought hope. He took immediate command of the situation. "Do not weep," he said, "for the girl is not dead; she is only sleeping." What a demonstration of the triumphant hope of the Christian faith.

A missionary preached the gospel in an African village for several years, but there was no response. Finally, one family decided to become Christians. Shortly afterward, however, the youngest son took seriously ill and was at the point of death. Immediately the villagers began to whisper among themselves that the evil spirits were punishing the family for forsaking their old religion. All predicted that the boy would die. In desperation the missionary fasted and prayed and begged the Lord to heal the boy. The lad's death, he felt, would bring defeat to the Christian cause in the village.

But in a few days the boy died, and the missionary conducted a Christian funeral for the family. Not long afterward the village elders came to the missionary and said, "We have decided to follow Christ; please baptize us." They went on to explain, "We watched carefully the funeral you conducted for the boy. There was no wailing or beating of breasts, only singing and prayer. If Christ can take away the fear of death, then He is worthy to be our Master."

Thought for the day: *A Christian need not fear death; Christ is the resurrection and life.*

Matthew 9:27—38   FEBRUARY 1

When he saw the crowds, he had compassion for them (v. 36).

In these verses three statements are made about our Lord. It is said of Him first that He *saw*; next, that He *felt*; and finally, that He *acted*. That He saw suggests *vision*; that He felt suggests *compassion*; that He went about preaching and healing suggests *consecration*. Three great spiritual lessons thus stand out boldly: 1) the need of vision; 2) the need of compassion; and 3) the need of consecrated action.

Jesus had *vision*—"He saw the crowds." It was more than physical observance, it was spiritual discernment. He saw not just a crowd of people, but individuals fainting, scattered, without a shepherd. He saw beyond the outer physical to the inner spiritual needs. Recall for a moment the incident of Jesus at the well of Sychar (John 4). The disciples saw only a woman who had come to draw water; Jesus saw a sinful woman in need of the water of life. They saw the well as a place of rest; Jesus saw it as a place of redemption.

Jesus had *compassion*. He was not simply touched for a moment with a mild pity. His heart was moved to the very depths. He suffered in His compassion for people. His heart bled and broke for sorrowing, sinful humanity. He was called "a man of sorrows and acquainted with grief" because He bore the griefs and carried the sorrows of others. His compassion led to an all-consuming passion, a life-long concern. He had one desire, one task, one goal: to redeem humankind—totally.

Jesus was moved to *action*. Emotion can never be a substitute for action. True compassion pours itself out in service. It manifests itself in some material way, in some practical effort, for our uplift and redemption. It is said of Jesus that "he went about doing good" (Acts 10:38). He went through all the cities and villages, teaching in the synagogues, preaching the kingdom of God, and healing all types of diseases. Vision led to compassion, and compassion to action.

Thought for the day: *We must see through the eyes of Jesus, feel through the heart of Jesus, and work through the power of Jesus.*

Matthew 10:1–4   FEBRUARY 2

He called to him his twelve disciples (v. 1).

The sending out of the twelve disciples marks the dividing line of Christ's ministry. Up to this time He has worked single-handedly. Now he feels the need of sympathetic fellowship and supplementary force. He wants those to whom He can impart Himself in close communion, and upon whom He can rely for the extension of the kingdom He is establishing.

Jesus chose His disciples from the humbler walks of life. They were fishermen, tax collectors, small tradesmen—simple, unaffected, elemental people. They had no wealth, no academic background, no social advantages. Think of anyone starting a world-wide movement today with such ordinary persons. A leader would normally seek out statesmen, financiers, socialites, movies stars, or trained experts.

Jesus is looking, not so much for outstanding people, as for ordinary people to whom He can entrust extraordinary tasks. He chooses us, not only for what we are, but also for what we may become by His grace and power. No person ever needs to think that he or she is too ordinary for Christ to use; our Lord can take the most unlikely one and make that person into an effective instrument for the kingdom.

When our Lord wanted to begin a movement of Christian missions that would be world-wide in its scope, He chose a humble shoemaker from Scotland, named William Carey, and through him aroused the missionary conscience of the Western world. When the time came for the first African to become a bishop in that vast continent, God raised up Samuel Crowther, a slave from the Yoruba tribe in West Nigeria. To be the first national bishop in the Indian church, God selected Samuel Azariah, a member of the lowest caste in Indian society. When God wanted an evangelist who would fearlessly call a nation to repentance, He reached out and picked up a young man named Billy Graham from the mountains of North Carolina. Our Lord can use anyone who is willing to surrender his all for kingdom service.

Thought for the day: *No one is ordinary in the hands of Christ.*

Matthew 10:5–15   FEBRUARY 3

You received without pay; give without pay (v. 8).

The King James Version translates this verse more smoothly than the Revised Standard Version. It says, "Freely ye have received, freely give." This does not mean that God's

42

servants should not receive their support. Christ states the contrary—"the laborer deserves his food." But through this instruction Christ emphasizes a basic principle of Christian life and service.

"You have received; now give." Here are the two aspects of spiritual living: Receiving and giving; having and sharing; experience and expression. We take from God and we turn around and give to others in need. We cannot give unless we first receive. But once we have received, we must give. Someone has said that there are only two things we can do with our religion: give it up or give it away. If it's no good, give it up and find something real. But if it's real, then give it away. The only way to keep what we have is to share it with others.

Then Jesus adds the significant word "freely." You have received *freely*, so give *freely*. All the gifts of God are free. They are not dispensed on the basis of merit; they cannot be earned or bought. They are the result of grace, that is, the "unmerited favor of God." And since we have received these gifts freely, we must distribute them freely. We cannot sell them or demand service for them. The servant of God is strictly prohibited from using his mission as a means of acquiring wealth. The good news that has been gratuitously bestowed must not be employed as a means of personal gain.

This means that we do to others as God has done to us. He forgave us; we forgive others. He loved us when we were unworthy; we love others even though we feel they are unworthy. He ministered to our needs; we minister to the needs of others. This is the Golden Rule of Christian service.

Thought for the day: *Seek the good of others; not their goods.*

Matthew 10:16–23   **FEBRUARY 4**

You will be dragged before governors and kings ... to bear testimony before them (v. 18).

43

Jesus never promised His disciples an easy time. He warned them beforehand that they would meet indifference, opposition, and even severe persecution. But note this significant fact. Jesus said, "You will be dragged before governors and kings for my sake, but this will give you the opportunity to bear witness for me." In other words, they were to turn every adversity into an advantage. And herein lies one of the secrets of power in the Christian life.

A young army officer said, "Weather, in war, is always favorable, if you know how to use it." That is the point—if you know how to use it. The fact is, everything that happens in life to the child of God can be used in some way to better a situation and to bring glory to God.

In 1899, David and Ada Lee, a missionary couple in Calcutta, India, received a telegram informing them that a terrible landslide in the mountain resort of Darjeeling had swept away six of their seven children, ranging in age from five to seventeen. It was a terrible blow to the Lees, but they were undaunted. They began an orphanage for destitute girls and later another for boys. They lost six of their own children, but over the next forty years, God gave them hundreds of children, and today the Lee Memorial Mission in Calcutta is still ministering to needy boys and girls from all over Bengal.

Just a few years ago an evangelist in Nepal baptized nine of his countrymen as Christians. The converts were in jail for a year, and the evangelist for five years. But while in prison the new Christians cleaned up the unsanitary conditions of the cells, and gave medical attention to some of the guards. The evangelist started a Bible class and won more converts to Christ in prison than when he was out. They turned adversity into opportunity.

Thought for the day: *Christians can find opportunity in every difficulty.*

A disciple is not above his teacher, nor a servant above his master (v. 24).

These words are both a warning and an encouragement to the followers of Jesus. They are a warning because they remind us that if our Lord Himself suffered opposition and persecution, then we can expect the same. They are an encouragement, however, in that they also remind us that Christ has been down the same road that we walk. He has met every experience that we face and has met it triumphantly. So we have One who can sympathize with us and help us.

When we suffer physical privations, let us remember that Jesus knew what it was to be hungry, thirsty, and poor. When we are tempted, we should recall that He "in every respect has been tempted as we are." When people seem ungrateful for favors done to them, we can remember that out of the ten lepers whom Jesus healed on one occasion, only one returned to give Him thanks. When people make fun of us, we remember that the people often laughed at Jesus; they called Him names; they said He was mad; they claimed He had a devil.

When rejected by our own family members, we can remember that Jesus "came to His own home, and his own people received him not." When we are lonely, we should remember that Jesus felt alone in Gethsemane and on the cross. It seemed as if the whole world had forsaken Him. When others lie and falsely accuse us, we can remember the many false witnesses who testified against our Lord at the time of His trial. When we are faced with martyrdom for His sake, we can remember that He willingly laid down His life for the whole world.

So when any trial comes along, if we look, we can see the footprints of the Son of God. He has passed that way, and He has conquered!

Thought for the day: *Christ identified with our tragedy; we can identify with His victory.*

Matthew 10:34—42

He who finds his life will lose it, and he who loses his life for my sake will find it (v. 39).

In common parlance we usually say, "Finders, keepers." But Jesus turned things around when he said, "Losers, keepers." Anyone who lives for himself will eventually lose his life; but he who lives for Christ and for others will save his life.

This principle is true in all realms of life. It is true in nature. If the seed tries to keep its identity, there will be no fruit. Only when it is willing to die and lose its identity, will it bring forth a harvest. Only when the wick is willing to burn itself out, will it give light to those who need it.

This principle is also true in the realm of human relationships. If we live selfishly for our own prosperity and enjoyment, life will turn sour on us. We will end up being dissatisfied and unhappy. But if we lose our lives in service and seek to bring joy and comfort to others, life becomes meaningful and exciting.

Too many people these days are interested in saving their lives. They are living for themselves, their own families, their own comforts, their own pleasure, their own prestige. And they make no lasting contribution. The world is no better off by their having lived. We need people today who are willing to lose their lives in sacrificial, vicarious living; who will spend their lives for others—their neighbors, their community, their country.

Several decades ago a celebrated socialite died in Paris. She had flitted from one party to another, from one thrill to another. When she died, her friends found 1,000 dresses in her wardrobe. That's all she left behind. On the same day that she passed away, General William Booth, founder of the Salvation Army, died in England. At his funeral they spoke of him as "the man with a thousand lives." A thousand dresses—a thousand lives. Which was the greater legacy?

Thought for the day: *Nothing spent for Christ is ever lost.*

Matthew 11:1–10   FEBRUARY 7

Are you he who is to come, or shall we look for another? (v. 3)

It is surprising that of all persons John the Baptist should be tempted to doubt. He had baptized Jesus. He had seen the Spirit of God descending upon Him. He had heard the voice from heaven saying, "This is my beloved Son." He knew that Jesus was the Messiah and had testified to this fact.

But even the greatest saint has moments of doubt, especially when everything seems dark. John the Baptist was in prison. The cell was dirty and dark and damp. He was all alone. The wicked Herod seemed to be winning all the battles. No miracles opened his prison doors, the day of God's victory seemed to tarry, and the Christ whom he had so gladly proclaimed made no haste to claim His kingdom. So John sent messengers to Jesus with the question, "Are *You* really the Messiah, or should we look for someone else?"

How did Jesus deal with John's doubts? He did not rebuke him. He didn't say, "Oh, my goodness, what's happened to John? He's backslidden." He knew the struggle John was going through, so He did not offer any intellectual proofs. Jesus merely encouraged John with the facts. "Tell John," he said, "everything is going according to schedule. The deaf hear, the lame walk, the blind see, the dead are raised up, and the poor hear the gospel preached." Jesus knew John's faith would revive.

When you are tempted to doubt, take the same practical approach. Stop and review your life; trace God's hand in your past. You were spiritually blind, now you see. You were dead in sins, now you have life. You were a moral leper, now you are

47

clean. You were insensitive to the Spirit, now you hear His voice. As you review your history, you suddenly realize it is His Story. You know He is still Lord and that His hand is upon you and the world.

Thought for the day: *Never doubt in the dark what God has told you in the light.*

Matthew 11:11–19   FEBRUARY 8

To what shall I compare this generation? (v. 16)

Jesus compared His generation to a group of children playing in the market place. One group suggested, "Let's play wedding; let's dance," and the others said, "We don't feel like being happy today." Then the first group suggested, "Okay, let's play funeral; let's mourn. But the others said, "No, we don't feel like being sad either." In other words, they were just downright contrary. No matter what was suggested, they didn't want to do it.

"Likewise," said Jesus, "John the Baptist came wearing odd clothes, observing a strict diet, and living in the desert, and you said about him, 'That man is crazy; he's cut himself off from society.' Then when I, the Son of Man, came attending weddings and accepting invitations to dinner, you said about me, 'This man is a party-goer; he associates with all kinds of people.'"

In this quaint illustration, Jesus pointed out the sheer contrariness of some people. When they do not want to obey the truth, they will find all sorts of excuses for their disobedience. Grown men and women can be much like spoiled children who refuse to play no matter what the game is.

Are we any different today? Of one preacher we say, "His sermons are not relevant"; of another, "His preaching is too personal." About one church we say, "Those people are all hypocrites," while of another we say, "Those people think they're all saints." About one evangelist we say, "That man

48

meddles in politics"; of another we say, "He doesn't attack the social injustices of our day." The fact of the matter is that in our minds we have decided we don't like preachers or evangelists anyway and that the church is an outdated institution. The first step in the Christian life is to make up our minds to be honest with ourselves, to face the truth with an open heart, and to obey the truth wherever we find it.

Thought for the day: *Would you rather be contrary—or close to God?*

Matthew 11:20–24   **FEBRUARY 9**

He began to upbraid the cities where most of his mighty works had been done (v. 20).

Great privilege always brings great responsibility. The cities of Galilee, such as Chorazin, Bethsaida, and Capernaum, had been given opportunities that had never come to Tyre and Sidon, or Sodom and Gomorrah. They had actually seen and heard Jesus Himself. Jesus preached to them often and performed many wonderful miracles in their midst. Out of Bethsaida He chose at least three of His disciples. Thus these places were highly favored. It is only natural, therefore, that Jesus would expect great things from the people of Galilee, and that He would upbraid them for not living up to their privileges.

The sin of these people was the sin of *indifference*. They did not attack Jesus or drive Him from their gates. They did not seek to crucify Him. They simply disregarded Him. But neglect can be as dangerous as willful opposition. Jesus condemned these cities because they did not repent. He had come among them, preaching, "The kingdom of heaven is at hand. Therefore, repent!" But they did not change their attitude toward their sin and turn toward God for mercy.

Many of us have had unusual privileges in our lives. We have had godly parents who nurtured us in the Christian faith.

49

We have attended churches where the pastors have faithfully proclaimed the Word of God. Perhaps we have attended Christian colleges. We live in a nation that upholds freedom of worship and guarantees our liberties. All these privileges simply add to our responsibility, for "to whom much is given, much will be required."

Christ faces us today with our most threatening sin—the sin of doing nothing. The sin of inaction is just as tragic as the sin of action; the sin of omission can damn us as easily as the sin of commission. Many times our defense is, "But I never did anything." That defense may be in fact our condemnation.

Thought for the day: *Do something with all those privileges of yours!*

Matthew 11:25–30   FEBRUARY 10

Come to me . . . I will give you rest (v. 28).

Everyone likes to receive an invitation—perhaps to dinner, a party, or a wedding. But here is an invitation that beats all invitations! It is a bidding to attend the feast of salvation. What makes the summons all the more significant is the Person making the offer. Suppose you received a sudden telephone call from the president of the United States, inviting you to come to dinner at the White House. You would count it a great honor. But here is the King of kings, the Lord of the universe giving you a special invitation. *"Come"* says Jesus lovingly, "come to *me.*" Not just to the church, but to the Savior.

"I will give you rest." What a glorious promise. Rest from your exhausting quest for the truth, for the way to know truth is not by intellectual search, but by knowing Christ who Himself *is* the truth. Rest from the burdens of legalistic religion, with its endless rules and regulations, for no one can satisfy the demands of the law. Rest from the crushing weight

of guilt, which cannot be lifted by ritual or ceremony. This is a deep-seated, abiding rest that only Christ Himself can give.

"Take my yoke upon you," says Jesus. He doesn't promise us a life of inactivity and ease. The "rest" He offers is a release from the drudgery of sin, not from the service of God. We quit working for the devil and we start working for God. But amidst all the toil, the rest still abides, for we serve under the leash of love, not under the lash of law.

A man came upon a young lad carrying a still smaller boy, who was lame, upon his back. "That's a heavy burden for you to carry," said the man. With almost a look of disgust the lad replied, "This is not a burden; this is my brother!"

Thought for the day: *The burden carried in love is always light.*

Matthew 12:1–8   FEBRUARY 11

Look, your disciples are doing what is not lawful to do on the sabbath (v. 2).

The Scribes and Pharisees reduced religion to a frightening list of "Thou-shalt-nots." Using the Ten Commandments as a basis, they developed hundreds and hundreds of needless prohibitions, that made worship a travesty and life itself a burden. This was especially true in regard to the keeping of the Sabbath Day.

Are we not guilty of the same approach even today? Have we not often presented the Christian faith in negative terms of prohibitions? "Thou shalt not smoke or drink; thou shalt not dance or play pool; thou shalt not go to the movies, etc." By so doing we have made the Gospel a burden instead of a blessing.

Bishop J. Waskom Pickett, one of God's choice servants in India, tells a story about himself as a young missionary. Asked to explain the Christian faith to a group of Hindu inquirers, he spoke for more than an hour, entirely in negative terms. Followers of Christ should not worship idols, should not drink liquor, should not gamble, should not eat the flesh of animals that had died of old age or disease, etc. When he had finished, a Hindu priest who was present, asked for the privilege of saying a few words. He said to the group, "I agree with what the missionary says, but I go further than he does. I tell you also not to eat any meat, or tomatoes, or beets, or eggplants." He merely added to the list of prohibitions drawn up by the missionary.

Commenting on the experience, Bishop Pickett testifies that he learned the hard way that Christians dare not reduce the Gospel to a body of denials. The church of Christ, he said, cannot compete with the other religions in denials and prohibitions, but no man-made religion can compete with the Christian Gospel in the richness and glory of its affirmations about God and humankind and life.

Thought for the day: *The Christian Gospel is a body of affirmations and not a system of denials.*

Matthew 12:9–21   FEBRUARY 12

Stretch out your hand (v. 13).

Jesus entered the synagogue and found there a man with a withered hand. Is this a picture of many church members today? They sit in church, well-dressed, performing the ritual, speaking the name of Christ, but their hands are withered, ineffective.

It seems clear from the Greek text that this man's hand had *become* withered. It had not always been thus. Once he was a strong man. Luke tells us that it was his right hand; tradition says he was a mason. Now his hand was paralyzed, useless.

The hand, in Scripture, often symbolizes spiritual truth. Jesus refers to a man who puts his hand to the plow and looks back (Luke 9:62). The hand of service can become a withered hand. An individual, once keen for the kingdom of God and winning others to discipleship can lose his desire to serve. Enthusiasm can die out in his heart. Jesus says to that person, "Stretch forth your hand."

Paul speaks about people "lifting holy hands" in prayer (1 Tim. 2:8). The hand of prayer may become withered. The individual becomes irregular, undisciplined in daily devotions. Vitality has seeped out of prayer life. Consequently defeat and discouragement abound. Jesus says to this person, "Stretch forth your hand."

In Galatians 2:9 Paul speaks about "the right hand of fellowship." This hand may also become a withered hand. Once it was a firm, strong, loving hand, extended in confidence, concern, and communion. Now it is withdrawn, paralyzed. Fellowship with other Christians is broken. Again Jesus says, "Stretch forth your hand."

So much depended on the mental viewpoint of the man who stood before Jesus in the synagogue. If he looked at the hand, healing seemed impossible. If he looked into the face of Christ, everything seemed possible. No matter how withered your hand has become, Christ wants to heal it—whether it be the useless hand of service, the paralyzed hand of prayer, or the withered hand of fellowship.

Thought for the day: *The healed hand becomes a helping hand.*

Matthew 12:22–32   FEBRUARY 13

He who is not with me is against me, and he who does not gather with me scatters (v. 30).

To realize the full impact of this statement, we must remember the context in which Jesus spoke. He had just healed a blind and dumb demoniac who was brought to Him. The man was delivered from an evil spirit and was able to see and speak once again. Some of the Pharisees standing nearby accused Jesus of casting out demons by the power of Satan. Jesus declared that He did so through the power of the Holy Spirit. This was a battle between Christ and Satan, between the forces of righteousness and the forces of evil. It was a fight to the finish.

In this war against Satan's strongholds there are only two sides. One is either *for* Christ or *against* Him; he is either *gathering* the harvest with Christ or *scattering* the grain with Satan. *There is no neutral ground!*

This holds true in all the major issues of life. If we do not strengthen the church with our presence, we are actually weakening the church through our absence. If we do not go to the polls on the question of local option, we are really casting our votes in favor of the liquor traffic. If we make no contribution to the cause of Christian missions, we are actually casting our votes for the withdrawal of all missionaries. If we refuse to give testimony to the police on the grounds that we don't want to get involved, we are in effect aiding and abetting the increase of crime. In all things in this world we must choose a side. Abstention from choice, or suspended action, is no way out because the mere refusal to give one side assistance is in fact giving support to the other.

Jesus demands that we make a choice regarding His invitations and demands. We must choose either to receive Him or reject Him. There is no middle ground.

Thought for the day: *There is no abstention in the vote for righteousness.*

Matthew 12:33–42   FEBRUARY 14

Behold, something greater . . . is here" (vv. 6, 41, 42).

Three times in this chapter our Lord declared His supremacy over all things and all people.

When the Pharisees criticized His disciples for plucking and eating ears of grain on the Sabbath, Jesus reminded them how King David and his friends, in order to satisfy their hunger, had entered the Temple and eaten the bread of the presence from the altar. Then Jesus said, "Something greater than the temple is here." He also went on to say, "The Son of man is lord even of the Sabbath." In other words, Jesus is greater than sacred buildings, rites or rituals, sacrifices or ceremonies. The temple stood for the presence of God, but in Jesus we have the very Person of God. He is Emmanuel, "God with us." The temple was the place of worship and sacrifice, but Jesus is the supreme sacrifice for sin, and He is the object of all true worship.

Again, when the scribes and Pharisees asked Jesus for a sign of His messiahship, He answered that there would be one great sign, that of Jonah the prophet. He was, of course, referring to His resurrection. Then Jesus went on to say, "The men of Nineveh . . . repented at the preaching of Jonah, but behold, something greater than Jonah is here," implying, "you have not repented." Jesus claims to be the greatest of all prophets and preachers. In fact, He is both the *subject* and the *object* of all true preaching. He Himself is the Good News. He is the object of our faith.

Finally, Jesus made reference to the Queen of Sheba's coming a great distance to hear the wisdom of Solomon. Then He said, "Behold, something greater than Solomon is here." Jesus is the end of all wisdom, for to know Him is to know God. To know Him is to know the truth. To be in touch with Him is to be in touch with reality.

Thought for the day: *Make Christ supreme; don't settle for anyone or anything less.*

Matthew 12:43–45   FEBRUARY 15

He finds it empty, swept, and put in order (v. 44).

This story that Jesus told is more than just a spooky ghost story. It is a parable full of the most practical truth.

55

The unclean spirit was banished from the house, but was not destroyed. In other words, one's life may be cleansed of evil, but the evil itself is not annihilated. It is always looking for an opportunity to make a comeback and to regain the ground it has lost. So when the unclean spirit returned to its former residence and found it "empty, swept, and put in order," it brought seven other evil spirits with it and set up housekeeping again.

The key word here is *empty*. It was good that the house was "swept and put in order." That was necessary. But the house was still empty, and an empty house is in danger. It needs a new housekeeper to keep it in shape. The Christian life consists of more than getting rid of old habits and old attitudes. Subtraction is important, but it is insufficient. It must be followed by addition. The heart must be cleansed of evil, but it must not be left empty. The empty heart must become the full heart. Christ must enter and set up housekeeping. Then alone will the house *stay* clean and be kept in order.

Well do I remember the first time I had to deal with a demon-possessed person in my missionary work. Upon hearing the command, "In the name of Jesus Christ come out of her," the unclean spirit immediately departed, and the woman became sane and peaceful. A miracle had taken place. Then I remembered the parable of Jesus. So I urged the woman to repeat a prayer after me, inviting Christ to come and live in her heart. The second miracle took place. A week later the woman returned to give her testimony and receive public baptism in the name of Christ. Jesus was now living in her heart.

Thought for the day: *The only permanent cure for an unclean spirit is the Holy Spirit.*

Matthew 13:1–9; 18–23   FEBRUARY 16

A sower went out to sow (v. 3).

With unforgettable vividness the parable of the sower brings a warning to those who hear the Gospel. There are different ways of hearing the Word of God, and the fruit that it produces depends on the mindset of the one who accepts it.

Hearing is important. Jesus said, "He who has ears, let him hear." "Hearing" means more than just listening with our ears. It refers to the frame of mind, of conscience, and of spirit. It signifies spiritual perception and understanding.

The four different soils symbolize four degrees of hearing. The *hard ground* stands for the *closed mind*. This is the mind hardened by prejudice, pride, an unteachable spirit, fear of the truth, or self-centeredness. The Word of God has not the slightest chance of gaining an entry into such a person's heart. The *rocky ground* symbolizes the *casual mind*. This mind is gushy, emotional, impulsive, shallow. It receives the Word for a while, but fails to retain it. The *thorny ground* illustrates the *confused mind*, divided between irreconcilable loyalties. In the beginning there is some growth and prospects of fruit, but conflict arises which kills productivity. The *good ground* is the *committed mind*, which is open, receptive, obedient, and persevering.

Hearing without doing is impertinent. It means that we are only playing with the truth; we are being frivolous; we don't really mean business.

Hearing converted into doing is imperative. It is necessary in order to produce fruit in our lives. It is necessary in order to build a solid foundation for our character. At the conclusion of His extended Sermon on the Mount, Jesus said, "He who *hears* these words of mine and *does* them is like a wise man who builds his house on the rock. And he who hears my words and *does not do* them is like the foolish man who builds upon the sand." It is the *doing* of the word that makes the difference.

Thought for the day: *The Gospel is not a story to be heard; it is a summons to be heeded.*

Why do you speak to them in parables? (v. 10)

As communicators of the Gospel we would do well to study the teaching methods of Jesus. He was the Master Teacher. His instruction was simple, yet profound; brief, yet comprehensive. Jesus communicated truth through word pictures. He used illustrations, similes, metaphors, analogies, and parables. He was particularly an expert in the use of the latter.

The parable has certain definite advantages. It arouses the interest of listeners. It makes abstract ideas concrete, and therefore enables the hearer to understand and remember the truth more easily. It compels the hearer to discover the truth. It reveals truth to the one who earnestly desires it, but conceals truth from the one who does not want to accept it. The burden is placed on the hearer.

I heard an Indian preacher tell the following parable to a group of illiterate villagers at the end of an evangelistic message. A monkey with poor eyesight went to the doctor for help. The doctor gave him a pair of glasses and sent him home. But the monkey did not know what to do with the glasses. He put them first over his ear, then against his neck, then on top of his head. But there was no improvement in his sight. Finally, in disgust, the monkey threw the glasses on the ground and broke them.

Then the preacher said to his listeners, "You have just heard the truth of God. What are you going to do with it? Apply it to your ears? Apply it to your heads? Just listen and nod in agreement? That is not enough. The monkey should have placed the pair of glasses on his eyes in order for them to do any good. Likewise, you must apply the truth of God to your heart and life, if it is to have any lasting effect."

I assure you that those villagers caught the preacher's point that day.

Thought for the day: *Why should preaching be dull when we have the best news to tell?*

Matthew 13:24–30; 36–43   FEBRUARY 18

Let both [weeds and wheat] grow together until the harvest (v. 30).

It is obvious that the world yields a mixed crop of good and evil. In the beginning God planted good in the world, and intended for everything to remain good. But Satan came along and planted evil among the good so now the two exist side by side.

We find good and evil existing within the same family. Sometimes the wife is spiritually minded, while the husband is a man of the world. Or the husband is a real man of God, while the wife is indifferent to spiritual things. Some of the children may be upright and obedient; others may be rebellious and delinquent.

In the church we find both wheat and tares. There are those who are born of the Spirit, sincerely love the Lord, and live exemplary lives. Then there are those who are merely nominal Christians, living in sin and defeat.

Sometimes it is difficult to distinguish between those who are in the kingdom and those who are not. A person may appear to be good, and in fact may be bad; another may appear to be bad and yet may be good. Thus it is not our business to judge people, for we are unable to know their inner motives and thoughts. God alone is the Judge, for He knows all things perfectly.

God allows evil to coexist with the good for a season. There is, of course, danger in this, for the evil may influence and undermine the good. But it also affords opportunity, for the good may influence and overcome the evil.

Sometimes, like the servants in the parable, we get impatient and want to take things into our own hands. We want to mete out judgment and destroy the tares. But God is ever patient. He always offers mercy before he pronounces judgment.

Judgment, however, though delayed, is certain. One day God will blow the final whistle, and will separate the good from the evil. Evil will be destroyed, but good will reign forever.

Thought for the day: *Evil often triumphs but never conquers.*

Matthew 13:31–33; 44–58   FEBRUARY 19

The kingdom of heaven is like a grain of mustard seed ... like leaven ... like treasure ... like a pearl (vv. 31, 33, 44, 45).

The kingdom, says Jesus, may be compared with a very small seed that grows into a large shrub. Or it may be thought of as leaven, which is unseen but spreads through the meal and affects every part of it. God's kingdom is small in its origins and quiet in its influence, but has great capacities for growth and bringing about change.

In the Telugu-speaking area of India, the American Baptist Mission had been working for thirty years (1840–1870) with so little success that it had come to be known as the "Lone Star Mission." Then one day a low-caste villager by the name of Yerraguntla Periah appeared on the scene, asking for baptism. A visit to his village revealed that almost 200 people were believers in Christ as a result of Periah's witness. This was the beginning of a great people's movement among the Untouchables of that area. Hundreds and then thousands began to come to Christ. Lutherans, Anglicans, Methodists, and others profited from the movement, which in the next thirty years brought a million people into the church. The tiny seed had grown into a large tree.

Again, Jesus says the kingdom is like a great treasure, a priceless pearl, for which one is willing to sell everything he has in order to purchase it. In other words, it is worth any sacrifice to enter the kingdom, for this is life's supreme goal.

At the age of fifteen, Sundar Singh, the son of Sikh parents in India, heard the voice of Jesus saying, "Come, follow me." The young lad answered the call and became a Christian. It cost him his family, his inheritance, his beautiful fiancée, and his standing in the community. His parents disowned him and tried to poison him. The community excommunicated him. But Sundar Singh found complete satisfaction and fulfillment in Christ, and became one of India's greatest saints.

Thought for the day: *In matters of the kingdom, the prize is worth the price.*

Matthew 14:1–12   FEBRUARY 20

He . . . had John beheaded in the prison (v. 10).

The story of Herod Antipas, king of Galilee, is one of the most tragic records in history. It graphically illustrates the disastrous effects of sin upon a person's life.

Herod's downfall began with the sin of lust. On a visit to Rome he seduced his brother's wife and persuaded her to leave his brother and to marry him. In so doing he broke two laws. He divorced his own wife without cause, and then married his sister-in-law.

John the Baptist was a faithful and courageous servant of God. He denounced sin wherever he found it—in pauper and plutocrat, in soldier and Pharisee. He publicly rebuked Herod for his sin and called upon him to repent.

If Herod had truly repented and set things right at this point, his whole story might have been different. But he refused to repent, and continued in his sin. Then he began to add to his guilt step by step. He threw John in prison and would have killed him, but he feared the reaction of the people. Finally, he was trapped by Herodias, his wife, and was forced to commit the sin of murder.

Throughout the story Herod appears as a man of weak character. He was more afraid of people than he was of God. He was more afraid of the sneers of his dinner guests than of committing a crime. He felt sorry (v. 9) for making a rash promise, but he showed no sorrow for his sin.

Herod paid heavily for his sin. The father of his legal wife, Aretas, king of the Nabateans, made war against him and soundly defeated him. When Jesus began his public ministry and performed many miracles, Herod was convinced that John the Baptist had returned in the flesh, and his guilty conscience tormented him day and night. Finally, the Emperor Caligula took Herod's province from him, and banished him to far-off Gaul to languish there in exile for the rest of his life.

Thought for the day: *The wages of sin is death (Rom. 6:23).*

Matthew 14:13–21   FEBRUARY 21

We have only five loaves here and two fish (v. 17).

When Jesus suggested to the disciples that they give the people something to eat, they insisted that eight months' wages were not adequate to buy bread for them (Mark 6:37). In other words they were saying, "We could not earn enough money in eight months to give this crowd a meal." Jesus asked them, "What do you have?" To which they replied, "There is a lad here who has five barley loaves and two fish; but what are they among so many? (John 6:9) One commentator suggests that the loaves were probably the size of our American dinner rolls. As for the fish, they were probably the size of sardines. It certainly did not seem like much. But Jesus said, "Bring them here to me." Then he took the loaves and fish, blessed and multiplied them, and fed a crowd of several thousand people.

In the hands of the Lord, little is always much. Moses had only a rod in his hand, but with the power of almighty God he was able to divide the sea so that the children of Israel could cross on dry land. The shepherd boy David had only a sling and five small stones in his hand, but with the strength of the Lord he was able to slay the giant and bring confusion to the Philistine army. Joshua had only three hundred men in his army, but with God on his side he caused the walls of Jericho to collapse; and he captured the city. Jesus started with only twelve ordinary men as His disciples, but today His followers number in the hundreds of millions around the world.

We may think that we have little of ability or talent or substance to give the Master. But if we give Him what we have, who can tell what He can do with us and through us?

Thought for the day: *Jesus doesn't merely add; He specializes in multiplication.*

Matthew 14:22–36   FEBRUARY 22

Jesus immediately reached out his hand and caught him (v. 31).

Peter was courageous enough to step out of the boat and try to walk on the water toward Jesus. But he made the mistake of taking his eyes off Jesus and looking at the wind and waves. He became afraid and began to sink. Then he cried out to Jesus, "Lord, save me." At that moment our Lord reached out a strong hand and saved him from a watery grave.

Down through the centuries many sinking in the sea of despondency have cried out to Jesus, "Lord, save me," and the Lord delivered them from their distress. There have also been those who were sinking in the sea of sin, and in mercy Christ reached out a strong hand and rescued them.

I shall never forget the testimony of a new convert in India. "I had fallen in a deep pit," he said, "and there was no way to get out. One day a man passed by and I cried out for help. He looked down at me and said, 'You must perform as many good deeds as you can, then you will get out of there.' And so saying, he went on his way. That was the voice of Mohammed. A second man passed by and said, 'This condition is the result of desire. Get rid of all desire and you can get out of this pit.' That was the voice of Buddhism. A third man looked down at me and said, 'This condition is the result of your *karma*—the sins of your previous life. Do the best you can in this life, and hope for something better in the life to come.' That was the voice of Hinduism. Then I looked up and saw a fourth man. When I cried out for help, He never said a word. He just reached down with a strong hand and pulled me out. That man," explained the convert, "was my Savior, Jesus Christ!"

Thought for the day: *Christ can save from the guttermost to the uttermost.*

Matthew 15:1–9   FEBRUARY 23

For the sake of your tradition, you have made void the word of God (v. 6).

The Pharisees complained to Jesus that His disciples transgressed the tradition of the elders by not washing their hands when they ate. They did not mean that the disciples' hands were dirty, but that the disciples had neglected the ceremonial washing which Jewish tradition required. Jesus counteracted the complaint by making a double charge against the Pharisees.

He denounced them because they obeyed the traditions of men but at the same time disobeyed the commandments of God. He also reproached them for being more concerned about clean hands than pure hearts.

Are we any different today from the Pharisees? We are very careful to observe tradition and custom. We try not to interrupt a person when he is talking; we don't talk with our mouths full; we don't break the queue. Men stand when a woman enters the room and when the National Anthem is played. We go through the proper channels of protocol. We say "please" and "thank you." But are we just as careful in observing the commandments of God? Do we love our neighbor as ourselves? Do we honor our father and mother? Do we pray for our enemies? Do we act toward others as we desire them to act toward us? We observe the traditions of men, but neglect the commandments of God. In this respect we are very much like the scribes and Pharisees.

Likewise, we are more concerned about outward cleanliness than about inward purity. We regularly bathe, brush our teeth, wash our hair, and polish our shoes. We wash our clothes, dust the furniture, sweep the rugs, and paint the house. We are careful to avoid bad breath and b.o. But are we as vigilant about keeping our minds free from impure thoughts; our speech free from gossip, abuse, and four-letter words? Are our hearts free from jealousy, bitterness, hatred, and lust? No! We wash our hands but not our hearts.

Thought for the day: *Cleanliness cannot take the place of godliness.*

Matthew 15:10–20   FEBRUARY 24

Out of the heart come evil thoughts . . . these are what defile a man (vv. 19, 20).

There is a lot of talk about pollution these days. Ecologists are warning us that we are polluting the air with poisonous gases, and our streams and beaches with poisonous chemicals. But Jesus warns us that the greatest pollution problem is not without—in the environment—but within, in the heart. This was clearly illustrated some time ago when a score of government pollution inspectors in New York City were arrested and charged with failure to enforce the antipollution laws. For several years they had been taking bribes from various companies and making out false inspection reports.

The Bible uses the word *heart* over 700 times. The word is used symbolically to denote the seat of our affections, emotions, desires, attitudes and motives. It is that great inner center where the mind, the emotions, the basic drives, the conscience, and the will all meet. It is the central motivating force of the personality, the organ of the soul, the citadel of the self. The chief picture used in the Bible is that of the heart being like a great inner secret spring out of which flows the stream of our lives. Thus Solomon writes in Proverbs 4:23: "Keep your heart with all vigilance, for from it flow the springs of life."

The human heart is the source of all our moral pollution. It is a veritable sewer pipe, pouring out a flow of deadly poisonous waters into the stream of our personality and thus into society. But, thank God, He promises to give us a new heart: "A new heart I will give you . . . I will take out of your flesh the heart of stone and give you a heart of flesh. And I will put my spirit within you, and cause you to walk in my statutes" (Ezek. 36:26–27). He gives a new heart to those who ask Him.

Thought for the day: *God is an expert at heart surgery, and He has never lost a case.*

Matthew 15:21–28   FEBRUARY 25

O woman, great is your faith! (v. 28)

On the surface of this narrative, it appears that Jesus was unkind to the woman, almost harsh. But it is important to remember that the tone of voice and facial expression with which a thing is said make a lot of difference. There is nothing in the story to suggest that the woman felt offended by the words of the Master. Actually, Jesus was merely trying to test her faith. And how marvelously did she respond!

At first Jesus tested the woman by His silence. When she

asked for help, "He did not answer her a word." This was surprising. She had heard of Jesus' compassion for needy people, but He seemed to pay no attention to her plea. Then Jesus tested her by reminding her that He was sent only to the lost sheep of the house of Israel. She was a Gentile and belonged to the Canaanites, the ancestral enemies of the Jews.

The woman's faith, however, seemed to become stronger with the testing. With undiminished fervor she fell at Jesus' feet and cried, "Lord, help me." At first she had recognized Jesus as the "Son of David." Now she acknowledged Him to be "Lord." First she stood and requested help; now she knelt and pleaded for mercy.

Then Jesus presented the most severe test. He said, "It is not fair to take the children's bread and throw it to the dogs." However, the woman was quick to observe that in using this common Jewish expression, Jesus used the diminutive word for *dog*, which denotes the household pet and not the scavenger of the street. Quickly seizing the opportunity, she replied, "Yes, Lord, yet even the pets eat the crumbs that fall from their master's table." She suggested that even Gentiles may receive something from His overflowing grace. When Jesus heard this, he said, "O woman, great is your faith! Be it done for you as you desire." Her faith had emerged triumphant.

Thought for the day: *Faith looks beyond the problem to the promise.*

Matthew 15:29–39   FEBRUARY 26

I have compassion on the crowd, because they have ... nothing to eat (v. 32).

Jesus had great compassion on hungry people. He was unwilling to send them away empty-handed, so He did something to satisfy their needs. I wonder how Jesus would feel and what He would do about all the hungry people in the world today.

Girdling the world at its equatorial bulge is a belt of hunger. Above it live the 1.4 billion inhabitants of the northern developed nations whose advanced industry and agriculture permit them the luxury of worrying about reducing diets instead of diet deficiencies. Below it are the potentially prosperous lands of the Southern Hemisphere's temperate zone. Along the belt live many of the 2.5 billion citizens of the underdeveloped nations, nearly all of them ill-fed; at least sixty percent are malnourished, and another twenty percent are starving.

To Americans hunger is a mild discomfort to be quickly alleviated. To most of the world it is a gnawing feeling in the stomach that turns into a daily compulsory fast. For such people hunger forms the context for all the rest of life. The United Nations Food and Agricultural organization tells us that from one-third to one-half of the world goes to bed hungry every night. Every day some 10,000 people die from starvation or from diseases related to malnourishment. In India some twenty-five million people are receiving less than five ounces of rationed grain a day, which is equal to 400 calories, or one-third of the food intake a human being needs to survive. This is a hungry world and it is becoming hungrier.

As Christians living in an affluent society we need to ask ourselves some questions. When so many around the world are hungry or starving, can we indulge in over-eating? Can we throw food away into our garbage cans? Can we plow under crops or kill millions of chickens just to keep prices up? What is our responsibility to a hungry world?

Thought for the day: *Maybe you can't feed the hungry multitudes, but try helping a few.*

Matthew 16:1–12   FEBRUARY 27

You know how to interpret the appearance of the sky, but you cannot interpret the signs of the times (v. 3).

The Pharisee was able to read the signs in the sky and predict the weather for the day, but he was unable to read the signs of the time and perceive that the kingdom of God was at hand. It is possible for a person to be knowledgeable about the things of the world, but at the same time to be completely ignorant of spiritual matters. A scientist may know many of the mysteries of creation, but nothing about the majesty of the Creator. One may be famous as a geologist and yet know nothing about the Rock of Ages.

The Pharisees did not know even the most basic spiritual truths, simply because they did not want to know. They asked Jesus for a sign of His messiahship when they already had an abundance of signs. One more sign, even of the greatest magnitude, would have made no difference. They had already made up their minds not to accept the truth. Their spiritual ignorance was not due to lack of evidence, but to lack of faith. The problem was not with the character of Christ's proofs, but with the condition of their hearts.

We often hear someone say, "Prove to me there is a God and I will believe in Him." But there is already plenty of proof. All one needs to do is look at the abundant provisions of God, the signs of His providential care, His wisdom and power manifested in creation, and His transforming grace demonstrated in the lives of countless people.

When the first Russian astronauts traveled in outer space, one of them came back and said, "We looked for God out there, but we didn't see Him." However, when one American astronaut made the same trip, he testified to an awesome feeling of the Presence of God all about Him. You see what you want to see.

Thought for the day: *A blind person's darkness is not dispelled by turning on more lights.*

Matthew 16:13–20   FEBRUARY 28

On this rock I will build my church, and the powers of death shall not prevail against it (v. 18).

69

There is fear in many quarters about the future of the Christian church. Many critics claim that the church is irrelevant, if not actually dead. Some governments are trying to wipe out the church. In such times as these the words of Jesus bring great comfort, assurance, and hope.

Christ is both the Founder and the Foundation of the church. *He* builds the church; we only assist Him. The church is a divine institution, not a human society or club. It is a spiritual fellowship comprising all those, who through faith in Jesus Christ, have been born of the Spirit. The foundation of the church is its confession that Jesus is "the Christ, the Son of the living God." Take away this cardinal truth, and the universal church will crumble.

Jesus says that the church is built on rock. Because it is a divine institution, it will stand the test of time. Nothing can shake it. Opposition, persecution, and all the combined forces of Satan will not be able to crush or wipe it out.

In the early days, the Roman government tried to stamp out Christianity by violent persecution. Christians were imprisoned, thrown to the lions, beheaded, and burned alive. But within 250 years the Emperor Constantine himself became a Christian and declared Christianity to be the state religion.

During the Middle Ages, the church suffered from inward corruption because of dishonest leaders and false teachings. Translators and printers of the Bible were burned at the stake. Then God raised up Martin Luther and purged the church. Today the Bible is the best seller around the world, and has been translated into hundreds of languages.

In modern times atheistic Communism has tried its best to exterminate religion in Russia and China, but the church still lives in these lands. The church has often been brought to its knees, but it has never been knocked out.

Thought for the day: *The church has many critics, but no substitute.*

*What shall it profit a man, if he gain the whole world
and lose his own soul? (v. 26).*

Several years ago an English artist drew a large painting
which attracted considerable attention from the public. He
pictured a young man playing a game of chess with the Devil,
and gambling for his soul. The young man had lost, and sat
dejected, his face buried in his hands. The Devil looked down
upon him in glee.

One day a famous chess player stood before the painting.
He took one look at the chess men arranged on the board and
immediately noticed something wrong. With a voice of
authority he said to those standing nearby: "Bring me a chess
board . . . place the men just as you see them in the picture."
Then he picked up one of the pieces on the board, moved it
to another position, and saved the game for the young man. It
seems the problem was a misplaced king!

That is exactly our spiritual problem today. We have
allowed other things to misplace Christ as King in our lives. It
may be money, comforts, position, honor, sex, or worldly
pleasure. So instead of living for God and for others, we are
living for ourselves; and we are in danger of losing our souls.

It is a tragedy when anyone loses all earthly possessions.
Our hearts are moved with compassion when we see pictures
of war refugees and tornado victims. It is an even greater
tragedy for a person to lose his health, for what good is wealth
if a person is too ill to enjoy it? Far worse is the loss of one's
mind, for then the person ceases to be human and becomes
a mere vegetable. But, says Jesus, the greatest tragedy of all is
for one to lose his soul. He can afford to lose his possessions,
or health, or even his mind, but he cannot afford to lose his
soul. It is worth more than the whole world.

Thought for the day: *Any exchange for one's soul is a poor bargain.*

Matthew 17:1—13 MARCH 1

They saw no one but Jesus only (v. 8).

As Jesus was transfigured on the mountain top, suddenly Moses and Elijah appeared and talked with Him about His coming death on the cross. Now Moses was considered by the Israelites as the supreme *Lawgiver* of the nation. It was through him that they had received the Commandments of God. Elijah was the first and the greatest of the *prophets*. The Jews looked back to him as the very voice of God. So when Peter realized the illustrious company he was in, he said impetuously, "I will make three booths here; one for you and one for Moses and one for Elijah."

But the moment Peter said this, a large cloud overshadowed the three disciples, blocking their vision completely. They could see no one. Then a voice from the cloud said, "*This* is my beloved Son . . . listen to HIM!" By his suggestion, Peter was virtually placing Moses and Elijah on a par with Jesus, the Son of God. It reminds me of the pictures I have seen on the walls of countless homes in India, where Gandhi and Buddha and Christ are portrayed as "the three great men of peace." But God will not permit this. His Son is unique; He stands alone; He demands a solitary throne.

Moses and Elijah were great men, but they were only human. They merely pointed forward by symbol and prediction to the atoning work of Christ. Jesus was more than human; He was the divine Son of God. In Him the Law of Moses and the prophecy of Elijah were fulfilled; furthermore, through His atoning death He brought salvation to the world.

When the disciples heard the voice of God through the cloud, they fell on their faces with reverence. Finally, when they looked up, "they saw no one but Jesus only." This is the

72

way it should be. When we put Christ in His rightful place, then we see Him in all His glory and power.

Thought for the day: *Jesus must be Lord of all, if He is to be Lord at all.*

Matthew 17:14—21   **MARCH 2**

I brought him to your disciples, and they could not heal him (v. 16).

The disciples of Jesus failed miserably on this occasion to minister to the needs of a desperate young man. It was a difficult case, no doubt, for the lad was both epileptic and demon-possessed. But Jesus had already given the disciples "authority over unclean spirits, to cast them out, and to heal every disease and every infirmity" (10:1). So they were not lacking in ability and authority. But as Jesus pointed out, it was their lack of faith that rendered His power inoperative.

How often the world seeks help from us as modern disciples of Christ, but because of unbelief we cannot help them. Some people, who have tried everything humanly possible to overcome their guilt and sin, turn to the minister for help. But since he does not believe in the deity of Christ or the supernatural, he is unable to lead them to a power beyond themselves. Others, who are ill and have tried everything that modern medicine has to offer, may look to the minister for help. But because he does not believe in divine healing, he fails to intercede for their physical restoration.

The unordained minister, the Christian in the pew, can fail just as miserably as the ordained minister in the pulpit. Perhaps the neighbors next door are grieving over the loss of a loved one, but because the "Christian" does not believe strongly enough in the resurrection of Christ, he/she is unable to offer any solace or hope. Perhaps the one who works in the same office or factory is facing some great trial in his life, but the "Christian" colleague does not believe sufficiently in the efficacy of prayer, and so fails to minister to the person's need.

Divine power for all human need is available, but we must exercise faith in order to make it operative in the lives of others. Jesus said, even a small faith, if real, can do the impossible.

Thought for the day: *It is not a great faith we need, but a small faith in a great God.*

Matthew 17:22−27   MARCH 3

Does not your teacher pay the tax? (v. 24)

The tax referred to here was the annual temple tax which was required for the support of the temple worship. The amount was one-half shekel, the days' pay for the ordinary working man. On another occasion, the Pharisees questioned Jesus whether it was lawful to pay the annual poll tax to the Roman government, and He answered, "Render to Caesar the things that are Caesar's" (Mark 12:17). Thus Jesus upheld both the religious and the civil tax, and set a good example by paying his dues.

Christianity and good citizenship go hand in hand. The true follower of Christ will accept and shoulder his duties as a citizen. He will be loyal to his nation and obedient to the laws of the land. Christians, in fact, ought to be the finest citizens, for in respecting the authority of God, they also respect the authority of government; in obeying the moral law, they also comply with civil law; in loving and serving God, they also love their neighbor and seek to minister to his needs.

In the early years of the Christian faith, the Roman Emperor Julian (332−363), an enemy of Christianity, highly praised the Christians for "their loving service rendered to strangers and their care for the burial of the dead." He testified that "there was not a single Christian who was a beggar," and that the Christians "cared not only for their own poor but for others as well."

A few years ago I heard the Hindu headman of a village in India pay a public tribute to the Christians of the community. He said, "They work hard; they help people in need; they obey the laws of the land; and they live quiet, peaceful lives. They are an example to all of us." The tribute was all the more remarkable when we remember that these Christians came from the despised, "untouchable" segment of Indian society. When they became Christians, they became good citizens.

Thought for the day: *Christians may not be the cream of society, but they are the salt of the earth.*

Matthew 18:1–6

Unless you turn and become like children, you will never enter the kingdom of heaven (v. 3).

Entrance into the kingdom of God does not depend on special privileges or personal greatness; it depends on a particular attitude of mind or set of the soul.

The first step is a *new direction*—"Unless you turn." The sinner is faced in the wrong direction—on the pathway away from God. The repentant must turn around and face toward God. It involves a complete about-face; a reversal of lifestyle. The forgiven one now strives to do God's will.

Then follows a *new disposition*—"become like children." This does not mean being childish in behavior but child-like in spirit. Humility becomes the basic characteristic. A child doesn't talk about the past, but looks ahead to the future and wants to grow up. Likewise, the new-born child of God can forget the past, face the future with confidence and hope. The desire now is to grow into a mature Christian.

Children are ever ready to ask for and accept a gift, without embarrassment or apology. They feel completely dependent upon their parents and willingly trust them.

Children are open and frank. Likewise, the child of God readily accepts the gifts of our heavenly Father; trusts Him in all things; and talks to Him with all frankness.

The new direction and new disposition result in a *new destiny*—"the kingdom of heaven." This is completely a new sphere of living, with new standards and goals. The Christian's destiny is now to become more like the Master every day.

The first step is our part. Christ waits for us to turn around and throw our wills on His side. The second step is His part; he gives us a new disposition. The third step is a cooperative affair. Christ supplies the grace and power as we supply the willingness and obedience.

Thought for the day: *To turn around toward God is to go forward, not backward.*

Matthew 18:7–14   **MARCH 5**

Does he not leave the ninety-nine ... and go in search of the one that went astray? (v. 12)

It would seem almost blasphemous to ask, "Did Jesus have any favorites?" The impulsive answer would be, "Certainly not. He was incapable of any favoritism." But what if the question were pressed: "Were there some people over whom He expressed a special concern?" It is not so easy to return to complete denial. The facts are, according to our Scripture passage, that Jesus Christ does express a special concern over certain people.

Jesus is concerned about the *lost one*. He clearly stated, "The Son of man came to seek and to save the lost" (Luke 19:10). Like the faithful shepherd who is disturbed when a sheep goes astray, Christ is distressed when a man or woman gets lost from the fold of His love and care. His concern leads Him to action. He actively goes out in search of the lost one and tries to lead him home.

Jesus is concerned about the *last one*. In the parable

which He told, the man had a hundred sheep; only one went astray. But the shepherd didn't say to himself, "Well, never mind about that one sheep; I still have ninety-nine left." Instead, he left the ninety-nine in the fold and went out after the one lost sheep. Christ is interested in the salvation of the very last person.

Jesus is also concerned about the *least one*. He said, "It is not the will of my Father who is in heaven that one of these little ones should perish." "Little ones" here refers primarily to the children, but it could also mean those who are insignificant in society—the drunk on skid row, the village urchin, the poor widow in the ghetto, the prisoner in the penitentiary. No one anywhere is beyond the concern and love of the Savior. He is interested in the redemption of every single individual.

Thought for the day: *Christ is concerned about the lost, the last, and the least.*

Matthew 18:15–18   MARCH 6

If your brother sins against you. . . . (v. 15).

Great harm can come to the church of Jesus Christ when its members fail to deal with offenses and grievances in a Christian way. Several years ago, an outstanding layman of a very ancient church in southeast Asia led a movement against the leaders of the church because he felt they were drifting from the teachings of the founders. Instead of settling the dispute within the framework of the church organization or through arbitration, the opposition group took the matter to the civil courts. Before non-Christian judges they argued over the details of Christian doctrine, including the nature of the Presence of Christ in the elements of Holy Communion. The whole affair seriously affected the witness and vitality of the church. In the end the church was split.

In this passage of Scripture, Jesus lays down certain

fundamental principles for dealing with offenses within the household of faith:

First, do not brood over a wrongdoing, but bring it out into the open. To harbor a resentment within yourself is to poison the mind and life. Any such feeling should be honestly faced and put into words.

Second, if you feel someone has wronged you, go to see that person. Talking behind the person's back or merely writing a letter will only aggravate the problem. Nothing can take the place of an honest, face-to-face interview that is pervaded with loving concern and a prayerful spirit.

Third, if a private, personal meeting fails to achieve its purpose, then take along some wise person or persons with you to help the process of reconciliation. Often a group of Christian brothers and sisters can achieve what one alone is unable to do.

Finally, if this attempt fails, take the matter to the entire Christian fellowship. There, in an atmosphere of prayer and love, personal relationships may be righted. Only after all these attempts at reconciliation have failed, should any discipline of the offending member be attempted.

Thought for the day: *Litigation destroys; reconciliation redeems.*

Matthew 18:19–22   MARCH 7

Lord, how often shall my brother sin against me, and I forgive him? (v. 21)

Jesus preached and demonstrated that God is a loving heavenly Father who forgives those who repent and turn from their sins. In His parable of the prodigal son, the father welcomed back the penitent son and restored him to full fellowship. To the paralyzed man whom Jesus healed and to the woman who bathed His feet with ointment, He said with tender compassion, "Your sins are forgiven." While He was dying on the cross, He cried out, "Father, forgive them, for they know not what they do."

Jesus also taught that we should forgive others in the same manner that God forgives us. He clearly said, "Only if you forgive men their trespasses, will your heavenly Father forgive yours." One of the petitions of His model prayer is, "Forgive us our debts as we also have forgiven our debtors."

But you say, "I simply cannot forgive that person. The wrong which he did me is too great." All right, then to be honest you should pray, "Lord, don't forgive me, because I am unwilling to forgive the other person." Is that what you want? Or you say, "I can forgive the person, but I can't forget about it." Then you should say to God, "Lord, please forgive my sin, but don't forget it. Keep throwing it up into my face." But God doesn't forgive that way. When He forgives, He also forgets; that is, He doesn't keep bringing up the past.

Again you say, "I will forgive and I will forget, but I can't keep on forgiving. There is a limit to forgiveness." All right, then to be honest you should say to God, "Lord, I expect you to forgive me only a few times, and after that you can quit." But God's forgiveness is unlimited. He doesn't keep score of the number of times He forgives. And He requires the same of us. We must be willing to forgive the other person over and over again.

Thought for the day: *Divine and human forgiveness go hand in hand.*

Matthew 18:23–35   **MARCH 8**

Should not you have had mercy on your fellow servant, as I had mercy on you? (v. 33)

We saw yesterday that divine and human forgiveness go hand in hand. Only if we are willing to forgive those who trespass against us, will God be willing to forgive our trespasses against Him. In order to drive home this truth, Jesus told the dramatic parable which we read for today.

In the parable we have a couple of contrasts. There is first the contrast between the size of the two debts. The servant owed his master ten thousand talents. The talent was the largest denomination used in the account of money or weight in those days, and was probably worth about a thousand dollars. Thus the entire debt was a hundred denarii, which was the equivalent of only about twenty dollars.

Then there was the contrast between the unlimited compassion of the master and the unreasonable severity of the servant. When the servant was confronted with his immense debt, he fell at his master's feet and asked for patience and time to pay up. In response, the master had mercy on him and forgave him the entire amount. But when the fellow servant asked for the same terms, the first servant seized him by the throat and threw him into prison. What a picture of ingratitude and callousness!

The point Jesus is making is this: nothing that men can do to us can in any way compare with what we have done to God, for our sin sent the Son of God to a cross. And if God has so freely forgiven us, then we must be willing to forgive others. We have been forgiven a debt which is beyond our means to pay. Surely, then, we can forgive the debts that others owe to us.

Thought for the day: *Treat others in the way you want God to treat you.*

Matthew 19:1–12   MARCH 9

The two shall become one (v. 5).

When a man and a woman are joined together in marriage, in what sense do they become one? Are they one because they now have the same surname? But so do other relatives of the family. Are they one because they live in the same house, eat at the same table, and sleep in the same bed? Not necessarily, for two people may be close physically, but far apart in mind and in heart. Are they one merely because they join their bodies together? This may be a beautiful outward symbol of, but can never be a substitute for, the deeper emotional and spiritual union that marriage involves.

Husband and wife should be *one in purpose*. Their chief aim in life should be to glorify God by doing His will. This provides the spiritual foundation for their home. It becomes the center around which all their ambitions and efforts revolve.

Husband and wife are *one in love*, a love which is sanctified by their common love for Christ. They love one another completely and unselfishly, so that they seek each other's well-being and happiness. Their mutual love fortifies them against outside temptations and against the hardships of life.

Husband and wife are *one in shared experiences*. They share the same joys and sorrows, the same trials and triumphs, the same losses and gains. When one suffers, the other feels pain; when one succeeds, the other feels honored. They rejoice in each other's advances, and grieve with one another's setbacks.

To be one certainly does not mean that husband and wife lose their identity and become one person, for they will always be separate individuals with minds and wills of their own. But they can both choose to unite in one purpose and one commitment, and thus become one in mind and heart. It is this spiritual unity that converts a house into a home and transforms a legal ceremony into a life-long companionship.

Thought for the day: *When two become one in Christ, it's the sweetest fellowship this side of heaven.*

Matthew 19:13–15   **MARCH 10**

Jesus said, "Let the children come to me" (v. 14).

Children were brought to him that he might lay his hands on them and pray (v. 13).

It was probably the mothers who brought their children to Jesus. What an inspiring sight! Most of the time when people came to Jesus and asked Him to lay hands on them, they needed urgent help and were motivated by a sense of desperation. Perhaps they were blind, or lame, or lepers. But in this case the mothers were motivated by love, desiring that He should simply pray for, and bless, their children. It is evident from the narrative that Jesus was not only "a friend of sinners"; He was also a friend of little children.

The Gospel writer tells us that "the disciples rebuked the people." Perhaps they felt our Lord was tired and needed a rest, and so they wanted to protect Him from unnecessary bother. However, it is evident that they also seemed to feel that the children were too insignificant to interfere with the work of the Master or to demand His attention and care. The response of Jesus was considerate and tender. "Let the children come to me," He said, "for to such belongs the kingdom of heaven."

Several years ago a godly Indian mother brought her baby to the altar at the great Maramon Christian Convention in South India. She asked the bishop to lay hands on the child and consecrate him for service in Nepal. (At that time Nepal was closed to the outside world.) Everyday the young lad repeated this prayer after his mother, "Lord Jesus, when I become a big boy, send me as a missionary to Nepal."

The young lad grew up and completed high school, and then was graduated from seminary the very year that Nepal opened its doors to the outside world. It was my privilege to be among those who laid hands upon Kunjukutty Athialy and consecrated him as the first Indian missionary to Nepal.

Thought for the day: *A mother's noblest act is to bring her child to Jesus.*

What good deed must I do, to have eternal life?
(v. 16)

When the young man came to Jesus, there were some things he did not need. He already had them. First, he had *riches,* for the account tells us that "he had great possessions." How he got them, the record does not say, but he probably had inherited a princely estate, and he may have been successful in administering his affairs. In any event, he was wealthy.

Then again, the young man had *rank.* Luke tells us that he was a ruler of the Jews. He was not one of the nobodies; he belonged to the aristocracy. He rated high in society. He was a man of prestige and influence, and was held in respect by the community.

The rich young ruler also had *religion.* This may sound startling, but it is true. He was a member of the orthodox church of his day. Jesus said to him, "You are asking about life. Let me try you on the commandments." The young man said, "Which?" Jesus enumerated several. Without a blush, the ruler looked into the face of Jesus and said, "All these have I kept from my youth up." He probably told the truth, for Jesus did not question him. He was a moral, upright young man, who rigidly observed the ethical requirements of his faith.

The young man had riches, rank, and religion—all these. But one thing he lacked. That was eternal life. This life cannot be purchased with money. It cannot be earned by position or status. It is not the reward of our good deeds. Morality is negative; life is positive. Morality is ethical; life is spiritual. Morality is achieved; life is imparted. Eternal life is the gift of God through Jesus Christ. "He who has the Son has life; he who has not the Son of God has not life" (1 John 5:12).

Are you looking for eternal life? You must receive it as a gift from nail-pierced hands.

Thought for the day: *The one with everything has nothing, if he lacks eternal life.*

Matthew 19:23–30

Lo, we have left everything and followed you. What then shall we have? (v. 27)

Peter's question negated his affirmation. It was true that he had left his boats, his fishing nets, his business, his home and his security, but he had not forsaken everything. Peter had not forsaken Peter. He had not fully surrendered himself. And so he was constantly getting entangled in his unsurrendered self. It showed up now and then in the form of pride, self-seeking, self-sufficiency, and self-will.

It is so easy for us to give things to Jesus—our time, our money, even our service—and yet not give ourselves. We give—but we don't give up!

A layman in India said to the congregation during a revival, "All these years I have given my tithes and offerings to the Lord, but I have never given myself." A young American missionary, who went as pastor to an English-speaking congregation in Bombay, confessed in a pastor's retreat: "I gave up my homeland, a good job, and a good salary to come to India to work for God, but I must admit that I have not really given myself to Him." The last thing we are ready to surrender is the self.

Jesus said, "If any man desires to be my disciple, let him deny himself." That is the first and most crucial step. Not just giving up comforts, or position, or pleasure, but denying self. This means to die to our own will and to make God's will the ruling principle of our lives.

Take the word *sin.* Right at the heart of the word is the letter *I,* which stands for the ego, the unsurrendered self. Now bend the *I* around until it becomes an *O,* and suddenly the word *sin* spells *son.* This is the road from sin to sonship—

when we cross from self-centeredness over to Christ-center-edness.

Thought for the day: *The self on our hands is a problem and a pain; in the hands of God it is a possibility and a power (Dr. E. Stanley Jones).*

Matthew 20:1–16   MARCH 13

Do you begrudge my generosity? (v. 15)

The telling of the parable was prompted by the remark that Peter made to Jesus. Peter said, "Lo, we have left everything and followed you; now what do we get?" He was merely expressing the principle by which we operate in all affairs of life, that is, the principle of reward for merit or payment for services rendered. A person studies for four years in college and is granted a bachelor of arts degree as a reward for meeting certain standards. An athlete competes in the mile race in the Olympics and is granted a gold medal for outrunning all competitors. A laborer works eight hours a day, five days a week, and at the end of the month receives a check as stipulated wages for work rendered. So Peter was saying, "Lord, we have given up our homes and our occupations in order to serve you; now what reward do we receive?"

In response, by means of the parable, Jesus said, "Peter, you don't understand. The kingdom of God does not operate on the basis of reward and remuneration. It operates on grace, the unmerited favor of God. Everything that God gives is of grace. We cannot earn what He gives us; we cannot merit or deserve it; we cannot put God in our debt. What God gives to us is given out of sheer generosity, out of the goodness of His heart. What God gives is not a reward or payment, but a gift. So no one can say, "Lord, I served you for fifty years, and this person served you only two years." Or, "I won more souls for the kingdom than this other person; I should get more than he does." Even to make such a suggestion takes the giving of

God out of the category of grace and puts it into the category of remuneration; and God doesn't operate that way. With Him it is grace, and grace alone.

Thought for the day: *The grace of God is the greatest leveling influence in the universe.*

Matthew 20:17–28   MARCH 14

The Son of man came not to be served but to serve, and to give his life as a ransom for many (v. 28).

Once again Jesus gives His disciples a lesson on humility. He points out two significant principles in the Christian life.

To the Christian *it is more important to serve than to be served.*People of the world enjoy being served. They like to be boss or supervisor and give all the directions. They delight in having others wait on them for needs and comforts. Position, prestige, and honor are their goals. But disciples of Christ take the attitude of servants. Their greatest joy is in ministering to the needs and welfare of others. They look upon their occupations or professions as a means of serving Christ and others. Christians look out upon the world with Christ-like eyes, seeing the distress, pain, and sin of people all about. They feel for the world with a Christ-like heart, as they empathize with others in their concerns. They reach out with Christ-like hands and seek to lift the fallen.

Again, to Christians, *it is more important to give than to get.* Jesus said that He had come to serve and also to give his life as a ransom for many. He was on His way to the cross, but the disciples were reaching out for thrones, and crowns, and scepters. People of the world look out for themselves, and in the end they lose themselves. Christians give themselves away and end up finding themselves. They bestow mercy, and receive mercy; they give out love, and receive love in return. They seek the happiness of others, and joy floods their lives.

Instead of asking, "How much can I get?" we must ask, "How much can I give?" This is the motivating principle of life.

Thought for the day: *When the prodigal son left home, he said, "Give me my money." When he returned home, he said, "Make me a servant."*

Matthew 20:29–34   **MARCH 15**

What do you want me to do for you? (v. 32)

It seemed like a foolish question for Jesus to ask. The two men were obviously blind. What else would they desire but to be able to see? However, behind Jesus' question lay a very important truth.

When the blind men first cried out for help, they merely said, "Lord, have mercy on us." But what did that mean? In what way did they want mercy to be expressed? Did they want the Lord to throw a few coins into their beggar's bowl? Or to give them a cup of cold water? You see, it was all so general. Jesus knew what the two needed and desired, but He wanted them to confess their need in specific terms. Only when they made a definite request—"Lord, let our eyes be opened"— did Jesus touch their eyes and restore their sight.

Whenever we come to the Lord for help, the first thing He asks us is, "What do you want me to do for you?" He already understands our problem more perfectly than we do, and does not need for us to pass on any information to Him. But He wants us to confess our need in a definite way. It is not enough to say, "Lord, I need your help," or, "Lord, I want your blessing." These are generalities. We must pinpoint the problem or the need. Do we need forgiveness for a particular sin? Then let's say it. Do we need cleansing from a particular impurity? Let's confess it. Christ can then meet us at the point of our need.

Pilots in the Air Force are able to pinpoint a particular object from a very high altitude and drop their bombs right in the center of the target. They call this precision bombing. Our Lord specializes in precision blessing. When we specify our needs clearly, He can zero in on the target and apply His grace to the very heart of the problem.

Thought for the day: *Specific requests bring specific answers.*

Matthew 21:1–11   MARCH 16

The crowds ... shouted, "Hosanna to the Son of David!" (v. 9)

Those few days from the Triumphal Entry of our Lord into Jerusalem to His crucifixion afford all the proof we need of the fact that popularity is a fleeting thing and that unregenerate humankind are a fickle, depraved lot. It was "hurrahs" on Sunday and hisses on Friday—from the same crowd!

When Christ entered Jerusalem, He was acclaimed and applauded by the multitude. When He went out, He was spat upon and jeered by the mob. He rode into Jerusalem over the garments spread out before Him by the enthusiastic crowd. He went out bearing a cross. As they welcomed Him to the city, they cried, "Blessed is he who comes in the name of the Lord!" As He was led out of the city, they cried, "Away with him, crucify him!" He was received into the city as if He were a conqueror and a king. He was led out as if He were a malefactor and a criminal. When He came into Jerusalem, palm branches were waved in salutation before Him. When He went out, a crown of thorns was placed on His brow in mockery. So overwhelming was the enthusiasm of His reception into Jerusalem that the Pharisees, His enemies, said, "Behold, the world is gone after him." So unpopular was He a few days later that not even the Roman governor, who found Him innocent, dared to risk the displeasure of the mob by setting Him free.

Is not the same spirit alive today? We sing, "Crown Him

With Many Crowns," on Sunday and then go out to crucify Christ with our deeds the rest of the week. We give Him our money at the worship service, but fail to give Him our time and devotion during the rush of daily activity. We need the redeeming grace of Christ just as much today as the people back in Jesus' day.

Thought for the day: *It's not how loudly we shout, but how straight we walk that counts.*

Matthew 21:12–17   **MARCH 17**

My house shall be called a house of prayer (v. 13).

We must admit that the average church in our country is *not* a house of prayer. In many churches there is no regular prayer service; there are no study-prayer groups. The one and only prayer that is offered during the entire week is the so-called "pastoral prayer," followed by the Lord's Prayer, in the Sunday morning worship service. A majority of church members do not observe a daily prayer time, nor do they return thanks before meals; in fact, they do not know how to pray.

Some Roman Catholic churches keep their doors open during the daytime to permit members who are passing by to drop in for a quiet time of prayer. Almost any hour of the day two or three of the faithful may be found kneeling in silent prayer. This at least is an improvement over the average Protestant church.

Perhaps the churches in Korea are closer to being houses of prayer than any other churches in the world. Every Korean church, regardless of the denomination, conducts a prayer service at 5:30 a.m. every day of the week. In the capital city of Seoul, with its more than 5000 Christian churches, thousands of Korean Christians may be seen making their way to these early morning services. The Wednesday evening prayer meetings are almost as well attended as the regular Sunday morning worship services. In the regular church services, when the pastor says, "Let us pray," the whole congregation prays out loud together. Each person, with eyes closed and hands clasped, looks toward heaven and earnestly expresses praises and petitions to God. It is this spirit of prayer that has made the Korean church one of the fastest growing churches in Asia and the Far East. For the past thirty-five years the Christian constituency has doubled each decade, and has grown from 350,000 to *ten million!*

Let us learn a lesson from the Christians of Korea.

Thought for the day: *The church advances most rapidly on its knees.*

Matthew 21:18–22   **MARCH 18**

... the fig tree withered at once ... if you say to this mountain ... (vv. 19, 21).

The withering of the fruitless fig tree is an acted parable. A fig tree is supposed to bear fruit. When Jesus approached this particular tree, He found it full of leaves, which was a sign of fruit; but there was no fruit. So He commanded the tree not ever to bear fruit again.

Jesus, of course, was speaking particularly to the spiritual condition of Israel at that time. God had chosen Israel in order to deliver His revelation to them, and through them to bring blessings to all the nations. But in spite of their outward profession of righteousness, they had failed to produce the fruits of righteousness and had failed to fulfill their appointed ministry. Therefore, as a nation, Israel was under judgment. However, Christ is also speaking to us today, as members of the household of faith. We are meant to bear fruit—the fruit of the Spirit in our own lives and fruit in the transformation of others. We have a calling to fulfill. If we fail in this calling, either as individuals or as a nation blessed with innumerable spiritual privileges, the judgment of God will be upon us just as surely as it was upon Israel. Thus here we have a lesson on the tragedy of fruitlessness.

When the disciples saw how quickly the command of Jesus took effect, they asked the Lord, "How did the fig tree wither at once?" This gave Jesus the opportunity to drive home a second spiritual lesson, namely, the *triumph of faith*. He said, "If you have faith, you can not only wither a fig tree, but you can remove mountains; that is, you can overcome all difficulties, you can do what is humanly impossible." "For whatever you ask in prayer," said Jesus, "you will receive, if you have faith." Thus the child of God does not operate on the formula: *difficulty, doubt, defeat;* but rather on the formula: *trial, trust, triumph!*

Thought for the day: *Faith and fruit are the hallmarks of the Christian life.*

Matthew 21:23–32   **MARCH 19**

Go and work in the vineyard today (v. 28).

The Christian is not called to a life of idleness but to a life of useful activity. The New Testament makes it clear that we are not saved by our works, but we are certainly saved *unto* good works. Works are not the cause of our salvation; but they are the natural result of our redemption. Jesus says to each one of us, "Go and work."

In order to be a worker for God, we must be His children. The command is addressed to the child—*"Son,* go and work." First we must be in spiritual relationship to God; then we can enter into partnership with Him in service. Unless we are sons and daughters we will have nothing to give to others. Only after we have personally experienced His grace and love in our own lives will we be able to share these blessings with others. The new birth, therefore, is a prerequisite for service.

We are called to work in God's vineyard. "Go and work *in the vineyard.*" The vineyard is made up of all those who have not, by repentance and faith, entered into the kingdom of God and have not accepted His will for their lives. The vineyard also consists of all areas of human relationships—social, political, economic—that have not accepted the lordship of Christ. The vineyard may be in one's own family circle; it may be in the office, the factory, the schoolroom; it may be across the street or across the seas. Each one of us has a plot in the vineyard where God wants us to plant, cultivate, and harvest.

Jesus says, "Go and work in the vineyard *today*." There is an urgency about the call. No time is to be wasted. The harvest is ripe and laborers are needed desperately. So Jesus urges us to "work while it is day, for the night cometh when no man can work." To delay is to miss the harvest.

Thought for the day: *Don't try to give God instructions; just report for duty.*

Matthew 21:33–46   MARCH 20

The very stone which the builders rejected has become the head of the corner (v. 42).

B. R. Ambedkar was born into an outcaste Hindu family in India near the beginning of this century. In those days caste discrimination was exceedingly harsh. Even the shadow of an "untouchable" falling upon a member of the higher castes could pollute him. "Untouchable" children were not permitted to sit in the same classroom with others.

But Ambedkar was an intelligent and ambitious young man. After high school, through the help of a friendly rajah (king), he was able to come to the United States and England, where he earned two doctoral degrees in law. When India gained her independence from Britain in 1947, the new government wanted someone to draft a constitution for the young republic, and they could think of no one more competent than Dr. Ambedkar. Thus, the lad who grew up in one of the despised castes of India eventually became one of its great political leaders. With a stroke of his pen in the new constitution he outlawed untouchability in India and declared all people equal.

If this could happen to an ordinary person in history, how much more could it happen to our Lord Jesus Christ. When He was upon earth, He was rejected and despised by His own people, but today He is acclaimed as Savior and Lord by millions who represent every race and nation and tribe around the world. There were those who called Jesus names in His day. They said He was mad, that He had a devil. Today His praises are sung in every land and all Christian prayer is offered in His name. He was once condemned to die on a cross between two thieves, but today He is the Lord of life, the Head of the church, and the coming King whom millions await with faith and hope. One day He will rule the world.

Thought for the day: *God may appear to lose a minor skirmish now and then, but He is going to win the final battle.*

Matthew 22:1–14   MARCH 21

Come to the marriage feast (v. 4).

Jesus compared the kingdom of God to a royal wedding feast. This makes the Christian life something special. God's invitation is an invitation to joy and fellowship—not to gloom and isolation. To think of the Christian life in terms of a long face, drudgery, restrictions, and binding regulations is to miss the whole point. It is a life of true inward joy and peace, of freedom, adventure and victory. It is a feast, not a fast.

The invitation is to all, regardless of race, color, position, or worth. God sends forth His messengers over and over again, calling men and women to the marriage feast. He is determined that the banquet hall will be filled and that His Son will be glorified.

But there are two warnings that we must heed. It is

possible for us to miss the feast—because we are preoccupied with other things and fail to hear the invitation. Country folk are too busy on the farm, doing the chores, milking the cows and plowing the land; they have no time for spiritual things. City folk are engrossed in their business, buying and selling, taking inventory, keeping accounts, and competing with one another; they also have no time for the kingdom. It is possible to be so busy making a living that we forget to make a life. We can be so involved in the details of everyday life that we forget to live.

The second warning has to do with the way we accept the invitation and participate in the marriage feast. We must be dressed in the proper wedding garment, which is the righteousness of Christ. If we depend upon our own merit, our own good deeds, our own righteousness, we shall never be fit candidates for the kingdom. We must come in the spirit of humility and utter dependence upon God and accept His righteousness, which He offers to us as a free gift in a nail-pierced hand.

Thought for the day: *There is no gate-crashing at God's feast; we must come in on His terms.*

Matthew 22:15–22   MARCH 22

Render ... to Caesar the things that are Caesar's, and to God the things that are God's (v. 21).

The Christian has dual citizenship. He is a citizen of the country in which he was born and lives, as well as a citizen of God's kingdom. Therefore he has a responsibility in both areas.

The Christian is in debt to his own country for many things. The state provides him with safety against the lawless, and it provides all public services such as highways, education, and provision for unemployment and old age. If he accepts the protection and privileges provided by the state, then he is under obligation to support the government. Christianity can never be identified with any particular political party or social theory, but Christians should always take their stand for law, order, and loyalty.

But the Christian is also a member of God's kingdom and is responsible to God in matters of conscience, faith, and principle. He owes his worship, service and obedience to the King of heaven. The two obligations—to God and to the state—may coincide for the most part, but there are times when they may conflict with one another. When the Christian is convinced that the action of the state is contrary to the will of God, then he will have to follow his conscience and be loyal to the higher law of the kingdom. Before the outlawing of state Shintoism in Japan, many Japanese Christians, who ordinarily were peaceful and law-abiding citizens, refused to go to the shrines and bow the knee to the emperor, as was demanded by the state. They had to suffer the consequences, but they were loyal to their Lord and Savior.

In all events, however—and this is the main point Jesus is emphasizing—the true Christian is at one and the same time a good citizen of his own country and a good citizen of the kingdom of heaven. He will never fail in his duty either to God or to people.

Thought for the day: *Obedience to God and loyalty to the state go hand in hand.*

Matthew 22:23–33   MARCH 23

You are wrong, because you know neither the scriptures nor the power of God (v. 29).

The Sadducees completely denied the idea of any life after death. So they came to Jesus with a catch question which, they believed, would reduce the doctrine of the resurrection of the dead to an absurdity. According to the Jewish system of Levirate marriage, if a man died childless, his brother was under obligation to marry the widow and to beget children in his brother's name. The Sadducees concocted an improbable case in which seven brothers, one after another, married the same woman. They asked, "In the resurrection, whose wife will she be?" To which Jesus replied, "If you knew the Scriptures and the power of God, you wouldn't ask such a question." Then he proceeded to show from the Scriptures that there is life after death because God is God of the living and not the dead.

It is right here that many of us go wrong in our theological thinking. We don't study the Word of God with sufficient care and depth to clear up many of our doubts and misunderstandings. Not that the Bible will answer all of our questions, but it will answer the basic questions of life and faith, and guide us into the truth. The Scriptures leave no room for doubt about such essential truths as the supernatural power of God, the deity and uniqueness of Christ, His vicarious death and bodily resurrection, salvation through faith alone, the second coming of our Lord, and the future judgment. Teachings on these subjects are clear for all to understand.

The basic question is really this: What is our attitude toward the Word of God? Do we consider the Bible as the product of human minds, and therefore just another piece of valuable literature? Or do we accept the Bible as a revelation from God to us, and therefore divinely inspired, and the sole authority for faith and practice? This makes a world of difference in our theological concepts.

Thought for the day: *The Bible is God's blueprint for life.*

Matthew 22:34–46   MARCH 24

Teacher, which is the great commandment in the law? (v. 36)

In response to this sincere question, our Lord gave a simple yet profound answer. He declared that the essence of all divine law is expressed in one word, *Love*. Love God and love people.

The Ten Commandments are for the most part negative: "Thou shalt not . . . thou shalt not." Jesus took the first four commandments, which have to do with our relationship to God, and fashioned one great positive commandment: "Love God with all your heart, mind, soul and strength." Then He took the next six commandments, which have to do with our relationship to others, and he fashioned a second positive command: "Love your neighbor as yourself." In these two commands all the law is fulfilled.

The first command, says Jesus, is to love God supremely, with every aspect of one's personality. We are to love God with all our *heart*, with all the sincerity of our *emotional nature*. We are to love Him with all our *mind*, with all the sanity of our *intellectual nature*. We are to love Him with all our *soul*, with all the intensity of our *volitional nature*. We are to love Him with all our *strength*, with all the vitality of our *physical nature*. One's whole self is to be brought under the sway of God. This makes for unified personality, for fixation of purpose.

Jesus follows the first great commandment with a second: "Love your neighbor as yourself." The two cannot be separated. They are like the two rails of the railroad track or like the two wings of a bird. To talk of loving God without loving people is a farce. It would be comparable to putting our arms around a person and then kicking him in the shins. Christian love is spelled with a capital *L*. The vertical stroke, representing our relationship with God, is immediately followed by a horizontal stroke, which represents our relationship to others. If we love God, we will love people.

Thought for the day: *Love* is the perfect tense of *live*.

Matthew 23:1–12   **MARCH 25**

They preach, but do not practice . . . they do all their deeds to be seen by men (vv. 3, 5).

97

Matthew 23 is a terrible indictment against hypocrisy, as illustrated in the character of the Pharisees. Jesus points out some of the basic characteristics of the pharisaic spirit, which is still very much alive today.

The religion of the Pharisees was characterized by *profession without practice*. Jesus said, "They preach, but do not practice." They interpreted the Law of Moses and told others what they should do, but they themselves failed to observe these same instructions. Sounds familiar, doesn't it?

A certain preacher who had received an honorary doctoral degree was once introduced to a group of people at an informal party. One of the ladies, on hearing him introduced as "Dr. So-And-So," asked him the question, "Doctor, where do you practice?" He replied, "Oh, I don't practice, I just preach." There's enough truth in this story to hurt. Many so-called Christians unfortunately do not practice what they preach. In the Christian life, profession and practice must go hand in hand.

Again, the religion of the Pharisees was characterized by a *desire for show*. Jesus said, "They do all their deeds to be seen by men." They wore phylacteries—small leather cases containing Scripture texts—bound upon the arms and forehead. It would have been better to allow the Word of God to dominate action and thought. They came out to pray in sweeping robes decorated with exaggerated tassels. It would have been better to clothe themselves with the garments of humility. They sought the seats of honor at the feasts and in the synagogues, and loved people's praise. But all this was to miss the point of true religion. The object of religion is not to bring glory to one's self, but to bring glory to God and to deepen one's relationship with God and people.

Thought for the day: *The Christian belongs in the workshop, not the showroom.*

You traverse sea and land to make a single proselyte (v. 15).

There is a big difference between proselytism and conversion. Proselytism is a change of *label;* conversion is a change of *life.* Proselytism is horizontal in nature, a change in position along the same level. Conversion is primarily vertical in nature, lifting a person from one level of living to another.

Proselytism may be illustrated by the Muslim cook in India who came to his employer, a Catholic priest, and asked to be baptized. The priest quickly poured water on the Muslim's head and said, "You are no longer Abdul (a Muslim name), but from now on, you are Da-ood (David)." After the ceremony the priest said to the new "convert," "There is one stipulation you must observe carefully. You are not to eat mutton on Friday, only fish."

For several weeks Da-ood obeyed his master, but one Friday special friends suddenly dropped by for a visit, and Da-ood felt he had to serve them mutton curry and rice. The aroma came to the attention of the priest, so he came to his servant and said, "Da-ood, I thought I told you not to cook mutton on Friday." But Da-ood insisted the meat was fish and not mutton. An argument ensued, and finally in desperation the cook said to the priest, "Sir, you are not the only clever one. You poured water on my head and said, 'You are no longer Abdul; from now on you are Da-ood. Well, I poured water on the meat and said, 'You are no longer mutton; you are fish'."

That is proselytism—a change in name without a corresponding change in nature.

Conversion may be illustrated by the Hindu university student in India who had recently been baptized as a Christian. Some of his fellow students met him and said, "Friend, we hear you have changed your religion."

"Oh no," answered the new Christian, "you have things

turned around. My religion has changed me!" That is conversion—a transformation of life.

Thought for the day: *People can make proselytes; only God can convert.*

Matthew 23:23–32 {MARCH 27}

First cleanse the inside . . . that the outside also may be clean (v. 26).

The Pharisees placed the emphasis on external observances, and overlooked the importance of the inner motive and condition.

Jesus commended the Pharisees for their good works. He said, "You fast and pray regularly; you give the tithe of your income; you cross a whole continent to make a single proselyte; you build tombs for the prophets; you keep the traditions of the elders. All well and good. But," said Jesus, "inwardly you are proud, you like to be saluted as 'Rabbi' in public. Inwardly you are selfish, you deceive the poor and the widows. Inwardly you are ambitious; you desire the upper seats at the feasts. Inwardly you are hypocritical; you fast and you pray only to be seen by others. You cleanse the outside of the cup and of the plate, but inside they are full of extortion and rapacity . . . You are like whitewashed tombs." Finally Jesus climaxed His discourse by this terse statement: "First cleanse the inside!"

Our main problem is within. We need an inner transformation, a clean heart. We need to be born again, to become new persons in Christ Jesus.

Religion emphasizes the *outer action*; the Gospel emphasizes the *inner condition*. Religion tries to work from the circumference to the center, from the outside to the inside. The Gospel goes straight to the center and works from the inside out. Religion ends in an *outer reformation*; the Gospel ends in an *inner transformation*. In other words, religion places the primary emphasis on *doing*, while the Gospel places the primary emphasis on *being*. Religion says, Do good and eventually you will become good; the Gospel says, Become good, and then you will naturally do good. The attempt to become good by doing good is like taking a bushel of apples and tying them onto a telephone post, thereby expecting the post to become an apple tree. Impossible! The tree must first *be* an apple tree; then it will produce apples.

Thought for the day: *True righteousness is not put on; it is put in.*

Matthew 23:33–39   MARCH 28

O Jerusalem... How often would I have gathered your children ... and you would not! (v. 37)

This is the pathetic cry of rejected love. One can almost see teardrops rolling down the cheeks of Jesus as He said these words.

Jerusalem was a city that had enjoyed many privileges and opportunities down through the centuries. God had sent to the city many outstanding prophets who fearlessly proclaimed His message and called the people to repentance and true righteousness. Jerusalem was the religious capital of the Jewish nation. The high priests and members of the Sanhedrin resided there. The magnificent temple was located there, and drew thousands of pilgrims from all around at the time of the main feasts.

What was the response of the residents and rulers of Jerusalem to all this? Instead of receiving the Word of God and obeying His commands, they stoned the messengers of God and even killed some of the prophets. But God was exceedingly patient with the Israelites, and in the end sent His Son as Prophet and Redeemer. We can safely infer from Jesus' statement that He must have visited Jerusalem on several occasions and confronted the people with His claims

and mighty works. The climax came when he rode triumphantly into the city as the long-expected Messiah and King.
But even at that moment the chief priests and rulers were
plotting his death by crucifixion. No wonder the agony of
Jesus was so intense.

Jesus will never force Himself upon any person or nation.
He fully respects the right of everyone to make his own free
choice. His is solely the appeal of love. He pleads with
outstretched hands; He calls lovingly by name. But He never
forces an entry into our lives. If we ever want Him to walk
across the threshold of our heart's door, we must respond to
His love and invite Him to come in. Once invited, however, He
will not hesitate to enter.

Thought for the day: *The greatest tragedy of all is to trample
on the love of God.*

Matthew 24:1–2, 15–22, 34   MARCH 29

*There will not be left here one stone upon another
(v. 2).*

Matthew 24 is one of the most difficult chapters in the
New Testament to understand. The problem rises because
Jesus in His discourse shifts back and forth between two great
future events—the destruction of Jerusalem and His own
second coming. So interwoven are these two series of
predictions that great care must be exercised in determining
which details should be assigned to each one. The best way to
study the chapter, therefore, is to concentrate on each subject
separately by gathering and reading all the verses that
describe that particular event.

In the passage assigned for today's reading, Jesus
describes some of the awful terror of the siege and the final
fall of Jerusalem, along with the complete destruction of the
temple. In less than fifty years the prophecy of Jesus was
tragically fulfilled. In A.D. 70 Jerusalem finally fell to the

besieging army of Titus, who later became the emperor of Rome. The horrors of that grim siege are described by the Jewish historian, Josephus. He tells us that the inhabitants became so desperate that they gnawed on the leather of straps and shoes, ate the dung of cattle, and even devoured the dead. He also informs us that 97,000 were taken captive and 1,100,000 perished by slow starvation and the sword. The magnificent temple was razed to the ground until not one of its massive stones stood upon another.

In all ages, among all peoples, it has been the tendency for people to associate religion with sacred places. The Hindus focus their attention on their ancient temples and the Ganges River. The Muslims center their faith in their magnificent mosques and Mecca. Jews still look upon Jerusalem as the Holy City. Christians are prone to boast of their ornate cathedrals and sanctuaries. But the Christian faith does not depend on holy cities and sacred buildings. It is founded on the person of Christ. Buildings may topple, cities, yes, even kingdoms, may fall, but Christ is indestructible and unchanging.

Thought for the day: *Our faith is grounded on the Rock of Ages.*

Matthew 24:3–14   MARCH 30

He who endures to the end will be saved (v. 13).

Jesus never promised His followers an easy life. He always urged prospective disciples to count the cost before making their choice. Even after they chose to follow Him, He warned them well in advance that trials and persecutions would come.

Jesus foresaw that persecution would arise from different sources. The delivering up to councils and scourging in the synagogues refer to Jewish persecution. The governor and kings refer to trials before the Roman courts, such as Paul faced before Felix and Agrippa. But most heartrending of all would be the betrayal by members of one's own family—brother against brother and daughter against mother. Thus persecution would come from religious leaders, civil authorities, and relatives of the family.

But Jesus impressed one thing upon His disciples. However severe the persecutions might be, His followers must not forget their mission. The Gospel was to be preached to all nations. Nothing should dim their vision or lessen their zeal. Even their appearance before kings and rulers should be seized upon as God-given opportunities to bear witness to the truth. And Jesus promised them that in these public trials the Holy Spirit would give them wisdom and strength. He would guide them in what they should say.

When we turn to the book of Acts we see how wonderfully this promise of Jesus was fulfilled. As Peter and John, filled with the Holy Spirit, addressed the members of the Sanhedrin in Jerusalem, it is recorded that the counselors "wondered and recognized that they had seen Jesus." As Stephen defended himself before this same group, it is said that "his face shone like that of an angel." Even as he was being stoned, he was able to cry out, "Lord, do not hold this sin against them."

Finally, Jesus promised nis disciples that "he who endures to the end will be saved." Their unfailing loyalty would be recompensed with eternal salvation. The future reward would make all the present trials fade into insignificance.

Thought for the day: *The cost of discipleship is great, but it's worth it.*

Matthew 24:23–35   MARCH 31

They will see the Son of man coming . . . with power and great glory (v. 30).

When Japanese troops overran the Philippines in the early months of World War II, General Douglas MacArthur, as he was being evacuated from the beach, boldly declared, "I shall return." Three years later the general kept his word. As he waded ashore in the battle area amidst cheers from the people, his first words were, "I have returned."

During His last days on earth, as Jesus faced death on the cross, the resurrection, and His final ascension to the Father, He clearly declared to His disciples, "I will return." The two heavenly messengers who witnessed the Ascension reiterated the promise when they said to the gaping disciples that Jesus will return (Acts 1:11). And one day when Christ steps on this earth again, He will say to all, "I have returned." This is the most certain event of the future.

The return of Christ will be personal and will involve His own visible presence. Jesus clearly said, "They will *see* the Son of man coming." The angels declared, "This Jesus . . . will come in the same way as you *saw* him go into heaven." Paul wrote, "The Lord himself will descend from heaven with a cry of command" (1 Thess. 4:16). The apostle John wrote, "Behold, he is coming . . . and every eye will *see* him" (Rev. 1:7).

In some ways the return of Christ will be in distinct contrast to His first coming to earth. He came first in weakness, as a babe; He will return in power as the King. He came in humility, lying in a manger; He will return on the clouds with glory. He came first to die and make atonement for sin; He will come again to judge the world and to rule over all humankind.

We Christians thus live in a sort of tension—between present fulfillment and future consummation. So Paul can say, "Now is the day of salvation," and Peter can talk about "the salvation ready to be revealed in the last time."

Thought for the day: *The King is coming!*

Matthew 24:36–51   **APRIL 1**

Of that day and hour no one knows . . . watch therefore (vv. 36, 42).

105

By means of revelation God has shared His secrets with us. Many things that were once mysteries were hidden from us but have now been made known to us through His Word and through His Son. No longer are we kept in the dark about spiritual truth. We know all that is necessary for redemption and effective living.

However, the Scriptures tell us that there is one great secret which God has never disclosed to anyone—not even the angels in heaven; not even the Son of man while He was on earth. This is the secret of the time of Christ's second coming. God has told us that there will be certain signs preceding the event, but He has not revealed to us the exact day and hour of the event itself. This is history's best kept secret.

The unpredictability of Christ's coming is a powerful incentive to holy living and to faithful service. John writes in his epistle, "Every one who thus hopes [for Christ's return] purifies himself" (1 John 3:3), that is, "keeps himself clean." Jesus reminds us to be about our Father's business, "for the night is coming when no man can work." In his second epistle Peter admonishes us with such words as "be mindful," "be not ignorant," "be diligent," "beware." Not knowing when Christ may come, we are to be especially careful to live holy and useful lives.

I heard a story once about a father who went away on business and was not sure when he would return. He simply said, "I will come back when my job is finished; perhaps the first of next week." Every day the children said, "Mother, Daddy may come this evening; we'd better get all cleaned up just in case." When Daddy finally came, his wife said to him, "You know, I've never had such an easy time keeping the children clean; they wanted to be sure and be ready for you whenever you came."

Thought for the day: *I must live and work as if Christ were coming today.*

The door was shut (v. 10).

This is the door of lost opportunity—a door which no one can open. It is closed forever whether by our death or by the return of the Lord Jesus Christ.

Death closes the door of further opportunity. As long as we are here in this life, the door is open. There is a chance, an opportunity, an invitation. The Savior, the Spirit, and the Word all say, "Come . . . now is the day of salvation; now is the acceptable time." But death closes the invitation and seals our decision.

For some—those living in the last days—it will not be death but the visible return of our Lord that will close the door of opportunity. When the Bridegroom arrives, the day of salvation will give way to the day of judgment. Then it will be too late to turn to the Savior. The door will be shut.

Jean Paul Sartre, the great existentialist atheist, wrote a famous play entitled *No Exit.* It's a play about hell. Three characters are locked in a dismal hotel room. There is no exit, no way of escape. After the Broadway play had made such a hit, one of its stars, Rita Gamm, was interviewed on TV. She was asked, "Miss Gamm, if you knew you were going to hell, what book would you take along to read?" She replied, "Well, I guess I would take the Bible to see where I went wrong." Unfortunately, the Bible tells us that then it will be too late.

The title of Sartre's play is interesting. *No Exit* is really a modern translation of the text, "the door was shut." The door has been eternally closed upon ourselves by our own choices. There is "no exit" from ourselves, thus no way to enter in. God's love is open, but we can forever shut the door on ourselves so that there is no way out.

Thought for the day: *While the door to salvation is still open, let us be sure to enter in.*

*The master of those servants came and settled
accounts with them (v. 19).*

The parable of the talents is a dramatic lesson on the
subject of Christian stewardship—one of the most important
and yet most neglected principles of the Christian life. The
concept of stewardship includes the following basic ideas:

1. God, as Creator and Redeemer, is sovereign Owner of
   all things and all people.
2. As an expression of His love, God grants to us various
   talents, abilities, and opportunities.
3. As His creatures, we are merely tenants, holding in
   trust what belongs to God, managing it as efficiently as
   we can, and using it for His glory and for the good of
   others.
4. One day we shall have to give an account to God of
   the way we have used the talents and opportunities
   that He has given us.

We are not equal in talent and opportunity. Some have
five talents, some two, others only one. But it is not the kind or
number of our talents that matters; it is how we use what God
has given us. God never demands from us abilities that we do
not have, but He does demand that we use to the full the
abilities that we possess. The temptation of the one-talented
person is to feel that his place in life is obscure and his
possibility for serving the Lord so insignificant that he fails to
use the one ability he has. But all that God requires is that the
individual use that one talent to the full.

Two important lessons of life stand out in the parable.
First, if we use what we have, we will receive more from God; if
we do not use what we possess, we will be deprived of what
was first given. The second lesson is that the only way to keep
a gift is to spend it in the service of God and others.

Thought for the day: *Users are keepers.*

As you did it to one of the least of these my brethren, you did it to me (v. 40).

Life has been defined as sensitivity. The lowest life is sensitive only to itself. The higher you go up the rung of life, the greater the degree of sensitivity. For example, the oyster puts its skeleton on the outside and its nervous system on the inside. Its shell completely encases its nervous system. It opens only to take in from the outside, and then closes up. Humans, on the other hand, have their skeleton on the inside and their nervous system on the outside. This is dangerous because it makes them sensitive to their environment.

The highest level of sensitivity is found in Jesus Christ. He said, "I was hungry and you gave me food, I was thirsty and you gave me drink, I was a stranger and you welcomed me, I was naked and you clothed me, I was sick and you visited me, I was in prison and you came to me." If we ask, "Lord, when did we do all this?" He answers, "As you did it to one of the least of these . . . you did it to me." In effect Jesus said, "I am hungry in everyone's hunger; I am bound in everyone's imprisonment." Here is perfect sensitivity and therefore perfect life.

You can tell how high you have risen on the rung of life by asking yourself the question, "How sensitive am I to the needs of others? How deeply do I care?" Some are sensitive only to themselves; others only to their families. Some are sensitive to their own group or to their own race. A few are sensitive to humanity as a whole.

To be Christianized is to be sensitized. The moment you come into contact with Christ, you begin to care. You lay down the burden of your own sin and take up the burden of the sin and suffering of others. No wonder Baron Von Hugel defined a Christian as one who cares.

Thought for the day: *If I care, then I will begin to share.*

She has done a beautiful thing to me (v. 10).

The woman who made this beautiful gift to our Lord was most probably Mary of Bethany, sister of Martha and Lazarus. It was the custom in those days to sprinkle a few drops of perfume on a guest when he arrived at a house or when he sat down to a meal. But it was not just a few drops that Mary offered. She broke the flask and anointed Jesus with the entire contents, a very precious ointment worth more than 300 *denarii*. This was the equivalent of almost a year's pay for an ordinary worker.

Mary's extravagance provoked the disciples' criticism. "Why this waste?" they asked. "This ointment might have been sold for a large sum and given to the poor." But Jesus accepted Mary's expression of love, and commended her for her dedication.

No gift is too costly to give to Jesus. There can be no extravagance in giving to the One who gave His all, even His very life's blood, for the whole of humankind.

Vida Chenoweth is reputed to be one of the world's greatest artists on the marimba. She has given concerts in Carnegie Hall in New York and played before presidents around the world. But one day Miss Chenoweth met Christ and felt His call to serve as a missionary in New Guinea. For several years she lived among the primitive Usarufa tribe in the mountains, helping to translate the New Testament into their language. Once while on furlough, after she had completed a brilliant performance with the Oklahoma Philharmonic Orchestra, a lady rushed forward in excitement, full of praise for the young artist. Then she suddenly blurted out, "What a waste to bury such unusual talent in the mountains of New Guinea and hide it from the world!" To which Miss Chenoweth quickly replied, "What a waste to bury the Gospel in the plains of Oklahoma and hide it from the people of New Guinea!"

Thought for the day: *Nothing is wasted when it is used for Christ.*

Matthew 26:14–25   APRIL 6

Truly I say to you, one of you will betray me (v. 21).

What a striking contrast between the anointing of Jesus by Mary of Bethany and His betrayal by Judas the disciple. On one hand we have a demonstration of generous love; on the other, diabolical treachery.

Though the Gospel writers give no explanation of the motive of Judas, we can readily distinguish certain ingredients in his character that might have prompted his deed. Undoubtedly there was *covetousness*. There are hints of this here and there in the Gospel narrative. It was primarily Judas who complained about Mary's wasteful extravagance in anointing Jesus with the costly ointment (John 12:5). Judas was treasurer of the apostolic band and used his position to pilfer from the common purse (John 12:6). He actually asked the chief priests how much they would give him if he betrayed Jesus into their hands.

Jealousy might have been another factor. Judas was probably jealous of the three disciples—Peter, James, and John—who formed the inner circle of Jesus' band. Perhaps he was afraid that when the rewards and places of honor were given out in the Lord's kingdom, he would come out on the short end.

Then undoubtedly there was *unholy ambition*. Like the rest of the disciples, Judas thought of the kingdom in earthly terms and dreamed of obtaining high position in it. But gradually he came to realize that Jesus had no intention of setting up such a kingdom so his dreams and ambition were shattered. It may be that in his disillusionment the love he once bore for Jesus turned to hate.

We shudder at the treachery of Judas. But wait a minute! Covetousness, jealousy, selfish ambition—are these strangers

111

to us today? Are these not the sins that still make people betray Him in every age? Judas was no exceptional monster; he is but an example of what anyone may finally do, if he fails to appropriate the divine cure for his besetting sin.

Thought for the day: *No one bears the name of Judas today, but many still share his shame.*

Matthew 26:26—35   APRIL 7

When they had sung a hymn, they went out to the Mount of Olives (v. 30).

Just think of it! Jesus was on his way to the Garden of Gethsemane to be betrayed. He was on His way to the cross to die. But He was able to sing! In the darkest hour of history, He was able to give thanks to God!

And because He sang, His followers can sing today, in any circumstances—in persecution, trials, sorrow, tragedy, and even death. When Paul and Silas were in prison, their feet in stocks and their backs bleeding, they "sang praises to God at midnight," and all the prisoners heard them. Their singing caused the prison doors to be opened by an earthquake, and all the bonds of the captives to be loosed.

Christianity is a singing religion, for we have something to sing about. David writes, "[The Lord] drew me up from the desolate pit, out of the miry bog, and set my feet upon a rock, making my steps secure. *He put a new song in my mouth*, a song of praise to our God" (Ps. 40:2—3). This is the biography of every Christian: from the *mire* to the *choir!*

In the New Testament, Paul exhorts us to "be filled with the Spirit." This, he declares, will result in speaking "in psalms and hymns and spiritual songs, singing and making melody to the Lord" (Eph. 5:19). The power of the Holy Spirit enables us to sing in the face of any situation.

At the closing of the age, when the saints gather around the throne of God, there will be a great multitude from all nations who will sing praises unto God Almighty. In Revelation, John writes, "They sang a new song, saying, 'Worthy art thou to take the scroll and to open its seals, for thou wast slain and by thy blood didst ransom men for God from every tribe and tongue and people and nation'" (5:9).

Thought for the day: *Christ helps us to quit sinning and start singing.*

Matthew 26:36—46   **APRIL 8**

Not as I will, but as thou wilt (v. 39).

Few, if any, of us can ever fully grasp the tremendous struggle that our Lord went through as He prayed in the Garden of Gethsemane. Mark tells us that His mind was "greatly distressed and troubled." Three times Jesus threw Himself on the ground and prayed in desperate agony.

But why all the struggle? Hadn't Jesus from the very beginning of His ministry made a total surrender of Himself into the hands of the Father? Didn't He affirm over and over again, "My will is to do the will of my Father"? Is there any question about the reality and depth of His surrender? Absolutely not. But there was a terrific struggle between the emotions of the moment and His will. There was the natural shrinking from the excruciating pain and shame of the cross. There was the horrifying realization that He was about to bear the sin of the world. But Jesus won the victory when He finally prayed, "Not my will, but thine, be done" (Luke 22:42). At that moment He reconfirmed the attitude of obedience and surrender that He had maintained from the beginning.

Who among us, even the most mature child of God, has not gone through a similar experience? We must not get the false impression that surrender is something we do once and for all and that that's the end of the matter. We can make a lifelong commitment. We can say, "I surrender all," and mean every word of it. But to put this commitment into practice, to actualize it, to make it real in concrete situations is a continuous, lifetime affair. Again and again, in each new crisis, we have to say, "Not my will, but thine, be done." But this is where the growing process takes place. We become stronger in our commitment, we become more sensitive to His leadings as we become more mature in our spiritual lives.

Thought for the day: *Surrender is more than a definite act; it is a daily attitude as well.*

Matthew 26:47–56   APRIL 9

The one I shall kiss is the man (v. 48).

We can readily trace the steps in the tragic downfall of Judas. To begin with, there was the growing pollution of his inner life, including his inordinate desire for money and his selfish ambition for power. When he realized that his dreams for a political kingdom were based on false hopes, disillusionment led to bitterness and perhaps even hate toward our Lord. Somewhere along the line he must have made a willful, deliberate choice to betray the Master into the hands of the chief priests and scribes. Thus unsolicited, he met with them in secret, made his offer, and settled on the price.

The manner in which Judas concluded his foul crime was in full keeping with its essential baseness. He was present at the Last Supper, dipped bread into the same dish with our Lord, and possibly received the elements of Holy Communion. Then he went straight to the Sanhedrin and gathered a motley crowd armed with swords and clubs. He led them to Gethsemane, where Jesus was engaged in solemn prayer, and handed Him over to His enemies with a kiss! Even today we shudder at the thought.

But before we are too hard on Judas, perhaps we should search our own hearts. Have we ever been guilty in the Communion Service of partaking of the bread and wine, symbols of our Lord's atoning death, without actually appropriating His saving or cleansing power in our lives? How often have we sung with gusto, "Oh, how I love Jesus," and then gone out to love the world of material comforts and gadgets? How many times have we called Him "master" with our lips, but failed to crown Him Lord in our lives? Have we never betrayed Christ to His enemies by false profession, hypocrisy, pride, bickering, and lack of love for one another? If we are honest with ourselves, we must admit that the spirit of Judas is very much alive today, at times in our own hearts.

Thought for the day: *Enough of betrayal! What is needed is portrayal of Christ's purity and love.*

Matthew 26:57–68   APRIL 10

Tell us if you are the Christ, the Son of God (v. 63).

What a striking contrast between error and truth we find in this passage.

The Gospel writer tells us that "the whole council sought false testimony against Jesus to put him to death." Instead of listening to the evidence first and then passing judgment, they had already predetermined the verdict and were seeking evidence to justify it. "But they found none." For the witnesses all turned out to be false, and they did not agree among themselves. Thus when the high priest asked Jesus whether He had any answer to make against these charges, our Lord "was silent and made no answer." He refused to defend Himself against false charges.

Then the high priest took the final step. He chose an approach that was absolutely forbidden by law, that is, asking a leading question in an attempt to make the person on trial incriminate himself. Bluntly he asked Jesus, "Are you the Messiah?" This time our Lord did not remain silent. He had to testify to the truth. Without hesitation and clearly, He answered, "I am" (Mark 14:62). He then added a quotation from Daniel which emphasizes the claim with a distinct prophecy,

"You will see the Son of man seated at the right hand of Power, and coming with the clouds of heaven."

Here Christ plainly claims to be God, and this is a claim that all must ponder. For it is either true or is not, and either way it eternally matters. If this claim is not true, there is no salvation for you and me; but if it is true, the entire world must face the fact. All Scripture and history declare that Jesus is truly the Messiah, the Son of the living God, and countless millions of people down through the centuries have verified the truth in their own lives.

Thought for the day: *Christ is not looking for lawyers to defend Him, but for witnesses to declare Him.*

Matthew 26:69–75   APRIL 11

I do not know the man (v. 72).

Matthew is a master at portraying scenes of striking contrast. He has just described the courageous confession of Jesus before the members of the Sanhedrin. When asked the question, "Are you the Messiah?" Jesus answered directly and without hesitation, "I am," even though He knew this would lead to His condemnation and death. Now Matthew describes the cowardly denial of Peter before a servant girl and a few bystanders. Peter was unwilling to confess Christ because he was afraid it would get him into trouble.

The fall of Peter can be traced to certain definite causes. There was his spirit of self-reliance. When Jesus made the prediction that all the disciples would fall away at the hour of trial, Peter quickly said, "Though they all fall away because of you, I will never fall away." Then when Jesus foretold Peter's denial, Peter announced boastfully, "Even if I must die with you, I will not deny you" (vv. 33–35). No doubt he expressed sincere devotion, but he betrayed his pride.

Because of his spirit of self-reliance and pride, Peter failed to draw on divine resources just when he needed them most.

In Gethsemane Jesus had urged His disciples to watch and pray so that they would not enter into temptation (v. 41). He reminded them that "the spirit indeed is willing, but the flesh is weak." In other words, their intentions might be bold, but they lacked the strength to carry them out. But instead of praying, the disciples fell asleep. Three times Jesus admonished the eleven to spend time in prayer, but each time he found them sleeping. Jesus especially singled out Peter and said to him, "Simon, are you asleep? Could you not watch one hour?" And because Peter failed to pray, he had no strength to withstand temptation when it came. Consequently he fell.

Self-reliance, pride, prayerlessness—these are the traits that usually lead any person to deny his Lord.

Thought for the day: *Prayer is not merely the preparation for the battle; it usually is the battle.*

Matthew 27:1–10   APRIL 12

. . . he went and hanged himself (v. 5).

Once again Matthew proves to be a master of contrasts. Back to back he presents the denial of Peter and the downfall of Judas. Whereas Peter "went out and wept bitterly" (26:75) and was later restored to fellowship with His Master, Judas "went out and hanged himself" and sealed his doom forever.

Peter had sinned grievously against his Lord. Three times he denied that he ever knew Him. But he realized the tragedy of his sin and sincerely repented of his cowardice and denial. On the morning of the resurrection he was one of the first to rush to the tomb, seeking the risen Lord. On the day of Pentecost he was gloriously filled with the Holy Spirit and became one of the pillars of the early church.

As for Judas, his treachery was the final step in a downward course. It is true he recognized and confessed his sin. He declared before the chief priests, "I have sinned in betraying innocent blood." The record tells us that he even repented and made restitution by returning the thirty pieces of silver for which he had sold his Lord. But then, instead of turning to Christ and seeking forgiveness, he committed suicide.

Judas was able to recognize his sin, but was unable to apprehend the love of God in Christ. He turned from his sin, but failed to turn to the Savior. If he had not taken his own life, he could have sought out the Master after the resurrection, received full and free forgiveness, and been restored to fellowship with the Lord and the disciples. He too could have been present at Pentecost. He also might have become a leader in the early church, perhaps a writer of one of the books of the New Testament; instead he cut off all hopes of restoration and salvation, and will be remembered throughout eternity as the despicable betrayer of our Lord.

Thought for the day: *God's grace is greater than our disgrace.*

Matthew 27:11–23   APRIL 13

What shall I do with Jesus who is called Christ?
(v. 22)

This is a question that every one of us must ask and answer. Jesus is on our hands; we must do something with Him.

What are some of the attitudes we may take toward Christ?

We may try to *put Him away*. The people of Jesus' day tried this, but found it impossible. They nailed Him to a cross and laid His body in a tomb, but death and the grave could not hold Him. On the third day He rose from the dead and was on their hands again. Even today we may try to get rid of Christ, but it is of no avail, for He is ever before us.

We may try to *put Him off*, in an attempt to postpone our decision to some future date. Like Governor Felix of Paul's day, we may look for "some more convenient day." But this is exceedingly dangerous, for the longer we delay the harder it becomes to accept the Savior. Delay tends to dampen our desire and harden our hearts. Furthermore, we can never be sure of tomorrow. Today is the moment of opportunity.

We may try to *put Him aside*. Some accept the matchless teachings of Jesus and try to put His principles into practice, but they don't want to receive the person of Christ Himself. Mahatma Gandhi of India is a classic example of this attitude. But this is an impossible position, for no one can live the life of Christ without His presence and power. It is only when He is dwelling within us that we can live up to the high standard which He has set before us.

Paul admonishes us to *"put on the Lord Jesus Christ"* (Rom. 13:14). That is, we are to cast off the garments of sin and be clothed anew in the righteousness, love, and power of Christ. We do this by receiving Him as personal Savior and Lord.

Thought for the day: *What we do with Christ in this life will determine what He does with us in the life to come.*

Matthew 27:24–31   APRIL 14

Having scourged Jesus, [Pilate] delivered him to be crucified (v. 26).

There is a tendency for us to blame the crucifixion of Jesus entirely upon the Jewish religious leaders of that day. But we dare not forget that it was the Roman governor, Pilate, a representative of the Gentile world, who gave the final consent to Christ's death. It was a combination of false religion and dirty politics that sent Christ to the cross.

Pilate was convinced of Jesus' innocence. He was astute enough to recognize that it was purely out of jealousy that the chief priests had arraigned Him. He also marveled at the silence and composure of Jesus, as He made no attempt to answer His accusers. Thus Pilate should have acquitted the Lord at once. But he wanted to please both rulers and people so he attempted to compromise with justice. He offered to release Jesus in place of the murderer Barabbas, but the crowd demanded Barabbas' release instead. Pilate then tried to satisfy the malice of the mob by inflicting upon Jesus the torture of a Roman scourging, but the people shouted all the more, "Crucify him! Crucify him!" Finally, through fear of being accused of disloyalty to the emperor in shielding one accused of treason, Pilate pronounced the death sentence and delivered Jesus over to the multitude to be crucified. And in so doing, he condemned himself.

Pilate furnishes the pitiful picture of one who lacks courage to follow his convictions and to obey the voice of conscience. He is a tragic example of those who are more interested in pleasing people than in pleasing God; who are more concerned about serving their own selfish ends than about upholding justice; who follow the path of expedience rather than that of truth. The temptation to compromise is ever before the politician, the business person, or even the preacher. In fact, it is a common temptation to all of us.

Thought for the day: *If one is not willing to stand for something, he is liable to fall for anything (paraphrased from Peter Marshall).*

Matthew 27:32–44   APRIL 15

He saved others; he cannot save himself (v. 42).

Not content with nailing Jesus to a cross, the chief priests and rabble shouted at Him in heartless derision. They hurled their words at Him like poisoned arrows, dipped in venom, shot from snarling lips.

"Aha," they jeered, "You boasted that you could destroy the temple and rebuild it in three days. You have nails in your hands. You have wood; go ahead and build it. You claim to be a miracle man; perform a miracle now. Come down from the cross and we will believe you." Then in ridicule they said to one another, "He saved others; he cannot save himself."

Could not Jesus have saved Himself? He might have compromised and made His kingdom political rather than spiritual. He could have called down twelve legions of angels and destroyed His enemies. Yes, He might have saved Himself, but He would not have become our Savior. For no one who saves himself can save others.

Was there no other way for Christ to save us? Could He not have started a monastery and spent His life in teaching others? Could He not have started a new religion? But again He would have been only a teacher or a philosopher, not a Savior. He came to seek and to save sinners.

Because He had no sin of His own, only Jesus could save us. One criminal cannot die for another. One sinner cannot save another. Since we have all sinned, no human can save humankind. Only the Son of God could take our place. The innocent had to die for the guilty; the sinless for the sinful. Jesus took upon Himself our sin, the sins of the whole world; and it crushed Him, it broke His heart. But because He did not save Himself, He stands today as the Savior of the world, able and willing to save all those who come to Him in repentance and faith.

Thought for the day: *The cross is not a picture of Jesus in trouble; it is a demonstration of God in action.*

Matthew 27:45–50 APRIL 16

My God, my God, why hast thou forsaken me? (v. 46)

These are words of unspeakable agony. The human mind will never be able fully to comprehend them.

During His public ministry Jesus had experienced every form of human suffering. He knew what it was to be hungry, thirsty, tired, tempted, and lonely. He was often ridiculed, abused, and even blasphemed. He was finally betrayed by one of His own disciples; He was forsaken by the rest. He went through the agony of a Roman scourging. They pushed a crown of thorns down upon his brow. Even at this moment He hung shamefully on a cross between two thieves, and suffered the pangs of death.

But through all of these experiences Jesus was strengthened and sustained by the unfailing presence of God. Though people had rejected Him, His heavenly Father was always near. Then suddenly on the cross it seemed that even the Father had abandoned Him, and He was completely alone in the world.

Sin always separates us from God. It puts up an insurmountable barrier between God and us. Jesus had never known this separation because He had never sinned. He was pure and spotless. But in this terrible, grim moment on the cross Jesus completely identified Himself with human sin. He became, as it were, a sinner and suffered the very consequences of sin—separation from God. It may be that the separation was only for a brief moment, but when we realize that Christ was coeternal with the Father, that He lived in unbroken communion with the Father, and that He was holy, we can in some small way comprehend the untold agony of that moment.

Thus we should never hesitate to go to Jesus when sin separates us from God, because He Himself has gone through this experience on our behalf and can fully empathize with us. There is no depth of human experience which the Savior has not shared and plumbed.

Thought for the day: *Christ suffered our agony that we might share His glory.*

Matthew 27:51–54   APRIL 17

The curtain of the temple was torn in two, from top to bottom (v. 51).

In the temple in Jerusalem hung a large curtain that separated the Holy of Holies from the rest of the sanctuary. That was the veil beyond which no one might proceed except the high priest, and that only once a year on the Day of Atonement. It was the veil behind which the Spirit of God dwelt.

Matthew tells us that at the very moment when Jesus expired on the cross, the curtain guarding the Holy of Holies was torn in two from top to bottom. No doubt an invisible power from above was responsible for this symbolic act. Up to this time God had been hidden and remote. No one knew what He was like; no one could enter directly into His presence. God demonstrated to the world in this dramatic way that the vicarious death of His Son had removed the barrier between Himself and sinners. We could now see the holiness and love of God and could walk straight into His presence without the aid of a human mediator. Sinners could now approach the very throne of God and find there forgiveness, cleansing, and power for a new life. No longer did God require animal sacrifice and the blood to be applied to the altar of the temple. The final and perfect sacrifice had now been made, and the blood of Jesus Christ was able to cleanse from all sin.

The tragedy is that many people around the world have not yet heard this message. Millions of people in India are still offering their sacrifices on the altar of the temple. They are still seeking to approach God through the mediatorship of the priest. The inner sanctum is off-limits to them. We need to declare to the world that Christ died for our sins and that the curtain in the temple has been torn in two from top to bottom.

Thought for the day: *The success of the cross produces access to the throne. God is no longer behind the curtain.*

Matthew 27:55–66   **APRIL 18**

There were also many women there, looking on from afar (v. 55).

Devout women played a significant role in the life and ministry of our Lord.

God chose Mary, a pious peasant woman of Israel to be the mother of Jesus, through a miraculous conception wrought by the Holy Spirit. Mary must have accepted her calling with an awesome sense of responsibility as she brought up her son in the admonition and fear of the heavenly Father. During His public ministry there were several women who followed Jesus and lovingly ministered to His comforts and welfare (see Mark 15:41). Among these were Mary Magdalene, Joanna, and Susanna (Luke 8:2, 3). Two sisters, Mary and Martha, opened to Jesus their home in Bethany, where He often took refuge from the jostling crowds. It was this Mary who anointed the Master's feet with costly ointment and was commended for her sacrifice and devotion.

In the passage of Scripture for today, notice the loyalty and courage of these women in the last days of our Lord's earthly life. When all the men had fled in fear, these women followed Jesus to Golgotha and stood by Him as He hung and died on the cross. When Joseph of Arimathea placed Christ's body in a tomb for burial, they were there to pay their respects. And as they were the last ones at the cross, they were the first ones at the tomb on Sunday morning. Matthew tells of this in the first verse of the next chapter. They were the first witnesses of the Resurrection and the first bearers of the good news that He was alive.

Down through the history of the church, women have continued to demonstrate their devotion and loyalty to the Lord. They have faithfully supported the church with their attendance, their gifts, and their service. They have gone as missionaries to the far corners of the earth to every continent, nation, and island. It is high time for us men to take a lesson from the women.

Thought for the day: *Men sing lustily, "Rise up, O Men of God," and then let the women do the work!*

*An angel of the Lord ... rolled back the stone, and
sat upon it (v. 2).*

Let your imagination run wild for a moment. Imagine that
after Jesus had been crucified and buried, Satan calls all his
devils together and says to them, "We have won our final
victory. We have killed the Son of God and finished him off
forever. I am calling for a ten-day celebration. Let us eat, drink,
and be merry."

Suddenly in the midst of the festivities, a nervous
messenger arrives on the scene and shouts, "The stone is
moving; the stone is *moving!*"

"How many are pushing on the stone?" Satan asks.

"Just one lone angel, Your Majesty," answers the messenger.

"Send up a dozen men to Jerusalem," orders Satan, "and
hold that stone in place. Meanwhile, on with the festivities!"

In a short while a second messenger arrives in agitation.
"That stone is still moving!" he screams.

"Send up a whole battalion of devils," shouts Satan,
obviously upset by the news. "That'll hold him! Back to the
celebrations!"

Not long afterward a third messenger arrives, disheveled
and shrieking, "The stone is still moving—we can't stop it!!' "

Now Satan takes things seriously. "Stop the festivities," he
cries. "Everybody up to the tomb in Jerusalem, we *must* hold
that stone in place!"

And so all hell puts its shoulder to the stone, but one lone
angel on the other side, with one hand behind his back and
the other gently touching the stone, rolls it away from the
tomb, turns it on its side, and *sits on it!*

But the irony of the whole episode is this: *The tomb is
already empty!* Jesus has already risen. The angel does not
roll away the stone so that Jesus can come out of the tomb.

He rolls it away so that His disciples can go in and see that Jesus is not there, that He is alive!

Thought for the day: *"The Christian does not deny the reality of death, but he certainly defies its finality"* (E. Stanley Jones).

Matthew 28:16–20   APRIL 20

Go therefore and make disciples of all nations (v. 19).

Christ began His public ministry by giving an invitation to sinners—"*Come* unto me, and I will give you rest . . . Come, follow me." He ended His ministry with a command to believers—"*Go* into all the world and preach the gospel . . . go and make disciples of all nations."

Go is a big word in the Christian faith. You can't spell *God* without *go,* you can't spell *good* without *go,* you can't spell *gospel* without *go.*

A few years ago I was seated on a plane beside a young, attractive girl with long black hair and a miniskirt. In conversing with her I discovered she was working as a go-go girl in a night club. I extended my hand and said somewhat enthusiastically, "Shake, I'm a go-go boy!" Seeing her consternation, I explained that I was a Christian, and that our Lord has commanded all Christians to go-go-go. "Go into all the world and preach the Gospel." This means that all followers of Christ are go-go boys and go-go girls.

The Great Commission was not an exclusive command for the immediate disciples of Christ. It is binding upon all Christians of all ages. Every follower of Christ is to be involved in mission, whether it be across the seas or across the street. Some need to go home and tell their loved ones what Christ has done for them. Some need to go next door and share the good news of Christ with their neighbors. Others must go across the tracks or into the ghetto and declare that God loves the poor and the downtrodden. Still others should go to the other side of the world and proclaim to all of every race and nation that Christ died for their sins. Whether it be near or far, we must all go somewhere and tell the good news.

Thought for the day: *It is not crossing the seas, but seeing the cross, that makes a person a missionary.*

Mark 1:1−8   **APRIL 21**

The beginning of the gospel ... (v. 1).

The Gospel is *news*. That means it is a vital report about events in history. The sovereign God *predetermined* these events. The prophet Isaiah *foretold* them. John the baptizer *prepared* the way for them. Our faith, therefore, is not based on the sinking sands of fancy or myth, but on the solid foundations of fact and mighty acts. God has stepped into the stream of human history. He has intervened decisively on our behalf. This is what the Gospel is about.

The Gospel is *good* news. These days newspapers and radio and television broadcasts are full of bad news—reports of strikes, riots, inflation, crime, violence, and conflict. It is good to hear something hopeful amidst all the confusion and despair. The Gospel tells us that God is *not against us* because of our sins, but is *for us* against our sins. When we were unworthy, He loved us. When we were helpless, He came to our rescue. When we were guilty, He offered us mercy. This is indeed *good news*.

The Gospel centers around a *person*. The distinctive feature of the Christian faith is not primarily its teachings, ethics, or creeds, but the person of Jesus Christ. Christianity is what it is because Christ is who He is. In all the major religions of the world, you can take away the founder without disrupting the religious system itself. For example, you can take Rama or Krishna out of Hinduism, and Hinduism as a philosophical system would still be intact. But in Christianity, if you remove the founder, you have nothing left. The person is all-important.

The Gospel centers around a *unique* person. Jesus is "The Son of God," that is, the God-man. He is fully human and fully divine. As human, He is so *like* me, I feel I can put my arm around Him and say, "my Brother." But as divine, He is so *unlike* me, I am forced to kneel and confess, "My Lord and my God!"

Thought for the day: *The Gospel is not good views, but good news.*

Mark 1:9–20   APRIL 22

Follow me (v. 17).

The Gospel is the good news that God has acted on our behalf. But His *action* demands a specific *reaction* on our part. The big question of the Gospel is this: What am I going to do about what God has done for me? It requires a verdict.

This verdict is primarily a response to the person of Jesus Christ. Herein lies one of the basic differences between religion and the Gospel. Religion says, "Here is an organization; join it. Here is a system of belief; understand and accept it. Here is a set of principles; practice them faithfully." On the other hand, the Gospel says, "Here is a Person, a unique Person. Believe Him; follow Him."

Christian experience is, therefore, basically a relationship to our Lord and Savior, Jesus Christ. To be a Christian in the New Testament sense of the term is more than just belonging to the church, or giving mental assent to the creeds, or seeking to practice certain teachings. To be a Christian is to put one's trust in Christ, enter into a personal relationship with Him, and follow Him from day to day.

Jesus said to Simon and his brother, Andrew, both fishermen, "Follow me, and I will make you fishers of men" (Matt. 4:19). To become a disciple of Christ is to become identified with Him in His redemptive ministry to the world. Christ came to seek lost people, and our task is to show them the way home. Christ died to reconcile all persons to God. But our duty is to call them to repentance and faith. Discipleship, therefore, is not a life of ease; it involves relationship with Christ and responsibility to others. It means becoming like Christ and bringing people to Him. And this is a lifetime vocation, not a temporary assignment.

Christ is still calling for disciples today. He walks into the office, factory, school room, coliseum, highway, and home, saying, "Follow me."

What will your answer be?

Thought for the day: Relationship *with Christ leads to* partnership *with Him.*

Mark 1:21—34   APRIL 23

He healed many who were sick (v. 34).

Does the Christian faith have any concern for the body? For the soul, yes; but for the body? It would indeed be strange for a faith based on the incarnation—the Word become flesh—to have no interest in the physical welfare of us all. We believe it does. A large section of the gospel record is given over to the healing ministry of Jesus. He was interested not only in our souls and minds but in our bodies as well.

However, Christianity is not primarily a healing cult. To keep the body in constant repair is not its chief aim. That would put us at the center and reduce God to the status of a cosmic bellhop to be summoned at will. God would be serving us; we would be using Him. The primary purpose of the Christian faith is to reconcile us to God, to redeem us from sin. But welfare of the body is a by-product.

Not all diseases are cured in this life. Some have to await their final cure in the general resurrection. We live in a mortal world, and the body breaks down some time or another. God will either heal the disease or He will give us grace to use it for His glory.

However, Christ is still the Great Physician and He continues to heal today. A few years ago a Japanese student, George Nakajima, studied at Asbury Theological Seminary. He suffered from acute stomach disorder and had to undergo two major operations. Then he faced a third operation and the outlook was grim. But the president of the seminary, along with two students, went to George's hospital room, laid hands upon him, and prayed that God would heal him. God intervened miraculously. In a short while George had fully recovered without surgery and was back attending classes. Today he serves Christ effectively in his homeland.

Thought for the day: *"Jesus Christ is the same yesterday, today, and forever."*

Mark 1:35—45   APRIL 24

He ... went out to a lonely place ... he went throughout all Galilee (vv. 35, 39).

There was supreme symmetry in the life of Christ. He combined perfectly the spiritual and the social, the desire for prayer and the love of service.

Jesus was a man of prayer. Often He withdrew from the crowd and went into the mountains or along the seashore to commune alone with His Father. Sometimes He prayed far into the night; sometimes He arose early in the morning. The Garden of Gethsemane was possibly a favorite retreat of His for meditation and intercession. Christ's disciples were so impressed by His prayer life, that on one occasion they entreated Him, "Lord, teach us to pray."

But apart from His devotional life, Christ was constantly among people—in the temple and synagogue, on the mountain side and the highways, in the market place and homes. He gave Himself fully to help the sinful and the suffering—no one could have done more for others than He did. He poured out His life in service.

Christ's inner life of prayer and His outer life of service were equally important to Him. The one did not crowd out the other; they complemented one another.

We always find it difficult to maintain this balance between personal meditation and social service. There is a tendency to accept the one and exclude the other. Some people drift into mysticism. They withdraw into the hermitage; they are too pious to serve. Others are satisfied with mere social service. They have no time for prayer or devotion. Service itself becomes their god.

Jesus would condemn either extreme. Worship without service is gross hypocrisy—to talk about serving God without ministering to the physical needs of people. Service without worship is sheer presumption—to talk about serving others without loving God. If we are to be worthy disciples of Christ, we must keep worship and service in perfect balance, just as He did.

Thought for the day: *Life is like a see-saw. It must be on center and balanced evenly on both sides. Get alone with God; then get out among people.*

Mark 2:1–12   **APRIL 25**

They removed the roof ... and ... made an opening (v. 4).

Here we have one of the most fascinating incidents in the ministry of our Lord. Four men carried a paralytic to Jesus. The narrative beautifully portrays the power of love, cooperative action, and vicarious faith. Let us look at these four men.

First, they came *bringing* (v. 3). The man was paralyzed and therefore unable to come to Christ on his own. These men had possibly met Jesus before and seen him heal. So they convinced the paralytic of His compassion and power and then brought the man to Him. They came cooperating, each one holding a corner of the stretcher. No one person was able to carry him, but four working together could. There are many who will never get to Christ without the help of others.

Second, they came *boldly, beseeching* (v. 4). In spite of many obstacles they were determined to reach Jesus. There was the *crowd*, selfishly blocking the way, jamming the place. They wouldn't move over and let a needy man get to Christ. Then there were *customs* hindering. The proper way to enter a strange home is through the front door. But there was no room at the door. So in desperation the four removed the tiles from the roof and let the man down into the presence of Jesus.

Third, they came *believing* (v. 5). The record tells us that "when Jesus saw *their* faith, He said to the paralytic. . . ." It was a vicarious faith that interceded for the patient. They already knew of the Master's power to heal. Doubtless "their faith" included the man's faith also, for when Jesus said to him, "Take up your pallet and walk," he immediately responded in obedience. The united faith of the four prompted and inspired the paralytic's faith. They made it easy for him to believe. So they came *believing* and therefore receiving. Faith both *seeks* and *secures.*

Thought for the day: *Our greatest responsibility and privilege is to bring needy people to Jesus.*

Mark 2:13–17   APRIL 26

He was eating with sinners (v. 16).

Matthew (Levi) was a tax collector on behalf of the Roman government. Tax collectors have never been popular, but in the days of Jesus they were actually hated. People never knew just how much tax they had to pay. The collectors extracted from them as much as they could, and then lined their own pockets with the surplus that remained after the demands of the law had been met. So in calling Matthew to be His disciple, Jesus offered friendship to a man who was socially despised. He invited into His fellowship a person whom all others would have scorned to call friend. And then when Jesus condescended to eat with Matthew and other tax collectors, He was accused by the Pharisees of being a friend of sinners. To which Jesus replied, "Those who are well have no need of a physician, but those who are sick; I came not to call the righteous, but sinners."

Hinduism believes in the possibility of incarnation. In fact, there are supposed to be ten incarnations of Vishnu, the second member of the Hindu trinity. In each case, according to the Hindu scriptures, an incarnation was necessary when wickedness became rampant upon the earth. Vishnu was obliged to incarnate himself in order "to destroy the wicked and deliver the righteous." But Christ came for exactly the opposite reason—to redeem the wicked. He came expressly as "the friend of sinners."

A few years ago some Russian atheists published a tract entitled, "The Friends of God." The tract described Moses the murderer, Abraham the deceiver, Jacob the thief, and David the adulterer. It ended with this question: "What kind of a God must he be to have friends such as these?"

But it is exactly here that we see the true character of God. He is merciful, gracious, and loving. He is willing to eat with sinners in order to redeem them and transform them into His children.

Thought for the day: *Since Jesus is the friend of sinners, then there is hope for me!*

Mark 2:18–28   APRIL 27

The sabbath was made for man, not man for the sabbath (v 27)

133

The religion of Jesus differed drastically from that of the Pharisees, particularly in regard to the attitude toward forms and ceremonies. To the mind of the Pharisees ritual constituted the very essence of religion. Ritual thus became an end in itself and led to strict legalism. To Jesus it was the principle or motive behind these ceremonies that was all-important.

The Jewish law had required but one fast a year, and that was on the Day of Atonement. But the rabbis had multiplied this observance to twice a week—on Mondays and Thursdays. The trouble with the Pharisees was that they were proud about their strict observance of the ritual, and in far too many cases their fasting was purely for self-display. It was to call the attention of others to their own goodness. Jesus taught that religious ceremony is proper, when expressive of true feeling, when fitting to the time and place. But when required or performed for selfish motives, ceremony may become perfunctory, meaningless, and eventually a farce. Our Lord thus strikes at the very heart of all ceremonialism in religion.

In regard to the Sabbath, the Pharisees had imposed so many regulations on its observance that the day had become a burden to the people. Even works of necessity and mercy were ruled unlawful. Everyone thus became a slave to legalism. Jesus insisted that religion does not consist in rules and regulations. He came not to patch up an old system but to offer something new. He demonstrated that persons are far more important than systems and rituals. True religion, he taught, springs from the heart.

The Christian life is not to be confused with any ritual. It cannot be bound up by any set of rules and requirements. Its very essence is a new life. It controls us, not by rules but by motives. Its symbol is not a fast, but a feast.

Thought for the day: *Christ came not to impose law, but to impart life!*

Is it lawful on the sabbath to do good or to do harm?
(v. 4)

Picture this drama in your mind. It is the sabbath day, and the scene is a Jewish synagogue. On one side you have the Pharisees, and on the other, Jesus. In the middle is a man with a paralyzed hand. They are all in the synagogue on the Sabbath for the same purpose—to worship God and to listen to the exposition of the sacred Scriptures. But what a difference in spirit and behavior!

Note the difference in the attitude toward the man with a withered hand. Jesus saw him as a person in need while the Pharisees saw him as an object of contention. Jesus looked upon him with love and compassion; the others had no concern for him whatsoever. The record tells us that Jesus was grieved at the hardness of their hearts.

Then note the difference in the attitude toward the Sabbath. The Pharisees had a very legalistic and narrow concept of the Sabbath as a day of taboos and prohibitions. To them religion was a matter of rituals, rules, and regulations. As a result they were more concerned about keeping the law than helping a needy person. On the other hand, Jesus believed that acts of mercy and necessity were lawful on the Sabbath. To him religion was not law, but service—it was love for God and love for people. So Jesus felt the man was more important than the rules.

The Pharisees criticized Jesus for breaking the law by working on the Sabbath. But could speaking the word of healing or stretching out the hand be considered acts of labor? Were not the Pharisees far more guilty of breaking the law of God by harboring hatred in their hearts and seeking for ways to kill Jesus?

The pharisaical spirit is still alive today in persons who carry out all the external acts of religion, but have no compassion for suffering people and never reach out to help them

Thought for the day: *Helping a person in need is more important than performing a ritual.*

Mark 3:7–19 APRIL 29

He appointed twelve, to be with him, and to be sent out to preach (v. 14).

Jesus is in the business of making disciples. He has a mission to perform, a world to redeem. And He needs men and women to help fulfill this task. So He calls us to be His disciples.

To be a disciple of Christ involves two things—being with Christ and being sent forth by Him. Relationship and partnership; communion and commission. The two go together.

Christ calls us first to be with Him. Discipleship begins with a personal relationship with the Master. It is more than signing a card, taking a course, or joining an organization. It is fellowship with a person, the person of Jesus Christ. We must spend time with Him; learn from Him, understand Him, and become like Him. Fellowship will then become an abiding friendship, which in turn will transform our lives. As the divine Savior, He will forgive our sins and cleanse us from all unrighteousness. As the great Teacher, Christ will instruct us and guide us into the truth. As sovereign Lord, He will reveal His will to us individually.

Christ then sends us forth. We are not only to be His companions, but His representatives as well. He calls us to be partners with Him in His world-wide redemptive mission. He wants us to share with others the good news of the Gospel. So he sends us into the factory, office, classroom, market, arena, and home to witness to His redeeming love and power. But He does not send us out alone, merely to do His work for Him. Through the abiding presence of His Spirit He accompanies us, empowers us, and works with us. It is an abiding partnership.

These two aspects of Christian discipleship are inseparable. One is the necessary preparation; the other, the logical consequence. The supreme privilege for any Christian is that of testifying for Christ; but the necessary qualification for such witness is personal association with the Lord.

Thought for the day: *We are saved to serve.*

Mark 3:20–30 **APRIL 30**

Whoever blasphemes against the Holy Spirit never has forgiveness (v. 29).

The Holy Spirit is God's Representative upon earth. Without the Spirit's aid no one would be able to recognize his sin and understand his need for a Savior. Apart from His enabling grace no one would be able to come to Christ. Thus the Holy Spirit is indispensable.

Our attitude toward the Holy Spirit is therefore all-important. Paul warns us against "grieving" the Spirit (Eph. 4:30). As a person with feelings, He can be grieved by our un-Christlike attitudes of resentment, anger, and hatred. Paul also cautions us not to "quench" the Holy Spirit in our lives (1 Thess. 5:19). He likens the Spirit to a flame, which may be dampened by our indifference and carelessness. But in the passage of Scripture for today Jesus warns us not to "blaspheme" against the Holy Spirit.

Jesus was casting out demons through the power of the Holy Spirit. But some of the scribes accused him of exorcising evil spirits through the power of the devil. They even claimed that Christ Himself had an unclean spirit (v. 30). This, Jesus said, is the unpardonable sin.

The emphasis here is not so much upon a single act as upon a protracted attitude of the mind, especially toward the Holy Spirit. There is only one condition for forgiveness and that is penitence. But if a person, by repeated resistance to the Spirit's overtures of love, has lost the ability to recognize goodness when he sees it, he has so twisted his moral values until to him evil is good and good is evil. Then, even when he is confronted by Jesus, he is conscious of no sin; he cannot repent and therefore he cannot be forgiven. That is the sin against the Holy Spirit.

Let us always be sensitive to the promptings of the Spirit and ever grateful for His ministry to us.

Thought for the day: *All that Jesus did* for *me on the cross, the Holy Spirit wants to do* in *me through His power.*

Mark 3:31–35 MAY 1

Whoever does the will of God is my brother, and sister (v. 35).

In these words Jesus lays down the conditions of true kinship. Kinship is not solely a matter of flesh and blood. It is essentially a matter of spiritual communion. Sometimes a person can feel much closer to someone who is not related to him than he does to members of his own family.

Jesus says that his true brothers and sisters are those who do the will of the heavenly Father. In other words, kinship is not a matter of profession but of performance. It is demonstrated by obedient action.

What is the will of God that He expects us to fulfill?

It is His will that we believe in His Son (John 6:29). God so loved the world that He sent His only Son into the world. Through the life of the Son the Father has revealed His essential being and character. Through the death of His Son He has provided us with redemption from our sins. Through the Resurrection He has gained for us victory over death and Satan. Now God expects us to believe in Christ as the true Messiah and to accept what He has done for us on the cross.

When we do this we become the children of God and enter into His family.

Further, "this is the will of God, your sanctification" (1 Thess. 4:3). He desires that we be separated from the world, cleansed from all impurity, and set apart for His service. Since He Himself is holy, He wants us to be holy.

Also it is God's will that we "give thanks in all circumstances" (1 Thess. 5:18). Whatever happens to us comes through the permissive (not necessarily causative) will of God, and all things work together for our good and His glory. So we should be grateful to God for His constant love and manifold good gifts in spite of all the trials and difficulties of life.

Thought for the day: *To do God's will is not always the easiest but is certainly the safest and happiest way in life.*

Mark 4:1–20   MAY 2

A sower went out to sow (v. 3).

There is one Sower, the Holy Spirit, and one quality of seed, the Word of God. But there are different kinds of soil, which determine the fortune of the seed.

There is the *hard soil,* trampled by people and beasts. The seed that falls on such a surface is unable to germinate. The birds of the air swoop down and devour it. Some hearers of the Word are so hardened by hostility or indifference that no message can find entrance into their hearts. No sooner has the truth been preached in their hearing than Satan comes and snatches it away.

There is the *rocky soil,* with a thin layer of earth over a shelf of limestone. The soil is good but it lacks depth. The seed sprouts all right, but because of shallow roots the plant quickly withers under the blighting sun. Likewise, there are those who readily accept the Word of God; their emotions are easily stirred. But they lack depth of conviction and, because of their superficial commitment, soon fall away when difficulties come.

There is also the *thorny ground*. The seed takes root and springs up with promise, but thorns grow and choke the plant so that it cannot bear fruit. Some people gladly accept the Word and begin the Christian life, but in time they are overcome by the cares and pleasures of life so that they turn away from the truth.

Then there is the *good soil* which bears fruit, possibly thirtyfold, or sixtyfold, even a hundredfold. By this figure our Lord describes the true hearers who not only receive the Word, but continue to practice it in spite of opposition and difficulties and who influence the thinking of others by their righteous lives.

People do not by nature resemble one of these types of soil. They *become* like hard or rocky or thorny soil by their own choice. It is possible for every person to be like the good soil.

Thought for the day: *Our response to the Word determines the harvest.*

Mark 4:21–25   **MAY 3**

Is a lamp brought in to be put under a bushel?
(v. 21)

A lamp is intended to give light and to enable us to see. Therefore, it is put in a place where it can easily be seen. Likewise, the Christian must shine in public and help to dispel the spiritual darkness all about.

Jesus warned His disciples against three different ways in which they might hide their light. First He said, "Don't put your lamp under a bushel." A bushel is a container to measure grain, and is, therefore, a symbol of trade. It is possible to allow un-Christian business methods to snuff out the light. It is also possible to put the light on top of the bushel, not under it, to make one's business a candlestand—a means through which his Christian life shines.

Again Jesus said, "Don't put your light under the bed." The bed is a symbol of inactivity or rest. By lying down on the job, by mere unconcern or indifference, we each may put out the light. Through carelessness we may bypass many an opportunity to witness for our Lord or to minister to the needy.

Then Jesus said, "Don't put your lamp under a vessel" (Luke 8:16). A vessel is an instrument used in the kitchen. So it is possible to allow preoccupation with household duties or the daily routine of living, to keep one's light from shining forth. On the other hand, it is possible to place the lamp on top of the vessel, to make even the menial task of life a means by which to bring glory to Christ.

Jesus said, "Put your lamp on a stand." Let your light shine forth, free from any obstacles or hindrances. You may throw open the doors of your business in the morning as one who throws open the doors of opportunity for the service of God and people. You may handle your ledgers with as great a sense of sacred mission as the minister handles the Bible in the pulpit.

Thought for the day: *Don't hide! Shine!*

Mark 4:26–34   MAY 4

The earth produces of itself (v. 28).

The parable of the sower, which we read two days ago, teaches the responsibility of those who hear the Word of God. This parable contains a lesson for those who proclaim the Word. The first parable depicts, by various kinds of soil, the heart responses of different hearers; this parable illustrates the right attitude of mind for one who preaches the Gospel.

The Christian sower is often inclined to become impatient about the harvest. We are anxious to see things happen, and we want quick results. We would like to see the kingdom of

God established right now. Through this parable Jesus teaches us that the farmer can sow the seed, but he cannot make the seed grow. In fact, he does not even understand how it grows, for the processes of life are mysterious. The seed has the secret of life within itself. All the farmer can do is to sow the seed faithfully, and then allow the process of growth to take its course.

This does not mean that he is unconcerned about the harvest, but he can do nothing to produce it. Certainly anxiety will in no way help or speed up the growth process.

The growth of the seed is *gradual*: "first the blade, then the ear, then the full grain." But it is also constant. Night and day, even while people sleep, growth goes on. In the end, the harvest is *sure*. Then the farmer can put in his sickle and reap the fruits of his labors.

This parable is not intended to make Christians satisfied with stunted growth or fruitless lives. It is designed to deter us from seeking to manipulate spiritual processes and to encourage us to await the gradual fulfillment of God's purposes. Happy are the Christian workers who have learned to wait patiently for the harvest when they have faithfully scattered the seed, to do their work carefully and to leave the results with God.

Thought for the day: *We do not create the kingdom; the kingdom is God's.*

Mark 4:35–41   MAY 5

A great storm of wind arose (v. 37).

I have encountered a great variety of weather on the high seas. There is, for example, the day of the *glassy sea,* when the air is still and the water so smooth it actually looks like glass. There is also the day of the *choppy sea,* when the wind is just strong enough to churn the sea and form white caps on the waves. Then occasionally there is the day of the *stormy sea*, when the clouds are black and the winds roar over the deep. Waves rise and fall like miniature mountains and valleys, causing the ship to pitch and roll at the same time.

Life is like this, days when things go smoothly and orderly and we can smile the whole day long. There are days when things don't go quite right, and we tend to become irritated or anxious. But at times everything seems to go wrong, and our hearts are filled with despair.

To follow the Master does not mean smooth sailing always or cloudless skies. Even when no sin or doubt is involved, even then the tempests burst; circumstances seem against us; the waves threaten to engulf us. But as long as Jesus is in the ship with us, we have reason to hope.

Notice the progression in the details of the narrative. There arose a great storm (v. 37). Then Jesus arose (v. 39a, KJV). Finally, there arose a great calm (v. 39b). It was Jesus' presence and power that made the difference. In the same way Jesus is able to speak the word of peace amidst the storms of life. In the storm of sorrow He tells us of the abiding love of God. In the storm of temptation He reminds us that His grace is sufficient. In the storm of death He says to us, "I am the resurrection and the life; he who believes on me shall never die."

Thought for the day: *In the presence of Jesus we can have peace amidst even the wildest storms of life.*

Mark 5:1–20   **MAY 6**

Clothed and in his right mind (v. 15).

In yesterday's lesson we observed that Jesus has power over *nature*. Today we read of His power over *human nature*. The story of the healing of the Gadarene demoniac is one of the most dramatic incidents in the ministry of our Lord.

In the New Testament the word *demon* is mentioned only once. On the other hand the adjective *demonic* occurs fifty-five times in the Gospels, and *unclean* or *evil* spirits twenty-eight times. Some people claim that "spirit possession" is merely a figurative expression for moral depravity, or more definitely, for mental disease or insanity. But the New Testament differentiates clearly between mental illness and spirit possession (see Matt. 4:24; 8:16). According to the late Dr. Kurt Koch, well-known German medico-psychologist, these two phenomena are characterized by a completely different set of symptoms. For example, if one prays for a mentally ill person, he or she will remain calm throughout. On the other hand, a spirit-possessed person usually becomes upset and often violent.

"Spirit possession" describes the mysterious but real invasion and control of human personality by actual malign spirits of supernatural power. During my service in India I have witnessed several cases of the phenomenon. I have talked to missionaries from various countries who have also encountered numerous cases. In many instances exactly the same symptoms as described in the Gospels have been evident. In every instance it has been the authoritative command in the name of Christ that has brought complete deliverance.

The Gospel narrative so simply yet powerfully describes the transformation wrought by Christ in the personality of the demoniac: Mark writes, "They ... saw the demoniac sitting there, clothed and in his right mind." Luke adds the further detail that he was sitting "at the feet of Jesus." What a beautiful picture of serenity and poise. Christ has complete power over the spiritual forces of evil. He can set people free.

Thought for the day: *Christ can calm the tempest of the sea; and the turmoil of the soul.*

Mark 5:25–34   **MAY 7**

A woman ... came up behind him ... and touched his garment (vv. 25, 27).

There is a big difference in this story between the crowd and the woman. Many in the crowd must have touched Jesus that day. They accidentally jostled Him, and their garments brushed against His. But they merely "thronged" about Jesus, so nothing happened. The woman did more than "throng"; she actually reached out and touched Him. It was a different kind of contact. As a result she was instantly healed.

Look for a moment at the touch of this infirm woman. It was the touch of *desperation*. She had been ill for twelve years. She had sought the help of many physicians and had spent all her savings. But instead of getting better, she got worse. Her condition seemed hopeless. So she reached out to Jesus as a last resort.

It was a *purposeful* touch. The woman was incurably ill, and she was tired of her condition. More than anything else in the whole world she wanted to be well and strong. So she intentionally slipped through the crowd, made her way right up to the Master, stretched out her hand and touched His garment. There was nothing accidental about that touch—she had made her plan and she carried it through willfully.

It was also the touch of *faith*. The woman believed that if she could only touch the Master's garment, she would be healed. Perhaps she had watched Him reach out His hand on other occasions, touch the sick, and heal them. So she was determined to make contact. And Jesus, perceiving the woman's faith, said to her, "Daughter, your faith has made you well; go in peace, and be healed of your disease."

Are we among the "throngers" or the "touchers"? Do we merely brush against the Savior casually and go on our way the same as before? Or do we really touch Him and rise in newness of life?

Thought for the day: *It takes little effort to throng about Jesus in the crowd. It takes determination and faith to touch Him and be healed.*

Jairus . . . fell at his feet, and besought him (vv. 22, 23).

There was a difference between Jairus and the infirm woman we read about yesterday. Jairus was a ruler of the Jewish synagogue, a man of prominence in the community. He was a person of comparative wealth and power. The woman was poor, weak, unknown, ceremonially unclean, and friendless. But Jesus treated them both alike, with the same courtesy and tender compassion. He is no respecter of persons.

One thing, however, was common to both the woman and Jairus. Both were driven to Jesus by a sense of desperate need. For twelve years the life of the woman had been made miserable by continual disease and suffering. She had tried every remedy. But she was getting worse. Her case seemed hopeless. As for Jairus, for twelve years his home had been brightened by the presence of a lovely daughter, an only child. Now she lay at death's door. Again, the situation seemed hopeless.

Jairus was so desperate that he was willing to push aside all obstacles. He forgot his *prejudices*. There can be no doubt that he must have regarded Jesus as an outsider, a dangerous heretic, one to whom the synagogue doors were closed. He forgot his *dignity*. He, a ruler of the synagogue, came and threw himself at the feet of Jesus, the wandering teacher. It must have taken a conscious effort of self-humiliation for a man in his position to come and beg help from Jesus. But to whom else could he go?

The very first step in the Christian life is this sense of desperate need. When a person realizes that he is nothing in himself, and that he can do nothing to save himself, then only will he fall at the feet of Jesus. But it is just at this point that the grace of God takes over, and the Spirit brings order out of chaos, hope out of despair, and life out of death.

Thought for the day: *We have a great need for the Savior; we have a great Savior for our needs.*

Mark 6:1–6   MAY 9

He marveled because of their unbelief (v. 6).

Jesus had just completed a successful tour in the environs of Capernaum where he performed a series of astounding miracles—stilling a storm, delivering a demoniac, healing incurable disease, raising the dead. As a result, His fame spread all through the countryside, and many believed on Him and followed Him. Then Jesus returned to His home town, Nazareth, and on the Sabbath day entered into the synagogue to teach. At first the response of the listeners was positive. Many were astonished at His teaching and they said among themselves, "Where did this man get all this wisdom?" And, recalling the reports of the many miracles Jesus had recently performed, they exclaimed, "What mighty works are wrought by His hands!"

But then they began to have second thoughts. They said to themselves, "Wait a minute; we know this man. He grew up in this town. Is He not the carpenter, who used to operate the workshop down on the corner? Is he not Mary's son, and are not his brothers living among us? What can be so unusual about this man?" And so they took offense at Him.

The people of Nazareth thought they knew Jesus, but they really didn't. They were so full of prejudice that they were unable to look beyond his humble birth and his familiar figure as a boy. All they could see was the carpenter and hometown lad. They failed to recognize Him as the Messiah. And because they did not understand who He really was, they were unable to put their trust in Him. And because of their lack of faith, Jesus was unable to perform any mighty works in their midst.

It is so important that we know who Jesus is—the Son of God, the Savior of the world. Then we can believe in Him and have full confidence in His grace and power. Our faith will

147

then release His power and produce miracles in our hearts and lives.

Thought for the day: *Don't let anyone whittle down the size of your God.*

Mark 6:7–13   MAY 10

He began to send them out two by two (v. 7).

Thus far we have observed the public ministry of Jesus. He served with a strong sense of divine appointment, knowing that the Father had sent Him into the world on a mission of utmost importance. His whole life was devoted to the fulfillment of this mission. So Jesus went about among the villages teaching and preaching. He proclaimed that the kingdom of God was at hand and called upon people to repent. He also ministered to their physical and emotional needs, as He cast out evil spirits and healed the sick.

Jesus had already appointed His twelve disciples (see 3:14) that they might "be with him, and ... be sent out to preach." But up to this point they had merely remained with Him, basking in His fellowship, observing, learning, and preparing themselves. Now Jesus decides to send them out on their first temporary assignment. Notice carefully that He passes on to them exactly the same mission in which He Himself is engaged. "They went out and preached that men should repent. They cast out many demons, and anointed with oil many that were sick and healed them." Their mission was an extension of His.

Jesus warned His disciples that the response to their preaching would be similar to that of His. At times many would receive their message and respond in faith. At other times people would reject their preaching and refuse to believe the Gospel. But certainly they could expect fruit.

Jesus also sent His disciples out with authority. Many of them were simple fishermen; one had been a despised tax collector. All came from humble backgrounds and common walks of life. But Jesus delegated His authority to them so that they preached and ministered with power.

Jesus is still sending forth His disciples in these days. Our responsibility is to continue the same mission that He began upon earth. And, thank God, we have the same authority and power at our disposal.

Thought for the day: *It is God's mission and God's power. Therefore, we cannot fail.*

Mark 6:14–29

[Herod] . . . was much perplexed (v. 20).

Herod Antipas was the ruler of Galilee, a man of position and wealth. But he was an exceedingly wicked man. He visited his brother in Rome, seduced his wife, Herodias, and persuaded her to marry him. When John the baptizer publicly rebuked him for this adulterous union, Herod was fearful and perplexed, but too weak-willed to confess his sin and set things right. Finally, trapped by Herodias and her daughter, Salome, he added the sin of murder to his record, by ordering the execution of John.

But Herod suffered from a guilty conscience. He had put away the prophet of God, but he could not silence the voice of God. Day and night he was haunted by the vision of a bloody head staring at him with glassy eyes from a silver plate. So when he heard of the mighty works that Jesus was performing and how everyone was acclaiming Him as a prophet, he exclaimed in fear, "Alas, John, whom I beheaded, has been raised from the dead."

In India they tell the story of a theft that took place in the king's palace. The king lined up his servants and questioned them one by one about the missing silver vessel, but each one pleaded innocent. Then the king distributed wooden sticks of equal length to the men and said to them, "Bring your sticks back to me this same time tomorrow evening. By that time the stick of the thief will have grown three inches longer, and he will be found out. When the guilty servant heard this, he became afraid, went home and cut three inches off his stick. The next evening he was caught—trapped by his own guilty conscience.

The only cure for a guilty conscience is for a person to repent and confess his sin before Almighty God, who will graciously pardon all transgressions, blot out the past, and enable him to begin a new life. Conscience will then become an ally, not an enemy.

Thought for the day: *'Tis better for one to lose his head than his soul.*

Mark 6:30—44   **MAY 12**

Send them away ... You give them something to eat (vv. 36, 37).

The contrast between the attitude of Jesus and the attitude of the disciples reveals two different reactions to human need. When the disciples saw the large crowd, how late it was, and how hungry the people were, they said to the Master, "Send them away." In effect they were saying, "These people are tired and hungry, but there are too many of them for us to handle. Get rid of them and let them shift for themselves, or let someone else worry about them. There's nothing we can do." But Jesus said to the disciples, "These people *are* tired and hungry. We can't send them away; we must help them. Why don't *you* give them something to eat?"

How often we are like those disciples. We see people all about us in difficulty and need, but we are not willing to get involved. We're too busy, or we just don't care enough. We try to push the responsibility for meeting their needs onto someone else. We send them away empty-handed. At such times Jesus always says to us, "Get involved. Do something to help these people."

Jesus wanted his disciples to get busy and act because He Himself intended to do something. He took the loaves, gave them to the disciples, and they in turn distributed them to the people (v. 41). Observe the three important words here—loaves, disciples, people. Notice also their order and relation. Where do we find the disciples? They are between the loaves and the multitude. How did the loaves get to the people? They were distributed through the disciples, for Jesus did not give directly, but by their hands.

We stand, as those disciples did, between the loaves and the multitude. We stand either as obstructionists, withholding the loaves from hungry people by our indifference, selfishness, and sloth; or else as Christ's faithful helpers, passing out the loaves from His hands to the multitude.

Thought for the day: *Christ provides an abundant supply, but He leaves the distribution to us.*

Mark 6:45–56   **MAY 13**

Take heart, it is I; have no fear (v. 50).

Certain mental and emotional states throw dust into the human machinery. Fear is one of them. It is perhaps the greatest enemy of mental, physical, and spiritual well-being. A few years ago, an article written by an eminent physician and published by *The Reader's Digest,* described fear—and its related mental states of stress, tension, and anxiety—as "the cause of all disease."

Now, not all fear is bad. Natural fear, which is a God-given instinct, protects us from potential dangers to our bodies. Were it not for this, we would frequently be injured. There is also the wholesome "fear of the Lord," a deep, reverential awe and an all-enveloping desire to be with Him and serve Him. But we are talking about the abnormal fear that can only bring harm to the individual—fear of the unknown, fear of the future, fear of people, fear of failure, fear of death, etc. Such fear destroys our peace of mind, enslaves our wills, and actually makes us sick in mind and body.

This incident and others that we have read about in Mark's Gospel give us the scriptural antidote for fear. To the disciples who sat trembling in the boat, Jesus said, "Take heart; it is I." The knowledge of His presence dispels our fears. When we are assured that He is still with us, even when trials, temptations, discouragement, and death stare us in the face, then we can take courage and overcome our fears.

On another occasion, when a storm rose on the Sea of Galilee and was about to engulf the disciples, Jesus said to them, "Why are you afraid? Have you no faith?" If we really believe in Christ as a Person, trust His word, and have confidence in His love and power, we shall never become victims of the numerous types of fear that press us on every hand. Faith is the ultimate cure for fear.

Thought for the day: *The fear of the Lord displaces all other fears (L. Gilbert Little, M.D.).*

Mark 7:1–13 MAY 14

You leave the commandment of God, and hold fast the tradition of men (v. 8).

The charge which the Pharisees preferred against Jesus was that "his disciples ate with hands defiled." This did not mean that the disciples ate with hands that were physically unclean. It meant they had neglected the ceremonial washing which was required by Jewish traditions. The hands had to be washed in a particular way, with water kept in special large stone jars. First, the hands were held with the finger tips pointing *upward*. Water was poured over them and ran down at least to the wrists. Each hand was then rubbed with the fist of the other. Second, the hands had to be held with finger tips pointing *downward*, while water was poured over them in such a way that it began at the wrists and ran off the finger tips. Only then were hands considered clean.

The charge gave our Lord an opportunity to rebuke the Pharisees for their hypocrisy, and as an example He cited one of their common practices. According to the law of God, one should honor his parents and provide for their needs. According to tradition, however, if one should pronounce over any property the word *Corban*, which means "a gift," this property would be regarded as dedicated to God. But the tradition also provided that, while the property could not be given to any other person, it could be used by the owner for his own gratification. Thus it was possible for a person to keep the tradition but at the same time disobey the commandments of God.

Here then Christ exposes ancient and modern hypocrisy. He shows how opposed ritualism may be to reality, tradition to truth, and decrees to duty. Clean hands can never be a substitute for an unclean heart; washing can never atone for wickedness, nor lip-honor for heart-hypocrisy. It is righteousness that God requires and not "religiosity."

Thought for the day: *People look on the outward appearance, but God looks on the heart (1 Sam. 16:7).*

Mark 7:14–23   MAY 15

What comes out of a man is what defiles a man (v. 20).

Yesterday we saw how our Lord rebuked the Pharisees for their legalism. They were more concerned about ceremonial cleanness than they were about moral purity; more meticulous about conformity to traditions than obedience to the commandments of God. There is no greater peril than that of identifying religion with outward observance. It is possible for

153

ethical religion to be buried under a mass of taboos and rules and regulations.

In today's Scripture, Jesus carries this idea a step further. He proclaims a truth that must have seemed startling, yes, even revolutionary, to those who heard it for the first time. He declared that real uncleanness is not a matter of the body but of the spirit. One is not defiled by that which enters his mouth, but by that which proceeds from his heart. Therefore, what one needs most, if he is to be clean, is not a washing of the hands but a cleansing of the heart.

Many years ago the cowboys of a little Western town were watching a silent movie. The plot centered around the usual triangle of a handsome hero, a beautiful heroine, and a villain. In the middle of the story, the villain kidnapped the beautiful girl, flung her on his horse, and rode off with her. This was too much for the cowboys. They pulled out their six-shooters and fired into the screen trying to stop the villain from carrying off the beautiful girl. They riddled the screen with holes, but the picture went on. The villain carried off the girl. Now, if just one of the cowboys had used his good sense, he would have turned and fired one shot into the projector and stopped the whole picture!

Many of us try to reform ourselves on the outside. But what we need most is a clean heart within.

Thought for the day: *Start with the projector if you want a beautiful picture on the screen.*

Mark 7:24–30   MAY 16

He could not be hid (v. 24).

A young man, recently converted, was engaged to work during the summer months in a lumber camp where the men were noted for being "rough and tough." His friends were worried whether he would be able to maintain his Christian experience in such company. At the end of the summer, when the young man returned home, his friends asked him, "Bob, how did the men treat you when they learned you were a Christian?" He replied, "No problem. I never let on I was a Christian." Evidently his "conversion" was not genuine enough to make a difference in his life.

But Jesus was different from all others, so different that "he could not be hid." Day after day He was constantly thronged by the multitudes so that at times he found little time to eat or sleep. Once in a while he tried to slip away from the crowd, into a quiet mountain place or by the seashore, in order to rest and commune with His Father. But the crowd always looked for Him and found Him.

Jesus could not be hid because He was different in His Person. All knew He was more than an ordinary man. Some said He was a prophet; others believed He was the Messiah. His character was so different. He was honest and pure, compassionate and loving—free from the common prejudices and bigotry of His day. His message was also different, exposing the hypocrisy and sin of the religious leaders. When He spoke, people said, "This man speaks with authority."

Jesus could not be hid because of His *works*. His fame spread far and wide as He ministered to the poor and sinful, fed the hungry multitudes, healed the sick, cast out unclean spirits, calmed stormy seas, and even raised the dead. All were convinced that no one could do such mighty deeds unless God were with him. His radiant life and unselfish actions revealed Christ to the whole world.

Thought for the day: *If we are hid in Christ, He will be clearly seen.*

Mark 7:31–37   MAY 17

He has done all things well (v. 37).

In almost all of the miracles of healing that Jesus performed, He merely spoke a few words or touched the sick person, and immediately healing took place. But in this particular case Jesus proceeded with great deliberation and performed a series of unusual acts. He put His fingers into the man's ears, spat on the ground, and touched his tongue. Then he looked up toward heaven and gave the command, "Be opened." And the man was healed.

Why did Jesus employ pantomime in connection with this healing? We must remember that the man was deaf so Jesus had to use sign language in order to communicate with him. Our Lord was acting out what he intended to do. He was showing the man what to expect. His ears would be opened; his tongue would be loosed. That's why Jesus touched the man's ears and tongue. When He looked toward heaven, He was reminding the deaf man that all healing comes from above—from the Divine Physician. Evidently Jesus was seeking to arouse the man's faith and expectation.

When the miracle took place, the man could hear perfectly and speak plainly. As a result, the people declared with astonishment, "He has done all things well." This is exactly the same verdict that God pronounced upon His own work at the time of creation (Gen. 1:31). He looked around at the things He had brought into existence and declared each time, "It is good." In the beginning everything was good, but human disobedience spoiled it all. When Jesus appeared among people, healing their bodies and redeeming their lives, He was actually re-creating that which had been ruined. He was restoring the beauty of God to a world rendered ugly by sin. And when the people saw this, they declared, "It is good."

Jesus is a specialist in all that He does. He heals perfectly, He delivers completely, He cleanses through and through.

Thought for the day: *Jesus never does a poor job. He does everything well.*

Mark 8:1–10   MAY 18

A great crowd had gathered (v. 1)

The feeding of the four thousand took place in the district called Decapolis (see 7:31), which literally means "the ten cities." These cities were on the east side of the Jordan River, within Syria, and were essentially Greek in character. It was in this same area that Jesus had healed the Gadarene demoniac (Mark 5:1–20). At that time the inhabitants had pleaded with Jesus to leave their cities, but now from that region a tremendous crowd of about four thousand assembled to hear His teaching. What caused the difference in the attitude of the people?

We remember that the cured demoniac had wished to remain with, and follow, Jesus, but Jesus had sent him back to his home and friends to tell them what great things the Lord had done for him. The man did more than that. He went throughout the whole Decapolis and proclaimed the news so that "all men marveled" (5:20). Is it just possible that part of this great crowd was due to the missionary activity of the healed demoniac? Were there people in the crowd that day who came to Jesus because they had heard a man telling of what Jesus had done for him? If so, we have here a marvelous illustration of what one person's witness can do for Christ.

Several years ago in India a villager, almost blind from cataracts, came to the mission hospital for an operation. In a short while he regained his vision and went home rejoicing. One day the missionary doctor looked out the window of his office and saw a strange sight. About twenty men in single file approached, holding onto a long bamboo pole. They were all blind with cataracts. At the front of the line was the man who had recently been operated on. When his friends heard what had happened to him, they wanted to come to the Christian surgeon for help. The testimony of one man had convinced them that there was hope for them too.

Thought for the day: *The primary calling of every Christian is to witness for Christ.*

Beware of the leaven of the Pharisees ... and of Herod (v. 15).

Leaven was a piece of dough that had been kept over from a previous baking until it became fermented. To the Jew fermentation was equivalent to putrefaction, and therefore leaven was a symbol of corruption or evil. So when Jesus says, "Beware of leaven," He is actually warning us to be on our guard against evil influences.

Jesus warns us against three types of corruption. He says, "Beware of the leaven of the *Pharisees,* that is, *formalism.* The Pharisees were more concerned with outward observances than with inner purity. They were careful to keep the traditions, but at the same time neglected the commandments of God. Today we are inclined to substitute membership in the church for relationship with Christ, and the practice of ritual for the pursuit of righteousness. This is to make a travesty of religion and miss the very heart of the Gospel.

Jesus also warns us against the leaven of *Herod,* which stands for *materialism.* The Herodians tried to build up happiness through the pursuit of pleasure and the gaining of power and wealth. This led to worldliness and irreligion. In a highly affluent society such as ours today, it is so easy to become entangled in the web of secularism and get our values all mixed up. We are inclined to feel that the supreme objective of life lies in material well-being and progress. We become more interested in the kingdom of gadgets than in the kingdom of God.

Jesus also warns us against the leaven of the *Sadducees* (Matt. 16:11), that is, *rationalism.* The Sadducees were skeptics who did not believe in resurrection, angels, or spirits. They over-emphasized human reason to the neglect of faith. And today we have in our midst those who deny the supernatural in revelation and in religion.

Against the insidious spread of these three forms of leaven, the church needs to be constantly on its guard.

Thought for the day: *The antidote for the leaven of the world is the Bread of Life.*

Mark 8:22–26   MAY 20

Then again [Jesus] laid his hands upon his eyes (v. 25).

The miracle we have just read is found only in Mark's Gospel. It is unique in the fact that it is the only miracle that can be said to have happened gradually. Usually Jesus' miracles of healing were completed suddenly. In this case the blind man's sight came back in stages. No explanation is given as to the reason; we can only speculate about the purpose of Jesus.

But possibly there are one or two significant lessons in this narrative for all of us. The ways of Jesus are varied. We cannot dictate to Him how He should operate. Sometimes he heals in person, sometimes from a distance. At times he lays hands upon the individual; at other times he merely gives a verbal command. Sometimes He uses pantomime; sometimes He does not. Sometimes He heals instantaneously, but occasionally He heals gradually. There is a pleasing variety in the methods Jesus employs.

Furthermore, there is variety in Christian experience, especially in the outward manifestations. Some people experience a great burst of emotion. They feel like jumping or shouting. Others are poised and quiet; they experience a great inner calm. Some speak in tongues; others do not. The important thing for me is not to deny the validity of the other person's experience just because "he didn't get it the way I did."

Can you imagine the blind man of this passage and blind Bartimaeus of Mark 10:46–52 meeting by chance sometime later and sharing their experiences of healing? One would have told how he was healed instantaneously with only a word from the Master's lips; the other would have described how he saw clearly only after our Lord had touched him twice. But it would have been foolish for either one to deny the healing of the other simply because Jesus had employed different methods to restore their sight. The important thing was that both had once been blind, but now they could see perfectly.

Thought for the day: Variety *in Christian experience does not deny its* validity.

Mark 8:27–33   **MAY 21**

Who do you say that I am? (v. 29)

With this question Jesus confronts every living person. Everything depends on the answer. For what we do with Him depends largely upon what we think of Him.

Who, then, is this Jesus? Is He just a *man*? Certainly He was human in every respect. Born in a manger, He worked at a carpenter's bench, walked our footpaths, slept on our hillsides, drank from our wells, was tempted like all of us, died and was buried. And yet He is more than human.

Is He just a great *teacher*? Again and again we read in the Gospels that Jesus went about teaching the people. Great crowds assembled to hear Him speak. His teaching was so profound that it is recorded "the people were astonished at his doctrine, for he taught them as one having authority." And yet Jesus is more than a teacher.

Is He just a *prophet*? This was the general opinion of Jesus as He walked and worked among the people. Some thought He was John the baptizer, or Elijah, come to life again. Others said, "He is *one* of the prophets." If there ever was a prophet who declared the message of God, who foretold the future, it was Jesus.

But Jesus is more than a great man, an unusual teacher,

or a famous prophet. Peter, when confronted with the question, declared under the illumination of the Holy Spirit, "You are the Christ, the Son of the living God." He was right! Jesus is the Anointed One, the Messiah, the Savior of the world. The angel said to Joseph, "Call His name Jesus, for He shall save His people from their sins." The angelic host sang over Bethlehem, "To you is born this day . . . a Savior, who is Christ the Lord." Paul wrote of Him, "At the name of Jesus every knee shall bow . . . and every tongue confess that Jesus Christ is Lord."

Thought for the day: *Jesus is more than a great man; He is the God-man.*

Mark 8:34–38

Let him deny himself and take up his cross and follow me (v. 34)

In these words our Lord lays down the challenge to discipleship. There are four distinct steps to be taken.

1. *Make Up*—"If any man would come after me." He who wishes to be a disciple of Christ must first *make up his mind* to follow Christ. Christ is a perfect gentleman and will not force anyone to join Him. The individual must choose of his own free will.

2. *Give Up*—"Let him deny himself." This is more than a giving up of our sins or turning our backs on the old life. It involves the surrender of the right to ourselves. The center of our lives must shift from self to Christ. We must pray as Jesus did in Gethsemane, "Not my will, but thine be done." Then we shall be able to testify in the words of the apostle Paul, "I am crucified with Christ."

3. *Take Up*—"Let him take up his cross." Taking up the cross does not mean enduring some great irritation, or burden, or distress, but accepting the concept of self-giving as the motivating principle of our lives. The cross not only has

meaning for us *objectively* as the *propitiation for our sins;* it also has meaning for us *subjectively* as the *principle for service.* We cannot bless unless we bleed; we cannot live for others unless we die to ourselves.

4. *Keep Up*—"And follow me." Here is a clear call for a consistent walk with the Master. We must not only accept Him as Savior, but follow Him as Guide and Lord. This means keeping in close touch with Him through prayer and the Word, walking by His side in faith and obedience from day to day, and remaining in the center of His will at all times. There are many who start on the way, but fail to follow through unto the end.

Thought for the day: *To follow Christ is more than taking a walk; it is going on a journey for life.*

Mark 9:1–13   MAY 23

This is my beloved Son (v. 7).

The New Testament affirms that Jesus is the *Son of God.* Mark begins his narrative by saying, "[This is] the beginning of the gospel of Jesus Christ, the Son of God." John concludes his gospel by stating, "These things are written that you may believe that Jesus is the Christ, the Son of God" (20:31). Throughout the epistles are many passages that refer to Christ with this title.

Many individuals gave witness to the sonship of Christ. Peter, speaking on behalf of the disciples, said, "You are the Christ, the Son of the living God." The Roman centurion, who supervised the crucifixion, exclaimed when he saw Jesus die, "Truly this man was the Son of God." The Gadarene demoniac, when confronted by Jesus, cried out, "What have you to do with me Jesus, Son of the Most High God?"

Jesus Himself claimed that He was the Son of God (John 10:36). It was for this reason that the Jewish leaders accused Him of blasphemy and clamored for His death. It was at this very point that the devil made the main thrust of his temptation—*"If* you are the Son of God, then make these stones bread . . . jump down from this pinnacle."

But the greatest witness of all was that of the heavenly Father. Twice during the public ministry of Jesus—His baptism and transfiguration—God spoke in an audible voice, saying, "This is my beloved Son; listen to him."

Jesus is not the Son of God after the human analogy of a parent with an offspring. The term *son* is only one way of indicating the relationship of Jesus Christ to God. It affirms the deity of Jesus and His unity with the sovereign God of the universe. For this reason Jesus was able to say, "He who has seen me has seen the Father, for the Father and I are One." As one young lad said, "Jesus is the best photograph that God ever had taken."

Thought for the day: *Jesus is God. Don't just tip your hat to him; give Him your heart.*

Mark 9:14–29   MAY 24

If you can do anything, have pity on us and help us (v. 22).

There is an interesting connection between this narrative and one found in chapter 1 (vv. 40–45). There we read the story of a leper, who knelt at the feet of Jesus and said, *"If you will* [i.e., if you want to], you can make me clean." Notice, the leper was confident of Jesus' ability to heal him—"you can make me clean"—but he questioned Jesus' willingness to do so. In response Jesus said, "I will" (i.e., I want to). Then He demonstrated His willingness, as He touched the leper and commanded, "Be clean." Immediately the man was healed.

In the passage for today we find the narrative of a father, who brought his epileptic son to Jesus. After describing the pitiful condition of the boy, the father said to Jesus, *"If you can do anything,* have pity on us and help us." In this case

163

the supplicant seemed to be confident of Jesus' willingness, but he questioned His ability to heal—"*if you can do anything.*" Then Jesus demonstrated His power by miraculously healing the boy.

Throughout His public ministry Jesus proved over and over again that He is both willing and able to help all those who come to Him with needs. He demonstrated His willingness by showing compassion for the sick, the hungry, and the sinful. He never turned anyone away. Jesus also demonstrated His ability or power by healing all manner of diseases, feeding the multitudes, stilling a storm at sea, walking on the water, and raising the dead. No case was too hard for Him.

But Jesus made it plain that His willingness and power must be matched by our *faith*. In this incident when the father said to Jesus, "Help us if you can," Jesus immediately threw back the challenge, "If *you* can [that is, it's up to you]! All things are possible to him who believes."

Jesus is always willing and able to help. Are we ready to believe?

Thought for the day: *Faith, f-a-i-t-h, means "forsaking all I trust Him.*

Mark 9:30—41   MAY 25

They had discussed with one another who was the greatest (v. 34).

In the first half of this Gospel the writer has a particular objective in mind. He reports in rapid succession a series of remarkable miracles that Jesus performed—the cleansing of a leper, the healing of a paralytic, stilling of the tempest on Lake Galilee, deliverance of a helpless demoniac, raising of Jairus' daughter from the dead, the feeding of five thousand, and then another four thousand hungry people. Mark is thereby building up a powerful case to prove that Jesus is truly the Christ, the long-expected Messiah. He is vividly portraying the *adequacy* of Christ for every situation. Our Lord is the God of the impossible.

But in the second half of his Gospel, Mark tells of a series of incidents about the disciples of Jesus, portraying their utter *inadequacy* for the mission that is ahead. Four of those instances are found in the ninth chapter, which we are now contemplating. A father brought his epileptic boy to the disciples, but they were unable to heal him (v. 18). When Jesus spoke to them about his imminent suffering and death, they were unable to understand his words (v. 32). They argued among themselves about who was the greatest in the kingdom of heaven (v. 34). They rebuked a man who was not a member of their group for casting out unclean spirits in the name of their Master. Impotence, lack of spiritual understanding, pride, bigotry—these were the sins of the disposition that harassed them.

Jesus realized the inadequacy of His disciples so He made provision for them. He was looking forward to that great day of Pentecost when He would pour out His Spirit upon these men, purify their hearts, and endue them with power from on high. The indwelling Spirit would illuminate their minds, turn their pride into humility, their bigotry into love, and their impotence into power. Many a twentieth-century disciple of Christ is suffering from the same spiritual condition, but thank God, the dynamic of the Spirit is still available to all.

Thought for the day: *Christ wants us to exchange our* inadequacy *for His* adequacy.

Mark 9:42–50   **MAY 26**

It is better for you to enter life lame than ... to go to hell (v. 45).

In this passage contrast is made between "hell" (Gehenna) and "the kingdom of God." Gehenna is the Greek name for the Hinnom Valley, southwest of Jerusalem, where Ahaz and Manasseh (2 Chron. 28:3; 33:6) had instituted infant sacrifices to the Ammonite god, Molech. After the reforms under Josiah, the valley was declared unclean, and consequently became the garbage dump for Jerusalem. It was a foul, filthy place that smouldered continuously like a vast incinerator and where loathsome worms bred on the refuse. Because of this the name Gehenna became symbolic for hell.

In contrast is the kingdom of God, a society upon earth in which God's will is done as perfectly as it is in heaven. It is characterized by life, order, peace, and purity.

Jesus is saying that the goal of doing God's will is worth any amount of sacrifice or self-discipline. Physically speaking, sometimes it may become necessary for one to consent to the amputation of a limb or some part of the body in order to preserve the life of the whole body. The same is true spiritually. It would actually be far better to lose some important part of the body and save our spiritual lives, than allow this member to become an instrument of sin leading us to spiritual death. The hand, foot, and eye are used here as three parallel figures to represent the common agents of temptation.

But we must not take this passage too literally. The emphasis is primarily upon a radical separation from sin. If anything in our lives becomes an occasion for sin or keeps us from doing the perfect will of God, it must be cut off. The process may be as painful as a surgical operation. It may seem like cutting off a hand or a foot, but if we are to enter the kingdom and find real life, it is necessary.

Thought for the day: *It is better to lose a limb than life.*

Mark 10:1–12   **MAY 27**

What ... God has joined together, let not man put asunder (v. 9).

Divorce has become one of the major social and spiritual

problems of our day. The number of dissolved marriages is growing at an alarming rate in American society. In 1960 one out of every four marriages ended in the divorce court; today it is slightly higher than one out of three. In a few states and certain metropolitan areas, the ratio is as high as one divorce to every two marriages. Nearly nine million children now live in fatherless homes. Once marriage was considered permanent, sacred, and fulfilling, but it is fast becoming a temporary union. Instead of a holy, beautiful relationship, marriage has become a selfish partnership that may be dissolved when either party finds another more desirable.

The Bible holds marriage in high regard; it was God's design from the very beginning. He made Eve for Adam because He saw that man was incomplete without woman. Marriage is often used as an illustration of deep spiritual unity. In the Old Testament, God's relationship with Israel is described as a marriage. When Israel turned to false gods, the true God charged the Israelites with adultery as a nation. In the New Testament, the born-again believer is described as being "wed to Christ." Our Lord's relationship to His church is portrayed under the analogy of the bride and bridegroom.

Jesus taught that marriage is a permanent relationship, and the only legitimate ground for divorce is adultery (see Matt. 19:9). The truth is that infidelity does in fact dissolve the bond and unity of marriage; divorce merely attests the fact.

The real thrust of Jesus' words in this passage is that the loose sexual morality of our day must be abandoned. Marriage must not be entered into lightly but thoughtfully; not just for pleasure but for responsibility; not as a temporary civil contract but as a permanent spiritual union.

Thought for the day: *Unity in Christ is the only sure foundation for a happy and fulfilling marriage.*

Mark 10:17–22   MAY 28

A man ran up ... he went away sorrowful (vv. 17, 22).

167

This is one of the great dramatic incidents in the life of our Lord. It has all the elements of a good story. It has movement, color, contrast, suspense and climax. It is not fiction; it is history. It is the tragic account of one who stood at the crossroads of life, made the wrong decision, and so far as we know, elected an eternal destiny of darkness.

Notice how the inquirer came to Jesus. He had so many good qualities to his credit. He was *eager*, he came running. He heard that Jesus was in town, so he didn't want to miss this opportunity to meet Him. He was *humble*; he knelt at Jesus' feet. Even though he was a man of wealth and position, he was willing to kneel in the dust of the road, for he knew he was in the presence of a great man. He was also *honest*, for he asked a question in keeping with his need. He had many things—riches, power, and morality—but he did not have eternal life. Finally, he was a *young* man (see Matt. 19:20). He stood at the threshold of life, but he knew that life was fleeting and short. He was earnestly seeking to make preparations for the future.

The pity of the story is the manner in which the young man left Jesus. He came running; he walked slowly away. He came eagerly, expecting; he went away sorrowful. He came with much; he returned empty-handed. He asked his question and received the answer; but he was not willing to pay the price. He wanted eternal life, but not enough to meet the conditions laid down by our Lord.

No one, having been confronted by Jesus, can turn his back on the Savior and go away happy. He will leave with a sad heart, with no hope for the future. For when one rejects Christ, he is rejecting life itself.

Thought for the day: *It costs much to follow Christ; it costs more to reject Him.*

Mark 10:23–31   **MAY 29**

[The disciple] . . . will . . . receive a hundredfold now . . . and in the age to come eternal life (v. 30).

A rich young ruler had just come to Jesus with an important question: "What must I do to inherit eternal life?" In response Jesus commanded him to "go sell all, and come, follow me." But the young man turned and walked away sorrowful, for he was not willing to part with his riches. As Peter watched this scene, he could not help but draw the contrast between the man and himself and his colleagues. So somewhat boastfully he said to Jesus, "Lo, we have left everything and followed you." The unspoken implication was, "Do we receive anything in return?"

It was not good taste on Peter's part to ask that question, pertinent though it seemed to him. Renunciation should never be for the sake of reward, but for love of the Redeemer. There is no place for the commercial element in the Christian life.

Yet Jesus was quick to point out that for renunciation there is reward. God will never be in debt to anyone. He keeps accurate records and one day will settle the accounts. Every sacrifice made for His sake and the Gospel's receives a hundredfold recompense in this life, and in the future, eternal life itself. The reward is neither in kind nor measure, for our Lord gives us much better and far more than we can ever renounce. He substitutes inward good for outward gain; new spiritual relationships for lost family ties; heavenly possessions for material substance. And his recompense satisfies the soul many times more than whatever we have surrendered ever could.

However, Jesus made it clear that to be a disciple is costly. He warned His followers that they would receive their reward *only with persecutions*. There would be rejection, slander, imprisonment, physical suffering, perhaps even death. Jesus also reminded his disciples that God does not always settle his accounts within this world of time and space. He has eternity in which to repay. The reward may not be immediate, but it is sure.

Thought for the day: *Jesus never used a* bribe *to induce people to follow Him. He always threw out a* challenge.

*The Son of man also came ... to serve, and to give
his life as a ransom for many (v. 45).*

An interesting feature in Mark's Gospel brings out an
important spiritual lesson for us all. In chapters eight to ten,
three times Jesus takes His disciples aside and warns them of
His impending suffering and death. But each time, immediately after Christ's solemn discourse, the disciples give a
display of carnal selfishness. The contrast is striking. On one
hand, we have the *self-giving* disposition of the Savior; on the
other, the *self-seeking* spirit of the disciples.

In 8:31—33, Jesus for the first time revealed to the
disciples that "the Son of man must suffer many things, and
be rejected by the elders and chief priests and the scribes, and
be killed." Immediately Peter spoke up and said, "God forbid,
Lord! This shall never happen to you." In return Jesus had to
rebuke Peter sternly.

In 9:30—34, Jesus again described His forthcoming
death. Immediately afterward the disciples argued with one
another about who among them was the greatest. Then Jesus
had to put a child in front of them and give them a lesson on
humility.

In chapter 10, which we are now contemplating, once
again Jesus warned His little flock that He was on His way to
the cross. Shortly afterward, James and John came to Jesus
privately and asked Him to grant them the privilege of sitting
on His right and left in the kingdom. Jesus had to remind
them that instead of a crown to wear, there was a cup to
drink—the cup of suffering.

Finally, Jesus climaxes His discourse with this matchless
statement: "The Son of man came not be served but to serve,
and to give his life a ransom for many."

At the heart of the Christian life is a cross. We are called to
be servants, not sovereigns. We are called to give ourselves for
others, not to use others for our own gain.

Thought for the day: *We cannot wear the crown, unless we bear the cross.*

Mark 10:46–52   **MAY 31**

Take heart ... he is calling you (v. 49).

A significant point in the story of blind Bartimaeus is this—no one took an interest in the man until they saw that Jesus was interested in him. At first the people looked upon Bartimaeus as a nuisance. So they told him to shut up and tried to keep him away from the Master. But when they saw Jesus' concern for the blind man, they began to look upon him as someone in desperate need. They said to him somewhat tenderly, "Take heart; the Master is calling you." Then they gently led him to Jesus.

This understanding of Christ's compassion for all types of people has inaugurated more social movements throughout the world than we normally realize. For a long time no one was interested in the untouchables of India. They were looked upon as the scum of society, as a people who were being punished for sins committed in a previous existence. Then when Christian missionaries realized that Christ loved the outcasts just as much as the Brahmins, they preached the Gospel to them and invited them to become the children of God.

For many years no one was interested in the lepers of Africa. They were considered unclean and were cut off from society. But when Christian doctors understood that Christ had compassion on lepers, they went among these people, ministered to them in their suffering, and invited them to become members of God's family.

For decades the tribal people of New Guinea looked upon the birth of a female child as a bad omen, and parents often left their girl babies in the bushes to die. But when Christ came their way, the Guineans suddenly saw that all children are the gift of God, and from then on they nurtured their baby girls with the same tender care and affection that they showed to their boys.

The world has never been the same since Jesus demonstrated that God cares for all people.

Thought for the day: *We dare not look upon anyone other than as a person for whom Christ died.*

Mark 11:1—10

Blessed be the kingdom of our father David (v. 10).

Until now Jesus has forbidden His followers to publicly proclaim Him as the Messiah. He has carefully avoided precipitating the inevitable crisis. But at last the hour has come. Jesus openly declares Himself to be the promised King of Israel. Accompanied by His disciples and acclaimed by the multitude, He rides into Jerusalem in a pageant of triumph.

The manner of Christ's entry is significant. He came riding on a donkey. Nowadays the donkey is an object of amused contempt, but in Jesus' day it was considered to be a noble animal—a symbol of peace. When a king went forth to battle he rode a horse; when he came in peace he rode a donkey. Thus Jesus was proclaiming Himself to be the King of peace.

The multitude, however, completely misunderstood the nature of Christ's kingship. They thought of kingship in terms of conquest and deliverance. They spread palm branches and their garments on the road. They shouted, "Blessed is the kingdom of our father David that is coming!" They believed that Jesus would restore to Israel the splendor and glory of King David's reign. So they hailed Him as King for what He could do for them, rather than for what they must do for Him. They cried, "King," with their lips, but failed to surrender their hearts.

From the pages of Italian history comes the story of Garibaldi, the famous Italian general. After he had driven the enemy from Italian soil and won independence for his people, they were faced with the question of who should be made king. Many said Garibaldi, savior of the country, should be crowned king. But others opposed the move. The dissension was so sharp that Garibaldi was finally banished to the island of Capri, which was given to him as a gift in token of his service to his country. How like so many who are willing to receive benefits from Christ's hands, but banish Him to some corner of their lives, thus denying His lordship.

Thought for the day: *It is* surrender, *not* shouts, *that pleases the King.*

Mark 11:12–14; 20–21   JUNE 2

He found nothing but leaves (v. 13).

Bible commentators have always had great difficulty in interpreting this passage. Several perplexing questions rise. Was it not unreasonable for Christ to expect fruit from the fig tree out of season? Was it not contrary to the character of Jesus to blast a tree that had disappointed Him when He was hungry? Was it not unusual for Christ to use His power in a destructive manner when all of His miracles were beneficial in nature? The answers to these questions are not easy to find.

However, most Bible scholars are convinced that this was an enacted parable, predicting the forthcoming judgment on the nation of Israel. God had placed His chosen people in an advantageous position among the nations of the world; He had bestowed upon them special privileges and opportunities; He had prepared them for the coming of the Messiah. However, when the Son of God visited His people, he found them making great professions of holiness and boasting of their superior goodness; but beneath all the pretense and hypocrisy He could find no fruit of righteousness. In fact He was about to be rejected by the very people who had been prepared for His coming. Thus He caused the fig tree to wither as a prophecy of the impending judgment of God upon the unfaithful, fruitless nation.

This parable was fulfilled in the experience of Israel. But is there not a message here for our nation today? God has blessed our land with tremendous natural resources and with a great spiritual heritage. He has permitted us to enjoy wealth, power, and position. We have boasted of religious freedom, equality, and justice for all. On our coins we have engraved the words, "In God we trust." But have our deeds always corresponded with our words? Are we even now producing fruits of righteousness proportionate to our superior spiritual advantages? Do we really trust in God? If not, God's judgment will fall upon our nation just as surely as it did on Israel. We'd better wake up before it is too late.

Thought for the day: *Privilege always entails responsibility.*

Mark 11:15–19   JUNE 3

My house shall be called a house of prayer for all the nations (v. 17).

By His dramatic act of cleansing the temple Jesus registered His indignation against certain sins of His day.

He protested, first of all, the practice of *injustice*. The moneychangers and the dove merchants exploited the pilgrims with exorbitant prices. For converting the pilgrim's national currency into the required temple coinage, moneychangers extracted a fee equivalent to one-half a day's wage for an ordinary worker. For doves to be used in the temple sacrifice, the merchants charged twenty times the regular price. Temple authorities thus treated the pilgrims, not as worshipers to be accommodated, but as victims to be fleeced for their own selfish ends. All this under the cloak of religion!

Jesus also protested the spirit of *irreverence* that was prevalent among the people. They had lost the sense of the presence of God in the Holy Place. They had profaned the

174

temple by commercializing its sacred activities. Jesus therefore rebuked them for their impropriety and indifference, and accused them of turning God's "house of prayer into a den of robbers."

Our Lord also expressed His indignation over the practice of *racial discrimination*. This incident took place in the outer area of the temple called "The Court of the Gentiles." At the end of this court was a low wall with inlaid tablets which warned Gentiles that death was the penalty for going beyond this point. Jesus was moved to anger by the exclusiveness of Jewish worship. He reminded temple leaders that God's house is to be "a house of prayer *for all the nations*," not just the Jews.

The sins of exploitation, irreverence, and racial bigotry are still among us today. We need to have the Savior stride through the corridors of our hearts and minds, overturning our prejudices and driving out our selfishness, until we once again become the sanctified temples of the Holy Spirit.

Thought for the day: *The beauty of God's House lies in the purity of its members.*

Mark 11:20–25   **JUNE 4**

Whatever you ask in prayer, believe that you receive it (v. 24).

In this passage our Lord lays down three basic conditions for effective prayer:

All prayer must be accompanied by *faith*. Faith, said Jesus, is so powerful that it can remove mountains. The word *mountain* here is used as an analogy depicting that which is difficult or impossible. Thus the prayer of faith can change difficult situations or even accomplish the humanly impossible. Our faith, Jesus emphasized, must rest in God. When we fully realize His wisdom and power, His dependability and faithfulness, then it is easy for us to believe in Him as a God who answers prayer.

Again, prayer must be offered in the spirit of *expectancy.* Jesus said, "Whatever you ask in prayer, *believe that you receive it,* and you will." Prayer must never be a mere formality or dubious ritual. It must grow out of an intimate relationship with the Father and always be vibrant with confident hope. In this attitude of expectancy the supplicant can thank God for the answer even before it is realized.

Several years ago a terrible drought blighted the southern part of India. The crops withered; the cattle died. In one village the little band of Christians decided to gather and pray for rain. When the pastor stood before his flock, he said to them solemnly, "My fellow Christians, you have assembled here for just one purpose—to pray for rain. Let me ask you a question: *"Where are your umbrellas?"*

Prayer must also be offered in the spirit of *love.* "Whenever you stand praying, forgive, if you have anything against any one." God is love, and always stands ready to forgive. He requires that we take the same attitude toward others. If we harbor bitterness, resentment, or hatred in our hearts against anyone else, we erect a barrier between God and ourselves, thus seriously affecting our communion with Him. To approach a forgiving God, we must be forgiving.

Thought for the day: *The prayer of a righteous man has great power in its effects (James 5:16).*

Mark 11:27–33   JUNE 5

By what authority are you doing these things? (v. 28)

The confrontation between Jewish leaders and Jesus on this occasion reminds me of a popular proverb in the Kanarese language of India: "Can the jackal stand in the presence of the lion?" Imagine puny, sinful men standing before the spotless Son of God and asking Him by what authority He operated!

The authority of Jesus is not a delegated authority like that of the president of the United States. One becomes president because the people make him president. His authority is given to him by the American people and by the Constitution of the land, and it lasts for only four or eight years at the most. Jesus, however, is not Lord because His disciples or the church have made Him so. He is Lord in Himself. We cannot make Him or unmake Him. It is for us to acknowledge and to accept Him as Lord.

Jesus had on many occasions demonstrated His divine authority before the people. He had demonstrated His authority over the human body by healing the sick. He had manifested His power over nature by stilling the tempest and miraculously feeding a crowd of five thousand people. He had shown his power over the spirit world by delivering the demon possessed. He had even exhibited his authority over death by raising a young girl from the dead. With all this evidence facing them, the chief priests and elders still demanded to know more of Jesus' credentials.

Modern critics of our Lord declare that they want more proof before they are ready to acknowledge His authority. The fact is that the accumulated evidence of Scripture, history, and personal testimony is already overwhelming. The real question at issue is not proof but obedience. Honest doubters are always deserving of sympathy; but professed seekers after truth, who are unwilling to accept the evidence on hand, condemn themselves by their intellectual dishonesty. An increasing knowledge of divine truth is conditioned upon humble submission of the will to what has already been revealed.

Thought for the day: *It is not further* evidence, *but simple* obedience, *that is needed.*

Finally he sent [his beloved son] to them (v. 6).

The meaning of this parable is not hard to find. The owner of the vineyard is God; the vineyard itself is Israel. The tenants are the rulers to whom God entrusted the spiritual care of His people. The servants sent by the owner are the prophets, whom the rulers of Israel had rejected or killed. The son and heir is Jesus, whom the elders at that very moment were conspiring to kill. But judgment was sure to come. God was getting ready to reject the faithless tenants and to hand over the keeping of the vineyard to the Gentiles. If anyone refuses his privileges and responsibilities, God will pass them on to someone else. This indeed is the chief lesson of Jesus' parable.

However, tucked away in the symbols of this parable are two more significant truths that we must not overlook. The first is that *Jesus Christ is God's last word in revelation.* "Finally he sent his son." This is in keeping with what the author of the letter to the Hebrews writes in his introduction: "In many and various ways God spoke of old to our fathers by the prophets; but in these last days he has spoken to us by a Son" (1:1). The prophets were servants, the messengers of God. They pointed to the coming of the Messiah. Jesus is the Son, the express image of God. He is the fulfillment of all the prophecies. Those who have seen Jesus have seen the Father.

The other truth is that *God will always have the last word in history.* We may strut about in defiance for a season. We may go so far as to stone the messengers of God and even nail His Son to a cross. But the day of accounting is coming when God will sit in judgment upon all people and recompense each one according to deeds done. The sinner will be expelled, but the Savior will be exalted.

Thought for the day: *We may speak a million words, but God will speak the last word.*

Mark 12:13–27

They asked him a question (v. 18).

In the eleventh and twelfth chapters of Mark's Gospel we find a series of questions that were put to our Lord by various groups of Jewish leaders. First the chief priests, scribes, and elders asked Him, "By what authority are you doing these things?" (11:28) Then the Pharisees and Herodians came to Him with the question, "Is it lawful to pay taxes to Caesar, or not?" Finally, the Sadducees came with a most unlikely story of a woman who was married to seven brothers and they asked Him, "In the resurrection whose wife will she be?"

Now there is nothing wrong with asking questions. It is the most effective way to get information. But everything depends on the motive behind the question. One may sincerely pose a question in an honest attempt to know the truth and dispel his doubts. He deserves a straightforward and honest answer. But someone else may ask a question in an attempt to discredit the truth or as a cover-up to avoid facing the truth. He is more interested in questions than in answers.

This is the spirit in which the Jewish leaders approached Jesus with their questions. They asked tricky, loaded questions in order to trap Him and get Him into trouble. But Jesus was quick to recognize and expose their hypocrisy. He realized that theirs was not an intellectual problem so much as a moral problem. They knew the truth, but were not willing to obey it. And often the modern skeptic or agnostic is guilty of the same attitude.

A young man once came to the famous evangelist Dwight L. Moody, and said to him, "Mr. Moody, I have several questions written down that I would like to ask you. If you can answer these to my satisfaction, I will return tomorrow night and surrender myself to Christ." The evangelist replied,

"Young man, you've got it all wrong. First surrender yourself to Christ, then come back tomorrow night and I'll try my best to deal with your questions."

Thought for the day: *The Christian life is not a question to be answered but a Person to be followed.*

Mark 12:28–34   JUNE 8

You shall love the Lord your God with all your heart ... mind and ... strength (v. 30).

The emphasis here is on the word "all." Our love for God is to be *complete*. He desires *all* our devotion. Isn't this true of us also? The wife wants all of her husband's love; the husband wants all of his wife's love. We are not satisfied until we have all. Can God be satisfied with anything less?

Our love for God must also be a *well-balanced love*, expressing every aspect of our personality. We are to love Him with all our *heart*, all our emotions; with all our *mind*, all our intellect; with all our *soul*, all our will; and with all our *physical strength*. The whole of our being is to be brought under the sway of God. This makes for an integrated personality, for fixation of purpose.

Many love God in an unbalanced and, therefore, weak way. Some love Him with the strength of the feelings and weakness of the mind. This makes the *emotionalist* in religion. Some love with the strength of the emotions and weakness of the will. This makes the *sentimentalist* in religion. Others love Him with the strength of the mind and weakness of the emotions. This makes the *intellectualist* in religion. Still others love Him with the strength of the will and weakness of the emotions. This produces the *legalist* in religion, the person of iron—very moral, but unloving and unlovable.

Imagine a young man proposing to his girlfriend in the following manner: "Young lady, I'm going to put before you an

Aristotelian syllogism, and I trust you will consider it thought-fully. The major premise is: 'It is not good for man to be alone.' The minor premise is: 'I am alone and I am lonely.' Now I hope you come to the same conclusion as I do." What do you think the girl would say? She probably would reply, "Young man, get off the premises!"

We must love with mind, heart, soul, and strength.

Thought for the day: *Love is the fulfillment of the law.*

Mark 12:35–44 JUNE 9

She . . . has put in everything she had (v. 44).

What a precious lesson in giving is found in this simple narrative. The contrast is between "many rich people who put in large sums" and "the poor widow who put in two copper coins." In our eyes the gift of the poor widow was meager and worthless, and the gifts of the rich were costly and great; but in the eyes of the Lord these offerings were comparatively worthless and the poor woman had given more than any of the others. For the others had thrown in what they could easily spare, while the widow had flung in everything that she had. It is not the size of the gift that matters, but the degree of sacrifice that is behind the gift.

There is a parable about a pig and a hen that were walking down the street together. They passed several restaurants, each displaying the sign, "Ham and eggs." The hen said to the pig, "Doesn't it make you feel important? These people couldn't get along without us. It's 'ham and eggs' wherever you go!"

With a grunt the pig replied, "It's all very well for you to talk. For you it's just a *contribution*; for me it's a *sacrifice!*"

Our offering to God must be more than just a contribution—it must be a sacrifice.

Here in the United States we have the highest income of all the nations. We are the best-fed, best-dressed, and best-housed people in all the world. And yet I'm afraid that our giving to Christ and His Church has been merely a contribution and not a real sacrifice. As a nation we spend billions of dollars each year on liquor, cigarettes, and gambling. We spend more in one year on dog food, or chewing gum, or cosmetics than we do for the spread of the Gospel around the world. Have we really learned to sacrifice for the kingdom of God?

Thought for the day: *The best way to measure our offerings is not by how much we give but by how much we keep.*

Mark 13:1—8 JUNE 10

Many will come in my name, saying, "I am he!" and they will lead many astray (v. 6).

Those words of Jesus are certainly an accurate description of the situation in our day.

Rev. Sun Myung Moon, formerly an ordained Presbyterian minister in Korea, has established the Unification Church here in the United States. He claims that Christ's mission was incomplete, that Christ redeemed the spiritual element in humankind but did not redeem the whole of society; thus the cross failed in its ultimate goal. Moon contends that he will establish the perfect family, which is the means of salvation, and thus complete the mission that Jesus began. Moon is looked upon by his followers, who number in the tens of thousands, as the second Christ.

On Sunday, April 25, 1982, a full-page ad appeared in the *New York Times* under the caption, "The Christ is Now Here." The ad claimed that the Christ is already here and will soon make himself known. "He will come not to judge, but to aid and inspire, and will deliver the world from hunger, injustice, and war."

A few years ago, Maharishi Mehesh Yogi, Indian guru and spiritual leader of the Transcendental Meditation movement in the West, boldly declared before an audience of 5000 New Yorkers gathered in the Felt Forum of Madison Square Garden: "This afternoon I can announce convincingly that this Transcendental Meditation will definitely create world peace for thousands of generations." He went on to say that "wars, famines, and earthquakes are all signs of tension. Meditation eliminates tension and thus eliminates the problems."

Many people are being led astray by the claims and teachings of these false prophets and pseudo-christs because they have not been properly instructed in the Word of God and have not been sufficiently confronted with the claims of Christ. The church must give its people a solid grounding in biblical truth and meet their spiritual needs through a personal experience with Christ.

Thought for the day: *Faithful preaching is the best antidote to false teaching.*

Mark 13:9–13   JUNE 11

It is not you who speak, but the Holy Spirit (v. 11).

Jesus never left his followers in any doubt that the way they had chosen was a difficult one. He repeatedly warned them of persecutions to come. But in the midst of all these trials, Jesus promised his disciples two things. He told them not to be anxious about what they would say before their captors, for in that hour the Holy Spirit would guide them and speak through them. And the persecution itself would become an avenue of witness for their Lord.

Church history gives us many illustrations of the fulfillment of Jesus' prophecy and promise. When Peter and John were dragged before the Jewish council in Jerusalem, they answered the questioning with such skill and boldness that the council members marveled at their words and testified, "These men have been with Jesus." When Paul stood on trial before Governor Felix and King Agrippa, his

183

testimony and arguments were so powerful that the two rulers actually trembled.

In A.D. 156, when anti-Christian persecution broke out in the province of Asia, Polycarp, bishop of Smyrna, was dragged before the proconsul and ordered to deny Christ and to "swear by the divinity of Caesar." The aged bishop replied, "For eighty-six years I have been [Christ's] servant and He has never done me any wrong; how can I blaspheme my King who saved me?" Polycarp was burned alive, but his death led to the end of persecution in Asia, and paved the way for those not so courageous as he to declare their faith in Christ openly.

In recent years Yusuf Roni, a staunch Muslim and head of the department of religion in Indonesia, was marvelously converted and began to witness for Christ. He was arrested and put in jail for five or six years. Finally he was allowed to defend himself, and his arguments, based on the Koran and the Bible, were so effective that he was released. Today he is an evangelist to his people.

Thought for the day: *The blood of the martyrs is the seed of the church.*

Mark 13:14—27   **JUNE 12**

They will see the Son of man coming with great power and glory (v. 26).

Christians look in two directions. We look back in gratitude to the first coming of Christ, when He came to earth to provide redemption for all of us. We also look forward with hope to the second coming of Christ, when He will return to establish His kingdom of righteousness upon earth.

Jesus taught clearly that His Second Coming is *certain.* At the Last Supper He said to His disciples, "*I will come again,* and will take you to myself" (John 14:3). In fact, His return to earth is the most certain event there is to be. It is more certain than death, for there will be at least one

184

generation that will not taste death when He comes. The Second Advent will be the next great cataclysmic event in salvation history.

The second coming of Christ will also be *personal*. Jesus said, "They will *see the Son of man* coming." The angels said to the apostles at the time of our Lord's ascension, "Men of Galilee, why do you stand looking into heaven? This Jesus, who was taken up from you into heaven, will come *in the same way* as you saw him go into heaven" (Acts 1:11). This implies that His return will be personal, involving His own visible presence.

This fact is brought out by the two Greek words used most commonly in connection with the Second Advent, namely, *parousia* and *ephiphaneia*; they mean "presence" and "appearance" respectively.

Jesus also declared that He will return *with great power and glory*. In His First Advent He came in weakness; He will return in power. He came in humility; He will return in majesty. He came as the Lamb of God; He will return as the Lion of Judah. He came to die, making atonement for sin; He will come the second time to judge the world and to rule. He came as Savior; He will return as King.

Thought for the day: *When he appears we shall be like him, for we shall see him as he is (1 John 3:2).*

Mark 13:28–37 JUNE 13

Take heed, watch; for you do not know when the time will come (v. 33).

Two extremes are to be avoided in regard to the doctrine of the second coming of our Lord. Some people take the attitude that the event may be so far in the future that it has no particular relevance to everyday living, and so they completely disregard the doctrine. Others become so obsessed with the idea of the Second Advent that it becomes for them practically the only doctrine of the Christian faith. It is so essential for the Christian to hold a sane and balanced view about this teaching.

Jesus stated clearly that the time of His return is unknown. There are signs, to be sure, which indicate to the careful observer that the Second Coming may be imminent, but no one can determine the exact day and hour. This is known only to the Father, and is perhaps the best-guarded secret in history.

However, though the time of the Second Coming is unknown, the event itself is certain and could take place at any moment. For this reason our Lord admonishes us to be constantly on our guard. Several times in this brief passage he tells us to watch, and He uses two different analogies to drive home the truth. The first is that of the doorkeeper who has been posted at the front gate, standing ready to receive the master of the house when he returns. The master warns the doorkeeper not to fall asleep, lest he return suddenly and take the servant by surprise. Then there is the analogy of the servant to whom the master of the house has assigned certain duties to be performed. Again, the master warns the servant not to be idle, lest he return suddenly and find the work undone.

The proper attitude of every believer is thus made clear. He must be *alert* and *busy; expectant* and *faithful*. For the Lord may return at any time.

Thought for the day: *Live each day as if Christ were coming at any moment; work as if He were coming a thousand years from now.*

Mark 14:1–11   JUNE 14

A woman came ... Then Judas Iscariot ... went (vv. 3, 10)

In an interesting way, Mark sets side by side the anointing

of Jesus by a certain woman and the betrayal of Jesus by Judas. What a tremendous contrast! On one hand an act of generous love; on the other, an act of terrible treachery.

The anointing of Jesus was the last act of kindness to him in His public ministry. The woman who performed the act was a perfect stranger; we don't even know her name. She brought an alabaster jar of costly ointment, broke it, and poured the ointment over the head of Jesus. Those watching exclaimed, "What a waste! The ointment could have been sold for more than 300 denarii (the equivalent of almost a year's wages), and the money given to the poor." The world always cries "waste" when a gift or a life is expended for Jesus. People cried "waste" when Dr. Tom Hale, brilliant surgeon, and his wife, Cynthia, accomplished concert pianist, left successful careers and went into the jungles of Nepal to minister to suffering people. They cried "waste" when Mother Teresa left her home in Yugoslavia and went into the miserable slums of India to minister to the destitute and dying.

True love never counts the cost. It always has an element of extravagance, even recklessness in its behavior.

In contrast to the loving act of the woman is the treacherous act of Judas. He was not a stranger. He was a disciple of Jesus, one who walked by his side, ate at the same table, saw every miracle, heard every parable. But he turned against Jesus and handed Him over to His enemies. Perhaps Judas had hoped that Jesus would restore the kingdom of Israel and he would have a high position in it. But when Jesus refused the earthly kingdom, Judas' hopes turned to disillusionment and his love for Jesus turned to hate. So he sold His Master for thirty pieces of silver. The big question is: "Was it worth it?"

Thought for the day: *Am I an anointer, or a betrayer, of Jesus?*

As they were at the table eating ... he took bread ... and he took a cup (vv. 18, 22, 23).

The Lord's Table is the most unusual table in all history. It is *the oldest table* in the whole world. In museums I have seen tables that belonged to ancient kings and queens and are a few centuries old, but the Lord's Table is almost 2000 years old. It has survived the rise and fall of many kingdoms and has lasted through countless wars, famines, and floods. And it will remain until Christ's return to earth.

The Lord's Table is *the longest table* in all the world. It stretches across the globe and embraces people of all nations, tribes, and castes. At this table are seated Asians and Europeans, Bataks of Sumatra and Karens of Burma, Ibans of Sarawak, and Nagas of India, high caste and low caste, rich and poor. All are one in Christ.

The Lord's Table is *the holiest table* in all the world. It is the table of our sinless Lord. The bread represents his broken body; the cup, his shed blood on the cross. At this table sins are forgiven, hearts are cleansed, and enemies are reconciled.

Some years ago in a small village in the Fiji Islands, a number of newly baptized Christians celebrated their first Communion service. Two young Fijians knelt at the altar to receive the elements. Suddenly one of them recognized the person kneeling at his side as the son of the man who had killed his father and drunk the blood out of his skull. Immediately the young man stood up and started back to his seat. But then he thought to himself, "This is foolish. Christ died for both of us. We are both His sons and disciples. The past is all forgiven. We are one in Christ." The young man immediately returned to the altar, put his arms around the man at his side, and with tears streaming down his face, took Communion with him.

Thought for the day: *At the Lord's Table all distinctions become meaningless.*

Mark 14:26–42   **JUNE 16**

He came and found them sleeping (v. 37).

Sleep is a pleasant and necessary part of our lives; it is essential to health and well-being. But sleep at the wrong time is unforgivable, and at certain times can be tragic in its results. The military guard who falls asleep at his post of duty, the driver who falls asleep at the wheel, the surgeon who drowses in the midst of a serious operation have certainly chosen the wrong time to sleep. There is a time to sleep and a time to be awake.

The disciples of Jesus often fell asleep at the wrong time, especially when they were supposed to be praying. When Jesus took Peter and James and John up into a mountain and there was transfigured, the three disciples were heavy with sleep. And now in this instance, in the Garden of Gethsemane, when Jesus exhorted his disciples to "watch and pray, lest you enter into temptation," again they fell asleep. Three times Jesus came back from his place of prayer and found them sleeping.

Of all the times for the disciples to sleep, this was the worst. The final hour for Jesus was at hand. He was about to be arrested, put on trial, and then nailed to a cross. He needed the sympathy, support, and prayers of those who were closest to him. But the disciples failed their Lord and failed themselves.

It is interesting, however, when we look into the book of Acts, to see the difference in the prayer life of the disciples. They suddenly became men and women of prayer. They prayed everywhere and at all times. In fact, sometimes when they were supposed to be sleeping, they were praying. When Peter was arrested and put in jail, the Christians in Jerusalem prayed all night for his release. When Paul and Silas were imprisoned in Philippi, they prayed and sang praises at midnight. What made the difference? It was the indwelling presence of the Holy Spirit. He inspired them to pray and taught them how to pray. And it is the Holy Spirit who can make a difference in our prayer lives today.

Thought for the day: *Prayer is the Christian's powerhouse.*

Mark 14:61b—72   **JUNE 17**

He broke down and wept (v. 72).

Peter was perhaps the most colorful of all the twelve disciples. He was rugged, aggressive, and at times impetuous. When Jesus was transfigured on the mountain, Peter was overwhelmed by the sight, and not knowing what to say, blurted out, "Master, let us build three tabernacles, one for you and one for Moses and one for Elijah." When Jesus asked the disciples, "Who do you say I am?" it was Peter who quickly responded, "You are the Christ."

Peter was also a man of courage. When Jesus came walking toward the disciples on the Sea of Galilee one night, Peter jumped out of the boat and started walking toward him. True, he became fearful, began to sink, and had to cry out for help. But he was the only disciple who tried to walk on the water. When Jesus was arrested in Gethsemane, it was Peter who fearlessly struck out with his sword in an attempt to defend his Master. Even after Jesus was led off to the Jewish council, Peter had the courage to follow the mob right into the courtyard of the high priest while all the other disciples fled.

But then Peter's courage reached the breaking point. Three times someone in the courtyard saw him and said, "You are one of his disciples, are you not?" Peter denied the charge each time and even started to curse. But when he suddenly heard the cock crow, Peter remembered the warning of his Lord, and "he broke down and wept." Here we see the difference between Judas and Peter. Judas betrayed his Lord and later even confessed his guilt when he cried out, "I have sinned in betraying innocent blood." But then he went out and committed suicide. Peter denied his Lord, but genuinely repented for his sin. Later he was restored to fellowship with his Lord. The same thing could have happened to Judas if he had waited for the Savior until the Resurrection.

Thought for the day: *If you rely on your own strength, you will deny your Lord.*

Mark 15:1–15 JUNE 18

Pilate, wishing to satisfy the crowd, released for them Barabbas (v. 15).

Barabbas was a notorious prisoner, a robber, and a murderer who had participated in an insurrection against the Roman administration. In character and spirit he stood in absolute contrast to the man called Jesus. Yet the crowd chose him over Jesus.

In so doing they chose lawlessness instead of law; violence instead of peace; hatred instead of love. But there is something highly significant in the whole affair. The very heart of the gospel is hereby disclosed—the sinless suffering for the sinful, the innocent giving his life for the guilty.

I like to imagine what happened to Barabbas on that fateful day. There he was lying on a bed of straw in a cramped, dark dungeon. The floor was creeping with vermin. He was hungry, lonely, and despondent. The time for his crucifixion was at hand. He was helpless and without hope. No chance of escape!

Suddenly the iron door creaked open and a Roman guard entered the cell. He kicked the prisoner and growled, "Get up, you dirty dog. You don't deserve it, but Pilate has ordered your release. Some man from Galilee—I believe his name is Jesus—will be crucified in your stead."

As if in a dream Barabbas stumbled out of the cell into

the bright morning sunlight. The streets of Jerusalem were silent, deserted. Then he saw a great crowd assembled on the hill of Golgotha outside the city. Soldiers were raising three crosses. So he rushed to the scene, mingled with the crowd, and observed every detail. He heard the shouts and taunts of the mob. He heard Jesus cry out, "Father, forgive them, for they know not what they do," and then, "It is finished."

Suddenly the truth dawned on Barabbas. He whispered to himself, "That is *my* cross. *I* was supposed to be crucified today. He is dying in *my* place." He rushed to the foot of the cross, threw his arms around the wooden pole, and cried, "My Lord, and my God."

But was that not *my* cross, too?

Thought for the day: *Jesus paid it all; all to Him I owe.*

Mark 15:16–32   JUNE 19

They led him out to crucify him (v. 20).

What were the ingredients of the crucifixion, the sins that sent Jesus to the cross?

1. *The robe of hypocrisy.* The soldiers put on Jesus a royal cloak, and knelt before Him to do him homage. They saluted Him, "Hail, King of the Jews!" But it was all in mockery. They called Him king, but treated him like a criminal. They struck Him with a reed and spat on him.

2. *The thorns of jealousy.* In 15:30, Mark states that Pilate "perceived that it was out of jealousy that the chief priests had delivered him up." They were jealous because Jesus drew such large crowds and was popular among the people. They resented the fact that Jesus "spoke with authority and not as the scribes."

3. *The scourge of hatred.* The Roman scourge was a long leather thong, studded here and there with sharpened pieces of lead that literally tore a victim's back to ribbons. The chief priests and Pharisees hated Jesus because He publicly

exposed the hypocrisy and corruption of their hearts. So they wanted to get rid of Him.

4. *The nails* that represented *the hardness of their hearts.* The religious leaders heard the marvelous teachings of Jesus, saw His miracles, and witnessed His sinless life. But instead of responding in faith, they hardened their hearts and rejected Him as Messiah.

5. *The wood of materialism.* Out of wood we make furniture and build houses, so the wood of the cross stands for the material things of the world. The Jewish leaders looked for a political kingdom. They expected the Messiah to drive out the Romans and restore the glory of Israel. Thus, when Jesus rejected the popular concept of the Messiah, the Jewish leaders were disappointed and angry.

Hypocrisy, jealousy, hatred, stubbornness, and material-ism—these are the sins that nailed Jesus to the cross. But are not these the prevalent sins of our time? Are we not guilty of crucifying Jesus afresh today?

Thought for the day: *There are no new sins in the world, only new sinners.*

Mark 15:33–39   **JUNE 20**

Truly this man was the Son of God (v. 39).

In Mark's Gospel three different titles are used to express the deity of Jesus. The first is *Christ,* which means "the Anointed One." When Jesus asked the disciples, "Who do you say that I am?" Peter quickly responded, "You are the Christ" (8:29). At Jesus' trial the high priest asked Him, "Are you the Christ?" (14:61). The second title is *Son of man,* used eleven times by Jesus Himself. He said, "The Son of man has authority on earth to forgive sins" (2:10); the Son of man is come "to give his life as a ransom for many" (10:45); one day we will see "the Son of man coming in clouds with great power and glory" (13:26; 14:62).

But the most important title given to Jesus is *Son of God*, which appears seven times in Mark. On two occasions, at Jesus' baptism and transfiguration, God spoke from heaven and said, "This is my beloved Son" (1:11; 9:7). Several times, when confronted by the Master, demonic spirits cried out, "You are the Son of God" (1:24; 3:11; 5:7). Then at the time of Jesus' death, the Roman centurion, who supervised the crucifixion, exclaimed with deep conviction, "Truly this man was the Son of God." The centurion was a hardened soldier. He had fought in many campaigns and seen countless men die, but he had never seen anyone die like this. Thus, God, humans, and demons all gave testimony to Jesus' deity.

So Christ was not only a man; He was also God. If He were just a man, his death was murder; as God, His death was a sacrifice. If he were just a man, they took his life from Him; as God, He laid down his life of His own will. If He were just a man, I will admire Him; if He is God, I give him my adoration. If He were just a man, I take my hat off to Him; if he is God, then I kneel and give Him my heart.

Thought for the day: *As man, Jesus is my Teacher and Example; as God, He is my Savior and Lord.*

Mark 15:40–47   JUNE 21

Joseph of Arimathea ... took courage and went to Pilate, and asked for the body of Jesus (v. 43).

Joseph of Arimathea was a respected member of the Jewish Sanhedrin, a religious man "who was also looking for the kingdom of God." Possibly he had seen and heard Jesus on several occasions and was a secret disciple of His. As a member of the council, he was no doubt present at the trial of Jesus and witnessed the whole chain of events. Most probably he was opposed to the death penalty for Jesus. But the sad fact is that he never spoke a word of defense on behalf of Jesus. He was too much of a coward to do so.

But then Mark tells us that Joseph "took courage" and went to Pilate and requested the body of Jesus. He took the body down from the cross, wrapped it in a linen shroud, and laid it in a tomb hewn out of rock, probably his own tomb. So we remember Joseph as the man who was silent when Jesus was alive, but gave Him his tomb when He was dead.

What changed the mind of Joseph and gave him the courage to approach Pilate? Perhaps because he witnessed the crucifixion. He heard the words of Jesus from the cross and saw His noble death. What the life of Jesus could not do, the cross of Jesus accomplished. When he had seen Jesus alive, he was attracted by His personality and teachings. But when he saw Jesus die, his heart was broken in love. He was convinced that Jesus was the true Messiah, the Son of God. Jesus Himself had said that when He was lifted up from the earth, He would draw all people to Himself (John 12:32).

I have seen the same reaction in audiences in India as they watched movies on the life of Christ. When they saw the miracles of Jesus, they clapped and cheered; but when they saw Him dying on the cross, they moaned and wept.

Thought for the day: *The life of Jesus challenges us; the death of Jesus changes us.*

Mark 16:1–8   JUNE 22

He has risen ... go, tell his disciples and Peter (vv. 6, 7).

Peter had made such a wonderful start for the Master. From just an ordinary fisherman along the shores of Galilee he had been transformed into a loyal follower of Jesus. His aggressive spirit and tireless devotion had endeared him to the heart of the Master who had taken him into the inner circle of the disciples.

But self-confidence led to a shameful denial of his Lord, and that too when his Lord needed him most. Peter proudly boasted that he would even lay down his life for Jesus, but when the crisis came he failed miserably. He sincerely repented and wept over his sin, but now his Lord was crucified, dead, and buried. If only he had found opportunity to confess his denial to the Master and ask for His forgiveness, things would have been different. But in the confusion of the trial and crucifixion this was impossible. And now Peter would have to carry his remorse with him throughout life. For the rest of his days he would be tormented by a guilty conscience.

Then came the glorious news: "He is risen!" And the angelic messenger who made the announcement said to the women at the tomb, "Go, tell His disciples *and Peter.*" Here was a special word for Peter. Of all the disciples, he was specially singled out. How the addition of those two words must have cheered his heart! The Master had not forgotten him; neither was He angry with him. Jesus knew that Peter had sincerely repented of his sin and He realized the remorse that Peter was undergoing. Jesus was far more eager to comfort the penitent sinner than to punish his sin.

The Resurrection, therefore, made a world of difference to Peter. It meant that he could see the Master again, that he could make his confession and be forgiven and restored to joyful fellowship with his Lord. Remorse was turned into rejoicing for Peter.

Thought for the day: *Because Jesus lives, He is able to forgive.*

Mark 16:9–20   **JUNE 23**

Go into all the world and preach the gospel (v. 15).

The Great Commission constitutes the marching orders of the Christian church. It is recorded in all four Gospels and in the book of Acts. Though all five statements are united in their central thought and aim, each one makes its own special emphasis through the inspiration of the Holy Spirit. Matthew emphasizes Christ's authority and presence. Mark emphasizes the universality of the commission. Luke stresses the content of the message and the power to proclaim it. John underscores the spiritual qualifications and demands.

Mark's statement of the Great Commission is simple yet grand and comprehensive. The emphasis is on crossing geographical frontiers. "Go into all the *world*." In other words, climb the mountains, cross the seas. Enter into every continent, country, city, and village. Set foot on every island. This is a universal task; everyone must be reached.

The emphasis is also on *preaching*—"Go ... and preach." Central to our task is proclamation of the Good News in Jesus Christ. We are not to be bearers of Western culture or the American way of life or a new system of philosophy. We are to preach Christ—crucified, risen, and victorious. He Himself is the good news. We are to preach for a verdict; for the Gospel is not only to be heard, but also to be heeded. It is not something to be looked at, but acted upon. "He who believes and is baptized will be saved; but he who does not believe will be condemned." Salvation by faith is the keynote here.

The Great Commission was not an exclusive command for the immediate disciples of Christ. It is binding upon all Christians of all ages. Every follower of Christ is to be involved in mission, whether it be across the sea or across the street. Every local congregation is to be engaged in mission, whether it be African, Indian, French, or American. All Christians, everywhere, must unite to take the Gospel to the whole world.

Thought for the day: *Some must go; some must let go; others must help go.*

Luke 1:1–4   **JUNE 24**

It seemed good to me also ... to write an orderly account for you ... (v. 3).

Is the Gospel narrative reliable? Can we put our full trust in its message? Luke, the historian, gives us the answer to these questions in the preface to his account. In a brief yet scholarly manner, Luke establishes not only his own trustworthiness as a writer, but also the historic worth and credibility of the gospel story. He wrote under the inspiration of the Holy Spirit—as all the writers of Scripture did—but he added to this divine impetus the human skills of scholarly research.

First of all, Luke tells us that he carefully gathered and studied all the available accounts of the ministry of Christ. He did not reject these as inaccurate, but as inadequate for the purpose he had in mind. For whereas Matthew wrote primarily to Jews, and Mark to Romans, Luke focused on the Greek world as his audience.

Then, too, Luke reminds his readers that he was living and writing amidst the scenes and in the very atmosphere of the events he was recording. These were fresh events, recently transpired in the midst of his contemporaries, and confirmed by eyewitnesses. Only after careful investigation did he sift his material and weigh the evidence in order to record established facts. These facts Luke relates "in order," in systematic arrangement with regard to time sequence, subject matter, and ultimate purpose. Since Theophilus, to whom Luke dedicates the book, was a man of education and official position, it was even more imperative that the writer present a document that was accurate, orderly, and well written.

Two lessons we can learn from this preface. First, the Gospel of Jesus Christ is not fancy, but fact; not theory, but history; not speculation, but revelation. Our faith is built, not on shifting sand but on solid rock. Again, just as Luke was not satisfied with anyone else's story of Christ and had to have his own, so we must not be satisfied with secondhand religion or a repeated tale. We must discover Jesus Christ for ourselves.

Thought for the day: *The Christ of history must become the Christ of experience.*

Do not be afraid, Zechariah ... your wife, Elizabeth, will bear you a son, and you shall call his name John (v. 13).

The systematic arrangement of Luke's Gospel becomes evident right from the start. First comes the prophetic announcement of the birth of John to Zechariah, his father, followed immediately by the announcement of the birth of Jesus to Mary, His mother. Then comes the narratives of the actual births of John and Jesus, interspersed with three magnificent hymns of praise. Both births were miracles: Mary was a virgin but gave birth to a son; Elizabeth was barren, but bore a son. In both cases the miracles were wrought by the power of the Holy Spirit. The angel Gabriel told Zechariah that his son, John, would be filled with the Holy Spirit from birth (v. 15); he told Mary that her son, Jesus, would be conceived by the Holy Spirit (see 1:35). The entire narrative shows how the saving events were initiated by the sovereign action of God for a specific purpose.

Gabriel unfolded the divine pattern of redemption. The Messiah, the Savior, was about to appear, but His coming was to be heralded by a special forerunner. The angel spoke with great definiteness about this person: he was to be named John; many would rejoice at his birth; he would be a Nazarite according to Old Testament standards, taking the vow of abstinence from wine and of total dedication to God; he would be filled with the Holy Spirit, lead his people to repentance, and prepare them for the coming of the Lord.

Even today the Christian is sometimes called upon to be a forerunner for Christ, particularly in isolated places where the Gospel story has not been proclaimed. And in order to be an effective herald for Christ, like John the Baptist, today's Christian messenger must be a person of sterling character and commitment. He must be totally dedicated to God, filled with the Spirit, and faithful to his message and mission.

Thought for the day: *Am I a foreruiner, or a forerunner for Christ?*

... the child to be born will be called holy, the son of God (v. 35).

The announcement to Mary of the birth of Jesus is recorded by Luke with unusual dignity and reserve. It is one of the most significant records in Scripture. The prediction is the crown of all prophecy and reveals the supreme mystery of the Christian faith, namely, the dual nature of our Lord, at once human and divine.

The same angel, Gabriel, who appeared to Zechariah, now appears again, this time not to an aged and distinguished priest amidst the splendors of the temple in Jerusalem. Now he comes to a humble peasant girl betrothed to a carpenter in an obscure village of Galilee. The angel tells Mary that before her marriage she is to become a mother, and she is to name the child Jesus, which means Savior. The child would be none other than "the Son of God."

The Virgin Birth of Christ has been one of the most controversial doctrines of the Christian faith. Some deny the teaching and contend that it is not essential to the total body of Christian truth. Others insist that the doctrine, rooted in Scripture and affirmed by church creeds, is vital to the whole nature and ministry of Christ.

What really is the significance of the doctrine of the Virgin Birth? In brief, it announces to the world that Christ did not come from within the stream of human history, but entered the world and history from without. He was not an ordinary human being, brought into existence by the natural means of procreation between a man and a woman. He was, and is, the divine Son of God who was "conceived by the Holy Spirit" and took upon Himself human nature and a human body. Christ is not a man who tried to become God; He is God who became man. He is not a mere man; He is the God-man. Only as such could He be the Savior of the world.

Thought for the day: *The greatest event of history is not that human beings landed on the moon, but that God landed on the earth.*

Luke 1:39–56   JUNE 27

[Mary] entered the house of Zechariah and greeted Elizabeth (v. 40).

In this passage we have the beautiful story of two noble women, Elizabeth and Mary, coming together for a friendly visit. The record tells us (1:36) that they were relatives, but we are not sure whether they were cousins or whether Elizabeth was Mary's aunt. Anyhow, it was more than blood relation that brought them together on this historic occasion. It was a common bond of divine intervention. Elizabeth was barren and beyond the age of childbearing, but God gave her a son whom she was to name John. Mary was a young unmarried woman, a virgin, but God was also giving her a son whom she was to name Jesus. One child was the Savior of the world; the other was a prophet, preparing the way for the Savior. So both women were expectant mothers; both children were miracle babies. What a significant get-together this was!

Elizabeth and Mary represent the glory and significance of motherhood. They serve as models for women of our day. The record tells us that Elizabeth was "righteous before God, walking in all the commandments and ordinances of the Lord blameless" (1:6). She was a woman "filled with the Holy Spirit" (v. 41). Mary was also a pious woman, touched by the Spirit of God, humble, and obedient. Her recorded hymn of praise to God, commonly known as the Magnificat, is one of the greatest hymns of all time. Both Mary and Elizabeth recognized that they were chosen vessels of God and that their sons were gifts from God sent for a special mission.

Modern life has robbed motherhood of much of its dignity and meaning. We need to recapture the biblical pattern for motherhood in our day. There is a sense in which every mother is chosen by God, every child is a gift from God, and every birth is significant in the plan of God. To be a mother is to be someone very special.

Thought for the day: *The hand that rocks the cradle can either* ruin *or* rule *the world.*

Luke 1:57–80   JUNE 28

His father Zechariah was filled with the Holy Spirit and prophesied (v. 67).

In the previous passage we saw the significant role that the two mothers played in the births and lives of John and Jesus. Now we see the equally significant role that the father assumes in the home. Zechariah, father of John the Baptist, now holds center stage. Like his wife, Elizabeth, Zechariah was "righteous before God, walking in all the commandments and ordinances of the Lord blameless." He, too, was "filled with the Holy Spirit" (vv. 6, 67).

It takes a righteous father as well as a righteous mother to have a true Christian home. Both parents must be godly in order to produce godly children. The father, in particular, can either help or hinder the sons and daughters in their concept of the heavenly Father. If Dad is cruel or harsh, an alcoholic or a wife-beater, the children will see God as a cruel tyrant or a stern judge who seeks only to control and punish. The very title "heavenly Father" will turn them off. On the other hand, if Dad is loving and compassionate, a man of integrity and piety, the children will rejoice to know that God is their "Father in heaven."

I once stood on Wall Street and said to myself, "This is the heart of America, the business center of our nation." Later I stood on the steps of the Capitol in Washington, and I said to myself, "No, this is the heart of America, for it is the political center of our nation." Then, standing in front of General Motors Corporation in Detroit, I said, "No, this is the heart of America, for it is the industrial center of our nation." But later when I sat in the living room of a humble home and watched father and mother and children listen to the reading of God's Word and then kneel in prayer, I said with conviction, "Now this indeed is the heart of America, for herein lies the strength of any nation."

Thought for the day: *Dad, what concept of the heavenly Father are you giving to your children?*

Luke 2:1–7   **JUNE 29**

There was no place for them in the inn (v. 7).

Luke tells us that when the baby Jesus was born, the family could find no room in the inn. So Joseph and Mary had to lodge in a stable and place their newborn son in a manger. Imagine it! Here is the Creator and Owner of the universe, the Lord of heaven, coming to His own world and His own people, and no decent place for Him can be found. Perhaps if He had descended from heaven in broad daylight with a great shout and much fanfare, a distinguished welcoming party might have received Him, and offered Him all necessary comforts. But our Lord slipped into the world quietly at night, unseen and unknown.

Are things different today? The Savior tries again and again to enter the world of human affairs, but everywhere is the sign, "Sorry, no room." No room in our homes, for we are too busy watching television and reading the newspaper. No room in our businesses, for we are too occupied in making money and seeking position. No room in our politics, for we are too engaged in maintaining power and fighting for our own interests.

A few years ago some church members were acting out

the story of Christ's birth at Christmas time. With great feeling they portrayed Joseph going from inn to inn and from house to house, seeking shelter for the night. In each case the answer was the same. "Sorry, no room." A young lad seated in the audience was so touched by the scene that he jumped to his feet and shouted out, "Mister, bring the baby Jesus to our house. We have plenty of room for Him."

It is time for us to make room for Christ in our lives. He is the only one who can turn chaos into order, sorrow into joy, conflict into peace, despair into hope, and defeat into victory.

Thought for the day: *When Christ comes in, many things will have to go out.*

Luke 2:8–20   JUNE 30

To you is born this day in the city of David a Savior, who is Christ the Lord (v. 11).

What a display the Lord of heaven put on in the sky that night when Jesus was born. An angel appeared to certain shepherds in a field, who were watching their flocks. A great light shone all around them, turning midnight into noonday. The angel shouted, "I have good news for you. The Savior of the world is here!" And suddenly a great heavenly choir burst forth in song, praising God and saying, "Glory to God in the highest, and on earth peace among men with whom he is pleased!"

A Savior is born. This is still the greatest news of all time. It is the good news that God has not left us in our predicament, but has come to our rescue. It is the good news that God is not against us because of our sins, but is for us against our sins.

The tragedy is that countless millions today still have not heard this good news. We need to announce it loud and clear across the whole world.

Legend has it that the news of the birth of his child was

brought to the Emperor Akbar of India by a relay of soldiers, stationed at calling distance from each other, all the way from the palace in Agra to the battlefield. When the day of delivery arrived, the news was given to the first soldier, who cupped his hands to his mouth and shouted, "A son is born; a son is born." The second soldier picked it up and shouted it out to the third, and so on down the line to the ears of the emperor.

As Christians, bearers of the Good News, we need to stand in our cities and shout forth: "A Son is born—the Savior of the world!" Others will shout it across the Atlantic to Europe; they in turn to the Middle East and on to Asia and the islands of the Pacific until everyone in the world has heard about the birth of the Savior.

Thought for the day: *The Gospel is not a secret to be hid, but an announcement to be made.*

Luke 2:21–32   JULY 1

My eyes have seen thy salvation (v. 30).

In this passage we have the third great hymn of praise concerning the birth of the Savior. The first was by Zechariah, father of John the Baptist; the second, by Mary, mother of Jesus; and now the third, by Simeon, a devout and righteous man who was looking for the coming of the Messiah. By the providence of God he was worshiping in the temple when the child Jesus was brought by his parents to fulfill the Jewish regulations. When Simeon saw the child, he lifted him up in his arms and began to praise God. With joy he cried out, "My eyes have seen thy salvation!"

Note two important truths inherent in this declaration. First, *salvation is personal.* Simeon said, "*My eyes have seen* thy salvation." This was not just something he had read about in a book or heard from others; it was something he had experienced for himself. Salvation, to be real, must be firsthand and personal. Only then will it be vital and dynamic.

A young man was praying for all the members of his family during morning devotions. When he came to his father, he paused for a moment and then prayed,: "Dear Lord, bless my father, and bring his religion down a foot-and-a-half. In Jesus' name. Amen." The boy knew that his father had much information about Christ, but no personal relationship with Christ. He had head knowledge, but no heart experience. And so he asked God to bring his father's religion down a foot-and-a-half, from head to heart.

The second important truth inherent in Simeon's declaration is this: *Salvation is in the person of Christ.* When Simeon said, "My eyes have seen thy salvation," he was speaking about the Christ child whom he held in his arms, not some abstract concept. Salvation does not reside in a set of teachings or system of philosophy; it is not found in a ritual or a creed. Salvation is in Christ and results from a relationship with Him.

Thought for the day: *Religion emphasizes principles and precepts; the Gospel emphasizes a Person.*

Luke 2:36—40   JULY 2

The child grew and became strong, filled with wisdom; and the favor of God was upon him (v. 40).

We need to add to this statement the last verse of this second chapter (v. 52), which reads, "And Jesus increased in wisdom and stature, and in favor with God and man."

Jesus, the God-man, is our perfect pattern for growth into maturity. His was a well-balanced and systematic growth. He grew in all areas of life, and He continued to grow.

Jesus, grew *physically.* Luke tells us he "increased in stature ... and became strong." No doubt working at a carpenter's bench and walking the hillsides of Galilee helped Jesus to develop a strong body. The fact that He was able to endure a Roman scourging and carry His own cross over cobblestone lanes is, in itself, a testimony to his physical stamina.

Jesus grew *intellectually*. Luke tells us he "increased in wisdom" and was "filled with wisdom." He was a student of nature and human nature. He was a student of the Word and could quote from the Old Testament in a masterly fashion. He saw through the subtle questions of His adversaries and silenced them with His wisdom. When He spoke, people were amazed at His teachings and insights.

Jesus grew *spiritually*. The record tells us that "the favor of God was upon him;" that He "increased in favor with God and man." He developed in His vertical relationship with His Heavenly Father—through prayer, worship, obedience, and feeding of the Word. He developed in His horizontal relationships with people—through compassionate concern, gentle manner, and loving service.

For a well-rounded personality, symmetric growth in all areas of life is essential. Some are careful to develop their bodies and guard their health, but do nothing to stretch their minds. Others seek education and knowledge but completely neglect their spiritual development. In order to be at our best for God and humanity, we need to grow in a balanced manner, physically, mentally and spiritually.

Thought for the day: *When we stop growing, we begin to die.*

Luke 2:41–52   JULY 3

Supposing him to be in the company they went a day's journey (v. 44).

It is possible for us to think that Christ is in our midst when He is not. The incident we have just read is a good illustration of this truth. Joseph and Mary had taken the twelve-year-old Jesus to the temple in Jerusalem for the celebration of the Passover. When the feast ended, they started the journey home, supposing that Jesus was in the caravan. But He had stayed behind, and they didn't discover until the next day that they had lost Jesus. He was not in their midst.

It is a somber fact that we can lose the presence of Jesus from our lives. Sometimes we can lose Him by sheer neglect, such as in the case of Joseph and Mary. They took for granted the presence of Jesus and didn't take the time to check whether or not He was in the company. In like manner, it is possible for us to lose the presence of Jesus by mere carelessness, perhaps by simply neglecting to spend time with Him in prayer or feeding on His Word. Sometimes we may lose Christ by harboring sin in our lives, and this is more serious. Perhaps we have been disobedient to His call or have transgressed His commandment. Then suddenly we wake up to the fact one day that Jesus is gone.

When we lose Jesus what should we do? The same thing that Joseph and Mary did. They went straight back to the very spot where they had lost Him—to the temple in Jerusalem. And so if we have lost Jesus at the point of our daily devotions, we need to go back to the place of prayer and reading of God's Word. If we have lost Him through disobedience, we need to get back into the center of His will. If we have lost Him by some particular act of sin, we need to confess that sin and seek forgiveness. Once again His presence will become real.

Thought for the day: *You can always find Christ at the place where you left Him.*

Luke 3:1–14   JULY 4

Prepare the way of the Lord, make his paths straight (v. 4).

John the Baptist was the first inspired prophet to break the silence of the centuries which had elapsed since the days of Malachi. He was an unusual man, with a special message and a special mission.

John the Baptist was not like the rest of the crowd. He was unusual in his *dress*—"He wore a garment of camel's hair, and a leather girdle around his waist" (see Matt. 3:4). He was unusual in his *diet*—"his food was locusts and wild honey." He was unusual in his *discourse*— he preached judgment and the wrath of God.

John, a *special man*, came with a *special message*. He boldly called the people to "flee from the wrath to come," and to "bear fruits that befit repentance." He warned the people that "every tree therefore that does not bear good fruit is cut down and thrown into the fire." He challenged the common person to be compassionate and charitable toward the poor; the tax collector to be honest and law-abiding; the soldier to be merciful to others and content with his wages.

John the Baptist had a *special mission* to perform. He was described as "one crying in the wilderness," a prophet sent by God to "prepare the way of the Lord." In those days when an Oriental king proposed to tour a part of his kingdom, he always sent a courier before him to tell the people to prepare the roads. Likewise, when the King of kings was about to enter the world, he sent his herald on ahead to prepare the way for his coming. Before the people would be ready to receive Christ, moral obstacles must be removed, individuals must repent and turn away from their sins.

The tone of John's message was particularly severe. He addressed the multitudes as a "brood of vipers," and exposed their pretense and hypocrisy. He challenged his hearers to show their repentance by their works and not to trust their descent from Abraham as securing their salvation.

Thought for the day: *Flee from sin and follow Christ.*

Luke 3:15–22   JULY 5

He who is mightier than I is coming (v. 16).

209

The personality and ministry of John the Baptist were so unusual that the people began to think he might be the Messiah. So they came to John and asked him plainly, "Are you the Christ?" To which John replied, "No, but the Christ is on his way. He is far greater than I am. I am not worthy even to untie the thongs of his sandals." Then John proceeded to describe more in detail the ministry of the coming Messiah.

First, John tells us that Jesus is to be the *Redeemer*. He says, "I baptize with water, but he will baptize with the Holy Spirit and fire." John's baptism was physical, symbolizing the washing away of one's sins. Jesus' baptism is spiritual, signifying cleansing from inner impurity. John called people to repentance; Jesus leads people to redemption.

Then John tells us that Jesus is to be the *Judge*. He uses the illustration of the Eastern harvester, sifting the grain. The winnowing fan was a large, flat, wooden shovel with which the farmer tossed grain into the air so that the heavy grain fell to the ground in a heap and chaff was blown away. Just as the chaff was separated from the grain, so Christ would separate the righteous from the unrighteous, the penitent from the impenitent.

John the Baptist was faithful to his message and his mission. He boldly denounced the sins of his day and called people to repentance. He did not speak of himself or seek to draw attention to himself; he spoke of Christ and pointed to him as Redeemer and Lord. What a model for Christ's witnesses and messengers today!

A couple of missionaries passed through London on their way from India to the United States, and went to hear two of the prominent preachers of the city. After the morning service, one missionary said to the other, "My, what a wonderful preacher!" After the evening service, they said to each other, "My, what a wonderful Savior!"

Thought for the day: *When we speak, whom do people see?*

For forty days ... [Jesus was] tempted by the devil (v. 2).

Temptation will come. This is an accepted fact of life. No stage of the Christian life, no degree of spiritual maturity, can exempt one from temptation in one form or another. There is a certain universality, a certain inescapableness, about temptation. Since life is as it is, since God has made us as He has, and since the world is what it is, temptation is bound to come sometime or other. Regardless of age, class, or position, all are subject to the onslaughts of the Evil One. You cannot build walls high enough, you cannot find a place of isolation lonely enough to keep out the devil. He is ready to meet you under any sky in all the world. If the Son of God Himself was tempted, how can we human beings expect to escape temptation? Yes, *temptation will come, but temptation may be overcome.* How? In the same way that Jesus overcame it: by the power of the written Word and the power of the Holy Spirit. After each temptation Jesus responded with the words, "It is written," and then He quoted a verse from the Old Testament Scriptures. The authority of God's Word can silence the voice of the tempter. No wonder the psalmist writes, "I have laid up thy word in my heart, that I might not sin against thee" (Psalm 119:11).

Then again, Jesus overcame temptation with the power of the Holy Spirit. This passage of Scripture begins with the two statements that Jesus was "full of the Holy Spirit" and was "led by the Spirit . . . into the wilderness." The passage closes with the statement that "Jesus returned in the power of the Spirit." If Jesus Himself needed the indwelling presence of the Holy Spirit to face onslaughts of the enemy, how much more do we?

The Word of God gives authority to answer the devil; the Spirit of God gives us power to rout him

Thought for the day: *"Temptation will come, but temptation overcome leads to a glorious outcome" (Paul S. Rees).*

Luke 4:16–30   JULY 7

The Spirit of the Lord is upon me (v. 18).

Jesus preached His first sermon in the synagogue at Nazareth. Using the Old Testament as a biblical foundation, he clearly outlined the program of His ministry. When we analyze the program, we find: 1) "Good news to the poor"— the economically disinherited; 2) "Release to the captives"— the socially and politically disinherited; 3) "Recovering of sight to the blind"—the physically disinherited; 4) "Setting at liberty those who are oppressed"—the morally and spiritually disinherited; 5) "The acceptable year of the Lord"—a new beginning on a world scale; 6) "The Spirit of the Lord"—the dynamic behind it all.

Just as Christ's personal growth was well-balanced in all areas of life—he increased in stature, wisdom, and in favor with God and man—so also His ministry was to be an all-inclusive, holistic program for total human needs: social, economic, physical, spiritual, and relational. He was to minister to individuals in all their frailties, and to confront society with all of its injustices. His goal? The kingdom of God upon earth.

The church should pattern its mission after that of our Lord. If we choose any other human model, we will get off track and onto some tangent, and miss the goal.

Some years ago my brother and I dropped into a coffee shop in Bangalore, India. To our surprise, on the front page of the menu was this sentence: "Give yourself a breakdown, drink our coffee!" When we questioned the waiter, he explained that the menu originally read, "Give yourself a break, drink our coffee." But a college student played a prank by adding the word "down," and when the restaurant needed a new set of menus, by mistake this particular copy was sent to the printers. So all the menus now read, "Give yourself a breakdown." When the model was faulty, everything went wrong.

We can't go wrong when we follow the Lord's pattern for ministry. His is the ideal program.

Thought for the day: *Our motto—The whole Gospel for the whole person for the whole world.*

Luke 4:31–37   JULY 8

They were astonished (v. 32).

Having announced the details of His program, Jesus immediately plunged into His public ministry. The rest of the chapter describes His teaching in the synagogues, delivering persons from evil spirits, healing all kinds of diseases, and preaching the good news of the kingdom.

Twice in this passage Luke tells us that the people were astonished at Jesus' ministry. First they were astonished at His *words*, for he spoke with authority (v. 32). When the rabbis taught, they always sought to buttress their statements with quotations from others. They would say, "There is a saying that . . . Rabbi So-And-So said that . . ." They always appealed to authority. But when Jesus spoke, He simply said, "I say to you." He needed no quotations or authorities to support Him. His authority came from within. This was something new to the people; here was a teacher who spoke as one who knew.

Then Luke tells us that the people were astonished at the *works* of Jesus. When with a single short command Jesus delivered a man from a demonic spirit, the people said to one another, "What is this word? For with authority and power he commands the unclean spirits, and they come out." In those days many sought to exorcise demons, but their methods were strange indeed. They recited a lot of mumbo jumbo and employed all kinds of weird paraphernalia. What a difference between all this hysterical formulae and Jesus' single calm

213

word of command. It was the sheer authority that staggered the people.

Christ's authority comes from His very personhood. He speaks and acts as He does because of who He is. He is not a mere human being. He is the divine Son of God. It is interesting that even the demons and unclean spirits recognized Him. They said, "We know who you are, the Holy One of God." Many today, supposedly wise and in their right minds, are not able to say this with conviction. It is time we recognized Jesus for who He really is.

Thought for the day: *We do not* concede *authority to Jesus; He* confronts *us with His own authority.*

Luke 4:38—44   JULY 9

I was sent for this purpose (v. 43).

When the people heard the words of Jesus and witnessed His works, they were astonished and gathered around Him in great crowds. They tried to hold on to Him and keep Him from leaving, but Jesus said plainly, "I must preach the good news of the kingdom of God to other cities also; for I was sent for this purpose." Then He departed from Galilee and entered Judea, preaching in all the synagogues .

Many of us today are trying to build a fence around Jesus. We have met Him and found Him to be so wonderful that we want to keep Him all to ourselves. Some try to shut Jesus up in their homes, but He wants to go across the street to the neighbors. Some want to keep Him in their section of town, but He wants to cross the tracks into the ghettos. Some want to keep Jesus within the boundaries of their nation, but He wants to cross the seas into every continent and island.

Where would the church be today if the early Christians had kept Jesus all to themselves? They realized that Jesus was on the move constantly so they decided to go with Him. Thus, Paul went with Christ from Palestine to Asia Minor and Greece.

Patrick went with Christ from England to Ireland. Augustine went with Him from Italy to Britain. Boniface went with Him from England to Germany. That's why we are Christians today.

John Williams was one of the first missionaries to the South Seas. He evangelized the people of Tahiti and established the church there. But then he realized that there were hundred of islands scattered all across the Pacific and that Christ did not want to be confined to one island. So he trained native missionaries, built a ship, and took them to island after island. As a result practically all that area of the world is Christian today.

Thought for the day: *If the church is following Jesus, it will go to the ends of the earth, for that's where He is going.*

Luke 5:1–11   JULY 10

Henceforth you will be catching men (v. 10).

Imagine it! A carpenter telling a group of experienced fishermen how to fish!

Simon, James, and John were partners in the fishing business. They had toiled all night on this occasion, but caught nothing. Then Jesus came along and said, "Put out into the deep and let down your nets for a catch." The interesting thing is that Simon and his partners didn't say, "Sir, you may be an excellent carpenter, but what do you know about fishing? The fish are just not biting today." Instead, they let down their nets a second time, and the catch was so abundant the nets began to break and the boats began to sink. As the fishermen stood in amazement, Jesus said to them, "Henceforth you will be catching men."

Note the steps that Simon, James, and John had to take in order to become fishers for the kingdom. First, *they recognized their inadequacy.* Their own unaided efforts had been in vain. In spite of all their skill and experience, they had tried and failed. Then again, *they were obedient.* Simon said to Jesus, "Master, we tried our best but caught nothing; nevertheless *at your word* we will let down the nets." They were willing to follow instructions, even though they didn't seem reasonable.

The amazing catch of fish made the three *aware of who Jesus really was and aware of their own spiritual condition.* So Simon Peter fell at Jesus' feet and cried out, "Depart from me, for I am a sinful man, O Lord." The first time Simon addressed Jesus, he called Him "Master" (v. 5). The second time he addressed Him as "Lord" (v. 8). Finally, the record tells us that Simon, James, and John *"left everything and followed him."* They left their boats and nets, their homes and business, to become His disciples and fishers of people.

Awareness of one's inadequacy and sinfulness, recognition of the person of Jesus and obedience to His will, willingness to forsake all and follow Him—these are the necessary ingredients for discipleship even today.

Thought for the day: *Christ says to us, "Let's go fishing today."*

Luke 5:12–16   **JULY 11**

[Jesus] stretched out his hand, and touched him (v. 13).

In Jesus' day leprosy was the most horrible and dreaded of all diseases. No treatment or cure for the disease was known. The leper was forced to leave home and family and become an outcast in society. Lepers had to call out, "Unclean, unclean," so that others would be warned to get out of the way. No one wanted to be near a leper; certainly no one wanted to touch one.

But Jesus had compassion on lepers. He allowed them to come into His presence; He even touched them. And His touch always brought complete healing. In this passage, we have another example of this fact. Luke tells us that Jesus stretched forth His hand and touched the leper and that immediately the leprosy left him.

When Christian missionaries first went to India, they came face to face with the caste system in Hindu society. Some groups were listed as "outcastes." They lived in segregated areas of town and performed all the menial tasks of the community, such as sweeping the streets and cleaning the toilets. Thus, they were considered "untouchables"—their touch or even their shadow would bring pollution and demand a ceremonial bath for purification.

The early missionaries were reluctant at first to baptize inquirers from among these low-caste people. They argued, "How can we build the church on the riffraff of society. We will never be able to win the high caste if we accept these untouchables." But as Bishop J. Waskom Picket said, "You can't judge Christianity by the type of people who receive it; you must judge Christianity by the type of people it produces." So the missionaries reached out and touched the low caste. Today our Indian bishops, superintendents, pastors, and lay leaders are persons who have come out of these despised castes of society.

A group of newly baptized Christians in India once said to me, "We may be untouchables, but God has touched us. We may be outcastes, but God has taken us in."

Thought for the day: *Touched by Christ, the "untouchable" becomes a toucher.*

Luke 5:17–26

Rise, take up your bed and go home (v. 24).

Several interesting facets sparkle in this intriguing story. First, we see *four men carrying another man.* The paralytic was unable to do anything for himself; he needed outside help. And so his friends just picked him up and brought him to Jesus. It is rare indeed, if not impossible, for a person to come to Jesus on his own. Usually it is through the concern, counsel, and aid of others that one is brought to Jesus. Just reflect for a moment. Who were the individuals in your life who led you to Christ? A parent, friend, Sunday school teacher, pastor, or even a stranger?

In the second place, we see the paralytic *entering the house through the roof and coming out through the door.* But there was no other way to get in. The crowd jammed the entrance and windows so the four bearers removed the twigs and mortar packed between beams of the roof, and lowered the paralytic's couch into the very presence of Jesus. It was an act of sheer desperation, but mingled with faith. When we come to Jesus we must have a sense of helplessness and urgency, along with a sense of hope and faith. The record tells us when Jesus saw *their* faith—the combined faith of all five men—He spoke the words of deliverance to the paralytic.

Finally, we see the paralytic *coming to Jesus lying on his bed, but leaving with the bed on him.* What a picture of complete deliverance! The man was no longer a captive to his condition. He was able to put the bed on his shoulder and walk off with it. And he got more than he asked for. Jesus saw the paralytic's need for healing of his soul as well as his body. So the Master not only said, "Take up your bed and go home," but He also said, "Man, your sins are forgiven."

Thus the miracles of Jesus were real proofs of His deity as well as expressions of His love; they were also parables of His willingness and ability to deliver from the guilt and power of sin.

Thought for the day: *When did I last bring anyone to Jesus?*

Luke 5:27–39   JULY 13

I have not come to call the righteous, but sinners to repentance (v. 32).

Hinduism and Christianity both believe in divine incarnation—God coming in earthly form. But the purposes of incarnation in the two religious systems are diametrically opposed to each other. Hinduism says that whenever evil gets out of control, or a demon goes on the rampage, then God (Vishnu) incarnates himself and comes to destroy the evil and protect the good. Hindus insist that there have been ten such incarnations so far in history—some animal and some human. Christian Scriptures tell us that only one incarnation took place—once and for all in the person of Jesus Christ. And the distinct purpose of His coming was not to destroy sinners and protect the righteous, but to redeem sinners and make them righteous. What a tremendous difference!

When Jesus said that He had "not come to call the righteous but sinners to repentance," He did not mean that some people are inherently righteous and do not need a Savior while others are definitely sinners and need a Savior. Paul tells us that "none is righteous, no not one." So all are sinners and all need a Redeemer. What Christ meant by the statement is this: some *think* they are righteous and therefore need no help, while others *know* they are sinners and long for help. The Pharisees and Scribes belonged to the first group; publicans and tax collectors made up the second.

This truth is illustrated over and over in the history of the church. The self-righteous Buddhists of Burma did not turn to Christ as a people, but the Karens of the forest, considered backward and stupid by the Burmese, believed in Christ by the tens of thousands. The Brahmins of India believed that they were being rewarded for good deeds of a previous life so they didn't need a Savior; but the despised untouchables recognized their spiritual poverty and gladly received Christ as Deliverer. In our churches, some trust in good works and miss God's gift of salvation while others confess their sins and come to Christ for forgiveness and cleansing.

Thought for the day: *Christ can save only those who want to be saved.*

The Son of man is lord of the sabbath (v. 5).

The fourth commandment of the Decalogue stipulates that the Sabbath is to be remembered as a holy day in which no work is to be done (Ex. 20:8–11). Worship and rest are to characterize the day. However, no particular instructions are given as to how the Sabbath is to be observed. So Jewish rabbis spelled out the details. This resulted in innumerable prohibitions and restrictions that upheld the letter but not the spirit of the law.

On two occasions the Pharisees accused Jesus and His disciples of breaking the Sabbath law. The first was when the disciples, while passing through the grain fields on a Sabbath, plucked and ate some ears of grain, rubbing them in their hands. In the eyes of the Pharisees the disciples were guilty of acts of reaping, threshing, and winnowing, all forbidden on the Sabbath. On the second occasion, the Pharisees criticized Jesus for healing a man with a paralyzed hand on the Sabbath. They were more interested in law than in life.

Jesus defended both actions by declaring that he was Lord even of the Sabbath and that works of necessity (like eating) and works of mercy (like healing) are legitimate on the Sabbath. He raised two basic questions regarding the nature of the day: Are people made for the Sabbath or is the Sabbath made for people? Shall the Sabbath be a burden or a blessing?

When we compare the Jewish observance of the Sabbath with the Christian observance of Sunday, is the situation any better today? If the Jews were guilty of excessive *legalism*, perhaps we are guilty of extreme *liberalism*. They were *repressive*; we are *permissive*. Anything goes on a Sunday nowadays. Malls are open; sales are held. People go golfing and fishing. Competitions and sports abound. The Pharisees made the Sabbath Day *miserable*. Christians today have made Sunday *pleasurable*.

It is time we reconsider the real meaning and objective of the Lord's Day and get back to basics.

Thought for the day: *Sunday is a holy day, not a holiday.*

Luke 6:12–19 JULY 15

He called his disciples, and chose from them twelve (v. 13).

Before every major decision in His life, Jesus prayed. It was only after he had spent a whole night in prayer, that He selected those who were to be His close companions and messengers of the kingdom.

It is significant that Jesus chose *twelve* disciples, corresponding to the number of the tribes of Israel. This, to the Jews, could not but point to His messianic claim and identify His works and His words with the fulfillment of the ancient prophecies.

Jesus used a minimum of organization. He enjoined no rules, but He made clear the cost of discipleship. He staked the entire future of His cause upon those twelve men. "Truth through personality" was His aim.

The disciples whom Jesus chose were men of marked contrast to one another in temperament, capacity, and record. Each of them brought to the Lord's service what he had. Andrew was a great-hearted man, of quick decision and fine courage; not showy or noisy but quiet and faithful. Peter was impulsive but generous; quick on the trigger but sincere and frank and courageous. Matthew was business-like, efficient and methodical. Thomas was slow on the uptake, cautious, and questioning yet steadfast and faithful. John was shy and reserved, deep and strongly affectionate but not soft, effeminate, or sentimental; a thoughtful man with a sensitive spirit; a man of directness in purpose and aim, unafraid and undaunted.

The history of this group is simply the story of transforming grace and of the consecrated use of varied aptitudes. Some of them were slow learners; they often misunderstood and misrepresented their Master; one ended disastrously. But Jesus never despaired of them, never cast them off, never rescinded His invitation; nor did he lower the degree of his companionship or relax His grip upon them. The story of the disciples is not that of "the perseverance of the saints," but "the perseverance of the Savior."

Thought for the day: *Christ uses all kinds of people to reach all kinds of people.*

Luke 6:20–36 JULY 16

Love your enemies, do good to those who hate you (v. 27).

In the socio-political movements of our day two particular strategies have been used to achieve the desired goals. One is *passive resistance*, in which the aggrieved persons resist oppression by bearing passively imposed wrongs and penalties. By so doing they hope to call attention to the wrongs, and thus gain redress. The oppressed says to his oppressors, "I will match my ability to suffer pain against your ability to inflict it, and I will wear you down."

The other strategy is that of *civil disobedience*. This involves choosing certain laws and regulations to disobey in order that by their disobedience and the bearing of consequent suffering, a larger end might be gained by changing the whole system and alleviating the injustice.

The method of Jesus, however, is different from either of these methods, and yet it sums up both and goes beyond each. It has within it passive elements of the first and the active elements of the second, but it adds a third: an active Offensive of Love on a higher level. Passively bearing a wrong is not enough, nor is it enough to precipitate a crisis in order to bear the penalty. You must add an element, the vital element that may be lacking in each—the active audacious offensive of love. Without this ingredient the whole effort will fail. It is this plus that puts soul into it.

So Jesus exhorts us to love our enemies and to do good to those who hate us; to bless those who curse us and to pray for those who abuse us. He Himself gave us the supreme example of this redemptive love as He hung on the cross. What made the death of Jesus different, in addition to the character of the sufferer, was the fact that out from Him went an active love toward those who put Him there, and that expressed itself in the prayer for His enemies, "Father, forgive them." That spirit wrested the offensive from their hands and turned the tragedy into triumph.

Thought for the day: *Love is the greatest force in the universe.*

Luke 6:39–49   JULY 17

Why do you call me "Lord, Lord," and not do what I tell you? (v. 46)

With the use of three different figures Jesus illustrates the nature of defective discipleship.

The first is the *log in the eye—a defective vision.* Jesus pictures a person trying to take a speck out of another person's eye who does not see the log in his own eye. This refers to the individual who does not recognize his or her own faults but who criticizes the faults of others. This makes the person a blind eye doctor who tries to perform an operation on someone else's eye. And Jesus asks, "Can a blind man lead a blind man?" The remedy for this condition is clear: take the log out of your own eye and then you will see clearly to take out the speck that's in your brother's eye." Recognize and confess your own self-righteousness and then you will be able to lead others to the Savior.

The second figure is that of *uncleanness in the heart—a*

defective spirit. An impure heart is like a rotten tree that produces bad fruit. Only a good tree can produce good fruit. In other words, the *fruit* is the product of the *root.* What's on the inside comes out, either as good or evil. So if you want good character, you have to go to the source. It's no use trying to reform yourself on the outside by your own efforts; you must be transformed on the inside by the grace of God. Make the tree good and the fruit will be good.

The third figure is that of *sand in the foundation—a defective will.* Jesus said that the person who hears His words but does not do them is like the man who builds his house on the sand; then when the storm comes the house crumbles. The only way to avoid this catastrophe is to build on the rock, that is, the rock of obedience. We must hear and obey; practice as well as profess.

Thought for the day: *By the grace of God defective disciples can become effective.*

Luke 7:1–10   JULY 18

He is worthy ... I am not worthy (vv. 4, 6).

The Roman soldier, who is the central character of this story, was no ordinary person. He was a centurion, the captain of a hundred men. The centurions were the backbone of the Roman army and were chosen for their leadership ability, good judgment, and courage. So he was a man of position and authority.

This centurion was unusual in several respects. He had an uncommon attitude toward his slave. In the eyes of Roman law, a slave was considered nothing more than a tool; he had no rights; his master could ill-treat him and even kill him if he chose. But this centurion loved his slave and would go to any trouble to save him. He also had an unusual attitude toward the Jews. In those days the Jews despised the Romans and called them pagans, while the Romans hated the Jews and looked upon them as religious bigots. But here we see a close bond of friendship between the centurion and the Jews. Though he was a military man, he was deeply religious, no doubt a Jewish proselyte, who believed in the one true God and the Old Testament Scriptures.

Because of all these fine qualities, when the centurion's slave became desperately ill and he sent certain Jewish elders to Jesus for help, they came to Jesus and said, *"He is worthy* to have you do this for him, for He loves our nation and he built us our synagogue." They made their urgent appeal on the basis of the centurion's worthiness; on the basis of his good deeds. But the interesting thing is that when Jesus got near the centurion's house, the centurion sent friends to Jesus, saying to Him, "Lord, do not trouble yourself, for *I am not worthy* to have you come under my roof . . . but say the word, and let my servant be healed." The Jewish leaders said, "He is worthy," but the centurion said of himself, "I am not worthy."

When we come to Christ we dare not trust in our own worthiness or merit; we dare not rely on our own righteousness or good works. The only way we can approach Christ is on the basis of His invitation, His willingness, and His love. Grace is our only plea.

Thought for the day: *It is not our worthiness, but His willingness that counts.*

Luke 7:11–17   JULY 19

When the Lord saw her, he had compassion on her (v. 13).

Yesterday we read the account of Jesus healing a slave. Today we read about his raising a young man from the dead. The two miracles present interesting points of contact and comparison.

In the first case, the miracle was performed at a distance;

in the second, in Jesus' presence. In the first, the subject was a servant; in the second, a son. In the first, the miracle was performed by request; in the second, without request. The first miracle was restoration to health: the second, resurrection from the dead. In the first case, a master was gratified; in the second, a mother. The first act of mercy was toward a rich Gentile; the second, toward a poor Jew. In both cases there was need, and in both Christ was equal to the need.

Jesus still blesses people without regard to nationality or class; still raises those dead in trespasses and sins; still restores the spiritually sick; still responds to faith wherever it is found; and still offers mercy to those who are expecting nothing. Sons and servants, saints and sinners, masters and mothers, and men and women everywhere may look to Him and live, may ask and receive.

Luke's primary purpose in recording this incident is to impress upon his hearers the sympathy and tenderness of the Man Christ Jesus. Jesus had not been asked to perform the miracle; He was moved solely by the mute appeal of human sorrow and distress. He was touched by the sad procession winding its way out to the place of burial; he was moved by the tears of the lonely mother, a widow, who had lost her only son and only means of support. So he stopped, touched the bier, and raised the young man from the dead, and *"gave him to his mother."* No picture could be more full of pity and compassion.

Thought for the day: *Christ has a strong hand and a sympathetic heart.*

Luke 7:18–30   JULY 20

Are you he who is to come, or shall we look for another? (v. 19)

There are different kinds of doubters. First of all, there is the *deliberate doubter*, where the doubt is rooted in the *will* of the individual. The person intentionally chooses to doubt, even when faced with all the evidence to the contrary. Like the Scribes and Pharisees of Jesus' day, who saw all His miracles and heard all His teachings and claims but refused to believe that He was the Messiah, the Christ. This kind of deliberate doubt becomes chronic unbelief, which is the root of all sin.

Then there is the *honest doubter*, where the doubt is rooted in the *mind*. The person is unable fully to accept the truth until certain legitimate questions are answered. Doubt rises either from lack of information or from faulty information. Or the person is not satisfied with the testimony of someone else, but has to know personally for himself. In either case, judgment is withheld until further evidence is produced. Like the disciple Thomas, who at first was slow to accept the fact of Christ's resurrection; but when he saw the nail prints in Jesus' hands, he knelt and confessed, "My Lord and my God."

Finally, there is the *depressed doubter*, where the doubt is rooted in the *emotions* or feelings of the individual. The person has been shaken by the circumstances and tragedies of life—accident, illness, loss, death—and begins to wonder where God is in all of this. He begins to doubt the goodness, the love, and the providence of God. Like John the Baptist, who had such an effective and successful public ministry, and then suddenly was thrown into a miserable, tiny dungeon, with no light, no companions, and very little to eat. Soon his depression led to doubt: "Is this really the Christ, or do we have to wait for another?"

Christ's prescription for the depressed doubter is still the same. He says to us as he said to John, "Look at the facts. Trace the hand of God in your own life and in the lives of others, and soon you will realize that He is still there amidst the tragedies of life, and that His grace and love still abound." He is God and there is no other.

Thought for the day: *Disperse your doubts with facts and faith.*

Your sins are forgiven . . . your faith has saved you; go in peace (vv. 48–50).

Look at the contrast between the two main characters.

The woman is *unnamed*. No mention is made of her name; she is simply referred to as "a woman." She was *unaccepted* by society, for she was a prostitute, a woman of ill-repute. All recognized her as "a sinner." She was *uninvited*, but her desperate need gave her courage to enter unbidden into the house of Simon, where Jesus was a guest. Above all, the woman was *undaunted*; nothing could stop her from meeting the Master.

No doubt the woman had already heard of Jesus. She had heard of His miracles and teachings, His compassion and love. She knew that He healed the sick and spoke the word of forgiveness to the sinner. So when she heard that Jesus was in town, being entertained in the house of Simon, she quietly slipped through the door and into the presence of Jesus.

The woman displayed all the qualities of genuine repentance and faith. She recognized she was a sinner and wept over her sins. When her tears began to wet the Master's feet, she wiped them with her braids of hair. Out of gratitude and devotion she kissed His feet and poured ointment on them. Her faith was genuine, for Jesus said, "Your faith has saved you; go in peace."

The attitude of Simon's mind and heart was entirely different. He was *self-righteous*, a Pharisee who took pride in his religious knowledge and performances; he felt *self-sufficient*, confident that he was a good man in the sight of God and society. Simon was conscious of no need and therefore felt no remorse and therefore received no pardon. The prostitute came forlorn and left forgiven; she came in penitence and left in peace. The Pharisee remained unconcerned and unforgiven.

The one thing that shuts a person off from God is self-sufficiency and pride. The greatest of sins is to be conscious of no sin; but a sense of need and a spirit of repentance will open the door to the forgiveness of God.

Thought for the day: *If we confess, He will forgive.*

Luke 8:1–15   JULY 22

Some [seed] fell into good soil and grew, and yielded a hundredfold (v. 8).

The parable of the sower is not only a warning to those who hear the Gospel; it is also an encouragement to those who preach the Gospel. Sometimes the servant of God may preach the Word faithfully and labor diligently, but still there seems to be no results. He begins to wonder if all the soil is good. There *will* be fruit; the harvest is sure. God's Word will not return void.

In Japan the spiritual soil has proved very hard, for the people are materialistic and secular-minded. But in Korea the soil is good. During the past thirty years the Christian constituency has doubled every decade. Likewise, the Islamic world has proved to be very resistant to the Gospel, but animistic tribes around the world have responded to Christ's invitation by the millions.

God's servants should diligently look for the good soil and plant the seed of God's Word there. Sometimes the Holy Spirit, through environmental factors, prepares the heart of a certain people for the coming of the Gospel. They are open and receptive. We should concentrate our efforts and resources for the winning of such people. Between 1820 and 1904 a certain mission labored in the area of Belgaum, India. At the end of that eighty-four-year period they could count only 200 converts from Hinduism. The missionaries became discouraged and turned the work over to another mission. In the next 20 years this second mission won over 12,000 people to Christ and established scores of congregations. Both missions were evangelical and worked hard. What then made the difference? The first group preached only to the high-caste Hindus; they were unresponsive—the hard ground. The second group preached to the outcastes; they were receptive—the good ground. We must learn to sow the seed where God has prepared the soil.

Thought for the day: *Those who sow in tears shall reap with shouts of joy (Psalm 126:5).*

Luke 8:22–25   JULY 23

He ... rebuked the wind and the raging waves ...
and there was a calm (v. 24).

Is the day of miracles past? Can God still calm stormy seas today?

In 1942 during World War II, my wife and our first child were with a shipload of missionaries being evacuated from India to the United States on the *S.S. Brazil.* As the ship zigzagged its way toward South Africa, one of the older missionaries, Dr. Corpron, was suddenly stricken with acute appendicitis. A younger doctor on board was ready to operate, but a ferocious storm, which had raged for several days, was tossing the ship about. The doctor said to the missionaries, "I cannot delay the operation beyond ten o'clock tomorrow morning. Otherwise, Dr. Corpron's appendix will burst and he will probably die." He urged everyone to pray for calm seas.

All night the prayer vigil went on, but the storm continued unabated. Suddenly, just before ten o'clock the next morning, the seas became as smooth as glass. Dr. Corpron was rushed to surgery and the operation was successful. Within minutes after the patient was back and strapped into his own bunk, the storm returned and the ship began to roll and pitch. But Dr. Corpron's life was saved.

The great revival that swept over the island of Timor in Indonesia during the 1960s was carried forward by teams of lay persons who went from place to place witnessing for Christ and calling people to repentance. The leader of Team 17 was a woman named Esther. One day the Lord spoke to her and said, "Go to Rote." At once the team hired a boat belonging to a Muslim and set out for the small island of Rote. On their way they ran into a severe gale. The Muslim said to the team, "If your God will answer your prayers and calm the storm, then I will believe in Him." The team prayed and within a few minutes the sea was completely calm. The Muslim was converted, and afterwards he renamed his boat *New Life.*

With God all things are possible. The Lord Jesus who stilled the storm on the Sea of Galilee is still alive today.

Thought for the day: *God who created the seas can also calm the seas.*

Luke 8:26–39   **JULY 24**

Then people went out to see what had happened (v. 35).

We divide the history of the world into two major blocks of time—B.C. and A.D. (before Christ and in the year of our Lord). The dividing line is the birth of Christ, when the Son of God entered the stream of human affairs. That was the most significant event of all time and has produced more revolutionary changes than any other single event in history.

We can also divide the history of every disciple of Christ into two sections: before Christ and after Christ. It is the coming of Christ into the life of the individual that makes the difference.

Look at the tremendous change produced by Jesus in the life of the individual about whom we read in today's passage of Scripture. "Before Christ" he was possessed with many demons, ran around naked, and lived among the tombs. He was often kept under guard and bound with chains and fetters, but he would break the bonds and the demons would drive him into the desert. What a picture of complete helplessness and despair. But notice the man's condition "after Christ." The demons were gone, and the man sat at the feet of Jesus, clothed and in his right mind. Then he told the entire city what Jesus had done for him. What a picture of complete deliverance!

Church history is full of magnificent illustrations of the before-and-after-Christ drama in the life of individuals and entire peoples. Recall such persons as Simon Peter, the apostle Paul, Martin Luther, John Wesley, Sadhu Sundar Singh, Toyohiko Kagawa, Charles Colson, and Malcolm Muggeridge. Remember such people groups as the untouchables of India, the Karens of Burma, the Bataks of Indonesia, and the Aucas of Ecuador.

In every case it was the coming of Christ that produced the change. By His power and grace He transformed lives and cultures so that murderers became missionaries, prisoners become preachers, headhunters became hearthunters, cannibals became evangelists, and skeptics became believers.

Thought for the day: *When Christ enters the scene, things will never be the same.*

Luke 8:40–42; 49–56   JULY 25

Only believe, and she shall be well (v. 50).

It is evident that Jairus, a ruler of the synagogue, had faith in Christ's power to heal, even though his faith was imperfect. It was more intelligent than the faith of the infirm woman who secretly touched Christ's garment, but it fell short of the faith of the centurion who believed that Jesus could heal even from a distance. Nevertheless, Jairus' faith was genuine. He pleaded with Jesus, "Come and lay your hands on [my daughter], so that she may be made well, and live" (Mark 5:23). He believed that Jesus could heal her.

But as Jesus and the crowd made their way toward the

home of Jairus, a messenger came running and said to the father, "Your daughter is dead; do not trouble the Teacher any more." No doubt Jairus must have felt the same way. While there was the least spark of life in the girl, there was some hope. Jesus could possibly restore her to health. But now it was too late; it was all over. Death had claimed its victim, and Jairus' faith was shattered. Even Jesus, he felt, could do nothing in such a situation.

Jairus failed to realize that there is no limit to the power of Christ. There is no situation too difficult for Him to handle. Christ is Lord over nature and can calm the stormy sea. He is Lord over human nature and can bring health to the body. He is Lord over death and can restore life. It was just as easy for Him to say to the girl, "Rise from the dead," as it was for Him to say to the storm, "Peace, be still," or to the infirm woman, "You are well; go in peace." So he said to Jairus, "Do not fear; only believe." And this is what He says to each one of us today, regardless of the situation.

Thought for the day: *Our extremity is God's opportunity.*

Luke 9:1–9   JULY 26

He called the twelve together . . . and he sent them out (vv. 1, 2).

The ministry of Jesus was gaining momentum. Everywhere great crowds surrounded Him. He definitely needed help. So He sent out the twelve disciples in order to multiply the effects of His own ministry. Until now the disciples had been His companions; henceforth they were to be more strictly messengers and representatives.

Note that before Jesus sent out the twelve, He empowered them for the task. They were ordinary men (such as fishermen and tax collectors) sent on an extraordinary mission. For this they needed extraordinary power. So Jesus gave them authority over all demons and power to cure all kinds of diseases.

Notice also the detailed instructions that Jesus gave to the twelve. 1) *The assignment*: to preach the kingdom of God and to heal; 2) *The equipment*: they were to travel light and accept the hospitality of the people to whom they ministered; 3) *The warning*: some would receive and some would reject them.

Finally, we read that the disciples were obedient to their commission. "They departed and went through the villages, preaching the gospel and healing everywhere." Their ministry was so effective and fruitful that news of their deeds reached even the ears of King Herod and caused him to tremble.

The directions Jesus gave to His disciples were peculiar to the time and circumstances. However, the principles behind them are valid for the Lord's messengers in our day. We all need power from the baptism with the Holy Spirit. Our authority comes solely from our Lord and the written Word. Our mission is twofold: to preach and to heal—spiritual and physical. We must never forget that people have bodies as well as souls and souls as well as bodies. As heralds of Christ we must not be encumbered with worldly cares and posses- sions, and we must always remember that the power which Jesus has conferred upon us is not for our comfort but other people's good.

Thought for the day: *Before you go out for Christ, first read the instructions.*

Luke 9:10–17   JULY 27

They took up what was left over (v. 17).

When the multitude was fed and all were satisfied, the disciples gathered up the broken pieces of bread and fish that were left over and filled twelve baskets full. Is this not a silent but clear lesson against waste? Even when a miracle could

234

feed people sumptuously, our Lord would not permit anything to go unused.

Several years ago an official from India toured the United States on behalf of his government. On the eve of His return, someone asked him for his impressions of our country. Among the various comments that he made, one thing he said was, "What has impressed me so much about this country is the size of the American garbage can!" People in certain parts of the world would be happy to receive the scraps from our tables.

God has blessed our nation with tremendous resources in land, forests, minerals, and oil. But we have taken advantage of our abundance and become a very wasteful people. Just think of the bottles, tin cans, containers, cartons, paper, rubber, scrap metal, cardboard boxes, and food that we simply throw away. It is only recently, when we have been faced with shortage in certain areas, that we have realized our wasteful habits and have sought to conserve our resources more carefully.

When our family lived in India, we threw nothing away. A piece of string, a bent nail, an old tin can, a sheet of newspaper—all were of some use to people who lived in poverty. In the face of dire need, waste is a sin.

It is also a sin to waste one's God-given talents and abilities. God has blessed many people with precious gifts who have dissipated those gifts through ingratitude, misuse, or pure laziness. God wants us to use His gifts for His glory and for the benefit of others.

Thought for the day: *God's generous giving and our wise using must go hand in hand (William Barclay).*

Luke 9:18–27   JULY 28

Whoever would save his life will lose it; and whoever loses his life for my sake, he will save it (v. 24).

235

As Sadhu Sundar Singh, the famous Indian Christian, and a companion trudged through a snow storm on a mountain path in Tibet, they suddenly came upon a man lying in the snow. Seeing that he was still alive, Sundar Singh lifted him up and started carrying him. His companion chided him for such stupidity and briskly walked on ahead. Several hours later Sundar Singh came across his companion's body lying frozen and lifeless in the snow. His own life, however, had been spared by his own exertion and the warmth generated by the man he was carrying.

Jesus said, "He who seeks to save His life will lose it, but he who loses his life will find it." This sounds like a contradiction, but it is a basic principle of life. The disciple of Christ must give himself in sacrificial service for Christ and others in order to find meaning and joy in life.

Too many people these days are interested in saving their lives. They are living for themselves or their own families, seeking their own comforts and pleasure and honor. The world is no better off for their having lived. We need people who are willing to lose their lives for Christ's sake in sacrificial living for others—for the community, nation, and world.

Jesus followed the same principle in his own life and mission. He lost himself in the Crucifixion and found himself in the Resurrection. He did not save Himself, but He saved others. Now He calls upon His disciples everywhere to deny themselves, take up their crosses daily, and follow Him.

Thought for the day: *He is no fool who is willing to give up what he cannot keep, in order to gain what he cannot lose (Jim Elliott, missionary martyr).*

Luke 9:28–37   **JULY 29**

When they had come down from the mountain ... (v. 37).

The transfiguration of Jesus was a mountaintop experience for Peter, James, and John. They not only saw Jesus, resplendent in all His glory, but they saw Moses, the giver of the Law, and Elijah, the greatest of all prophets. What more could a pious Israelite ask for in his lifetime? Peter's immediate response was (and no doubt he spoke for his two colleagues), "Lord, this is a great place to be. Let us build three tabernacles and just stay here." But he forgot about the work to be done down in the valley.

We all enjoy, and we need, occasional mountaintop experiences. It is wonderful just to bask in the fellowship of our Lord and to get a new vision of His glory and power. For awhile we simply forget the problems and the pains of everyday life—Christ's presence seems so real, His joy so overwhelming. But blessed as the mount is, we cannot remain there forever. The valleys below are full of trouble and desperately need divine help.

It is of the very nature of life that we must come down from the mountain. *Solitude* but not *isolation* must be part of the Christian walk. The solitude is necessary for one to keep his contact with God; but if a Christian shuts himself off from others, if he closes his ears to the appeals of the needy, then even the sense of God's presence will become dim. The *solitude* is not meant to make us *solitary*. It is meant to make us better able to cope with the demands of daily living.

Again, we must not forget that right after a great mountaintop experience, there often comes one of our greatest trials or strongest temptations. The gloom is never far from the glory. Where Christ is most prominent, Satan is most persistent. It is a time to be on guard.

Thought for the day: *We receive equipment on the mountain for engagements in the valley.*

Luke 9:37–43a   JULY 30

Jesus . . . healed the boy, and gave him back to his father (v. 42).

Jesus is in the business of restoring people to a life of usefulness.

Look at the Gospel record for evidences of this truth. In Luke 7:1–10 we have the story of Jesus healing a beloved slave and giving him back to his master for continued affection and service. This is followed by the account of Jesus raising a young man from the dead and giving him back to his widowed mother (7:15) for companionship and support. In the same chapter is the moving story of the prostitute who came uninvited to Simon's house and anointed Jesus' feet with tears and ointment. Jesus transformed her and restored her to a life of respectability and usefulness in the community.

In Luke 8 is the graphic description of Jesus delivering a man from several unclean spirits and sending him home to tell what God had done for him. Jesus took the demoniac from the tombs and gave him back to his community as a witness. In Luke 9 we have the story of Jesus delivering a young man from demonic spirits, and Luke writes that Jesus "gave him back to his father."

Modern history is also full of evidences of Christ's restoring ministry. We think of Adjai Crowther of Nigeria, captured and sold as a slave; Christ freed and transformed him and gave him back to his Yoruba people as their first pastor and bishop. We remember also Ko Tha Byu of the hills of Burma, a man who murdered thirty-five people and was sold as a slave; Christ redeemed him and gave him back to his Karen people to become their first evangelist. Here in the United States we remember Mike Warnke, slave to Satan and drugs; Christ delivered him and gave him back to society as witness and friend. And we recall Chuck Colson, disgraced and imprisoned for the Watergate crime; Christ redeemed his life and gave him back to the American people as evangelist and reformer.

Thought for the day: *What sin takes away, the Savior gives back, and more.*

He who is least among you all is the one who is great (v. 48).

Jesus was constantly challenging the accepted values of society. He said, "Don't hate your enemies; love them . . . don't try to save your life; lose it . . . don't strive to be master; be the servant of all . . . don't seek to be great; be willing to be the least . . . don't reach for the top; take up the towel."

The world has turned the values of life topsy-turvy. It is as if someone slips into a department store during the night and switches all the price tags, so that when customers arrive the next morning, they find balloons selling for $1,000 and refrigerators for 50¢. Jesus came to turn life's values right side up; he came to restore the price tags. The least would be the greatest.

When Jesus spoke these words, the disciples had just had an argument among themselves about who was the greatest of them. It is possible that Peter, James, and John precipitated the argument. They constituted the inner circle of the twelve, and had just returned from the Mount of Transfiguration where Jesus was glorified and Moses and Elijah appeared before them. No doubt they felt superior to the other disciples and had boasted about this unusual experience.

Jesus reminded His disciples (and He reminds us today) that God's standards for greatness are not the same as those of the world. It is not position or prestige or power that makes for greatness; it is humility and the willingness to serve others, regardless of recognition or reward.

Mother Teresa of India is probably one of the best living examples of this principle. Wearing a simple cotton sari and having no possessions of her own, she lives among the destitute and the dying in the slums of Calcutta, just to bring hope and love to the dregs of society. She certainly has taken the place of the least. But today, as recipient of the Nobel Peace Prize, Mother Teresa is known around the world for her humble spirit and sacrificial service. Truly she is one of the greatest.

Thought for the day: *Don't seek to be great; seek to be useful.*

Luke 9:51–62

No one who puts his hand to the plow and looks back is fit for the kingdom of God (v. 62).

In this passage we find three potential disciples. The first and the third were volunteers, the second was invited. All three cases portray some of the hindrances to true discipleship.

The first of the three men typifies the *impulsive disciple.* He was swept along by his emotions, by the sight of the crowds following the Master and by the thought that it would be a great privilege to be in such company. Not for a moment had he realized that following Jesus might involve sacrifice and pain. So Jesus advised him, "Before you follow me, count the cost." Jesus never induced people to follow him under false pretenses. He always pointed out the price to be paid and the demands to be met.

The second man represents the *insincere disciple.* When Jesus said to him, "Come, follow me," he made excuses. He said, "I have to take care of my father first. I will follow you after his death." (How many years that would be nobody knows.) Jesus responded, "Others in your family can take care of your father, but I have a different plan for you. Leave all and follow me now." No tie, however tender, can be regarded as a sufficient excuse for refusing to follow Christ. His call takes priority over all other calls and duties in life.

The third man in this passage represents the *delaying disciple.* He was not rash; he had counted the cost. It was not his intention to make an excuse. He was sincere in his decision to follow Christ, but he simply wished to delay—at least long enough to go home and say "good-bye' to his family. Jesus replied, "If you have decided to follow me, you can't look back. You have to keep your eyes ahead on the task and the goal."

Thought for the day: *If you would follow Christ, you must put Him first.*

Luke 10:1–16

The harvest is plentiful, but the laborers are few (v. 2).

Here is Jesus announcing a labor shortage in the work of the kingdom. As He looked out upon the land, He realized that in countless villages He had not yet set foot; multitudes had not yet heard His message. And the number of His disciples was small. The harvest was indeed plentiful, but workers were few.

If this was true in Jesus' day, how much more true it is in our day. In spite of all we have accomplished in the past several centuries, the task of world evangelization is far from complete. In fact, because of the world population explosion, our task is becoming greater and greater all the time. In Jesus' day the population of the world was possibly only 300 million; today it is five billion. The number of non-Christians around the world doubled between 1900 and 1965 and will triple by the year 2000. This means that there are more people to be reached for Christ than ever before in the history of the church—actually around three and a half billion. Among these are a billion Chinese, 850 million Muslims, and 650 million Hindus.

Jesus exhorts us to pray that the Lord of the harvest will send out many more laborers into the field, not just white Anglo-Saxons, but missionaries of all colors and races— yellow, brown, and black; Koreans, Japanese, Indians, Filipinos, and Africans.

Can prayer make a difference in the labor shortage? It certainly can! In 1727 the young Moravian church in Germany began a prayer vigil that lasted around-the-clock for 100 years. Within the next sixty-five years of this period this small evangelical community sent out more than 300 missionaries across the world. In 1810 a group of college students at Williams College in Massachusetts went into a field regularly and prayed for "the conversion of the heathen world." This resulted in the formation of the first mission society in the United States and the beginning of a missionary movement that eventually encircled the globe.

Thought for the day: *What can I do to relieve the labor shortage in God's work?*

Luke 10:17–24   AUGUST 3

Rejoice that your names are written in heaven (v. 20).

Jesus had sent out seventy disciples from His larger circles of followers, to go into every town and place where He Himself planned to go. The number seventy was to the Jews a symbolic number, for it was the number of elders who were chosen to help Moses with the task of directing the people in the wilderness; and it was the number of the Sanhedrin, the supreme council of the Jews. The seventy were sent out two-by-two to prepare the way for the preaching of Christ.

When the seventy returned they were radiant with the triumphs they had witnessed. They reported that even the demons were subject to them. When Jesus saw their elation, He cautioned them against unwholesome attitudes. He warned them not to boast about their accomplishments and reminded them that it was the sin of pride that had toppled Satan out of heaven when once he had been the chief of angels. He also reminded them that the power behind all their miraculous deeds was not their own, but had been given by Himself to them.

The response of Jesus, however, did not end on a negative note. He had to warn the disciples of certain dangers, but He did not want to dampen their joy. On the other hand, he sought to give them a nobler motive for their rejoicing. He said to them, "Don't rejoice over the number of demons you cast out and the number of miracles you performed, but rejoice that your names are written in heaven." He also reminded the disciples how privileged they were to see and hear all things that many kings and prophets had longed to see and hear but could not. Then our Lord Himself shared in the exultation of His followers, "rejoicing in the Holy Spirit," and returned thanks to the Father for what He was accomplishing through the humble messengers whom he had chosen.

Thought for the day: *It is better to boast about Jesus than to brag about yourself.*

Luke 10:25–37

You shall love . . . your neighbor as yourself (v. 27).

The parable of the Good Samaritan is one of the most meaningful stories that Jesus ever told. It so clearly reveals to us the attitude of the Christian toward those who are in need.

The Christian is one who *cares*. When the Samaritan saw the man beaten and lying in the ditch, "he had *compassion* on him." Compassion is a beautiful and strong word. It goes beyond mere pity. Pity means to *feel for* someone. It shakes its head and says, "Too bad; poor old chap." Compassion means to *feel with* the other person. It says, "It's bad, and so bad I must do something about it. I know how I would feel if I were in this person's place." When one meets Christ, he becomes sensitized to the sorrows, suffering, and sins of others. He begins to care.

The Christian is also one who *shares*. The Samaritan's attitude was different from that of the robber and the priest. The robber's attitude was, "What's yours is mine, I'll take it." The attitude of the priest was, "What's mine is mine, I'll keep

it." But the Samaritan said, "What's mine is yours, I'll share it."
So he shared all that he had with the wounded traveler—his
time, his energy, his wine, his donkey, and his money. The
Christian looks upon himself not as the owner but the steward
of his possessions, and is willing to use them for the good of
others.

The Christian is also one who *dares*. The Samaritan was
willing to take certain risks in order to help the stricken man
lying along the roadside. He dared to upset his travel
schedule, to expose himself to the dangers of the highway,
and to disregard the racial prejudices and taunts of his fellow
Samaritans. Likewise, in our efforts to help others, we may
often have to exhibit a spirit of daring and cut across the
customs, traditions, prejudices, and selfishness of our day.

Thought for the day: *Love needs demonstration not
definition.*

Luke 10:38—42   AUGUST 5

Martha was distracted with much serving (v. 40).

In this chapter of Luke's Gospel, we find, back-to-back,
two important records. The first is the dialogue between Christ
and a certain lawyer (remember yesterday's meditation).
When the lawyer asked, "Who is my neighbor?" Jesus told the
beautiful story of the Good Samaritan. A man was beaten up
and left for dead on the roadside. Two men came along, a
priest and a Levite—both religious men. But they passed by
without even lifting a finger to help the poor man in the ditch.
They were in too much of a rush to make it to the temple in
Jerusalem for the evening service. Then along came a
Samaritan, a person of a different social grouping, and in
compassion he stopped to minister to the destitute traveler.
By this story, Jesus was saying that *worship without service
is a farce*. Our faith must be expressed in deeds.

Immediately after the parable, Luke records the dialogue

between Jesus and Martha of Bethany (our lesson for today). Jesus was visiting the home of Mary and Martha, two sisters. Mary sat at the Master's feet and listened to His teaching. "But Martha was distracted with much serving." She was an activist, running back and forth between the kitchen and the parlor. Then Jesus gently rebuked her, saying, "Martha, you are anxious and troubled about many things; one thing is needful. Mary has chosen the good portion." In essence He was saying that *service without worship is equally a farce.*

The combined force of these two paragraphs is that *both worship and service are essential*; concern for both spiritual and material matters is necessary. In like manner, both evangelism and social action are essential ingredients of the Christian life and mission. We must be concerned for the total welfare of humankind. We must minister to the total needs of all persons.

Thought for the day: *Worship and work go hand in hand.*

Luke 11:1–13   AUGUST 6

Everyone who asks receives, and he who seeks finds, and to him who knocks it will be opened" (v. 10).

Jesus was the master Pray-er. There was something so meaningful and moving about His prayer life, that the disciples came to Him and said, "Lord, teach us how to pray." In response Jesus gave this beautiful discourse on prayer.

First, Jesus gave His disciples what is commonly known as the Lord's Prayer. This is more than just a formula to be repeated; it is a model of the basic ingredients of prayer. It includes our relationship to God and our relationship to people. It includes adoration, confession, petition, and intercession. It covers past sin (forgiveness), present need (bread), and future trials (deliverance).

To encourage His disciples in their prayer life Jesus gave the parable of the importunate host who went to his friend at midnight, asking for bread. We are not to infer from this story that prayer is merely an attempt to overcome the reluctance of God. We don't have to batter at God's door until we finally wear Him down and compel Him to give us what we want. Jesus is saying that our petitions should rise out of a sense of urgent need and should be characterized by intensity and persistence. But the main point He makes is this: If an irritated, unwilling householder can, in the end, be coerced by a friend's shameless persistence into giving him what he needs, *how much more* will God, who sincerely cares for us, be willing to listen to our petitions and supply all our needs?

Jesus further encouraged prayer by reminding His disciples that they were praying to a Father. If an earthly father, with all of his imperfections and limitations, will grant good gifts to his children, *how much more* will the heavenly Father grant good gifts to His children. He will give not only good gifts, but the greatest of all gifts—the Holy Spirit.

So ASK (make your request); SEEK (go after it); and KNOCK (keep at it).

Thought for the day: *Prayer is laying hold of God's readiness, not His reluctance.*

Luke 11:14–28   AUGUST 7

When he comes, he finds [the house] swept and put in order (v. 25).

In the parable of the unclean spirit, Jesus teaches the church an important lesson—the peril of the empty heart or the danger of a spiritual vacuum. According to the story, the unclean spirit left the man, wandered around for a while, then returned. Finding the house clean and empty, it brought seven other spirits to dwell there. Jesus said that the last state of the man became worse than the first.

There are two important facts to remember about any spiritual vacuum. The first is that it offers the church a

246

tremendous evangelistic opportunity. When people are without a strong commitment to any particular faith or ideology, they are usually more open to new ideas, and thus to the Christian message. They are approachable and winnable. In many areas of the world today—such as South Korea, Latin America, and Africa—the church is seizing the present opportunity for evangelism and is experiencing spectacular increases in the number of conversions and local congregations.

However, there is also a negative side to the spiritual vacuum. It not only provides an open door for evangelism and church growth, but it is also fraught with potential danger; people will not remain in a spiritual vacuum for long. As Dr. E. Stanley Jones often warned us, "Nature abhors a vacuum, and human nature abhors a vacuum." If the gospel of Jesus does not move into the spiritual vacuum fast enough, then a man-made "ism" or ideology will move in. People are made so that they have to believe in something; they must commit themselves to something or someone. This means that there is a certain urgency about this whole business of world evangelization. We must not, we dare not delay. A people who are open to the gospel today may not be open tomorrow. If we don't act now, it may be too late.

Thought for the day: *The only cure for the empty heart is the fullness of Christ.*

Luke 11:29–36   AUGUST 8

Be careful lest the light in you be darkness (v. 35).

In the Scriptures, light is a symbol of righteousness, and darkness is a symbol of evil. John tells us that "God is light" and Jesus claims to be the "Light of the world." Paul speaks of the "light of the gospel of Christ" and testifies that he was called to turn Gentiles "from darkness to light." He reminds the Christians at Ephesus that once they were in darkness but now had become light.

As the light of the gospel has penetrated into many areas of the world, it has dispelled spiritual darkness, transforming individual lives and society. People have given up their idols and turned to worship the living God. They have given up such practices as cannibalism, headhunting, temple prostitution, infanticide, and intertribal warfare. They have started ministering to the destitute and needy.

But while darkness is becoming light in some areas of the world, in other areas light is becoming darkness. This is particularly true of Western Europe and North America. For decades and even centuries, we have had so much light—Bibles, churches, and pastors everywhere; Christian literature in abundance; preaching on radio and television and from the pulpit. We have heard the Good News over and over again until it has become old news. People have become indifferent and careless. Some have willfully rejected the light. And now the light is turning into darkness—gross darkness at that, for the greater the light has been, the greater the darkness becomes. So we are besieged with pornography, divorce, crime, gang warfare, drugs, alcoholism, immorality, homosexuality, occultism, and Satan worship.

Jesus' warning comes to us with renewed force today—"be careful lest the light in you become darkness." Before it is too late and the darkness becomes complete, we need to repent of our ways and turn back to God, the Scriptures, and the church and start walking in the light once again.

Thought for the day: *Am I part of the solution or part of the problem?*

Luke 11:37–54   AUGUST 9

You Pharisees cleanse the outside of the cup and of the dish, but inside you are full of extortion and wickedness (v. 39).

Jesus again and again exposed and denounced the hypocrisy of the Pharisees. The basis of hypocrisy is insincerity. The hypocrite is never genuine; he is always playacting. God would rather have a blunt, honest sinner than someone who puts on an act of goodness.

The Pharisees manifested their hypocrisy in two basic ways. First, *they majored on externals*. They were more concerned about outer physical cleanness than about inward spiritual wholeness. They were meticulous about following custom, ritual, and ceremony, but at the same time neglected the development of the inner spirit. Jesus' comment was that if they were as particular about cleansing their hearts as they were about washing their hands they would be better persons.

The Pharisees not only concentrated on externals, they also *majored on nonessentials*. They were careful to tithe the small herbs that they grew in their gardens. They were careful to perform the detailed ceremonial washing before meals. They sought after the best seats in the synagogues and salutations in public. But at the same time they neglected the more important qualities of justice and generosity toward people, and love for God.

We dare not criticize the Pharisees of Jesus' day and forget our own hypocrisy in these days. We are upset about a spot on our dress or trousers; we are concerned about dust on the living room floor; we are outraged at the pollution of the air, rivers, and ocean. But how concerned are we about the purity of our minds and hearts and the integrity of our desires and motives? We are careful about the appearance of our sanctuaries and the observance of our ritual. But how concerned are we about the injustices of society and lack of commitment to our Lord? We must start concentrating on our inner spirit and the basic virtues in life.

Thought for the day: *People look on the outward appearance; God looks on the heart (1 Sam. 16:7).*

Even the hairs of your head are all numbered (v. 7).

Is God really interested in me—my needs, my problems? Or is He too busy running the universe, too big to be bothered about puny little me? After all, there are five billion people in the world. How could God be bothered about one single individual?

For the answer to this question we go to Christ, who in turn reveals the heart of the heavenly Father.

Listen first to the words of Jesus. The shepherd leaves the ninety-nine sheep in the fold and goes out in search of the one lost sheep. The woman forgets the nine coins in her purse and diligently searches the whole house to find the one missing coin. Jesus says that God is so concerned about the individual that He knows even the number of the hairs on his or her head.

Then look at the works of Jesus. Note how often He turned from the crowd to minister to one person in need—a leper, a sick slave, a sick wife, a paralyzed man, a ruler's daughter, a blind man. In the Garden of Gethsemane, when a large crowd came to arrest Jesus, one of his disciples tried to defend his Master and cut off a man's ear with his sword. In the midst of all the turmoil, Jesus stopped to put the ear back in place and heal the man. Even on the cross amidst all the pain and suffering, Jesus found time to minister to one repentant thief.

We know that God is interested in every individual; He cares for each person. He knows each person by name and by need.

Once a minister visiting a family noticed several children in the home. He asked the mother, "How many children do you have?" She began to count them off on her fingers, "John, Lucy, Mary, David. . . ." When the minister interrupted, "I don't want their names, I just asked for the number." The mother replied indignantly, "They have names, not numbers!"

Thought for the day: *In God's sight everyone is a VIP.*

Luke 12:13–31   AUGUST 11

A man's life does not consist in the abundance of his possessions (v. 15).

The rich farmer in the parable made two basic mistakes. First, *he lived only for himself.* Notice the frequent use of the personal pronouns in all his statements: "my crops . . . my barns . . . my grain . . . my goods . . . my soul . . . I will put down . . . I will store . . . I will say . . . ." He failed to realize that God is the real owner of all things, and that possessions are not to be used for selfish ends but for the kingdom of God and the good of others. Again, the rich farmer *lived only for this present world.* All his plans were made on the basis of life in this world. He forgot that there is a world to come, and he made no preparations for the future. When death suddenly took him by surprise, he found he had nothing to take with him.

It is possible to be materially rich but spiritually poor. It is also possible to be spiritually rich while being materially poor.

A number of years ago I was a guest in the palace of one of India's noted *rajahs.* He was dressed in costly silk and adorned with expensive jewelry—gold, diamonds, rubies, and emeralds. We sat on opulent Persian carpets and ate out of silver plates and bowls. I was dazzled by the rajah's wealth and possessions. But there was no faith or love in the home. At the time, the rajah was living with a beautiful night club dancer from Europe. The man was fabulously rich in the world's goods but was a spiritual pauper.

The next day I was invited into the humble home of a Christian family. Before we had light refreshments, the father read a portion of Scripture and then led in prayer. From the conversation that followed, I discovered that all six members of the family were committed Christians. Two of the children were in full-time Christian service. The family was poor in the world's goods, but wonderfully rich toward God.

Thought for the day: *True riches are in God, not in goods.*

Luke 12:32–48   AUGUST 12

Fear not, little flock, for it is your Father's good pleasure to give you the kingdom (v. 32).

Jesus spoke these words to his twelve disciples. They were an insignificant band, with no social standing or financial backing. At the time the Jewish leaders were against them, and later the Roman government would join the opposition. But in their lifetime alone, the disciples witnessed the spread of the Christian movement throughout Judea, Samaria, Syria, Asia Minor, Greece, and as far as Rome itself. By the year 313 A.D., the emperor himself had become a believer and Christianity had become the official religion of the Roman Empire.

This phenomenon has happened again and again in the history of the church. Adoniram Judson went from the United States to Burma in 1812. He preached for several years before he had his first convert. He was imprisoned as a spy for two years and suffered untold hardships. His wife became ill and died. But he faithfully labored on. Today a vital church in Burma numbers over two million members. The Karen church in the hills of Burma is one of the most indigenous churches in the world.

In 1856 William Butler arrived in India as the first American Methodist missionary. The following year the Indian Mutiny broke out and Butler had to flee to the mountains for safety. On Sunday morning the little band of twelve Indian Methodists met together for worship, and the pastor, Joel Janvier, preached on this very same text. Suddenly they were attacked by a group of mutineers. One young woman, Maria Bolst, was killed by a sword; the rest of the congregation was scattered. Today Methodist churches are found all across India, with a membership of approximately 650,000.

When the missionaries were forced out of China in 1949, only a million Chinese Protestant Christians were in the land. Today, in spite of all the suffering and persecution, the estimated number of Christians is between 35–50 million.

Thought for the day: *By the grace of God, a tiny flock can become a tremendous force.*

Luke 12:49–59   AUGUST 13

Do you think that I have come to give peace on earth? No, I tell you, but rather division (v. 51).

These words are indeed surprising to us. When Jesus was born, the angels over Bethlehem praised God and sang, "Peace on earth, good will toward men." Jesus Himself said to his disciples, "Peace I leave with you; my peace I give to you." Very often when Jesus healed or offered forgiveness to an individual, He said to the person, "Go in peace." We usually think of the gospel as a reconciling force, restoring peace. But here Jesus clearly announces that He has come, not to bring peace, but division.

There is a paradox here. The coming of Jesus certainly brings peace to people as they find forgiveness and deliverance from sin. It brings peace between groups or peoples who once hated one another, but then experienced the love of God in their hearts. In the early church, the division between Jew and Gentile was broken down by the Gospel. In our day we have seen tribal groups, who once incessantly fought among themselves, lay down their arms and start living in peace, whenever the Gospel has penetrated their lives.

But at the same time we have seen many cases where the coming of Christ has brought division in the home or society. Someone in a Muslim or Hindu family professes faith in Jesus Christ, and suddenly the rest of the family turns against that person with hatred and cruelty. Here in the West, we often experience division in the community when Christians take a stand on a social or moral issue, and people with vested interests rise up in protest and opposition.

We realize immediately that Christ does not intentionally bring division among people, but it is the varying response of people to the claims of Christ that brings division. Some accept Him as Lord, while others reject Him. Immediately, there is division. We must always strive for peace but be prepared for division.

Thought for the day: *Loyalty to Christ must take precedence over all other loyalties.*

Luke 13:1–17   AUGUST 14

Woman, you are freed from your infirmity (v. 12).

Luke describes in detail the woman whom Jesus healed. He tells us that she had a "spirit of infirmity"—not "an evil spirit" (demon possession), or simply "an infirmity" (a physical illness). There was something wrong in her inner spirit—deep down in her emotions—that affected her physically. "She was bent over and could not fully straighten herself." So here was a case of an inner emotional state resulting in an outer physical condition.

The woman in this story is a picture of many people even today. Some "spirit of infirmity"—wrong emotion or attitude—is affecting their physical welfare and keeping them in bondage. Often it is *a deep feeling of inferiority*, an inner nagging sense that you are no good, that you will never amount to anything, that no one could possibly love you, that everything you do is wrong. To such a person the Spirit says, "You are unique in the sight of God. He loves you and has a place for you. You are special to Him. And remember, you are a son/daughter of God. Nothing can be more noble." Like the little boy who said, "I know I am somebody. God made me, and He don't make no junk."

Sometimes the spirit of infirmity is *a perfectionist complex*, that inner feeling that no matter what you do, you can never achieve adequately. You never do enough; you are never able to please anybody, especially yourself. You are always striving, always feeling guilty, always driven by the "tyranny of the ought." And of course, you can never please God. He increasingly becomes a demanding tyrant, who moves out of reach every time you think you have arrived. To such a person the Spirit says, "God is not a cruel slave driver but a loving Father. Your relationship to Him does not depend on your achievements or your perfection. You are saved by grace and grace alone. So stop striving and start surrendering; stop trying and start trusting.

Thought for the day: *Christ is a specialist in internal medicine.*

Luke 13:18–35   AUGUST 15

When once the householder has ... shut the door, you will begin to stand outside and to knock at the door (v. 25).

We need to put this verse alongside the words of Jesus in Revelation 3:20—"Behold, I stand at the door and knock; if anyone hears my voice and opens the door, I will come in to him." This signifies *the door to the human heart.* Jesus, who as Creator and Redeemer, should be on the inside, stands as a stranger on the outside, seeking to get in. Patiently he knocks and he calls. It is up to the person on the inside to heed the voice of Jesus, open the door, and invite him in. So this is a door which is shut, but can be opened.

The picture painted by our key verse for today is just the opposite. Here a person stands outside the door of the household, knocks, and calls out, pleading for entrance. This signifies *the door to the kingdom.* But Jesus says, "It is too late; the door is shut." The person on the outside may say, "Lord, I ate and drank with you; I heard you preaching in the streets." But the Lord will say, "I know you not; depart from me, you worker of iniquity." So this is a door that is shut and cannot be opened. The door to the kingdom will be opened only to those persons who have opened their heart's door to the King.

Jesus made it unmistakably clear that there is a time of opportunity and there is a time when there is no longer opportunity to repent and believe the Gospel. Death closes the door of further opportunity; death seals our decision. As long as we are in this life, the door is open. There is a chance, an invitation. Death, however, ends this time of probation and makes it final. That is why the Scriptures always emphasize the urgency of our commitment. *"Now* is the day of salvation; *now* is the acceptable time." Tomorrow may be too late.

Thought for the day: *One day is too long to be without Christ.*

Luke 14:1–14 AUGUST 16

Every one who exalts himself will be humbled, and he who humbles himself will be exalted (v. 11).

Humility is one of the rarest and yet noblest of all virtues. It is so delicate a grace that to claim it is to disown it. One person may say of another, "He or she is a humble person," but when someone says of one's self, "I am humble," it echoes with a hollow ring. People cannot consciously strive to be humble; they become humble as they become more Christlike in their inner disposition.

Jesus again and again tried to teach his disciples a lesson in humility. In the Sermon on the Mount he said, "Blessed are the poor in spirit, for theirs is the kingdom of heaven ... Blessed are the meek, for they shall inherit the earth." When the disciples argued as to who was the greatest among them, Jesus said, "He who would be greatest among you, let him be servant of all." At the last supper he gave them a demonstration of the servant attitude when he took a basin of water and washed their feet.

Humility has always been one of the inevitable characteristics of great people. When Billy Graham came to India for evangelistic meetings, the most frequent comment about the evangelist was, "He appears to be a very humble man." E. Stanley Jones said on a number of occasions, "I am not fully Christian yet; I am just a Christian in the making."

Have you ever noticed that only the smaller birds sing? You've never heard a note from the eagle in all your life nor from a turkey nor from the ostrich. But you have heard from the canary, the wren, the lark, and the cardinal. The sweetest music comes from those Christians who are small in their own estimation and before the Lord.

When you are tempted to be proud or boastful, picture Jesus with a basin and towel in his hands.

Thought for the day: *It is possible to be too big for God to use, but never too small.*

Luke 14:15–24

They all alike began to make excuses (v. 18).

Listen to the excuses given by the invitees to the great banquet. How pathetic and flimsy they sound. One said, "I have bought a field, and I must go out and see it." Surely he had not bought the land unseen! Another said, "I have bought five yoke of oxen, and I go to examine them." Surely he had not been fooled into giving good money for lame or blind oxen! A third person said, "I have married a wife, and therefore I cannot come." We might ask, Why didn't he bring his wife along to the sumptuous feast—free at that? The truth of the matter was that none of the invitees wanted to come. They were all absorbed in their selfish interests and had no intention of coming. The excuses were nothing but a cover-up.

People are no different today. They make all kinds of excuses why they do not follow Christ or become members of His church. Some years ago the Reverend H.H. Elford, pastor in Minnesota, gathered all the excuses people usually make for staying away from church, and with a touch of irony listed "Nine Reasons Why I Don't Go To The Movies." Do any of these sound familiar?

1. The manager of the cinema never calls on me.

2. Every time I go they ask for money.

3. Not all people live up to the high moral standards of the films.

4. I went so much as a child, I've got all the entertainment I need.

5. The performance lasts too long. I can't sit still for an hour and a half.

6. I don't care for some of the people I meet at the cinema.

7. I don't always agree with what I see and hear.

8. I don't think they have very good music at the cinema.

9. Most people go to the cinema in the evening, and that's the only time I am able to be at home with my family.

Thought for the day: *No excuse is worth missing God's feast.*

Luke 14:25—35   AUGUST 18

If any one comes to me and does not hate his own father and mother . . . he cannot be my disciple (v. 26).

These words of Jesus sound harsh. But Matthew helps us understand this strange language with his phrasing: "He who loves his father and mother more than me, cannot be my disciple." The word "hate" has its roots in an Aramaic word

258

which means "to love less," so it really boils down to this: When the chips are down, a disciple will act as though he hates even his dearest loved ones if the claims of human affection ever come into conflict with the claims of Jesus.

Jesus, by these words, was trying to distinguish between a *dabbler* and a *disciple*. A dabbler, according to the dictionary, is one who follows an art or another branch of knowledge in a superficial manner or as a mere pastime. What a tragedy that many followers of Jesus are just dabblers; they follow him in a superficial manner, as a mere pastime, giving only a little of their time and energy. Jesus made it plain that the very basic assumption of being a disciple was His demand for priority over every other human claim for our lives and our loves. He said clearly, "Whoever of you does not renounce all that he has cannot be my disciple." He demands undivided allegiance, unqualified loyalty.

In India as a certain pastor conducted a testimony meeting in his church, many members gave witness to Christ's saving power in their lives. At the conclusion of the service, the pastor said, "Now we are going out to put our faith into practice. We are going into the outcaste section of town to minister to these poor untouchables and show them God's love." One man, a convert from a high caste in Hinduism, stood up and said, "Pastor, I'm sorry I can't join you; I'm saved all right, but not that far!" He was a half-hearted dabbler, not an out-and-out-disciple.

Christ is looking for disciples, not dabblers.

Thought for the day: *Dabblers usually become dropouts; disciples become dynamic.*

Luke 15:1–7   AUGUST 19

I have found my sheep which was lost (v. 6).

The fifteenth chapter of Luke's Gospel has been called "the lost and found department of the New Testament." Three things were lost—a sheep, a silver coin, a son—but all were found!

One of the most revolutionary ideas that Jesus proclaimed was that God seeks lost people. This concept completely reversed the almost universal belief that we must seek God. Jesus declared that *God* always takes the initiative. Because He is love, He is therefore concerned about our plight and is active in His pursuit of sinful humanity.

Several years ago while traveling on a train in northern India, I had a long conversation with a Hindu gentleman. He told me he had traveled thousands of miles on many pilgrimages during his lifetime. He had bathed in many of the sacred rivers and worshiped at many of the famous shrines. Even then he was on another pilgrimage.

"Why do you make so many pilgrimages?" I asked him.

"I am seeking God," he quickly replied.

Again I asked, "After so many pilgrimages have you not found him?"

He hung his head sadly. "No, I cannot say that I have found God yet," he said. "But I hope to find Him one day."

I then told him the good news of Luke 15. I emphasized the truth that Jesus came into the world to seek sinners, and through Him we can know God. Before we parted I gave him a copy of the New Testament as well as my name and address.

A few weeks later I received a letter from him. "Dear Sir," he wrote, "I have made my last pilgrimage. When I realized that God through Christ was seeking me, and put my trust in Him, He suddenly became real and personal to me. Now I can sincerely say, 'I have found God, or better still, He has found me.' "

Thought for the day: *God is only a step away. Turn around, and there He is!*

Luke 15:8–10   AUGUST 20

I have found the coin which I had lost (v. 9).

The sheep and the silver coin were both lost through carelessness. However, the former was lost through its own carelessness while the latter was lost through the carelessness of someone else. The woman of the house misplaced the coin, or dropped it unknowingly, so when she needed it, it was gone.

Many people are lost spiritually through the carelessness of others. Sometimes children are lost because parents are careless. The parents are so busy making a living and keeping house, that they have no time to sit down with their children and talk to them about spiritual matters. Sometimes a neighbor is lost through the carelessness of the Christian next door. The Christian visits his friend and talks about so many subjects—politics, inflation, sports, hobbies, the weather, etc.—but never says anything about his relationship with Jesus Christ. It is possible for church members to be lost through the carelessness of the pastor, who is so busy running the machinery of the church that he has no time to visit his people and confront them with the claims of Christ.

We should constantly ask ourselves, "Is there someone who is lost in my family, congregation, or community because of my carelessness?" It is a solemn thought.

When the coin was lost it did not lose its value. It was not marred or defaced. But it was out of circulation and therefore useless. So the lady of the house pushed aside the furniture and swept all the rooms until at last she found the lost piece of silver. Immediately the coin regained its usefulness.

God seeks lost people in order to put them back into circulation. He wants them to use their talents and skills for His glory, and spend their lives in the service of others. Just as a fifty-cent piece buys merchandise hundreds of times when it is spent and re-spent, so God can multiply our lives many times over as He circulates us in His service.

Thought for the day: *God will sweep the universe to find a lost soul.*

This my son was dead, and is alive again (v. 24).

You can't sin without something dying. Sin kills the power to discriminate between right and wrong. You can compromise with truth so long that you lose the power to know it. Sin deadens the affections so that you become hard and calloused and insensitive to sin. The more you do wrong, the less you respond to the call of God. Sin also kills your power to act in accordance with conscience and intelligence. The prodigal son *went* into the far country by his own will, but he was *sent* into the fields to work by another's will. He didn't want to do his father's will; he had his own way, and ended up enslaved to a stranger.

Everything in life has a price. You pay a price to be bad, in loss of freedom and self-respect. The price for sin's delight is far beyond what you get. You also pay a price for goodness—in self-denial, prayer, discipline. But you receive far more than you expect. When you buy evil, you get what you want immediately and pay the price in installments—like buying a car. When you buy goodness, you pay in advance and get the reward later—like going to college.

When the prodigal son headed for home, his father saw him a long way off and ran to meet him. They say that love is blind. Not at all! Love is far-sighted. The father saw him at a distance, he embraced him and gave him the kiss of forgiveness. When the son said, "Treat me as one of your hired servants," the father responded by treating him as a son. He gave him a new robe, a ring, and a pair of shoes—all signs of sonship and honor. He hired the local band and held a feast. And the son, who was once dead, began to live again!

Thought for the day: *We are not at home in this world until we are at home with God.*

He was angry and refused to go in (v. 28).

This is not the parable of the prodigal *son*, but the parable of the prodigal *sons*. Both boys were prodigal. One was a prodigal who went into the *far country*; the other was a prodigal who stayed at *home*. One was prodigal of his father's *substance* with *riotous* living; the other was prodigal of his father's *love* with *respectable* living. Both sons were sinners. One sinned in his outer *actions*; the other in his inner *reactions*.

The elder brother made three mistakes in his thinking that led to the tragedy of his life. He was mistaken about his *relationship*. He thought if he stayed at home, ate at his father's table, and worked in his father's field, then he was in right relationship with his father. But fellowship is not just a matter of physical contact. It is basically spiritual communion; kinship of mind, oneness of heart. It is possible to be *in* the church, but *out* of the kingdom.

The elder brother was also mistaken about his *responsibility*. He thought if he plowed the field, harvested the crops, and filled the barns, his duty was at an end. But at the same time he failed miserably in his responsibility to his brother. He did not go in search of him, and even grumbled when he came home. God is not satisfied with church members whose only concern is to raise the budget, repair the building, and pay the conference benevolences. God wants His people to be concerned about lost sons and daughters.

The elder brother was also mistaken about his *resources*. He said to his father, "You never gave me a kid, that I might make merry with my friends." The father answered, "Son . . . all that is mine is yours." The young man didn't have because he didn't ask. How like so many Christians who live far below their spiritual resources in Christ!

Luke 16:1–15

No servant can serve two masters (v. 13).

Nowadays a person can take on two jobs and work for two people. He can do one job in his working time and another in his spare time. He could, for example, be an office worker by day and a musician by night. But in Jesus' day, a slave belonged completely to his master. He had no spare time; every moment of his day and every ounce of his energy were devoted to his master. In the same way, Jesus insists, serving God can never be a part-time or spare-time job.

Many people try to serve God *and something else.* Some seek to serve God *and possessions.* They spend their time and efforts for material gain and physical comfort. Others try to serve God *and position.* They desire to climb the ladder of success and make a name for themselves. Still others attempt to serve God *and pleasure.* They love to have a good time and enjoy themselves. But God will not share his throne with anything else in the world.

Many people today also try to serve God *and someone else. They acknowledge that God is God, but believe that He is one among many gods. They acknowledge Christ as a Savior but not the one and only Savior.* Muslims claim that Christ is a great prophet, but only one in a long line of divinely appointed prophets. Hindus believe that Christ is an incarnation of God, but He is only one of ten or eleven different incarnations thus far in history.

A few years ago a group of Hindus in India decided to convert to Buddhism. Reluctant to remove the idol they had been worshiping, they simply installed a new image of Buddha at its side. The incident was reported in the *Times of India* under the caption, "Shiva and Buddha to co-exist in temple." But God will not share his throne with anyone else. He must be Lord of all or not at all.

Thought for the day: *It is not* God and, *but* God alone.

Luke 16:19–31 AUGUST 24

There was a rich man ... at his gate lay a poor man (vv. 19, 20).

In this parable of the rich man and Lazarus, Jesus by no means implies that it is sinful to be rich or that all poor people will be saved. Being rich was not the man's crime. After all, Abraham, to whom he called out in heaven, had been a rich man on earth. Being rich, the story hints, was the man's opportunity. His crime was self-indulgence and lack of compassion. He had much, but he lived for himself, and did nothing for the poor and needy.

What does this parable say to affluent America in this day? God has blessed our country with rich minerals and vast resources. To this we have added our scientific knowledge, our industrial genius, and work ethic. So today we are the richest nation in the world. But poor people are right on our doorstep, in our ghettos and slums, and on our borders. And millions of poverty-stricken people suffer in countries all across the world.

We in America have so much while in other countries they have so little. Our annual per capita income is around $9,000; in one-half of the world it is less than $200. Whereas Americans spend seventeen percent of their income on food, in India they spend sixty-seven percent. While we Americans have one doctor to every 600 persons, only one per 11,000 is available in Haiti. We Americans are only six percent of the world's population, but we consume forty percent of the world's resources. If all the world's people tried to live under the current standard of a North American, only eighteen percent could remain alive; the other eighty-two percent would die because of lack of resources.

How much compassion do we have for the Lazaruses who sit at our gates? Are we willing to use our affluence, not for our own selfish ends and comfort, but for the alleviation of the suffering and misery of the world?

Thought for the day: *To have is to owe.*

Luke 17:1–10 AUGUST 25

If you had faith as a grain of mustard seed ... (v. 6).

The disciples came to James and said, "Increase our faith!" Jesus responded by saying, "If you had faith as a grain of mustard seed [that is, small but sincere], you could do the impossible."

Two important lessons stand out from this conversation. First, Jesus is trying to tell us that *it's not a great faith that we need, but a small faith in a great God.* It's not the degree of our faith, but the character of the One we trust, that makes the difference. I shall never forget the time a village Christian in India brought his sick water buffalo to me and asked me to pray for its healing. Now, I had prayed on many occasions for a sick person to be healed, but a water buffalo? That animal was the only thing the villager owned; if it died, his family would probably starve. I knew that God was interested in people, but was He interested in water buffaloes? Anyway, I put my hand on the animal's head and prayed for it, and God healed it. I am sure it was more the villager's faith than mine which brought the healing. His faith was so simple but genuine.

Again, Jesus is trying to tell us through this principle that *it's more important to use the faith we already have than to seek for a bigger faith.* The more we exercise our faith, the stronger it becomes. If we believe that God is a loving heavenly Father, that He cares for our welfare, and that He is faithful to hear and answer prayer, then we can come in confidence to the throne of grace and make known our petitions. Faith, after all, is simply taking God at His word. He will never go back on His promises.

Thought for the day: *Faith is not believing that God can , but that God will!*

Luke 17:11–19 AUGUST 26

He fell on his face at Jesus' feet, giving him thanks (v. 16).

Ten lepers were healed, but only one came back to express thanks to Jesus. There was a note of sadness in the voice of the Master when He asked, "Where are the nine?"

There is nothing so hurtful as ingratitude. Just recently I heard a lady say, "You know, I was married for forty-two years before my husband and I were divorced, and in all that time he never once spoke a word of appreciation for the meal I set before him."

So often *children are ungrateful to their parents.* Parents take care of their children's needs from birth and pay all the bills, but never once do some children say, "Mom, Dad, thank you for all you have done for us." And then when the parents become old and feeble, they are considered a nuisance.

So often *we are ungrateful to other people.* We forget that we are dependent upon the services of others for many of the necessities and comforts of life. We feel that the world owes us everything so we never stop to say "thanks."

Often *we are ungrateful to God.* We fail to offer thanks before a meal. In time of bitter need we pray with desperate intensity, but when the crisis is over, we soon forget God. He has given us this beautiful world in which to live; He has showered us with innumerable blessings; He has given us His only Son for our redemption. How often do we stop to give Him thanks?

On the other hand, *gratitude can be so comforting*. About twenty years ago I helped a student from India who was suffering from loneliness and depression. He has never forgotten the kindness. Every year, without fail, he sends me a card on my birthday. Whenever I go to India, he comes to visit me. Now he is a bishop in his church, and whenever he comes to the United States on business, he visits me. I am humbled by his deep sense of gratitude.

Thought for the day: *Gratitude must become a daily attitude.*

Luke 17:20–37   AUGUST 27

The kingdom of God is in the midst of you (v. 21).

People are far more guilty of *reducing* the kingdom of God than *rejecting* it outright. Reducing it and, therefore, limiting it.

The people of Israel reduced the kingdom to a *political kingdom*. They looked forward to a messiah who would drive out the Romans and restore the throne of David. Even after the resurrection of Christ, the disciples still thought of the kingdom in national terms. They asked Him, "Lord, will you at this time restore the kingdom of Israel?" But Jesus always insisted that His kingdom "is not of this world."

Some Christians have sought to reduce the kingdom to an *ecclesiastical kingdom*. They claim that the church, with all its manufactured claims to infallibility, is the kingdom. But the Christian church, while it holds within itself the best life of the kingdom, cannot lay claim to the kingdom of God as its exclusive possession. The kingdom is absolute; the church is relative. The kingdom judges and corrects the church, and the church is potent to the degree that it obeys the kingdom and embodies its life and spirit.

Today some church leaders have reduced the kingdom of God to a *materialistic kingdom*. So to become a follower

268

of Christ is to become successful and prosperous, for "God wants His children to have the best"—plenty of money in the bank and a luxury car in the garage. But the Word makes it clear that "the kingdom of God does not mean food and drink but righteousness and peace and joy in the Holy Spirit" (Rom. 14:17).

Jesus said, "The kingdom of God is in the midst of you." That is, *He* is the kingdom. The King and the kingdom are one in that Jesus is the embodiment of the kingdom. He is the kingdom of God putting on sandals and walking. This means that if Christ is living in you, the kingdom of God is in you. When Christ reigns within, then His Spirit and virtues are manifest in your individual life and in all of your social relationships.

Thought for the day: *We belong to an unchanging King and an unshakable kingdom.*

Luke 18:1–8   AUGUST 28

They ought always to pray and not lose heart (v. 1).

In these words Jesus emphasizes two important principles of prayer:

1. *Prayer must be a continuous habit*—We "ought always to pray." This cuts across the common pattern of prayer followed by many of us. For us, prayer is something irregular, sporadic—a very present help in time of trouble. We pray only when we face a tough situation or major problem. When there is a severe drought, we pray. When a loved one lies in a coma, we pray. When a relative is seized as a hostage, we pray. Prayer is regarded as an emergency action of short duration. Either it works and we get what we want, or it fails and we get no results.

Christ suggests that we think of prayer as a way of living. It is an attitude, a response, a discipline with continuity. It is daily communion with a loving heavenly Father. Constant prayer keeps us aware of our Father's presence and care and seeks to bring our lives into harmony with His will. The more constant our prayer, the more assurance that we will not go astray.

2. *Prayer must be persistent*—"pray and not lose heart." In order to drive home this point, Jesus tells the story about a judge "who neither feared God nor regarded man." A poor widow kept coming to him for justice against her adversary, and though the judge cared nothing about justice or the widow, he vindicated her in order to get rid of her.

Now Jesus does not liken God to an unjust judge; he is contrasting God to such a person. What Jesus is saying is this: If in the end, an unjust and rapacious judge can be wearied into giving a widow justice, *how much more* will God, who is a loving Father, give His children what they need? We should pray with persistence and present our petitions with the assurance that God does hear and in His own time will answer.

Thought for the day: *More things are wrought by prayer than this world dreams of (Lord Tennyson).*

Luke 18:9–14 AUGUST 29

Two men went up into the temple to pray (v. 10).

What a study in contrasts! Note first the difference in the two men. One was a Pharisee—learned, high in society, religious, always strict about form and ceremony. The other was a tax collector—unlearned, low in society, nonreligious, unconcerned about form and ritual. Both men had a good intention—they went to the temple to pray. Could there be a finer motive? Is anything more necessary? And both men chose a good location—they went to the temple to pray. They went to God's house, the house of prayer.

But then note the difference between the two prayers that were offered. The Pharisee's prayer was more lengthy and based on comparison: "I am not like all other men ... or even like this tax collector." It was a proud prayer. The Pharisee praised himself and told God how good he was: "I am not a robber, evildoer, or adulterer. I fast twice a week and give tithes of all that I get." There was no spirit of repentance in his prayer. On the other hand, the tax collector's prayer was brief but sincere. It was full of meaning and came from the speaker's heart. It was a humble prayer, confessing sin and pleading for mercy. He stood at a distance, hung his head in contrition, beat his breast, and said, "God, be merciful to me a sinner."

Finally, notice the contrast in the results of the two prayers. Jesus said the tax collector went home justified, forgiven, but not the Pharisee.

What is my motive, my manner of prayer? Are my prayers sincere? Meaningful? Fruit-bearing? It is so easy for us to fall into the same pattern as the Pharisee. Like the Sunday school teacher, who, after giving a splendid lesson on the parable, said to the class, "And now, dear children, let us bow our heads and thank God that we are not like that ugly Pharisee!"

Thought for the day: *In prayer, motive is more important than manner.*

Luke 18:18–30   AUGUST 30

Sell all that you have ... and come, follow me
(v. 22).

The real character of the young man who came to Jesus can be summed up by four statements of contrast:

1. *He was so rich and yet so poor.* We know he was wealthy because the account says "he was very rich." He possibly inherited a vast estate of money, houses, and lands. But in spite of this, he stood as an anxious beggar at the gates of life. Money is incapable of purchasing life's real values; it is powerless to furnish lasting satisfaction to the human soul.

271

2. *He was so good and yet so bad.* When the inquirer asked Jesus how he might gain eternal life, Jesus quoted the Ten Commandments. The young man immediately responded, "All these I have observed from my youth." What a moral, upright gentleman! And yet he committed the greatest sin that any one can commit, and that is to turn his back on Jesus Christ. He was unwilling to put aside the idol of his heart—his possessions—and to follow Jesus.

3. *He was so wise and yet so foolish.* He was wise because he asked an intelligent question. Also, he did the wisest thing possible to find the answer to his question; he went straight to the Author of Life. But then how foolish he was. Having received the answer to his query, he rejected the source of life itself. The height of human folly is to turn one's back on Jesus Christ.

4. *He came so near, but went so far.* He knelt at the Master's feet and talked to Him. He found a way into the very heart of Jesus, for "Jesus looking upon him loved him" (Mark 10:21). But then he decided he could not pay the price, so he turned and walked away sorrowfully. He was on the very doorstep of eternal life but failed to enter in.

Thought for the day: *To reject Christ is folly; to follow Him is wisdom.*

Luke 18:31–43   AUGUST 31

Receive your sight; your faith has made you well (v. 42).

This story of the blind man offers an excellent study in how to have one's needs met by Jesus Christ. It summarizes for us all the necessary ingredients for a saving relationship with Him:

1. *Awareness of need.* The condition of the supplicant was apparent to all. He was both blind and poor, sitting as a lonely beggar at the side of the road. What a picture of utter

helplessness! But the man was conscious of his condition and open to even the slightest ray of hope.

2. *Seizure of opportunity.* When the blind man heard that it was Jesus who was passing by, he realized that here was a chance that came only once in a lifetime. So he cried out for help.

3. *Earnest persistence.* To the people listening to Jesus' teaching, the uproar was a nuisance, so they tried to silence the beggar. But he shouted all the more. Though his sight was defective, his lungs were not, and he used them to good advantage.

4. *Sense of urgency.* When the blind man heard that Christ wanted to see him, he threw aside his cloak, sprang to his feet, and came to Jesus. He realized that he had no time to delay.

5. *Acknowledgment of Christ's lordship.* The supplicant addressed Jesus as "Son of David" (Messiah) and "Lord." He recognized that Jesus was more than an unusual teacher or great prophet.

6. *Direct and emphatic request.* When Jesus asked the supplicant what he desired, he quickly responded, "Let me receive my sight." Jesus already knew what the man needed, but He wanted him to make his own confession.

7. *Sincere faith.* The blind man had faith in the willingness and ability of Christ to restore his sight. When Jesus perceived this, He said, "Receive your sight; your faith has made you well."

8. *Grateful discipleship.* As soon as the man received his sight, with a grateful and joyful heart, "he followed Jesus in the way."

Thought for the day: *When the persistent seeker and the compassionate Savior meet, there is salvation.*

Luke 19:1–10   **SEPTEMBER 1**

Today salvation has come to this house (v. 9).

273

This is the story of a little man, a crucial day, and a great salvation.

Luke tells us several things about the man Zacchaeus. First, he was *short of stature*—a physical fact of no particular significance except that it made it difficult for Zacchaeus to see anyone in a crowd. Again, he was a *wealthy* man —an economic fact, slightly more important, because he had accumulated his wealth by fraud and extortion. As a result, Zacchaeus was a *despised* person—a social fact that brought the contempt of others and loss of self-respect. Nobody liked Zacchaeus, and he knew it. Finally, most important of all, he was a *sinner*. He had gone the way of sharp bargaining, greed, and oppression, and was condemned by all. No doubt Zacchaeus felt lonely and despised, and was dissatisfied with his life.

Then came the crucial day. Jesus, noted as "the friend of sinners," was passing through town. This was the chance of a lifetime for Zacchaeus. He was determined to see Jesus. So he ran ahead and climbed a sycamore tree. When Jesus approached, he looked up and called out, "Zacchaeus, come down; I want to come to your house today." Zacchaeus would have been satisfied with a glimpse of Jesus, but Jesus wanted to come to Zacchaeus' house and spend time with him.

What was the response of Zacchaeus? He made haste (urgency); he came down from the tree (obedience); and he welcomed Jesus gladly. Later in the day he declared his willingness to make full restitution for all his dishonesty—a true sign of repentance.

The result? Jesus said, "Today salvation has come to this house!" A great salvation indeed, for it completely changed the life of this despised and miserable tax collector, Zacchaeus.

This account begins by stating that Zacchaeus "sought to see" Jesus, and it ends by announcing that "the Son of man came to seek and to save the lost."

Thought for the day: *A seeking sinner plus the seeking Savior equals salvation.*

Luke 19:11–27   SEPTEMBER 2

Trade with these till I come (v. 13).

This parable is essentially the same as the parable of the talents recorded in Matthew's Gospel (25:14–30), but there is one slight difference in the details. In the Matthew account, the employer gave varying sums of money to each servant, while in the Lukan version, the nobleman gave the same amount to each one. The parable of the talents teaches us that while abilities and opportunities for serving Christ may differ, those who are equally faithful will receive equal rewards. The parable of the pounds tells us that when abilities and opportunities are the same, greater faithfulness will receive greater reward.

We learn two important principles from this parable:

1. *Use what you have, or you will lose it.* The nobleman reprimanded the servant who took his money, wrapped it in a napkin, and hid it. He didn't condemn the servant because he failed to show a profit of ten or five (as two of the other servants did), but because he made no profit whatsoever. We can infer from the words of the nobleman that if the servant had increased his pound by even one, his master would have been satisfied. But he did nothing and made nothing. So the nobleman commanded, "Take the pound from him." If we don't use the opportunities, the gifts and abilities that we have, they will be taken from us. *Use or lose*—that's the way it works.

2. *If we use what we have, more will be given to us.* The nobleman commanded the other servants to take the one *mina* from the unprofitable servant and give it to the man who had made ten pounds. Then Jesus commented, "To every one who has will more be given." It is a rule of life that when we use the gift that God has given us, it will become even

more effective; when we use the opportunity we have, God will entrust us with greater responsibilities.

Thought for the day: *Don't freeze your possessions; multiply them.*

Luke 19:28–40

The Lord has need of it (v. 31).

"The Lord has need of it" evidently was sufficient grounds for the disciples to untie the colt and bring it to Jesus. Note that there seems to have been no reluctance on the part of the owner to comply with the request.

Christ is still in need of instruments, especially human instruments, in order to carry out his mission in the world. As someone has said, "Christ alone can save the world, but Christ cannot save the world alone." He has chosen to work through people.

Our Lord looked down and saw a promising young civil engineer on the campus of the University of Cincinnati, and said, "I need this young man." So Earl Arnett Seamands gave up his selfish ambitions and went to India, where he built over 175 village churches. Our Lord looked down and saw a humble preacher boy from the hills of North Carolina, and said, "I need this young preacher." As a result, Billy Graham has preached to millions of people across the world and led countless numbers to faith in Jesus Christ. Our Lord looked down and saw a young girl with a beautiful and exciting voice, and said, "I need her." And so Sandi Patti has blessed hundreds of thousands of people with her Spirit-filled music. Our Lord looked down and saw a young preacher with a great heart of compassion for young people, and said, "I need such a man." So David Wilkerson left his pastorate and went to work among teen-age gangs on the streets of New York.

A doctor traveling along a highway suddenly came upon the scene of a tragic accident. He stopped to minister to the driver of the car who was lying in a pool of blood in the ditch. He tried his best to save the man's life but failed. For a long time after that the doctor kept saying to himself. "If only I had had my instruments with me, I could have saved his life."

Thought for the day: *Christ needs me and the world needs me.*

Luke 19:41–48   SEPTEMBER 4

When he drew near and saw the city he wept over it (v. 41).

Luke tells us that Jesus wept over the city of Jerusalem. Does He also weep over the cities of the world today—New York, Chicago, Los Angeles, Bombay, London, and Bangkok? I believe He does.

I believe that Jesus weeps over *the poverty* in our cities, with people living in substandard conditions in the ghettos and slums. His heart aches when He sees ten to twelve persons jammed into one small hut, with no facilities for water or sanitation. I believe Jesus weeps over *the crime* in our cities, where gang wars prevail, muggings are frequent, and life is cheap. And His heart is broken by *the sins* of the city dwellers—pornographic bookstores, x-rated movies, topless bars, prostitution, and drugs.

We have allowed the devil to take over our metropolitan areas. In many cities across the world, Christian churches have pulled out of downtown sections and fled to the suburbs, allowing the heart of the city to become a cesspool of crime and vice. This is tragic. We are going to have to tackle the citadels of evil afresh.

In years past, the church has been definitely rural-oriented. This was proper at the time, for the majority of people lived in villages and small towns. But the situation is different now. Concentrations of people are in the cities. Furthermore, it is in the cities that political and economic power resides and where major decisions affecting the nations are made. Cities set the pace for society. All the fads, fashions, and new lifestyles originate in the city and then spread out to the countryside. As spokes in a wheel lead to the hub, so all roads lead to urban centers. Cultural centers, skyscrapers, mass media for communication, and the majority of leaders are all in the city. The church around the world will now have to become more urban-oriented in its thinking and planning, if it is to win the world for Christ.

Thought for the day: *Jesus is weeping while people are sleeping.*

Luke 20:1–18   SEPTEMBER 5

What then will the owner of the vineyard do to them? (v. 15)

The parable of the cruel vinedressers dramatically portrays both the patience and the judgment of God. In love he sent messenger after messenger, prophet after prophet, and eventually His own Son, seeking for the fruit of righteousness in the lives of His chosen people. God did not give up after the first attempt; he gave Israel chance after chance to repent and change its ways. But in each case, the response was the same. The people persecuted and killed the prophets, and then rejected and crucified the Son of God. Finally, patience gave way to judgment and Israel's place was given over to the Gentiles.

We can trace the patience and judgment of God operating in our lives today. He sends person after person into our lives to remind us of His love and offer of salvation. That person may be a parent, friend, pastor, TV evangelist, or even a stranger. God gives us opportunity after opportunity to repent and turn to the Savior. But if we reject His overtures of love and persist in our sins, one day we will have to face the judgment.

A number of years ago a young man in England, who was about to drown in the River Thames, was rescued by a stranger who happened to pass that way and hear his cry for help. A few years later that same young man was arrested on a charge of murder and condemned to die. When the verdict was announced in the courtroom, the prisoner rushed up to the judge and said, "Your Honor, don't you remember me? I am the one you saved from drowning a few years ago. Now you are sending me to my death. Is this fair?" The judge replied, "Young man, that day I was your savior; today I am your judge."

If we don't accept Christ as Savior today, one day we will have to stand before Him as Judge of the universe.

Thought for the day: *Better to receive Christ as Savior than to meet Him as Judge.*

Luke 20:19–26   SEPTEMBER 6

Render . . . to God the things that are God's (v. 25).

In our day few question the obligation to pay taxes to the government. If a person lives in a state and enjoys the protection and privileges of it, he should be willing to support the state. But Jesus would remind us that we also have an obligation to God—that we should render to God the things that are His.

We should render to God our *worship*. He is the Sovereign Lord, the Creator and Redeemer, and is worthy of our praise. On Sunday our place is in the Lord's house with the Lord's people, singing His praises and listening to His Word. In actuality, however, only a small percentage of the American people is in church on Sunday. Forty-three percent of the population don't belong to any church, while two-thirds of the church members don't attend church regularly. They are on the highway, or in the parks, or at home watching television. We are not giving to God the worship that is due Him.

We should also render to God our *tithes*. He is Creator and Owner of all things. We are merely tenants or stewards of what He has placed in our hands to be used for His glory and the welfare of others.

Then again, we should render to God our *obedience*. We should uphold His standards of righteousness and morality; we should accept His lordship and plan for our lives. But millions of Americans are trampling His commandments underfoot and doing their own thing. They are living as if there were no God and certainly no absolutes.

It is time for the American people to take spiritual inventory and start rendering to God the things that rightfully belong to Him.

Thought for the day: *It is more serious to rob God than to rob the government.*

Luke 20:41–47   **SEPTEMBER 7**

David ... calls him Lord; so how is he his son?
(v. 44)

The supreme question in the Christian faith concerns the person of Christ. Is He to be regarded as man or God, or at once God and man? Where is He to be placed in the scale of being?

Among the Jews the most popular title of the Messiah was "Son of David." That is what the blind man at Jericho called Jesus (Luke 18:38, 39), and that is how the crowds addressed him at his entry into Jerusalem (Matt. 21:9). The popular idea of the Messiah was that under Him the throne of David and the golden age of Israel would be restored. Thus it was a dream of political power.

In this passage of Scripture Jesus reminds His hearers that David himself in the Psalms spoke of the Messiah as his

Lord. This means that the Messiah is more than just the son of David; He is Lord. He is more than a human person; He is divine. So here we have one of the clearest claims of Jesus to be the divine Savior of the world that we find in all the four Gospels. The ideal Man is also the incarnate God.

This claim to deity is not something that the followers of Jesus have concocted on His behalf, but is something that Jesus claimed for Himself. In many different ways He declared His divine nature. He said, "I am the light of the world." "I am the bread of life" "I am the way, the truth, and the life." "I am the resurrection and the authority to judge the world." These are indeed fantastic claims.

If Christ is not all that He claims to be, then nothing matters. We can brush Him aside and forget Him. But if He *is* all that He claims to be, then nothing *else* matters. We are face-to-face with Christ; He is on our hands; and we must ask the all-important question: What shall I do with Jesus who is called Christ?

Thought for the day: *Jesus is Lord!*

Luke 21:1–4   SEPTEMBER 8

This poor widow has put in more than all of them (v. 3).

Well do I remember an incident that happened back in the '30s, in the days of the Depression. I was a budding young preacher, struggling to make both ends meet. One Sunday afternoon in a town in Illinois, I preached to a small group of people in a rented hall. After the message, the lay leader said to the congregation, "If you would like to express your appreciation to Brother Seamands, after the benediction slip a gift into his hand." One man gave me a ten-dollar bill, which in those days was a good sum of money. Needless to say, I was delighted. But I was almost moved to tears, when a shabbily dressed, elderly woman untied a knot in a dirty

281

handkerchief and handed me four pennies. I kept them safely in a small tin box just to remind me that God does not look at the amount, but at the motive of the gift.

William Barclay reminds us that two things determine the value of any gift. First, there is *the spirit in which it is given.* A gift which is made grudgingly, or out of a sense of duty, or for the sake of self-display, loses much of its value. The only real gift is that which is given spontaneously and cheerfully, out of the overflow of a loving heart. Then there is *the sacrifice which is involved* in the gift. Some gifts may be large, but they are given out of vast resources, and do not cost the giver anything. Other gifts may be small, but they are given out of meager resources—yes, even out of poverty—and with a good deal of self-denial or sacrifice. In God's sight such gifts have the greater value. A gift shows our love only when we ourselves have had to do without something, or have had to work doubly hard in order to get it.

Thought for the day: *We can best measure our offerings, not by how much we give, but by how much we keep.*

Luke 21:5–19   SEPTEMBER 9

This will be a time for you to bear testimony (v. 13).

The Christian is one who can turn calamity into opportunity. Jesus warned His disciples that severe persecution lay ahead. They would be dragged before high priests, governors, and kings and would be cast into prison. "But," said Jesus, "all this will be a time for you to bear witness for me." And He further encouraged the disciples by promising them that in the hour of testing He would give them "a mouth and wisdom, which none of your adversaries will be able to withstand or contradict." So they were to turn prisons into pulpits, trials into testimony, and persecution into proclamation.

The book of Acts is a record of the fulfillment of Jesus' prophecy and promise in the ministry of the apostles. When

Peter and John were put on trail before Annas the high priest in Jerusalem, they took the opportunity boldly to proclaim Jesus Christ as Savior and risen Lord. When Paul was made to stand before Governor Felix and King Agrippa, he seized the opportunity to tell them the story of his conversion and to declare Jesus as the Anointed One of God. While he was in prison in Rome, he witnessed to his guards and wrote letters to his converts.

While riding to school one day, a Chinese Christian came upon the scene of an accident. Someone had run over a little girl with his bicycle and sped on his way. The Christian stopped to minister to the wounded girl, but just then the police came along and jumped to the conclusion that it was he who had caused the accident. So they threw him into jail for a week. Feeling sorry for himself, he began to complain to God, but an inner voice said, "You have often prayed for these prisoners. Now is your opportunity. Get up and witness to them." Before his release, the Christian student had won several of the inmates to faith in Jesus Christ.

Thought for the day: *Opposition becomes opportunity when Jesus is near.*

Luke 21:20–28 SEPTEMBER 10

They will see the Son of man coming in a cloud with power and great glory (v. 27).

Both the Old and New Testaments are filled with promises of the Second Coming of Christ. There are 1,845 references to it in the Old Testament, and a total of seventeen Old Testament books give it prominence. Of the 260 chapters in the entire New Testament, there are 318 references to the Second Coming, or one out of every thirty verses. Twenty-three of the twenty-seven New Testament books refer to this great event. Paul mentions it fifty times. For every prophecy on the First Coming of Christ in the Bible, there are eight on His Second Coming.

When we look across the world, our hearts are filled with fear and dismay. All around we see injustice and oppression, crime and abuse, poverty and pain, terrorism and war. We see nations rise and fall, institutions change and crumble. We wonder if there is anything really unchanging, dependable, and secure. And then we hear the voice of Jesus saying, "When these things begin to take place, look up and raise your heads because your redemption is drawing near." To the Christian there *is* an unchanging Lord and an unshakable kingdom.

Evil people and evil institutions may seem to flourish for awhile, but God will have the last word in history. One day He will return to earth with His big ring of keys and say to humanity, "Ladies and gentlemen, it is closing time." Yes, closing time for injustice, oppression, and war; closing time for crime and drugs and all forms of evil. God will establish His kingdom of righteousness and peace, and He will reign forever and ever. Then the Utopia for which we have prayed and long hoped for will become a reality.

When Neil Armstrong landed on the moon, it is estimated that one billion people were watching. When Christ returns to earth, "every eye will see him."

Thought for the day: *Look around and lose heart; look up and find hope.*

Luke 21:29–38   SEPTEMBER 11

Heaven and earth will pass away, but my words will not pass away (v. 33).

The words of Jesus will never pass away because they constitute the *truth, eternal truth*. They are truth because He Himself *is* the truth. His words will never die, they will never be out of print. His words will always be up-to-date and relevant for every generation.

Down through the centuries people have tried to discredit the words of Jesus and have even attempted to destroy the Bible itself. But today more Bibles are being printed in more languages than ever before in history.

Voltaire, the eighteenth-century French philosopher, once predicted in public that the Bible would soon be discarded and forgotten. But after his death, the very house in which he lived in Paris became a center for the British and Foreign Bible Society.

When Mao Tse-tung was chairman of the Communist Party in the People's Republic of China, his picture and statue appeared all across the country. His words and teachings were published in a little Red Book and distributed all over China and throughout Southeast Asia. Millions and millions of copies were printed. The Communists boasted that the Red Book was the best seller in all history. But today Chairman Mao has been discredited by his own people, his statues have been torn down. The little Red Book is out of print, and his words are discredited and forgotten.

During the so-called Cultural Revolution, sponsored by Chairman Mao, the Red Guards burned Bibles by the thousands and tried to wipe out the Christian church. But the words of Jesus reached into the homes of China by radio from the Far East Broadcasting Company in Manila. Today there are more Chinese Christians than ever before in history. A new modern press built by the Amity Foundation in Beijing now publishes Chinese Bibles by the hundreds of thousands.

Thought for the day: *Yes, heaven and earth may pass away, but the words of Jesus will live forever.*

Luke 22:1–13   **SEPTEMBER 12**

Satan entered into Judas called Iscariot (v. 3).

The story of Judas is a warning to all of us. It reminds us that it is possible for a person, who was once a disciple of Jesus, to turn his back on the Lord and go out into eternal darkness.

Judas had a good start. When he heard the call of the Master, like the others, he forsook all—home, family, and business—and followed Jesus. He had the same opportunities as the rest of the disciples. He heard the marvelous teaching of Jesus, observed his sinless life, and witnessed every miracle he performed. Along with the other disciples, Judas was given authority over demonic spirits and commissioned to preach the kingdom of God and heal all diseases. His name, Jesus said, was written in the Lamb's Book of Life.

Then something happened in the heart and mind of Judas. It didn't happen suddenly; it was a gradual apostasy over a period of time. Certain sinful desires, over which Judas never gained full control, began to surface and develop. One was his love for money. John, in his Gospel, tells us that Judas was a thief and stole from the disciples' common treasury. In the end his avarice drove him to the place where he was willing to barter his Lord for thirty pieces of silver. The other sin in his life was unholy ambition. When he saw the power and wisdom of Christ, he dreamed of the restoration of the kingdom of Israel and a prominent position for himself. But when it became increasingly clear that Jesus' kingdom was not a worldly kingdom, Judas became disillusioned and resentful, and decided to betray his Master to the enemy.

And then came the climax. Satan entered into Judas. No doubt Satan could not have done so if Judas had not opened the door. There is no handle on the outside of the human heart. It must be opened from within. What a tragic ending to a life that was so full of promise!

Thought for the day: *The road to hell is gradual and silent.*

He took bread ... broke it and gave it to them,
saying, "This is my body" (v. 19).

The broken bread was a symbol of the broken body of
Christ on the cross. Our salvation was possible only through a
broken Savior.

In Gethsemane His will was broken when He prayed in
agony, "Not my will but thine be done." On Calvary His body
was broken when they drove the nails into His hands and feet.
In the hour of death, His fellowship with the Father was broken
when he cried in torment, "My God, my God, why have you
forsaken me?" He who was our Substitute and who was made
sin for us had to take upon Himself the proud, unbroken ego
of fallen humanity, and had to be broken at Calvary in
humanity's place. That is the hidden meaning of the words of
the Master: "This is my body which is *broken* for you."

We as sinners also need to be broken. When we look at
the broken Savior on the cross, and then realize the depth of
our own sinfulness, our hearts are broken in true humility and
repentance. The proud, self-justifying, self-reliant self has to
come as a lost, undone sinner whose only hope is a justifying
Savior. David had it right when, at the supreme moment of his
own total brokenness, he cried out from the depths of his
heart, "The sacrifice acceptable to God is a *broken* spirit; a
broken and contrite heart, O God, thou wilt not despise" (Ps.
51:17).

We as believers or disciples also need to be broken.
Immediately after Jesus had spoken of His broken body, His
disciples began to argue about who was the greatest among
them. They were proud and self-seeking, and therefore unfit
for service. If it is true that Christ had to be broken to make
possible the salvation of the world, it is just as true that we
must be broken to make this salvation *actual* in the hearts of
people. The cross is not only the provision for sin; it is also the
pattern for service.

There is no redemption apart from the broken Savior. There is no forgiveness apart from the broken sinner. And there is no blessing apart from the broken believer.

Thought for the day: *Brokenness leads to wholeness and usefulness.*

Luke 22:28–38   **SEPTEMBER 14**

Simon, Simon, indeed Satan has asked for you, that he may sift you as wheat, but I have prayed for you (vv. 31–32, NEB).

This verse implies that there is not merely one sifting, but two distinct siftings. One is Satan's; the other is Christ's. One is destructive, the other constructive. One is for the purpose of blighting, the other for the purpose of blessing. When Satan has done his sifting, no wheat will be left; nothing but chaff. When Christ has done His sifting, no chaff will be left; nothing but clean, pure grain. Satan wants people to make them his tools; Christ wants people to make them his instruments.

A beggar, ragged and dirty, came one night to Dante Gabriel Rosetti's home. He laid some sketches down on the table and asked the artist, "Tell me, sir, what do you think of these?" With one swift glance Rosetti answered, "They are excellent. Who drew these?" No answer. The old man laid another group of sketches on the table and asked a second time, "What do you think of these?" "Very inferior," was the reply. "Who drew these?" The old man was silent for a moment, then said, "I am the author of both sets of sketches. The first set I drew many years ago. These others I tried to draw the other day." And then almost in terror he continued, "Sir, these represent what I might have been. These others represent what I have come to be." A genius had gone down through drink. He had fallen into Satan's sifter and gone through.

Peter fell into Satan's sifter for a brief while and got into serious trouble, but then repented and came back to his Lord. Christ put Peter into His sifter at Pentecost and through the fire of the Holy Spirit burned up all the chaff and left only the pure wheat. Peter became God's chosen instrument to interpret Pentecost to the crowd in Jerusalem, to the believers in Samaria, and to the household of Cornelius. He became the author of two of the most beautiful and precious letters of the New Testament.

Thought for the day: *Better to be an instrument of Christ than a tool of Satan.*

Luke 22:39–53 SEPTEMBER 15

When he rose from prayer, he came to the disciples and found them sleeping (v. 45).

We note in this passage two distinct patterns of prayer life—that of our Lord and that of the disciples. Jesus had a regular and consistent prayer life. It was natural for Him to lift His voice in prayer to His heavenly Father, in any place and at any time. Sometimes He rose early in the morning and prayed. Sometimes He prayed all night. He often withdrew from the crowds to some quiet place, in order to commune with the Father and be strengthened in the inner man. Before every major decision, He sought the Father's will through prayer. Now we see Jesus on the Mount of Olives, agonizing in prayer just before His arrest and crucifixion. And because He prayed, He was able to face the grueling trial and agony of the cross triumphantly.

Then we note the irregular and inconsistent prayer life of the disciples. In the gospel narratives we find no references to their praying on any particular occasion. In fact, as we pointed out previously, every time the disciples were supposed to be praying, they were sleeping. Here in Gethsemane we have the classic example of this. While Jesus was spending several hours in agonizing prayer, the disciples were fast asleep. If ever they needed to pray, it was at that moment just before the storm broke. And because they failed to pray, they were overwhelmed by temptation and suffered a crushing defeat.

Paderewski, the famous concert pianist, said that if he failed to practice for just one day, he could tell the difference in his playing. If he neglected to practice for two days in a row, the experts could see the difference; three days, and the whole audience would know. In the same way, if we fail to pray one day, we can tell the difference in our lives; two days, and our family members will see the difference; three days, and everyone will notice the change.

A person's prayer life, to be effective, must be consistent, habitual.

Thought for the day: *Get on your knees; then stand on your feet.*

Luke 22:54–71

When they had kindled a fire . . . Peter sat among them (v. 55).

If we take this passage of Scripture and add it to the second chapter of Acts, we will discover three interesting vignettes in the life of Peter.

The first is that of Peter *near the fire.* When Jesus was arrested and brought into the high priest's house, Peter followed at a distance and entered into the courtyard. In so doing he exhibited both courage and fear. Evidently he was apprehensive of being found too close to Jesus and His accusers so he stayed back with the fringe of the crowd and followed at a distance. But at the same time he had enough courage to enter into the courtyard. The rest of the disciples had all fled and taken refuge in their homes. Some of the servants of the household had built a fire in the middle of the courtyard so Peter joined them and warmed himself by the fire.

The second picture is that of Peter *in the fire*. He soon got into trouble. Just a few hours earlier he had boasted before his Master that he was ready to follow Him to prison and even to death. But then when a maid and two other servants confronted him and said, "You are one of Jesus' followers," Peter vehemently denied the charge three times. Next we are told that "the Lord turned and looked at Peter." Something in that look must have pierced that very soul of Peter, for he immediately "went out and wept bitterly."

In the third vignette we see Peter *on fire*. After Christ's resurrection, Peter was reconciled to his Lord, and was later present in the Upper Room on the Day of Pentecost. He was no longer the cowardly, fearful Peter. Now filled with the Holy Spirit, he boldly proclaimed Christ to the multitudes in Jerusalem. He became the interpreter of Pentecost to the new Christians in Samaria and to the household of Cornelius. Today we remember Peter not so much for his denial but for his faithful leadership in the early church.

Thought for the day: *God can pluck us out of the ashes and set us on fire.*

Luke 23:1–17   SEPTEMBER 17

Herod . . . had long desired to see [Jesus] . . . hoping to see some sign done by him (v. 8).

People desire to see Jesus for different reasons; sometimes for diametrically opposite reasons.

At the time of Jesus' birth, wise men from the East came to Jerusalem asking, "Where is he who has been born king of the Jews . . . We . . . have come to worship him." King Herod told them, "Go and search diligently for the child, and when you have found him bring me word, that *I too may come and worship him.*" Now the wise men and King Herod said exactly the same thing, but with opposite motives. The wise

291

men actually went and worshiped the Christ child, but Herod wanted to learn of His whereabouts so that he might kill Him.

In the same way, we see a difference in the reasons Zacchaeus and Herod desired to see Jesus. (This Herod is not the same one who ruled at the time of Jesus' birth.) Zacchaeus had heard much about Jesus and "sought to see who [he] was" (19:3). Realizing his sincerity, Jesus spoke to him tenderly and went home with him for a visit. At the end of the day, Jesus was able to say to him, "Today salvation has come to this house." So Zacchaeus saw Jesus and his life was changed.

Herod the tetrarch, on the other hand, desired to see Jesus merely out of curiosity. He had heard much about the miracles of Jesus, and was hoping that Jesus would perform one of his "magic tricks" to entertain him. But Jesus, seeing through his motive, refused to speak even a word in his presence. So Herod with his soldiers treated Him with contempt and mocked Him. He refused to take Jesus seriously and treated Him as a joke.

The only way to come to Jesus is with sincerity and humility, recognizing Him for who He is—Savior and Lord— and then kneeling at his feet to worship Him in spirit and in truth.

Thought for the day: *Our reason for seeing Jesus will determine the result of meeting him.*

Luke 23:18–31   SEPTEMBER 18

I have found in him no crime deserving death (v. 22).

The chief priests of the Jews accused Jesus of blasphemy, because He claimed to be the Son of God. For such a heinous crime they demanded that Jesus should die, but the death penalty could be pronounced only by the Roman governor. So they brought Jesus before Pilate. The Jewish rulers knew that the charge of blasphemy would find no sympathy with the governor so they fabricated three political charges. They accused Jesus of being a revolutionary, with inciting people not to pay taxes to Caesar, and with claiming to be a king.

When Pilate examined Jesus carefully, he found Him innocent of all charges. Three times he declared that he found no crime in Him (vv. 4, 14, 22). Herod also found no fault in Him (v. 15). Note further that the penitent thief on the cross said of Jesus, "This man has done nothing wrong" (v. 41). Even the Roman centurion who carried out the crucifixion testified, "Certainly this man was innocent!" (v. 47)

A remarkable movie on the life of Christ attracts large crowds in India these days. Entitled "Man of Mercy," it was produced by a Hindu director with an all-Indian cast. The scene of the crucifixion always evokes a strong emotional response from the audience. Many moan and weep when they see Jesus dying on the cross. In one village where the movie was shown, when it came to the crucifixion event, a man jumped up, ran up to the screen and with frantic gestures shouted, "Don't do that. This man is innocent. You've got the wrong person."

Yes, all have declared that Jesus was innocent and the cross was a travesty of justice. Why, then, was He crucified? Herein lies the very essence of the Gospel. A sinner, a guilty person, could not have become the Savior of sinners. Only the innocent, sinless God-man could take our place and die for our sins. His life was not taken from Him; he voluntarily laid down His life on our behalf. He turned the injustice and tragedy of the cross into our redemption.

Thought for the day: *The cross was not a* human tragedy, *but a* divine triumph.

Luke 23:32–43   SEPTEMBER 19

There they crucified [Jesus], and the criminals, one on the right and one on the left (v. 33).

Three crosses and three men. But what a difference between Jesus and the other two.

On the middle cross, the *cross of redemption*, Jesus died *for our sins*. The two men at His side were guilty criminals being punished for their sins. They were mortals, subject to death at one time or another. Jesus on the other hand, was sinless, innocent of any wrongdoing. Moreover, He was more than just a human being; He was the divine Son of God. He was therefore immortal, not subject to death. But he voluntarily laid down His life for the sins of the world. He took our sins upon Himself and died in our place.

The second cross was the *cross of repentance*, where one of the criminals died *to his sin*. He watched carefully how Jesus conducted Himself in the hour of death. He listened to every word He spoke. He heard Jesus cry out, "Father, forgive them; for they know not what they do." And suddenly a change took place in the heart of this hardened criminal. He repented, confessed his sin, and asked the Lord to remember him when He entered into His kingdom. Jesus, in his dying moment, said to him, "Today you will be with me in Paradise." He died as a redeemed sinner.

The third cross was the *cross of retribution*, where the other criminal died *in his sins*. He, too, saw all that Jesus did, and heard every word He spoke on the cross, but instead of repenting for his sins and asking for mercy, he hardened his heart and cursed Jesus like the rest of the mob. And with the Savior of the world dying at his side, this criminal died as a sinner, unforgiven, unredeemed.

Today the middle cross is our only hope. But the big question is: On which side of the cross are you and I? On the side of repentance and redemption? Or on the side of impenitence and retribution?

Thought for the day: *My sin is either on Christ or on me.*

Certainly this man was innocent! (v. 47)

The death of Christ was an event of such cosmic significance that it affected all people and all history.

Nature itself reacted to His death. The sun hid its face and darkness covered the whole land for three hours—a fit symbol of the blackest crime in the history of humankind. Though men and women did not tremble for their sins, the earth shook beneath the load. Tombs were opened and saints walked about in the city, signifying that Christ had destroyed the power of death (Matt. 27:51-53).

Christ's death had an impact upon the religious world also. It brought an end to the age of law and ushered in the era of grace. The veil of the temple, which had covered the Holy of Holies, was rent from top to bottom, making it possible for sinners to enter directly into the presence of God for forgiveness and cleansing.

The Roman centurion, who personally directed the crucifixion, was so moved by the death of Christ that he glorified God and testified that the One whom he had crucified as a criminal was indeed a righteous man. Possibly he represented that vast host of believing Gentiles that was yet to enlist under the banner of the cross.

The mob of common people, who had been hounded by their rulers to cry out for Christ's death, were so disturbed by the shameful and tragic turn of events, that they returned to the city, "beating their breasts" in an agony of remorse. A few days hence many of these same people would respond to the preaching of Peter on the day of Pentecost and become the first members of the Christian church.

The last group around the cross consisted of those saddened disciples who "stood at a distance" and gazed in bewilderment upon the scene. But in only two days their sorrow would be turned into joy and they would begin to understand the significance of all that had taken place. The cross would no longer be the symbol of defeat, but of victory.

Thought for the day: *The cross is the pivotal event of all history.*

Luke 24:1–12   SEPTEMBER 21

Why do you seek the living among the dead? (v. 5)

An Indian evangelist was preaching in the market place of a village when a Muslim stepped out of the crowd and interrupted him, saying, "We Muslims have something in our religion that you Christians don't have." "What is it?" asked the preacher. "When we go to Arabia," explained the Muslim, "we can stand at the tomb of Mohammed and say with confidence, 'Here lies the body of our prophet.' But you Christians have no tomb at which you can worship." With a smile the evangelist quickly replied, "Thank God, we Christians have no tomb because we have no corpse!"

As Christians we do not worship a dead body, but a Living Lord. All human graves are respected for their *tenancy*. Someone stands by a particular grave and says, "Here lies the body of my loved one or friend." But Christ's tomb is respected for its *vacancy*. As the angel at the tomb announced, "He is not here; He is risen." And because Christ is *not here* in the tomb, therefore He is *everywhere*. He is our eternal contemporary. Because He is not in the grave, He is with us in the office, in the school, in the factory, in the home, in the shop. He is with us wherever we go.

Since Christ is alive, He is more than just history; He is news. Suppose you picked up the newspaper tomorrow morning and read the headline, "President Kennedy Assassinated." You would say to yourself, "That's not news; that's history." But supposing you read the headline, "Christ Died for Our Sins." Even though He was crucified almost 2000 years ago, it would still be up-to-date news. And it would be good news, the most important news any day, any year, any century!

Through the Resurrection, Christ stands today as Victor over Satan, sin, and the grave. And because He has triumphed, we shall also triumph.

Thought for the day: *As Christians we work, not to the victory, but from the victory.*

Luke 24:13–32   **SEPTEMBER 22**

Their eyes were opened and they recognized him (v. 31).

Luke is the only one who gives us this fascinating post-resurrection story. Several details stand out and demand our attention.

While the two disciples were walking from Jerusalem toward Emmaus, Jesus suddenly appeared and walked along with them. But they were so blinded by discouragement and sadness that they could not recognize who He was. The One on whom they had set their hopes for the redemption of Israel had been shamefully crucified on a cross. True, He had mentioned something about returning to life on the third day, but it was now approaching evening of the third day and still there was no sign of him.

Two things helped to open the eyes of the disciples. First, when Jesus opened up the Scriptures and helped them to see God's hand and purpose in all the recent events in Jerusalem, their hearts burned within them. Then when they sat at the table together in Emmaus and Jesus broke bread, blessed it, and gave it to them, their eyes were finally opened and they recognized Him as their Lord.

No story tells us more impressively the truth that the Savior walks with us all the way of our earthly journey. It is pathetic, however, that our eyes are so often dimmed by unbelief that we fail to realize His presence. We walk and are sad while we could be rejoicing in His companionship. When circumstances are good and things are going smoothly, it is easy for us to feel that Jesus is near. But when circumstances change and we are confronted by loss, sickness, or even death, we begin to wonder where Jesus is. Yet all the time He is close by our side.

Jesus not only walks with us today, he also instructs us out of the Scriptures so that the events of life take on new meaning. He enters into our homes and brings rich blessings as He breaks to us the bread of life. He is the divine Companion, Teacher, and Host.

Thought for the day: *The presence of Jesus turns sadness into gladness.*

Luke 24:33–43 SEPTEMBER 23

They told what had happened on the road (v. 35).

Mission is an intrinsic part of the Gospel. As soon as the two Emmaus Road disciples recognized that it was the risen Lord who sat at the table with them, they returned to Jerusalem to tell the good news, impelled by a sense of urgency. Luke writes that "they rose *that same hour*" and returned to the city. Notice that they had just walked from Jerusalem to Emmaus, a distance of seven miles so the round trip would make a total of fourteen miles for the day. Besides, night was already upon them when they started out. One would think that the two would have waited until morning to make the return journey to Jerusalem. But, no, they couldn't wait. Jesus was alive, and His disciples must be told!

Are we Christians today gripped by the same sense of urgency to tell a lost and dying world that Jesus died and rose again for our redemption? It is estimated that possibly two billion have not yet heard the name of Jesus.

A missionary was preaching to a group of Hindus in a village in India. After the message, a man came up and said,

"Sir, this is a wonderful story you told, of a man who loved us so much that He gave His life for us. How long have you known this story?" he asked.

"All my life," answered the missionary.

"And what about your father, and grandfather?" the Hindu asked. "Did they also know this story?"

"Yes," replied the missionary. "We've known about Jesus for many generations."

A puzzled look came across the man's face. "Sir," he said, "you people have known this story for a long, long time, but I am hearing it for the first time in my life. And I am already an old man. Tell me, sir, where have you been so long? Why have you come so late?"

Thought for the day: *No person has the right to hear the Gospel twice, when others have not heard it even once (J. Oswald Smith).*

Luke 24:44–53   **SEPTEMBER 24**

Tarry in the city of Jerusalem until you are endued with power from on high (v. 49, NKJV).

During His public ministry Jesus spoke three significant words: Come, Tarry, and Go. The first was an invitation to the sinner to come and find rest. The second was an exhortation to the believer to receive the fullness and power of the Holy Spirit. The third was a command to all disciples to go and preach the Gospel to the whole world. Coming without going would be incomplete; going without tarrying would be ineffective.

Notice that Jesus instructed His disciples to tarry *in the city*. The city is the place of congested populations and concentrated problems. It is the place of complex relationships and conflicting responsibilities. It is the place of storm and stress, of tension and temptations. Jesus was trying to show His disciples that the power of the Holy Spirit is adequate for the toughest, most adverse environment. If He can keep us victorious in the large city, He can keep us victorious anywhere.

Jesus also specified that the disciples were to tarry in the *city of Jerusalem*. Why not Jericho, Capernaum, or Nazareth? In the first place, Jerusalem was the scene of the crucifixion. It was there that the Master suffered what seemed to be His greatest defeat. He wanted to demonstrate to His disciples that through the Holy Spirit He would turn the place of greatest tragedy into the place of greatest triumph. In the very city where He had been crucified, He would build His church.

Furthermore, Jerusalem was the place of defeat for the disciples. It was there that they had fled and hidden and denied their Lord. Jesus wanted to show them that the place of their greatest defeat would become the place of their greatest victory. Where they had once scattered like sheep, they would now gather the lost sheep into the Father's fold. And if they could be triumphant in Jerusalem, then victory would be theirs wherever they went.

Thought for the day: *The human spirit fails, unless the Holy Spirit fills.*

John 1:1–18   SEPTEMBER 25

To all who received him, who believed in his name, he gave power to become children of God (v. 12).

Religion places the primary emphasis on *doing*, on *outer conduct*: Do good and you will become good. The Gospel places the primary emphasis on *being*, on *inner character*: be good and then you will do good. But how does this *being* take place? The apostle John makes this clear in verse twelve.

Being is by *becoming*: "To them he gave power to become the children of God." In one sense we are all the children of God by *creation*; we owe to Him our very existence and preservation. But we *become* sons and daughters of God

300

only by re-creation, by spiritual new birth. We must undergo radical transformation in our very inner being so that we become new persons in Christ Jesus. Thus, being is by becoming.

Becoming is by *belonging*: "To all who *received* him." We cannot make ourselves children of God; we have to enter into relationship with His Son. In his first epistle John writes, "He who has the Son has life; he who has not the Son of God has not life" (5:12). When we are born of the Spirit, Christ comes to dwell in us. He takes us over and makes us over. He lives the Christian life through us. So being is by becoming and becoming is by belonging.

Belonging is by *believing*: "To all . . . who believed in his name." We enter into relationship with Christ by putting our trust in Him as Savior, and entrusting ourselves to Him as Lord. Faith is the link that binds us to Christ. Faith is the hand that reaches out and accepts His offer of salvation and eternal life. So being is by becoming, becoming is by belonging, and belonging is by believing.

Am I a child of God today? Have I received Christ into my life and put my trust in His name?

Thought for the day: *We become children of God not by turning over a* new leaf *but by taking on a* new *life.*

John 1:19–34   SEPTEMBER 26

This is he who baptizes with the Holy Spirit (v. 33).

Two baptisms are mentioned in this passage of Scripture: the baptism with water and the baptism with the Holy Spirit. In the first baptism, the agent is the minister of God, the subject is the repenting sinner, and the element is water. Thus, the minister baptizes with water the individual who confesses and forsakes his sins. In the second baptism, the Agent is Christ, the subject is the child of God, and the element is the Holy Spirit. That is, Christ baptizes the believer with the Holy Spirit.

It is a misunderstanding of Scripture that in churches today so much emphasis is placed on the baptism with water while the baptism with the Holy Spirit is almost totally neglected. People are so careful to have their children baptized, or to receive baptism themselves. But many go on through the Christian life year after year without the all-important baptism with the Holy Spirit. They are more concerned that the minister of the church should baptize them than that Christ Himself should administer His baptism.

Several years ago the saintly Bishop J.M. Thoburn of the Methodist Church in India was preaching on the subject of the baptism with the Holy Spirit at a camp meeting in the United States. At the close of the message, he stepped from behind the pulpit and said to the congregation, "Dear Christian friends, I must confess that I am unable to administer this baptism of which I have been speaking. But before the service I was talking to a friend of mine, and He promised to be present and to administer this baptism to any who desire to receive it. That person is the Lord Jesus Christ Himself. He is, here and He can baptize you with the Holy Spirit right now." A large number of people responded to the invitation.

It is Christ's intention to baptize and fill you with the Holy Spirit. Make it your intention today.

Thought for the day: *The baptism with the Holy Spirit is not excess baggage but essential equipment for service.*

John 1:35–42   SEPTEMBER 27

He first found his brother Simon, and ... brought him to Jesus (vv. 41, 42).

Among the disciples of Jesus, Andrew is remembered as the soul winner. He is mentioned three times in the Gospel of John, and each time we find him introducing someone to Jesus.

In this passage of Scripture we note two important factors

in Andrew's preparation for becoming a soul winner. First, he responded wholeheartedly to the witness of John the Baptist, who pointed his finger at Jesus and said, "Behold the Lamb of God." Andrew immediately left everything behind and followed Jesus. He spent the whole day with Him, asking questions, listening to His teaching, and observing Him as a person. Convinced that Jesus was the Messiah, he felt impelled to tell this to someone. So he went to his brother Peter and said, "We have found the Messiah!" Notice, he did not employ theological exhortation or apologetic argument. He did not invite Peter to a religious ceremony. He testified to what he had seen and experienced for himself. He simply said, "We have found the Messiah." And he took him to Jesus.

We next read of Andrew in chapter six, where he brings to Jesus the young lad with the five loaves and two fish. With this meager lunch Jesus was able to feed 5000 hungry people in the wilderness. Then in chapter twelve, when certain Greeks came and said to Philip, "Sir, we wish to see Jesus," Philip wasn't sure what to do. So Andrew, without hesitation, escorted them into the presence of Jesus.

The Christians of China have demonstrated to the world the effectiveness of the personal witness for Christ. When they were driven underground by persecution during the Red Guard movement, they had only one means of witnessing for Christ—quietly as person to person. But the number of Christians in China may be fifty times what it was in 1949.

Thought for the day: *Am I a soul winner or just a breadwinner?*

John 1:43–51   SEPTEMBER 28

Philip found Nathaniel and said to him, "We have found him [the Messiah]" (v. 45).

In yesterday's meditation we saw how Andrew witnessed to his brother, Simon Peter, and brought him to Jesus. Today we see Philip doing the same thing with his friend Nathaniel. Again we are reminded of the responsibility and privilege that we have of witnessing about Christ to others.

Why is it so important to witness to others of our experiences with Christ? Because in so doing, He becomes more real to us. If we don't, His presence becomes dim in our lives. Can light be light without shining? Can a stream be a stream without flowing? Can love be love without manifestation? Likewise, can a Christian remain Christian without Christianizing? If we are not expressing our Christian faith, it will fade out. It may linger as a form, but it will die as a force. It may linger on the edge as a marginal influence, but centrally and fundamentally it will not be a transforming redeeming power. Nothing is really ours unless we share it.

When Dr. Merton S. Rice, the famous preacher, was a pastor in Duluth, a banker was his close friend. He played golf with him on occasion. After Dr. Rice had moved to Detroit the new pastor spoke to the banker about being a Christian and joining the church, to which the banker replied, "Well, if it is as important as you say, then why didn't Dr. Rice, with whom I was so friendly, ever speak to me about it?"

This word was sent on to Dr. Rice, who, when he heard it, took the first train from Detroit to Duluth, went straight to see the banker, fell at his feet and asked him to forgive him for doing him the wrong of never speaking to him about Christ. The banker was won, and so was Dr. Rice! From that time on he became committed to an evangelistic emphasis in his ministry in which he won multitudes to Christ.

Thought for the day: *Witnessing for Christ is not a* problem; *it is a* privilege.

John 2:1–12   SEPTEMBER 29

There was a marriage at Cana in Galilee ... Jesus also was invited (vv. 1, 2).

How significant it is that Jesus began His public ministry and performed His first miracle at a wedding ceremony! It demonstrates that our Lord was no recluse or killjoy. We sometimes think of Jesus as only "the man of sorrows." He was that in the light of the incalculable burden he bore as the world's Redeemer. Yet our Lord must also have been a popular dinner guest, who loved to mingle with people and enjoy their fellowship. That He was often invited into homes, that young children often flocked around Him indicate that he had a pleasant personality. He was no gloomy, morose recluse.

Jesus' presence at a wedding feast rebukes the foolish notion that religion robs life of its joy, or that loyalty to Christ is inconsistent with good times and innocent pleasure. It corrects the false impression that sourness is a sign of sainthood, or that gloom is a condition of godliness. Some religious people are suspicious of all joy and fun. They connect religion with black clothes, the sour face, and the hushed voice. They forget that Jesus came to give us life, yes, life more abundant. The Christian life is one of true joy and gladness.

Then again, the presence of Jesus at a wedding feast was a testimony to the sanctity of marriage. This is something we need to remind ourselves of these days. Many in modern society treat marriage too lightly, even as a joke. We read in the newspapers of people getting married in the strangest places—under water, in a stream, in a balloon basket, on the skating rink, etc. Many people regard marriage as a temporary contract; they walk into it backwards, so they can step out of it any time they like. If more people would take Christ into their courtship, into their marriage and homes, we would have far less divorce today. We need to regain the sanctity and significance of the marriage relationship.

Thought for the day: *Jesus is not a killjoy, He spills joy wherever He goes.*

Many believed in his name ... but Jesus did not trust himself to them because he knew all men (vv. 23, 24, 25).

Some people are genuine believers and some are not. Some people have been attracted by certain things in the ministry of Christ—such as His miracles or teaching—and have yielded to Him a certain superficial allegiance. But the Master knows their inmost hearts and does not respond to them. Faith is more than giving mental assent to the truth. Genuine faith results in action. James writes in his epistle, "Faith by itself, if it has no works, is dead ... Even the demons believe—and shudder" (2:17, 19).

This sounds like an absurd analogy, but we can believe every word in the Bible and yet be eternally lost. We have to act out our faith. Faith is essentially an act of the will— entrusting ourselves to the person of Christ. We believe that the Bible is God's Word, that Jesus died to save sinners, that He can forgive sin—certainly. But that moment comes when our faith looks up to Him and we say in our hearts: "Lord Jesus, I believe you died for *me*. I believe you forgive me *now*. And I entrust my whole life into your keeping; in sickness and in health, in adversity and in prosperity; in sorrow and in joy. I believe you can take me safely through the voyage of life to the other shore." That is faith!

The true test of faith is this: Did something happen in your life? Oh, I don't mean a great burst of emotion, a flash of lightning, or a sudden vision. But was there a real change in your life? Were the springs of your character transformed? Did you come into touch with the living Christ?

The manager of a store saw a boy kicking the candy-vending machine, big tears streaming down his face. "What's the trouble, son?" asked the manager. With a choking voice the boy replied, "I put my money in the machine, but nothing happened!"

That's the trouble. A lot of people profess to believe, but nothing happens. When faith is genuine, something will happen. Our lives will be changed.

Thought for the day: *Faith means: Forsaking-All-I-Take-Him.*

John 3:1–12

Unless one is born of water and the Spirit, he cannot enter the kingdom of God (v. 5).

Here we are face-to-face with the dire necessity of the new birth. Remember, it was Jesus Himself who spoke these words—not the pope, nor the bishop, nor a professor of religion, but the Son of God Himself. He spoke them to a religious person (a Pharisee), a man of authority and prestige (a ruler of the Jews). And Jesus today would say the same thing to everyone in the world: "You must be born again." This is a universal human necessity.

The birth that Jesus is talking about is not physical but spiritual. According to a basic biological principle, like produces like. From the vegetable comes the vegetable. From the animal comes the animal. From the human comes the human. Likewise, from the Spirit comes the spiritual. Physical birth can produce only physical life. It takes a spiritual birth to initiate spiritual life. People, therefore, require two births. They have to be conceived by their parents in order to receive physical life and enter into this world. They must also be conceived by the Spirit of God to receive spiritual life and enter the kingdom of God.

I was talking to a man in India who professed to be a Christian. I asked him, "Are you a born-again Christian?" "Oh yes," he said, "I am." Then he went on to explain. "You see, my grandfather was a Hindu, but he heard of Christ and was converted. So my grandfather was a Christian; therefore, my father was a born Christian, and I am a born-again Christian."

He was serious but dead wrong. For the new birth comes not by physical procreation, but by spiritual regeneration.

The new birth is more than just patchwork or an outer reformation. It is an inner, moral transformation. Like the young man who testified at the close of a summer Christian ashram, "I came here expecting the Lord to do some repair work on me, but instead He has given me a brand-new engine!"

Thought for the day: *God has no grandchildren, only children.*

John 3:13–21 OCTOBER 2

God so loved the world that he gave his only Son, that whoever believes in him should not perish but have eternal life (v. 16).

John 3:16 has been called "the Gospel in a nutshell." If we were to lose all the Bible except this one verse, we would still have enough divine truth to lead us from death to life.

This verse tells us that God took the initiative for our redemption. When we were unworthy, He cared for us. When we were helpless, He came to our rescue. His matchless love was the motivating force in this outreach. God so *loved* the world that He *gave*. He gave His son. Jesus also loved us and gave His life for us. The purpose behind all this was that we "should not perish, but have eternal life."

During World War II, a father and his son were walking down the street at night. The lad noticed in several of the homes a bright silver star hung in the window. "What do those stars mean?" he asked his father. "Son," replied the father, "It means that family has given a son to die for his country." There was a long silence, and then suddenly the young lad noticed a lone star shining brightly in the heavens. "Look, Daddy," he cried with excitement, "God also has given a Son to die for us!"

It is true that God has freely provided this salvation, but we must appropriate it. God has acted in response to our *need*; now we must act in response to God's *deed*. The big question of the Gospel is this: *What have you done about what God has done for you?* Have you given life for life, love for love, devotion for devotion? The Word tells us that "whoever *believes* in him [will] not perish but have eternal life." We appropriate God's gift by *faith*. That means believing that God loves us and has given his Son for us and believing that Christ loves us and has given His life for us. This is the road from death to life.

Thought for the day: *Thanks be to God for his unspeakable gift (Paul).*

John 3:22–30   **OCTOBER 3**

He must increase, but I must decrease (v. 30).

This is the record of the setting star and the rising Sun. John the Baptist was the setting star. He had been sent by God as the forerunner of the Messiah to prepare the hearts and minds of people for the coming of Christ. Courageously he called men and women to repentance and to "make straight the paths of the Lord." Those who repented he baptized with water as a public witness to their commitment. Regarded by many as a great prophet, John was popular among the common people and drew large crowds wherever he went.

Then suddenly the Sun appeared on the horizon. Jesus commenced His public ministry and began to perform many miracles and to preach the kingdom of God. All eyes turned to Him; great crowds followed Him. So John's disciples said to him, "Your popularity is waning. The masses are leaving you and going after the One whom you baptized on the other side of Jordan. You are being displaced."

John's answer is significant. He replied, "I told you I am

not the Christ, but only His forerunner. I am only 'the friend of the bridegroom.' The bridegroom is now at hand. This is no occasion for sorrow. My work is completed, my joy is full. From now on 'he must increase, but I must decrease.'"

This should be the motto of every Christian. The Christian world revolves around Christ, not the person in the pulpit or the person in the pew. *Christ* is the Sun, the light of the world. At best we are only reflections of His light. *He* is the Savior; we are merely witnesses of the salvation that He offers. We need to follow the advice of a great preacher to other preachers: "Remember, our Lord and Savior Jesus Christ has made you fishers of people, and a good fisher keeps himself well out of sight. Let your Master be always to the fore and yourself in the background."

Thought for the day: *No star can ever take the place of the Sun (Son).*

John 3:31–36   OCTOBER 4

He who believes in the Son has eternal life (v. 36).

Eternal life—what a beautiful phrase! But what does it mean? We tend to think of eternal life as life with endless duration—existing on and on. That is part of it. But when the New Testament speaks of eternal life, the emphasis is not on quantity or length; it is on the quality or character of that life. It suggests a relationship to God, not time.

Eternal life stands in contrast to biological life. The latter is humankind's natural or temporal existence; it is derived and fleeting; it has much less impact on the personality. Eternal life is God's own life within us, with this one major difference. With God, eternal life has neither beginning nor end, whereas with human beings, it has a beginning in their salvation experience, but no end. God's eternal life was implanted in humankind at creation (Gen. 2:7), but was forfeited in the tragedy of the Fall. It was subsequently provisionally restored to us through Christ's redemptive work. It is now freely offered to all who will receive it (John 1:4). The wondrous message of the Scripture is that God is willing to share His life—to share Himself—with human beings.

Eternal life is primarily a relationship to God through Jesus Christ. John writes, "He who has the Son has life; he who has not the Son of God has not life (1 John 5:12). Since Christ is the life, when we receive Him, His life is imparted to us. This life is both present and future, both now and throughout eternity through the resurrection of the whole person.

The text tells us that eternal life is granted to those who believe in the Son of God. Such belief is not to be confounded with belief in this or that historical statement concerning Him. No recital of creeds, however elaborate, can avail in the least. Genuine belief in Christ results in our following Him, accepting the ideals He sets before us, keeping His commandments. Belief in Christ is not a theory, but a practice; not a substitute for action, but the most powerful incentive to it.

Thought for the day: *Eternal life is a present possession and a future prospect.*

John 4:1–26   OCTOBER 5

Jesus said to her, "I who speak to you am he"
(v. 26).

John three and John four, when put side by side, make an interesting study in contrasts. Chapter three is about a man; chapter four, about a woman. Chapter three took place at night; chapter four took place at noon. Chapter three has to do with a ruler; chapter four with a prostitute. The ruler was a Jew; the prostitute, a Samaritan. She believed in Jesus; we have no certain knowledge whether Nicodemus believed or not.

The narrative of Jesus and the Samaritan woman is an

excellent study in the progress of faith; it demonstrates how faith may be gradually enlarged and strengthened. The Samaritan woman looked upon Jesus, at first, as merely a man, a weary traveler, a Jew; than as a prophet, and finally as the Messiah or Savior of the world.

First of all, she saw *a man*. Tired and thirsty, Jesus asked her for a drink. This surprised the woman, for it was not considered proper for a rabbi to speak to a woman in public, especially a social outcast. Furthermore, Jesus was a Jew and Jews usually had no dealings with Samaritans. But Jesus sought to break down all barriers of sex, social distinction, and race in order to win the woman's confidence.

Then when Jesus, a perfect stranger, revealed to the Samaritan woman all her sinful past, she was convinced that He was more than an ordinary rabbi; He must be a prophet. So she raised theological questions on the subject of worship. Jesus answered with such clarity and authority that the woman said, "Sir, I know when the Messiah comes, he will teach us all things." To which Jesus replied, "I who speak to you am he."

And suddenly the woman believed. No further questions, no demand for evidence or signs; she took Jesus at His word. Convinced that He was the Messiah, she ran back to town to tell everybody. Her curiosity about a man developed into respect for a prophet and finally into faith in the Messiah.

Thought for the day: *Faith, like muscle, grows strong with exercise.*

John 4:1–26 — OCTOBER 6

Sir, give me this water, that I may not thirst, nor come here to draw (v. 15).

In this beautiful story we have an outstanding example of soul-winning. Look carefully at the steps employed by the Master in dealing with this needy individual.

1. *Jesus sought her soul.* This was the only thing the Samaritan woman had of any value. With her virtue gone, her reputation soiled, her character marred, and her body given over to lust, she was ready for the junkyard of the universe. But Christ looked beyond all this and saw something of eternal value in this sinful woman. She had a soul that needed to be saved, a life that needed to be redeemed. Once delivered from her wretched past, she could become a mighty power for God and the good.

2. *Jesus secured her interest* by referring to something she knew and offering her something she wanted. She knew about the water in the well, but not of the water of eternal life. She knew of the well of Sychar, but not of Christ, the fountain of spiritual satisfaction. Suddenly her curiosity was aroused and her desire quickened. What was this "living water"? Who was this Stranger?

3. *He shocked her conscience.* Jesus tactfully commanded her to go call her husband, but she had no lawful husband. She had lived with five men. Suddenly her conscience was smitten; her sin came before her eyes. She had to face the question squarely; there was no sidetracking of the issue. Jesus never treated sin lightly, for to Him it was a moral tragedy. He loved the sinner but hated the sin. If the Samaritan woman wanted the living water, there was only one way. She must repent, confess, and forsake her evil life.

4. *He satisfied her heart.* What the woman had sought in vain for many years through sinful pleasure, she now found in a moment of time through the presence of the living Christ. Her heart was satisfied, her life changed. So she left her water pot behind and went home with the spring of living water down inside of her.

Thought for the day: *He that winneth souls is wise (Prov. 11:30, KJV).*

Many Samaritans from the city believed in him
because of the woman's testimony (v. 39).

These days we tend to place great emphasis on preparation for personal evangelism. We conduct many seminars and
workshops to train Christians in various methods of leading
people to Christ, such as The Four Spiritual Laws, Evangelism
Explosion, house-to-house visitation, and so on. These are all
helpful and ought to be pursued. But we need to learn an
important lesson from this story of the Samaritan woman,
namely, *motivation is more important than method.* Unless
people are motivated from within to speak for Christ, no
amount of training will turn them into effective witnesses.

Note this interesting contrast in the story for today. The
Samaritan woman found the water of eternal life that Jesus
had talked about. Her heart was satisfied, her life changed. So
she forgot the well and the water pot and ran back into town,
saying, "Come, see a man who told me all that I ever did. Can
this be the Christ?" She knew no theology; she had no training
in methods. She simply told how she had met Christ and what
had happened to her. So convincing was her testimony and
so remarkable was the change in her attitude, that the whole
town believed and came out to see the Messiah for themselves.

Now look at the disciples. They too went into town, but
what did they bring back? Bread and fish! They had all the
training, they knew the theology, but they never said to a
single person, "The man we believe to be the Messiah, the
Christ, is seated at the well just outside town. Wouldn't you like
to come and meet him?" All they did was shop for lunch.

So the woman went into town and brought back
practically the entire town. The disciples went into town and
brought back bread and fish. What our church people need
today is strong inner motivation that will impel them sponta-

neously to witness for Christ. This comes from a genuine experience with Christ and a daily walk with Him.

Thought for the day: *When people are motivated they will be activated.*

John 4:43–54

Jesus said to him, "Go; your son will live" (v. 50).

The majority of the healing miracles of Jesus were performed when He was physically present. He often reached out and touched the person who was sick. However, at least on two occasions—that of the Centurion's servant and the nobleman's son—Jesus healed by word of mouth from a distance. Time and space were unable to imprison His power.

Even today we are discovering that through intercessory prayer, we, the disciples of Jesus, can release the power of Christ to heal or change situations all the way across the world.

Several years ago an elderly saint of God here in the United States was impressed in the middle of the night to pray for her missionary in India. At that very hour—mid-morning in India—E. Stanley Jones, physically broken and spiritually depressed, knelt to pray in a back pew of the Lucknow Methodist Church. By the power of long-distance intercessory prayer he arose healed, a new man.

In January 1962, members of a Christian congregation in Oregon prayed for their missionary in Guatemala during the Sunday morning worship service. At the same hour—one o'clock in Central America—John Astleford of the Friends Mission was attacked in his van by two hitchhikers, while driving from Chiquimula to Guatemala City. Instead of pushing the van off the cliff as they first intended, the hitchhikers shot him in the mouth with a pistol and then fled with his money. Though weakened by the loss of much blood, John Astleford was enabled by an unseen power to drive the remaining forty miles over a difficult mountainous road to the capital city and the Presbyterian Hospital. There he stumbled out of the car into the emergency room. After several weeks of medical treatment and plastic surgery, John fully recovered and returned to his ministry.

Time and space are still incapable of limiting the power of Christ. He is the same yesterday, today, and forever.

Thought for the day: *Through prayer we can release the power of God around the world.*

John 5:1–9

Rise, take up your pallet, and walk (v. 8).

John's description of the scene at the pool of Bethsaida is pathetic. In the shade of the covered colonnade lay "a multitude of invalids, blind, lame, paralyzed." Among them was a man who had been ill for thirty-eight years. In accordance with tradition, they all eagerly waited for an angel to come from heaven to stir up the waters so that they could jump into the pool and be healed.

Then came Jesus. Notice how he dealt with the man who had been ill for so many years. He first asked a *question*: "Do you want to be healed?" It seemed like a foolish question, but Jesus wanted to know whether the man really had the *desire* to be different. Maybe he had given up all hope after so many years; perhaps he was content to remain as an invalid for the rest of his life. But his answer indicated clearly that he did want to be healed, but didn't know how it would be possible. He had no one to help him into the pool when the water was agitated.

Jesus than gave a *command*: "Rise, take up your pallet, and walk." This must have seemed impossible to one who had been unable to walk for thirty-eight years. But he responded both with *obedience* and *faith*. I like to think that the healing took place just as he made the effort to stand, inspired by faith in Jesus' word. For God's commands, when obeyed, are always His enabling acts.

Jesus deals with us in the same manner today. He starts with the question: "Do you really desire to be changed; or would you rather continue with your lifestyle? Do you really want to be free; or do you enjoy being a slave to your selfish desires?" Then He gives us a command; not the same command that he gave the lame man, but one in keeping with our problem: Go, call your husband; go, bring your income-tax form; go, restore what you have taken unlawfully; go, be reconciled to your brother. As we respond by His grace in obedience and faith, the healing, the deliverance, will take place.

Thought for the day: *Jesus delivers those persons who want to be delivered.*

John 5:9b—18   OCTOBER 10

See, you are well! Sin no more, that nothing worse befall you (v. 14).

Yesterday we saw how Jesus, in dealing with the impotent man at the pool of Bethesda, first asked him a *question*— "Do you want to be healed?" And then gave him a *command*—"Rise, take up your pallet, and walk." Now we see Jesus, when he meets the man for a second time, giving him a *warning*—"Sin no more, that nothing worse befall you." Physically the man was well, but spiritually he still had a soul, a life to be redeemed. Jesus' desire for the man was that he be as well on the inside as he now was on the outside. It is well for us to remember that people are not only sick and need to be healed; they are not only hungry and need to be fed; they are not only ignorant and need to be educated; but they are also lost and need to be redeemed.

Jesus took a holistic approach to people. He ministered to their bodies by healing their infirmities; He ministered to their

317

minds by teaching them the truth about God and life; and He ministered to their souls by speaking the word of forgiveness. He wanted people to be whole in body, mind, and spirit. Jesus never used His healing powers as a bait to induce people to listen to His words or to believe in Him as the Christ. It is true that many did believe in Him because of their healing, but He never said to people, "Unless you believe in me, I will not heal you." He healed solely out of compassion and love. But at the same time He never separated the physical from the spiritual. He didn't minister to one element to the exclusion of the other. Jesus knew that the human personality is a unit. Sometimes people get sick in body and mind and pass on illness to their souls. Sometimes they get sick in their souls and pass on illness to their minds and bodies. So he ministered to the total person.

Christ is the great example for all of us today. Let us be sure that in our individual and corporate ministries we minister to the total person and not just a part.

Thought for the day: *Jesus wants us to be* whole, *not just* well in body.

John 5:19–24   OCTOBER 11

He who hears my word and believes him who sent me, has eternal life; he does not come into judgment (v. 24).

The Bible brings us both bad news and good news. The bad news is that "all have sinned and fall short of the glory of God" (Rom. 3:23) and "the wages of sin is death" (Rom. 6:23). The Word tells us that "we shall all stand before the judgment seat of God" and "each of us shall give account of himself to God" (Rom. 14:10, 12). On that day the verdict will be "guilty—condemned to die!" But note this solemn truth: the condemnation is not merely confined to the future. It is in the here and now. As John writes in 3:18, "He who does not

318

believe is *condemned already*." So the verdict is already given; it will be finalized at the judgment. All of this is indeed distressing news.

But, thanks be to God, there is also the good news—exciting news! Jesus said that "God sent not the Son into the world to condemn the world, but that the world might be saved through him" (John 3:17). Paul writes that "the wages of sin is death, but the free gift of God is eternal life in Christ Jesus our Lord (Rom. 6:23). "There is therefore now no condemnation for those who are in Christ Jesus" (Rom. 8:1). Our text for today tells us that "he who . . . believes . . . has eternal life; he does not come into judgment, but has passed from death to life."

Note that just as condemnation and death are in the present, so also justification and eternal life are also here and now. The believer is already acquitted; the verdict is "not guilty" because his judgment has already been borne by Christ on Calvary. Christ has taken his place. So the believer has no fear of the judgment. His judgment is over. Now that's good news—the best news!

The dividing factor between the condemned and the acquitted is one's attitude toward Jesus Christ—either of belief or unbelief. He who believes in Jesus is released from the judgment. He who does not believe is already judged.

Thought for the day: *Faith in Christ can turn bad news into good news.*

John 5:25–30   **OCTOBER 12**

The father . . . has given him authority to execute judgment, because he is the Son of man (vv. 26, 27).

Yesterday we saw that Christ is the Savior of the world. Today we see that He is also the Judge of the universe. "But," some ask, "how can the same person be both Savior and Judge?" The answer is: In the same way that the sun in the sky is both giver and destroyer of life. The sun provides warmth and life to the plant so that it provides vegetables and fruit for our nourishment. But the moment you cut the plant and sever it from its roots, the same sun begins to wither and kill the plant. It is a difference in relationship between plant and sun. Likewise, when we are in right relationship to Christ through faith and obedience, He grants us life and spiritual fruit; when we are in wrong relationship to Christ, through unbelief and disobedience, immediately there is decay and death.

Judgment is inherent in the very nature of God and the universe. God is a holy God. He is irrevocably opposed to all forms of evil, and committed to upholding His moral law. Sin must be punished. Human government operates in the same way. Government cannot willy-nilly acquit all guilty criminals in the name of compassion and mercy. That would lead to breakdown of law and order; it would invite chaos. Crime must be punished.

Then again justice demands retribution. In human affairs we often see unrighteousness prospering; we see the guilty going scot-free. So many of the verdicts of today are unjust or partial or tentative that we cry out, "Is there no real justice in the world?" Both reason and conscience cry out for the verdict of a higher court. One day everything will be set right by the Supreme Court of the universe.

Christ Himself is the Judge. Human justice is often rendered unfair by injured pride, prejudice, intolerance, contempt, self-righteousness, or even ignorance; but Christ's judgment is always right and perfect. He alone has full knowledge, is absolutely holy, and perfectly loving. He is the *perfect* Judge.

Thought for the day: *Christ would rather be your Savior than your Judge.*

You refuse to come to me that you may have life
(v. 40).

Jesus had been making the most startling and far-reaching claims, and his opponents kept pressing Him for evidence. In response, Jesus here calls four witnesses to testify on His behalf.

The first is the human witness, John the Baptist. Many acclaimed him as a prophet; some even thought he might be the Messiah. But John said clearly, "I am not the Christ; he is coming after me." Then when Jesus appeared on the scene, John the Baptist pointed to Him and said: "Behold the Lamb of God. This is the Son of God."

The second and greater witness is the divine witness—God Himself. God testified to the divine Sonship of Jesus by the miracles which He accomplished through Him—healing the lame and blind, cleansing the leper, casting out evil spirits, and raising the dead. These were acts that only the omnipotent and all-wise God could perform. God also witnessed to Christ through His written revelation. The Old Testament Scriptures testify to the Son by prophesying every detail of His life and ministry. The Gospels witness to His sinless life and glorious victory over death.

In spite of all these witnesses and accumulative evidence, the Jewish leaders still did not receive Jesus as the Christ, the Son of God. They claimed to believe in God and the Scriptures; they claimed to be loyal to Moses; but still they would not believe their witness. Jesus chided them for the hardness of their hearts.

Is the situation any different today? It's not more evidence that people need; the witnesses are many. What they need is to act upon the evidence they already have. Many are like the man engaged in debate, who, when confronted with overwhelming arguments by his opponent, cried out, "Don't confuse me with the facts. I have already made up my mind!"

The big question for all of us is: Do I really have the will to believe?

Thought for the day: *I will make it my aim to accept Christ's claim.*

John 6:1–14   OCTOBER 14

There is a lad here (v. 9).

What a never-to-be-forgotten day that was for the lad! Little did he dream, as he started out that morning to hear the great Preacher, what the day would hold for him.

Several things impress us about this lad. First, he stayed close to Jesus and was therefore available at the time of need. He could have remained on the fringe of the great crowd as a casual spectator and allowed his mind to be distracted. He might have stopped to chase lizards or butterflies. But no there he was—right up front, mingling with the disciples, right next to the great Teacher. He was observing every deed and listening to every word.

When Jesus needed the lad's lunch, he offered it gladly. We cannot imagine our Lord forcefully taking it away from him. The lad might have held on to his loaves and fish for his own use. But that would have meant merely satisfying his own appetite for a few hours, and then he would have passed on and nothing would ever have been heard of him. Happily he chose to surrender the little that he had to the Lord, and thereby become a partner with Him in ministering to the needs of thousands of others.

We are also impressed that the young boy gave *all* he had. He could have kept back a couple of loaves and one fish in order to be sure he had something to eat. But he unselfishly gave all. The Lord Jesus accepted his gift, multiplied it by His divine power and made it the means of feeding more than 5000 people. The lunch was small, to be sure, but in the hands of Jesus it was sufficient for all. How happy the lad must have been as he related the miracle to his parents that evening when he got home. We can imagine how his eyes sparkled as he said, "Mom, Dad, Jesus and I fed them all!"

Thought for the day: *Jesus often takes* little *people and* little *things and does a* big *job with them.*

John 6:16–24   OCTOBER 15

It is I; do not be afraid (v. 20).

Fear is the most devastating of all human emotions. It has been described as private enemy number one. Fear brings unwholesome physical results such as restlessness, sleeplessness, disturbing dreams, and feelings of exhaustion. It affects the mind by paralyzing the brain so that it is impossible to reason and act efficiently. Out of fear arise unhappy emotional states, like loneliness, hatred, and resentment. Fear also has its destructive spiritual consequences, paralyzing and keeping the soul from creativity and fruitfulness.

The key to overcoming fear is found in the words of Jesus—"It is I." An awareness of the presence of Christ and faith in His person will dispel all fear.

One stormy night little Johnny was fast asleep in his own room. His father, realizing that the storm might frighten the lad, slipped upstairs to Johnny's room and sat quietly by his bed. On a sudden loud clap of thunder, the boy awakened and began to cry. In the dark, his father reached out, gently touched his son's hand and said, "Johnny, daddy's here; don't be afraid." Immediately the lad was at peace.

When the storms of life sweep over us and we become afraid, we hear the tender voice of the Master, saying to us, "Do not be afraid; I am with you." When temptations assail, He whispers, "Don't be afraid. I know what you are going through. I, too, was tempted, and I can give you strength to overcome." When suffering or loneliness besiege us, Jesus speaks softly to us, "Don't be afraid. I am no stranger to these feelings. I went through untold suffering and loneliness on the cross, and I give you my presence and peace." When death hangs a crepe on the door, Jesus says to us, "Don't be afraid. I have conquered death. Trust in me and you also will rise again."

In the presence of Christ we find peace and joy—the perfect antidote to fear.

Thought for the day: *Fear is* destructive; *faith is* creative.

John 6:25–34   OCTOBER 16

What must we do, to be doing the works of God?
(v. 28)

A universal conviction from time immemorial declares that a person by living a good and moral life can earn the favor of God. Religion has been equated with good works. For example, Hinduism says that by performing good *karma*(good deeds), such as charity to the poor, respect for all life, religious rites and ceremonies, one will gain *moksha* or salvation. Islam teaches that by performing faithfully the five religious duties—reciting the creed daily, praying five times a day, giving alms to the poor, fasting, and making the pilgrimage to Mecca—one will please God and find entrance into Paradise. Even the nominal Christian feels that by being a good parent, a helpful neighbor, and a faithful church member, one will eventually make it to heaven.

The question posed by the Jews to Jesus is typical of this universal belief: "What must we *do*, to be *doing the work* of God?" When the rich young ruler came to Jesus, he asked a similar question: "What must I *do* to inherit eternal life?" The whole emphasis was on doing something. In both instances the questioners expected Jesus to lay down rules and regulations and a list of things they should do. But that is not what Jesus says at all. To the rich young ruler He said, "Do you want to know what to do? Follow me!" To the Jews he said, "Do you want to know what work to do? Believe in me whom God has sent."

Jesus says the same thing to us today: "Believe in me; follow me. Get into right relationship with me." The Christian life starts with a Person, not with principles and precepts. It starts with faith, not with works. Good works are not the cause of our salvation, but the inevitable result. After we have come into right relationship with Christ, then plenty of room for good works exists. But we must start at the proper place—the person of Jesus Christ. No other beginning place can be found.

Thought for the day: *The one work that God desires most is faith in His Son.*

John 6:35–40 OCTOBER 17

Him who comes to me I will not cast out (v. 37).

What a beautiful promise! Jesus declares that He will not turn anyone away; He will receive everybody, regardless of race, color, caste, creed, social position, or spiritual condition. All are welcome.

Jesus demonstrated this promise over and over again in His public ministry. He never turned anyone away. When the lame, the blind, the lepers, the demoniacs came to Him, He offered healing and deliverance. He welcomed people of position and prominence, like Nicodemus, a member of the Sanhedrin; the Roman centurion who pleaded for his servant; and Jairus, ruler of the synagogue, who sought healing for his daughter. But Jesus also welcomed the social and moral outcastes like Mary Magdalene, the Samaritan woman at the well, the woman taken in adultery, and the thief on the cross. Several times when Jesus was surrounded by crowds, the disciples were irritated and said to Him, "Master, send them away" (that seemed to be their theme song), but Jesus always had compassion on the people and received them.

Jesus is still fulfilling His promise in our day. Several years ago Sadhu Sundar Singh, the famous Indian Christian, was invited into the home of a robber chief, in a lonely spot at the foothills of the Himalaya Mountains. While they ate together, Sundar Singh told his host the story of Christ and witnessed to him. When he came to the story of the thief on the cross, the man began to weep. Then he said to the evangelist, "I want to show you something." He led Sundar Singh to a nearby cave and showed him a pile of bones and putrefying corpses. "These are my sins," said the robber chief. "There are the people I robbed and killed. Tell me, will your Jesus accept a sinner like me?" Sundar Singh answered, "Friend, even if this pile of sins were as high as the Himalaya Mountains, Christ would accept you and forgive you." The robber knelt there in the presence of his sins and surrendered his life to Christ. He became a radiant witness for Christ.

Thought for the day: *Christ's invitation has no limitation.*

John 6:41–51 OCTOBER 18

I am the bread of life (v. 48).

Bread is the staff of physical life; without it life cannot go on. In the same way, Jesus is the essential of spiritual life; without Him real life can neither begin nor continue. Since the human person is a physical-spiritual being, he/she needs both earthly bread and the bread from heaven.

Two important spiritual truths are inherent in this analogy of Jesus, the living Bread. First, just as *bread brings sustenance* to our physical bodies, so also Christ, living within, sustains our spiritual lives. The steak and potatoes that the football player ate for lunch give him the energy to run for a touchdown. The meat and vegetables that the swimmer has eaten give her energy to swim up and down the pool. Likewise, the living presence of Christ and the truth of His Word provide a person energy to live for and serve Him.

In the second place, just as *bread brings satisfaction* to the hungry person, so the living Christ satisfies the immortal longings and insatiable hunger of the human heart. People are hungry for truth—and He alone can give truth. People are hungry for life—and He alone can give life, yes, life more abundant. People are hungry for love—and Christ alone can give them the love that outlasts sin and death.

Almost daily we are bombarded with news about famine and starvation in certain parts of the world, particularly in Africa. We see pictures of pitiful human bodies that are no more than skeletons, and our hearts are moved with compassion. We seek to rush bread to these suffering people as fast as possible. All this is well and good. But at the same time we must not forget the tremendous spiritual hunger that prevails all across the world. People are dying for lack of the living bread that comes down from heaven. We must be as concerned about feeding them spiritually as we are about feeding them physically.

Thought for the day: *People need bread for their souls as well as for their bodies.*

John 6:52–59   **OCTOBER 19**

Unless you eat the flesh of the Son of man and drink his blood, you have no life in you (v. 53).

We have before us a difficult passage to understand. These words of Jesus may even sound gruesome to us; they smack of cannibalism. But actually a deep and significant truth is hidden in these words.

The key to understanding this passage is found in the word *appropriation*. Remember, Jesus has just declared to the people, "I am the bread of life." That is, He is the basic essential of spiritual life. Without Him there is no life. He gives life and sustains it. Now He declares that unless we eat His flesh and drink His blood, we have no life in us. In other words,

Christ has to be appropriated; He must be received into the very center of our being. As long as He remains a historical figure in a book, He is external to us. But when He enters into our hearts and lives within us, then we can feed upon the life and strength that He imparts to us.

Suppose you are seated at the dinner table and a sumptuous meal is placed before you: juicy T-bone steak, baked potato with sour cream, lima beans, honeyed carrots, fruit salad, fluffy rolls, and apple pie with whipped cream for dessert. Now, you could sit and stare at this delicious meal until your eyes bulge and your mouth waters. You could discuss with your dinner mate the value of the food set before you—the number of calories, the inherent vitamins, the possible satisfaction and energy. But the food will mean nothing to you until you actually put it into your mouth, chew, digest, and assimilate it into your system.

In the same way you can look at Jesus, you can read and talk about Him, you can carry on extensive debates and theological discussions about Him, but you will never receive His life and power until you take Him into the very center of your being, and make Him your own personal Savior and Lord.

Thought for the day: *Christ appreciated is potential life; Christ appropriated is actual life.*

John 6:60–71   OCTOBER 20

After this many of his disciples drew back and no longer went about with him (v. 66).

In the Scripture lesson for today, we see three different responses to the teachings and person of Jesus Christ.

To begin with, we note those followers of Jesus who *turned back*. At first they followed Jesus because they were intrigued by the amazing miracles he performed, especially the feeding of the five thousand. But Jesus, knowing their hearts, said to them frankly, "You seek me, not because you saw signs, but because you ate your fill of the loaves." They were bread and fish disciples ("rice Christians"). So when Jesus talked about being the bread of life, and the necessity of their eating His flesh and drinking His blood, they found all this to be too heavy. They were not willing to pay the price and meet the demands so they "drew back and no longer went about with him."

Then we have the one disciple, Judas Iscariot, who just gradually *drifted away*. Jesus must have chosen him because of his gifts and potential. No doubt he was sincere at the outset and entered wholeheartedly into the ministry of Jesus. But gradually, step by step, he began to drift away. Disillusionment turned to bitterness; greed into treachery. Finally he became a tool of Satan and betrayed his Master for the paltry sum of thirty pieces of silver.

The eleven disciples made up the third group. They *held fast*. When Jesus saw many of His followers turning back, He turned to His immediate disciples and said, "Will you also go away?" To which Simon Peter quickly replied, "Lord, to whom shall we go? You have the words of eternal life; and we have believed, and have come to know, that you are the Holy One of God." What a magnificent confession of faith! These men had counted the cost and were willing to meet the demands of discipleship, however difficult they may be.

God forbid that we should turn back or drift away. May He grant us courage and strength to hold fast to the end.

Thought for the day: *Hold on to Christ; He is your only hope.*

John 7:1–9   OCTOBER 21

The world cannot hate you, but it hates me because I testify of it that its works are evil (v. 7).

The "world" that Jesus is referring to in these words is

that segment of human society that rejects the authority of God and His standards of conduct and relationships. The world sets itself up as the final authority and determines its own patterns of behavior. In the very nature of things, this automatically sets the rule of society over against the reign of God. The two are incompatible; they are at cross purposes.

Jesus said to His brothers, who did not believe in Him as the Messiah, "The world cannot hate you." As long as people are in line with the spirit and practices of the age, they will not be molested or hated. They just flow along with social tides. The moment we call into question the basic assumptions, biases, and lifestyle of a godless society, the world rises up in hatred and opposition. When Martin Luther King challenged the injustices of racial bigotry and led a courageous movement for civil rights, he became a marked man and finally the victim of an assassin's bullet. When Mahatma Gandhi spoke out against the animosity between Hindus and Muslims in his country, he was considered a traitor and shot to death by one of his own group. When Nelson Mandella of South Africa publicly denounced the government policy of apartheid, he was arrested and thrown into prison.

The world hated Jesus because He testified against its evil works. He exposed the sham and hypocrisy of those who claimed to be religious leaders. He probed the inner motives of those who made a good outward appearance but inwardly were deceitful and corrupt. When His purity clashed with the sinfulness of humankind, He had to give His life. But He didn't die as a human martyr for a just cause. As the Son of God, He offered Himself as a sacrifice for the sin of the world. The world hated Jesus, but He loved the world and redeemed it.

Thought for the day: *The love of God is greater than the hatred of people.*

John 7:10–13   **OCTOBER 22**

While some said, "He is a good man," others said "No, he is leading the people astray" (v. 12).

The August 15, 1988, issue of *Time* had a picture of Christ on the cover with the caption, "Who is Jesus? A startling new movie raises an age-old question." The feature article concerned the heated debate among scholars sparked by Scorsese's new film, *The Last Temptation of Jesus.*

The question, "Who is Jesus?" *is* indeed an age-old question. People have debated the issue for the last 2000 years, and the verdicts have run the whole gamut of opinions, everything from good man to God-man, from divine to demoniac, from seducer to Savior, from the bastard son of a Roman soldier to the Son of God, conceived by the Holy Spirit and born of the Virgin Mary. This is the paramount question of all time, for the answer will determine the course of history and the final destiny of each person.

John seven is significant because it describes the various reactions of the people to Jesus during His public ministry and the different verdicts concerning who He was. In this and the next three devotionals let us trace these responses.

In the passage of Scripture for today, we find two verdicts concerning Jesus. Some people said, "He is a good man." They did not recognize Him as the Messiah or Son of God, but at least they had a positive attitude toward Christ. His life was blameless, and His deeds helpful to others. But this verdict, though true, is not the whole truth. Jesus was indeed truly human, but He was more than human.

Another group said of Jesus, "He is leading the people astray," that is, "He is a deceiver." They condemned Him for breaking Sabbath regulations and claiming to be the Son of God. To them Jesus was evil.

Which is it? Is Jesus a good man or an evil man? Is He merely human or is He more than human? The answer is a matter of life and death.

Thought for the day: *Every person must make a verdict about Jesus Christ.*

This man has learning ... you have a demon (v. 15, 20).

Today we have two more divergent responses to the question, "Who is Jesus?"

Some people, when they heard his teaching, were amazed and said, "How is it that this man has learning, when he has never studied?" It was the practice in those days for a religious leader to attend a rabbinic school and sit at the feet of an accredited teacher, one of the great rabbis. Only then was he entitled to expound Scripture and to talk about the law. But Jesus had never been to such a school, and still he was able to interpret the Scriptures with great insight and clarity. Furthermore, no rabbi ever made a statement on his own authority. He always began by saying, "There is a teaching" ... or "Rabbi so-and-so said ..." But Jesus never used quotation marks; He spoke on His own authority. So the people were amazed and said, "No man ever spoke like this man." To them Jesus was the master Teacher.

In response, Jesus told His listeners that His teaching came from God, and so was true. Therefore, He could speak with authority.

The second group of people went from admiration to denunciation. When Jesus asked, "Why do you seek to kill me?" they answered, "You're crazy, you have a demon. No one is seeking to kill you." They accused Jesus of having an evil spirit within Him. In response, Jesus said to them, "Why are you angry with me and accuse me of breaking the Sabbath, when I brought healing and wholeness to an impotent man? You yourselves perform an act of surgery on a person on the Sabbath, when it becomes necessary to keep the Mosaic law of circumcision. So be careful how you judge me."

So which is it? Is Jesus merely a great teacher to be

admired, or is He more? Is He a good man or a mad man with a demon? The answer, again, is a matter of life and death.

Thought for the day: *Jesus desires more than just admiration as a teacher.*

John 7:25—36   OCTOBER 24

When the Christ appears, will he do more signs than this man has done? (v. 31)

We have traced two sets of verdicts concerning Jesus thus far: good man versus deceiver; and marvelous teacher versus mad man with a demon. Now we look at the third.

Some of the people who heard and saw Jesus, at first raised the possibility that He might be the Christ. However, on second thought they concluded, "But how can this be, for we know where this man comes from. His home is in Nazareth. And we know his parents and his brothers and sisters." This was contrary to the popular belief that when Christ appeared, He would come mysteriously and unexpectedly out of nowhere. No one would know where He came from. So this ruled out Jesus as the Christ.

In response to these remarks, Jesus made two fantastic claims. He said it was true that they knew where He came from, but it was also true that ultimately He had come from God. Second, He said that they did not know God but that He did. The authorities were shocked by these statements, and from now on, in their eyes, Jesus was not only guilty of Sabbath-breaking, but far worse, also of blasphemy.

But then some who witnessed the amazing miracles that Jesus performed asked, "When the Christ appears, will he do anything greater than this man has done?" And they believed on Him as the Christ. They saw the evidence, took it at face value, and made their verdict.

So the choice before us is clear. Is Jesus the Christ, or is He not? Is what Jesus claimed about Himself true, or is it not?

If what He said about Himself is false, then He is indeed guilty of the worst form of blasphemy. But if what He said is true, then without doubt He *is* the Christ, the Son of God. This leaves us with a choice: we must either accept Him fully or reject Him completely. There is no middle ground.

Thought for the day: *Jesus still asks people today, "Who do you say that I am?"*

John 7:37–39

He who believes in me ... "Out of his heart shall flow rivers of living water" (v. 38).

Jesus said to the Samaritan woman at the well, "The water I give you will become in you a spring." Then on the great day of the feast he said to the crowd, "He who believes on me ... 'Out of his heart will flow rivers of living water.'" Note, in you a spring; out of you rivers. In us, the Holy Spirit is like a spring; an artesian well that is constantly fresh and never runs dry. Out of us the Holy Spirit flows like rivers, bringing the water of life to thirsty people all around us. Thus, the Spirit-filled life is not like a vessel filled with water up to the brim and then left standing. Rather it is like a vessel placed under an open faucet so that the water is incessantly flowing in, the vessel is always full, and the water is constantly flowing out.

The infilling of the Holy Spirit is not an end in itself. The Spirit flows *in* only so that He may flow *out*. As E. Stanley Jones used to say, "The Holy Spirit is like electricity. He never goes in where He can't come out." The infilling of the Spirit is for the supplying of *my own needs*; the outflowing is to help me supply *the needs of others*. The infilling is for *Christian character*; the outflowing is for *Christian conquest*. The infilling goes to my *innermost heart*; the outflowing goes to the *outermost world*.

The spring–rivers analogy emphasizes the fact that the infilling and outflowing of the Holy Spirit are without measure.

Life is no longer a reservoir with limited resources so that if we draw on them we have only so much left; therefore, we must ration or conserve them. Life now becomes a channel attached to infinite resources so there is no danger of exhausting the supply. We do not have to dole out our resources; for the more we give, the more we have. We are now living the inexhaustible life.

A little girl said, "My heart is small and can't hold much of the love and grace of God. But it can overflow an awful lot!"

Thought for the day: *The* fullness *of the Holy Spirit is in order to usefulness.*

John 7:40–52   OCTOBER 26

There was a division among the people over him (v. 43).

We come now to the last set of responses from the people concerning the person of Jesus.

First, we note three divergent verdicts. Some people thought that Jesus was the *prophet* whom Moses had promised (Deut. 18:15). Others declared categorically, "This *is* the *Christ!*" Still others argued that Jesus could not be the Christ, because He was from Galilee and the Messiah was to come form Bethlehem. (Evidently these people were not aware of the fact that Jesus was born in Bethlehem.)

Then we note three different reactions to Jesus. The officers reacted in bewildered *amazement.* They had been sent by the chief priests and Pharisees to arrest Jesus, but returned empty-handed, saying, "No man ever spoke like this man!" They recognized Jesus as a *super teacher.* The chief priests and Pharisees then reacted in utter *contempt.* They derided the officers by saying, "Has this man deceived you also? Have any of the authorities or of the Pharisees believed in him? Only the ignorant and accursed crowd follow him." They looked upon Jesus as a *deceiver.* Finally, we see the reaction of Nicodemus, who sought to defend Jesus by reminding the Pharisees that no person could be condemned without first having opportunity to answer for himself.

Now we can gather up all the various reactions to Jesus and give a composite answer to the age-old question, Who is Jesus? He was truly a *man*, fully *human* like we are, so we feel we can put our arms around Him and call Him "Brother." But He was more than a man; he was the *God-man—God incarnate* in human flesh. He was so like us, yet so unlike us. He was a great teacher and the greatest of all prophets, but He was more than teacher-prophet. Jesus is the *Christ* the *Anointed One*, the *Son of God*, the one and only *Savior of the world*. So just when we are about to put our arms around him and call him "Brother," He steps in front of us and says, "Go sell all, and come follow me."

Thought for the day: *Don't let anyone whittle down the stature of your Lord.*

John 8:1–11   OCTOBER 27

Neither do I condemn you; go, and do not sin again (v. 11).

We have here another dramatic and deeply significant incident in the life of Jesus. Let us look at it from three different angles.

1. *Confrontation*: This was yet another attempt by the scribes and Pharisees to ensnare Jesus in a dilemma. The question they asked was a trap. If He were to say, "No, don't stone her," then He would be guilty of breaking the Mosaic law and condoning adultery. If He were to say, "Go ahead and stone her," then He would collide with Roman authorities, for they alone had power to impose and execute the death penalty. So either way Jesus would be in trouble.

2. *Challenge*: Jesus did not answer the question immediately. He stooped and with His finger wrote something in the

dust. Some have suggested that He wrote the sins of the woman's accusers as they peeked over His shoulder; that would have scared them half to death. Others have suggested that Jesus tried to turn the attention of the crowd away from the adulterous woman, half-clad and couched in the dust, and thus save her from all the embarrassment. It would be just like Jesus to do such a thoughtful thing. Finally, He stood up and said, "Let him who is without sin among you be the first to throw a stone at her." All could hear the deathly silence, and then one by one the accusers slunk away like a pack of whipped dogs. The woman was left alone with Jesus.

3. *Compassion*: It was at this point that human misery and divine mercy met. The men had looked upon the woman as a thing, a tool; Jesus saw her as a person. They wanted to condemn her; Jesus wanted to redeem her. So He said to her, "Is there no one left to accuse you?" She answered, "No one, Lord." (Notice, the Pharisees had addressed Him as "master" or "teacher," but the woman called Him "Lord.") Then Jesus said to her most tenderly, "Neither do I condemn you; go, and do not sin again." So the sinful woman went home forgiven, a new person. Her accusers went away unforgiven and self-condemned.

Thought for the day: *Jesus loathes the sin but loves the sinner.*

John 8:12–20   **OCTOBER 28**

I am the light of the world (v. 12).

In the Scriptures the coming of the Messiah is more than once referred to as a light to illumine the world's darkness. Isaiah writes, "The people who walked in darkness have seen a great light" (9:2). John writes, "The true light that enlightens every man was coming into the world" (1:9). Now Christ declares: "I am the light of the world." In what way is He light to all humankind?

1. *Light illuminates.* It dispels the darkness and helps us to see. Supposing we are in a dark room. All around us are many objects, but we can't see what and where they are. The moment we turn on the light, everything comes into view—the chairs, table, sofa, television set, book shelves, pictures on the wall, and so on. In the same way the light of Christ dispels the darkness of our minds and leads us to a true knowledge of the nature and character of God. Jesus shows us what God is really like.

2. *Light exposes.* When we shine a light into the corner of a room or into a closet, we are able to see the dust and dirt that have accumulated. The powerful light of the x ray reveals that which cannot be seen by the naked eye. Likewise, when the light of Christ shines into our hearts, all the sin and filth are disclosed. We begin to see ourselves as we really are and as God sees us. Then we realize our need of inner cleansing.

3. *Light shows the way.* If we try to walk along a path in a wooded area in the dark, we find ourselves falling into the ditch, or bumping into trees, or getting entangled in bushes. If we carry a flashlight, we can walk safely and steadily forward in the light. In the same way, if we walk in the light of Christ, it will save us from the pitfalls of life, and enable us to see the path of righteousness which leads us safely home.

4. *Light gives life.* The light of the sun is essential to all life. Forest trees push their tops up into the light; flowers turn their faces to the sun. John tells us that "in Christ was life, and the life was the light of men" (1:4). The light of Christ in our hearts generates and sustains our spiritual lives.

Thought for the day: *The light of the Savior brings life to the sinner.*

John 8:21–29   OCTOBER 29

I always do what is pleasing to [the Father] (v. 29).

As followers of Christ, can we honestly give this same

testimony: "I always do what is pleasing to my heavenly Father"? This should be the intent and goal of all Christians, even though their performance may never be perfect.

The question naturally arises: How can we please God?

1. *By believing in Christ.* When the people asked Jesus, "What must we do, to be doing the work of God?" Jesus answered, "Believe in him whom he has sent" (6:29). The writer of Hebrews says, "Without faith it is impossible to please [God]" (11:6). God is pleased when we accept His Son, believe in Him, and follow Him. For it is through the Son that He grants us eternal life.

2. *By being genuine.* The psalmist says that God desires "truth in the inward being" (51:6). This rules out pretense, sham, outer facade, double-talk, two-facedness. It means having a right spirit within—honest, sincere, humble, truthful. The outer appearance and inner reality are identical; the spoken word and the inner motive coincide. People can say of us, "Those persons are real; we know where they stand; we can depend on them."

3. *By fulfilling His will* God is engaged in a world-wide mission of redemption, reconciliation, and healing. His desire is that all peoples upon the face of the earth should hear of His love and Christ's redemptive work on the cross. He has chosen to work through human instruments and He has a place for each one of us in His plan. We are pleasing to God when we share His vision and mission and become partners with Him in this business of world evangelization and social reform.

A young soldier, accused of deserting the army in battle, stood before the famous general and conqueror, Alexander the Great. "What is your name?" asked the general. "Alexander, Sir," was the reply. Three times the general asked the question and received the same answer, "Alexander, Sir." Then the general leaned forward and said in a booming voice, "Young man, you have a choice. Either change your actions or change your name!"

Thought for the day: *Is my life pleasing to God?*

John 8:31–38   OCTOBER 30

If the Son makes you free, you will be free indeed (v. 36).

People may live in a nation like the United States, where they enjoy all the basic freedoms of life—freedom from fear, freedom from want, freedom of speech, freedom of worship, freedom of free enterprise, and so on—but still not possess the greatest freedom of all: personal, spiritual freedom. On the other hand, many people living under totalitarian regimes are deprived of their inalienable rights, but still may be free in mind and in spirit.

Jesus said that "everyone who commits [that is, practices] sin is a slave to sin." How true this is! All around us we see people who are slaves to either lust, or material possessions, selfish ambition, greed, pleasure, alcohol, cigarettes, or drugs. They are bound by the chains of sinful habits and cannot free themselves. Their minds are darkened and their wills enslaved. But Christ is the Great Emancipator. He can snap the fetters of sin and deliver us completely from all unholy desires and destructive habits. Then we are free indeed.

When President Abraham Lincoln was assassinated, his body lay in state for several days in the Capitol. Thousands filed by the casket to get a last glimpse of this great man and to do him homage. Among the crowd was a black mother and her young son who was about five years of age. She lifted him up as high as she could so that he could see over the heads of the people, and then said in a loud clear voice, "Honey, take a good, long look, that's the man who gave his life to set you free." Today we have the privilege of pointing to Christ on the cross and saying to people all over the world, "Take a good look at the Man hanging there. He's the One who died to set you free!"

340

He breaks the power of canceled sin,
He sets the prisoner free;
His blood can make the foulest clean;
His blood availed for me.

Thought for the day: *No chains are too strong for Christ to break.*

John 8:39—47   OCTOBER 31

If you were Abraham's children, you would do what Abraham did (v. 39).

The Jews considered themselves secure in the favor of God simply because they were descendants of Abraham, whom they regarded as the greatest figure in all religious history. They kept reminding Jesus that they were "the children of Abraham." In response, Jesus said to them, "If you were really Abraham's children, you would act like Abraham. He was a man of complete obedience and implicit faith. But where is your obedience? Where is your faith? Abraham received God's messenger, but you seek to kill him." In other words, Jesus was saying that it was not flesh and blood that made a true descendant of Abraham; it was moral quality and spiritual fidelity.

The reaction of the Jews was to make an even bolder claim. They said, "We are Israelites. We are not idolaters like the Gentiles. We have only one God. He is our Father and we are his children." To which Jesus replied, "If you were really the children of God, you would listen to his words and you would receive his Son." In other words, it is not physical descent, but spiritual disposition that is the true sign of a child of God.

The Jews of Jesus' day have their parallel even in our day. Many are relying for their spiritual security on their history or heritage. Lutherans boast, "We are the children of Martin Luther, the leader of the Protestant Reformation." But do they emphasize the great doctrine of justification by faith as Luther did? Methodists say, "We are the children of John Wesley," but do they believe and act as Wesley did? He emphasized the experience of the warm heart and the expansion of the world parish. He preached sanctification and perfect love; he promoted a social holiness that dealt with the social evils of his day. Are Methodists doing the same today? Heritage and tradition are great, but the "faith of our fathers" (and mothers) needs to become *our* faith—*our* experience and *our* convictions—even today.

Thought for the day: *Our manner of living must correspond to the banner we bear.*

John 8:46–59 NOVEMBER 1

Which of you convicts me of sin? ... Before Abraham was, I am (vv. 46, 58).

Here Jesus claims that He is both *sinless* and *timeless*. No human being could make such claims; only God Himself.

Both friend and foe testified to the *sinlessness* of Jesus. Listen to their witness:

Pilate: "I find no crime in this man" (Luke 23:4).

Pilate's wife: "Have nothing to do with that righteous man" (Matt. 27:19).

The Roman centurion: "Certainly this man was innocent" (Luke 23:47).

The thief on the cross: "This man has done nothing wrong" (Luke 23:41).

Writer of Hebrews: ". . . in every respect [Jesus] has been tempted as we are, yet without sinning" (Heb. 4:15).

Peter: "He committed no sin; no guile was found on his lips" (1 Peter 2:22).

Because Jesus was sinless He is both our Example and Savior. People will let us down. But Jesus, never! He is our perfect example. Furthermore, He alone can be our Savior because only the sinless could die for the sinful; only the innocent could give himself for the guilty. No other Savior is possible.

Jesus is *timeless*. He is able to say, "Before Abraham was, I *am*." His entry into the stream of human history was only a part of His timeless existence. In Jesus, the eternal God showed Himself to humankind. Thus, we cannot say of Jesus, He *was*. We must always say, He *is*. This means that Jesus is *changeless*. He is "the same yesterday, today, and forever." He is our *contemporary*. He is with us now, today, to comfort, guide, sustain, strengthen, and deliver. He will never leave us nor forsake us.

Thought for the day: *Jesus is never out of date; He is always relevant.*

John 9:1–12   NOVEMBER 2

Who sinned, this man or his parents, that he was born blind? (v. 2)

The question asked by the disciples poses the unsolved problem of the ages: Why do people suffer? Down through the centuries people have proposed a variety of answers to this question. The Hindu contends that all suffering is the result of one's own *karma*, accumulation of evil deeds committed in a previous existence. This makes the individual himself responsible. The Muslim claims that all suffering is due to *kismet*, or the will of Allah, which makes God responsible for all evil. The Buddhist teaches that existence involves suffering, and the way to escape suffering is to cease to exist, and that happens when one gets rid of all desire.

Jesus' response to the disciples' question is significant. He said, "It was not that this man sinned, or his parents, but that the works of God might be made manifest in him." By this Jesus did not intend to teach that suffering is never the result of sin. (For example, we know that many cases of

congenital blindness have been caused by venereal disease.)
Neither did He intend to imply that God intentionally wills
disease in order to demonstrate His healing power. Jesus did
not seek to explain the origin of suffering. What He said was
this: "We don't know why this man was born blind, but what is
important is that here is an opportunity to show what God can
do." So He healed the man.

In the Christian life the important question is not *why*—
why do we suffer? But *how*—how do we react to suffering?
Do we allow tragedy and suffering to crush us, to destroy our
faith, and make us bitter and despondent? Or do we, by God's
help, overcome suffering, grow stronger in our faith, and
thereby become witnesses to God's sustaining grace? Instead
of raising theological questions when faced with the tragedies
of life (as the disciples did), we can look upon such events as
situations and opportunities for God to work and bring glory
to His name (as Jesus did).

Thought for the day: *By God's grace* tragedy *can be turned
into* triumph.

John 9:13–25   NOVEMBER 3

*One thing I know, that though I was blind, now I see
(v. 25).*

This story of the healing of the blind man has a certain
irresistible charm. Intense drama and subtle humor pervade
the dialogue between the Pharisees and the man who
recovered his sight.

The Pharisees were in a dilemma. That a notable miracle
had taken place they could not deny. Only God could open
the eyes of a man blind from birth, but would God break the
Sabbath by healing on that day? In their opinion, anyone who
would do that must be a sinner. So they tried to discredit the
miracle. They declared that this was not the man who sat by
the roadside, begging each day; it was someone who looked

like him. But the man himself and his parents testified that he and the beggar were one and the same person.

"Who is this person who healed you?" asked the Pharisees.

"I don't know," replied the man.

"How did he heal you?"

"He put clay on my eyes, and I washed in the pool of Siloam and now I see."

"Well, he must be a sinner," declared the Pharisees.

To which the man answered, "I don't know who the man is, or whether he is a sinner or not, but one thing I do know. I was blind, but now I see!"
This the Pharisees could not deny.

Nothing is more powerful and convincing than the personal witness. As Christians we may not be able to answer all the questions people raise about the Trinity, the person of Christ, the Bible, and so on. But we can tell the world what Christ has done in our lives. He has opened our eyes; He has forgiven us; He has transformed our lives. That's what really matters.

A converted alcoholic was accosted by skeptics. "Surely you don't believe all that stuff in the Bible, like Jesus turning water into wine," they taunted him. The man replied, "I don't understand all that, but this I do know. For me Christ has turned liquor into bread!"

Thought for the day: *Don't argue with skeptics; just witness.*

John 9:26–34   NOVEMBER 4

They reviled him . . . And they cast him out (vv. 28, 34).

The drama and subtle humor of this story continue in the dialogue between the Pharisees and the man healed of blindness.

For a second time the Pharisees asked him. "How did he open your eyes?"

There is a touch of sarcasm in the man's reply: "I have already told you and you don't seem to listen. Could it be that you are considering becoming his disciples?"

In response the Pharisees *reviled* him; they heaped abuse upon him. They said sarcastically, "You may be his disciple, but we are disciples of Moses. (They loved to boast of their pedigree). We know that God spoke to Moses, but as for this fellow, Jesus, we don't even know where he comes from."

"Now that is indeed strange," replied the man. "You are religious leaders. You do not know where he comes from, and yet he opened my eyes. Never since the world began has it been heard that anyone opened the eyes of a man born blind. This man, Jesus, must be from God or he never would be able to do such a marvelous thing!"

Note the increasing anger and hostility of the Pharisees. *Abuse* now turned to *insult*. The Pharisees said to the man, "You are nothing but a sinner like this man Jesus. You are ignorant and uneducated, and you are trying to teach us, who are experts in religious affairs!" Then finally they resorted to *threatened force*. The writer says briefly, "And they cast him out"; that is, they excommunicated him from membership in the local synagogue.

It is possible for persons to be highly educated and conversant with religious matters, and yet not know God and be totally ignorant of the truth. On the other hand, people who are poorly educated and lacking in theological training may know God intimately and be in touch with the truth. Everything depends on people's response to the claims of Christ and whether they are willing to accept the truth or not.

Thought for the day: *Unbelief leads to folly; faith leads to wisdom.*

*He said, "Lord, I believe"; and he worshiped him
(v. 38).*

Three important lessons stand out in the Scripture
passage for today:

1. *The tender compassion of Jesus.* This is one of the
most touching scenes in the whole life of Christ. We see
Jesus, the divine Light and Life, going in search of an ordinary
beggar, a person at the bottom rung of society, who had just
been excluded from membership in his synagogue. Here was
Jesus engaged in follow-up work in the task of personal
evangelism. He wanted the man to know he was not alone,
that he was loved. He wanted to lead the man into further truth
and to bring his faith to maturity.

2. *The growing faith of the man.* The man born blind
first regarded our Lord as "the man called Jesus" (v. 11), a
wonderful man, no doubt, but still just a man. Then when he
pondered the magnitude of the miracle, he recognized Jesus
as a prophet (v. 17), a person who lives close to God and
brings God's message to mankind. Finally, when Jesus
revealed His true identity, the man believed in Him as the "Son
of man" and worshiped Him. When people walk in the light
they already have, they always receive additional light.

3. *The increasing blindness of the Pharisees.* In contrast
to the simple faith of the man was the stubborn unbelief of the
Pharisees. They recognized that a notable miracle had taken
place and knew in their hearts that only one sent from God
could perform such a miracle. But they deliberately rejected
the facts and denounced Jesus as a deceiver, even a sinner.
So at the conclusion of the story, the man who was blind from
birth had received not only physical sight but spiritual insight
as well. As for the Pharisees, they rejected the truth and
entered into gross spiritual darkness. Their condemnation lay
in the fact that they knew so much and claimed to see so well,
yet they failed to recognize God's Son when He came.

Thought for the day: *Better to be blind and see, than to have eyes and not see.*

John 10:1−10 **NOVEMBER 6**

I came that they may have life, and have it abundantly (v. 10).

We find three common attitudes toward life:

1. *Life as a Tragedy.* This is the attitude of the confirmed pessimist, one who is always looking on the dark side of life. Some one has defined the pessimist as one who turns out the lights to see how dark it is. Such persons look at life through dark glasses, and the heavens always look cloudy. Afraid to face life, they run away from its trials and difficulties. "I'm here through fate so I guess I'll have to make the best of it," they say through clenched teeth. And when life is over, like the dying actor to those around, they exclaim, "Let down the curtain; the farce is over."

2. *Life as a Comedy.* This is the attitude of the pleasurist, who feels that life is "made for fun and frolic" and nothing else. Such persons look at life as a joke and play the part of the fool. They take no responsibilities, are always nonchalant and frivolous. Their philosophy is that of the epicurean: "Eat, drink, and be merry, for tomorrow we die."

3. *Life as a Victory.* This is the attitude of the true Christian, who has made Christ Lord and found abundant life in Him. Christians face life in the strength of Christ and are ready for anything. They see the joy in life and yet its serious side, and triumph in all the circumstances and affairs of this world. They are true optimists, trusting in Christ and looking with hope for the kingdom.

The pessimist is *tired* of life: the pleasurist *trifles* with life; the Christian *triumphs* in life. The pessimist *runs away* from life; the pleasurist *runs after* life; the Christian is *running over* with the abundant life. The pessimist looks at life as a *job*; the pleasurist as a *joke*; the Christian as a *joy*. To the pessimist life is *painful*; to the pleasurist it is *pleasureful*; to the Christian it is *purposeful*. The pessimist says, "We're here through *fate*; the pleasurist, "We're here for *fun*; the Christian, "We're here for *faith*."

Thought for the day: *Christ helps to face the music, even when we don't like the tune (Phillips Brooks).*

John 10:11–18   NOVEMBER 7

I am the good shepherd. The good shepherd lays down his life for the sheep (v. 11).

In this passage Jesus describes the difference between the true and the false shepherd. In claiming to be the Good Shepherd, Jesus sets Himself apart from both the false shepherds of the Old Testament—kings, priests, and prophets—who perverted the truth and led the people astray; and also the hypocritical Pharisees who posed as the religious leaders of their day. Note the contrasts:

1. The true shepherd *"enters the sheepfold by the door."* He is divinely appointed and has authority in himself. The false shepherd, like a thief, "climbs in by another way." He is an unauthorized leader, exercising self-assumed authority (v. 1).

2. The true shepherd *"calls his own sheep by name and leads them out,"* and *"the sheep follow him, for they know his voice"* (vv. 3, 4). An intimate relationship exists between shepherd and sheep. As for the false shepherd, he is a stranger to the sheep; they do not know his voice and will not follow him (v. 5).

3. The true shepherd *cares for his sheep, protects them, and is willing to lay down his life for them* (v. 11). The hireling, or false shepherd "cares nothing for the sheep" (v. 13), and flees for his life when he sees the wolf coming (v. 12). He is more concerned about saving his skin than protecting his sheep.

These words of Jesus can be fitly applied to the true and

false shepherds of the Christian congregations of our day. False shepherds are those who lack a genuine call to ministry, who care more about status and salary than about people and their spiritual welfare, who fail to feed their sheep on the Word of God, and are unable to protect their flock from the wolves of heresy and worldliness. True shepherds are those who are genuinely called by God, care for and love their people, nurture them on the truth, and are willing to lay down their lives in sacrificial service for the spiritual welfare of their congregations.

Thought for the day: *Jesus, the Good Shepherd, is the perfect model for shepherds of all time.*

John 10:19–29   NOVEMBER 8

No one shall snatch them out of my hand (v. 28).

In yesterday's meditation we noted the difference between the motivation and service of the good shepherd and that of the false shepherd. Today we note the benefits that the sheep receive from the faithful service of the true shepherd.

First, the sheep receive *life*. Jesus said, "I give them eternal life, and they shall never perish." They also find *satisfaction*. The sheep are free to go in and out of the fold to find pasture (v. 9). Then they also receive *protection*. Jesus said, "My sheep . . . follow me . . . and no one shall snatch them out of my hand." As long as we willingly remain in the hands of Jesus, we are safe from the enemy. This does not mean that we will be exempt from temptations and trials, but none of these things will be able to destroy or crush us.

A British soldier approached an evangelist after the sermon and said, "Sir, is it possible for a British Tommy to stand upright in the army?"

Taking a pen out of his pocket, the evangelist asked the soldier, "Is it possible for the pen to stand upright in my hand?" He stood the pen upright in the palm of his hand and then let it go. Naturally it fell down flat.

The soldier replied, "No, it is not possible."

"Now watch," said the evangelist, as he stood the pen upright in the palm of his hand and held on to it with the other hand.

"But you're holding it!" exclaimed the soldier.

"That's just the point," replied the evangelist. "As long as you allow Christ to hold you in His hand, you will stand upright."

Twenty-five years later the evangelist was preaching in a church in Bangalore, India. A British soldier, now much older and wiser, said to him, "Sir, it is true! A British Tommy can stand upright in the army. I have allowed Christ to hold me for the past twenty-five years, and He has never let me down."

Thought for the day: *There is perfect calm in the palm of Christ's hand.*

John 10:30–42   **NOVEMBER 9**

Do you say ... "You are blaspheming," because I said, "I am the Son of God?" (v. 36)

The main purpose of John's Gospel is to inspire faith in Jesus as the Son of God, Giver of eternal life (v. 28). To prove the deity of Jesus, the writer first of all records the great "I am" statements of our Lord which may be summarized as follows:

I am the Messiah (4:26)
I am the Bread of Life (6:35)
I am from above (8:23)
I am the Eternal One (8:58)
I am the Light of the world (9:5)
I am the Door (10:7)
I am the Good Shepherd (10:11)
I and the Father are one (10:30)
I am the Son of God (10:36)

I am the Resurrection and the Life (11:25)
I am Teacher and Lord (13:13)
I am the Way, the Truth and the Life (14:6)
I am the True Vine (15:1)

As further proof of Christ's deity, John records eight of His outstanding miracles (besides the Resurrection), six of which are found only in this Gospel. The list includes the water turned into wine; the healing of the nobleman's son, the man at the pool, and the man born blind; feeding the 5000; walking on the sea; the raising of Lazarus; and the miraculous catch of fish.

All through the gospel we note the two constrasting responses to these claims and signs. Some rejected the evidence, accused Jesus of blasphemy, and took up stones to kill Him (v. 31). Others accepted the evidence and believed on Him (v. 42).

All the evidence is before us today and we are faced with the same alternative: either *reject* or *receive; blaspheme* or *believe*. Christ is the great Divider of the human race, and it is our *faith* or *unbelief* that determines on which side of Christ we are on—the side of life or the side of death.

Thought for the day: *My* decision *about Christ will determine my* destiny.

John 11: 1—16   NOVEMBER 10

Are there not twelve hours in the day? (v. 9)

This question of Jesus suggests a certain fundamental attitude of life. It avoids, on one hand, an easy-going, nonchalant attitude, and on the other, a fretful anxiety. We do well if we follow the example of Jesus.

1. *We must live calmly.* There are a *full* twelve hours in the day. Tremendous tasks were heaped upon Jesus, but we never see Him fretful or nervous. He had all kinds of interruptions and disturbances, but no unrest; all kinds of

opposition, yet an amazingly unruffled spirit. Christ was confident that His life was God-ordered, that He was in the Father's care.

David Livingstone was confident in the same faith when he said, "I am immortal until my work is done." A person can't talk that way unless he is fitting in with utter flexibility to the pattern of God for his life. Time after time, Livingstone was laid low by fever and attacked by wild beasts; but time after time God raised him up. When asked for the secret, he quoted the promise of Jesus: "Lo, I am with you always, even to the end of the age."

2. *We must live selectively*. There are *only* twelve hours in the day. The things Jesus did *not* do are almost as wonderful as what He did. You can tell the difference between an ordinary artist and a real genius by this: a real artist subordinates all details to one dominant impression he is seeking to produce. Life is like that, if it is going to be a success. Some passion must control; some motive must dominate. Everything else must be subordinate. The ignoble must be dropped entirely; the unimportant must take second place. We must recognize the importance of selecting and discarding the trivial. Too many people spend themselves on the irrelevant.

Many things in this demanding world are not necessarily vicious, but we cannot afford to give attention to them if we are going to be effective disciples. Other things are bigger and more worthwhile. The Christ-controlled life represents a blend of passion and poise, of calmness and earnestness. Only Christ can give it and sustain it.

Thought for the day: *For to me to live is Christ and Christ alone.*

John 11: 17–27   **NOVEMBER 11**

I am the resurrection and the life (v. 25).

The verb tenses in this passage are significant. Martha said to Jesus, "Lord if you *had been* here, my brother would not have died." Here the *past tense* signifies lost opportunity. If Jesus had been on the scene when Lazarus took sick, Jesus could have healed him. But He wasn't present, so Lazarus died. The implication of Martha's words was: It's too late now; the opportunity for healing has past.

When Jesus said to Martha, "Your brother will rise again," She replied by saying, "I know that he *will rise* again in the resurrection at the last day." Here the *future tense* represents belief in the life to come, which gives hope for the future.

Finally, Jesus said to Martha, "I *am* the resurrection and the life," the *present tense* signifying an immediate reality. He went on to say that even if believers die physically, they will never die spiritually. This takes the sting out of death for the Christian. Death is no longer a dead end, but a door leading to a higher form of life.

My father, E.A. Seamands, missionary for over forty years, was visiting a group of Christians in a village one day. There he met a man who was in the last stages of the dread disease of leprosy. Already his nose and ears, fingers and toes were eaten away. But he was a radiant Christian, rejoicing in the salvation that Christ alone can give. The leper led my father to a tree just outside the village and pointed to a trench that was now about three feet deep. "Do you see this trench?" he asked. "This is my grave. I come here every day and with the stubs of my hands I dig a little deeper. I am preparing for the day when I will leave this wretched body and go to be with my Savior forever." To the leper death was not an end, but just the beginning of life.

Jesus never preached a funeral sermon. He broke up every funeral He ever attended. Death could not exist where He was. When the dead heard His voice, they sprang to life.

Thought for the day: *Death is God's anesthesia while He is changing our bodies* (E. Stanley Jones).

Jesus wept (v. 35).

In an informal church gathering many were quoting their favorite Scripture verses. These represented some of the most sublime and best loved statements in God's Word. Suddenly a lad called out, "Jesus wept," and immediately a ripple of laughter filled the room. But I thought to myself, Why should we laugh at this verse? It is the shortest verse in the Bible, but it's packed with meaning.

The question naturally arises, Why did Jesus weep when He knew that He was about to restore Lazarus to life? Herein lies the significance of this verse. Jesus did not weep over the death of Lazarus, but wept in sympathy over the anguish that Mary and Martha and friends of the family were experiencing from the loss of their brother and friend, Lazarus. This underscores the humanity of Jesus. He was not only fully God, but fully human as well. So when He saw the people weeping, "He was deeply moved in spirit and troubled."

The Greeks believed in an isolated, passionless god, who was untouched by the joys and sorrows of others. They argued that if a person is capable of feeling gladness or grief, then it means that someone else can have an effect over, therefore power over, that person. Now, no one else can have any power over God; that would be unthinkable. So God must be totally incapable of feeling any emotion whatsoever.

What an entirely different picture Jesus gave of God! He showed us a God whose heart is torn with anguish over the sufferings of His people, a God who is actually afflicted with our afflictions. To the Greek reader of this gospel, those two little words, "Jesus wept," would bring the most astounding message possible: that God understands and cares.

A mother, who lost her son in one of the bloody battles in Vietnam, cried out in anguish, "Where was God when my son was being killed in Vietnam?" An understanding pastor replied softly, "He was watching His own Son being put to death on a cross!"

Thought for the day: *Jesus is the best photograph God ever had taken.*

John 11:38—44   NOVEMBER 13

Lazarus, come out (v. 43).

If yesterday's passage underscored the full humanity of Jesus, today's passage emphasizes His deity. The focus shifts from human sympathy to divine power.

All through this Gospel the evangelist lays stress upon both the humanity and deity of Jesus. As man, Jesus accepted an invitation to a wedding feast; as God, He turned the water into wine. As human, Jesus became thirsty; as God, he offered the water of life. As human, He experienced hunger; as God, He said, "I am the bread of life." As man, He wept over the death of Lazarus; as God, He was able to say, "Lazarus, come out." I remember Dr. H.C. Morrison, founder of Asbury Theological Seminary, saying in one of his sermons, "There was so much power in the voice of Jesus that He had to specify Lazarus by name. If He had said only, 'Come out,' *all* the dead would have risen!"

In each of Jesus' "signs," an act of faith and obedience precedes the miracle itself. At the wedding feast in Cana, Jesus commanded the participants to "fill the jars with water"; then he turned the water into wine. To the impotent man at the pool of Bethsaida Jesus said, "Rise, take up your pallet and walk"; and at once the man was healed. To His disciples in the desert Jesus said, "Make the people sit down"; then he multiplied the loaves and fish and fed the 5000. To the man born blind Jesus said, "Go, wash in the pool of Siloam"; "so he went and washed and came back seeing." And now in this passage Jesus says to the people standing at the tomb of Lazarus, "Take away the stone"; then he cried out, "Lazarus, come out." All the miracles of Jesus were in response to obedience and faith of the people involved.

The deeper meaning of this amazing miracle is that Christ has robbed death of its sting and the grave of its victory. He demonstrated by deed the truth of His word: "I am the resurrection and the life."

Thought for the day: *Christ has conquered our greatest enemy—death.*

John 11:45–57   NOVEMBER 14

It is expedient for you that one man should die for the people (v. 50).

As in the case of every miracle that Jesus performed, the raising of Lazarus resulted in divided reaction among the people. Many who witnessed the miracle believed in Christ. They were open to the evidence and responded in faith and adoration. But the priests and Pharisees persisted in their unbelief, willfully choosing to reject the truth, simply because it threatened their interests.

Why did the same evidence leave some believers and others doubters? Subjective factors made the difference. Faith is the result not only of experiencing the evidence, but responding to it. Repeatedly in the Gospel the evangelist stresses the fact that a person's attitude and motive are the determining factors in belief. He emphasizes that the responsibility for unbelief is not with God but with the people; not with the revelation but with the recipients of it. The problem is not inadequate evidence, but refusal to accept the evidence. We see the same spirit all about us today.

When the priests and Pharisees heard the news of the raising of Lazarus, they called a council meeting. "If we don't put an end to these miracles," they said, "every one will go after this man Jesus, there will be an uprising, and then the Roman government will step in and destroy our temple and

357

our nation." Then Caiaphas, the high priest, made his two-edged statement, "If you had any sense," he said, "you would know that it is far better that one man should die for the nation than that the whole nation should perish." He meant that it was better to kill Jesus than to invite trouble with the Romans. Jesus must die to save the Jewish nation. What Caiaphas did not realize, however, was that a far more significant meaning lay hidden in his words. Jesus was to die—not only for the Jewish people, but for the whole world. He was to be the sacrificial atonement for the sins of all people. Caiaphas' statement thus turned out to be a prophecy of the vicarious death of Jesus.

Thought for the day: *One died that all may live.*

John 12:1—8   NOVEMBER 15

The house was filled with the fragrance of the ointment (v. 3).

The home of Mary, Martha, and Lazarus in Bethany is for us the model of a Christian home. When Jesus first came to Bethany, Martha (the eldest) received Him into their home (see Luke 10:38). This was the beginning of a long and intimate friendship that changed the lives of the two sisters and their brother. Jesus transforms every home He enters.

Have you ever invited Christ into your home? Does He have first place in your family? Is your home a place of prayer, where the Bible is honored and where love reigns supreme?

After Jesus raised Lazarus from the dead, out of gratitude the family planned a special dinner in Christ's honor. Note how each member represents one particular aspect of the Christian home.

1. *"Martha served."* The first time Jesus entered the home, He rebuked Martha for being too preoccupied with serving. He urged her to sit at His feet and listen to His message. But on this occasion there was no rebuke. Martha

was a good cook and used her culinary skill to serve Christ with a loving heart. She was a symbol of *the loving service of devotion*.

2. *Lazarus sat at the table with Jesus.* He was a symbol of *the silent witness of transformation*. He had been dead four days. Everyone in town knew this fact. Now he was alive and well at the table with Jesus, eating, and enjoying the fellowship. He didn't have to say a word. Everyone who saw him sitting there knew that a miracle had taken place. It was a testimony to the love and power of our Lord.

3. *Mary anointed the feet of Jesus* with precious, costly ointment, bought with her savings; and she wiped his feet with her hair. She was a symbol of *the loving sacrifice of consecration*. Out of love she gave the best she had to Jesus. As a result, the house was filled with fragrance.

Loving service, total consecration, and the witness of a transformed life—these characteristics make a house a Christian home.

Thought for the day: *Is Christ the Master of my home?*

John 12:9–19   **NOVEMBER 16**

They came, not only on account of Jesus but also to see Lazarus, whom he had raised from the dead (v. 9).

The raising of Lazarus from the dead had caused a stir in the countryside. Here was a man who had died, was in the tomb for four days, and now was walking around hale and hearty. People were talking about it all over town. Crowds gathered just to catch a glimpse of Lazarus, and many believed in Christ as a result.

Nothing is so powerful as the witness of a transformed life. People may be impressed by the size and beauty of our sanctuaries; they may be impressed by the wonderful institutions of the church and its noble humanitarian service. But nothing influences people more than to see a person alive and whole, who had been dead in trespasses and sins, a person who was once in bondage to evil habits, now free in spirit; someone who was once ill-tempered and self-seeking, now kind and thoughtful.

The jungle camp meeting at Dharur in India has been the spearhead of the evangelistic work in the South India and Hyderabad Conferences of Methodism for several decades. This camp or *jathra* (religious festival) was started back in 1923 by my late father, E.A. Seamands, and his missionary colleague, M.D. Ross. It now attracts 100,000 village people each year. Many villagers come to the camp, hear the gospel message in word and song, and go back home new persons in Christ.

One day a Hindu village headman met my brother David and with a puzzled look, asked, "What has happened to these people? What kind of idol do you have over there at the Dharur Jathra? David tried to explain that there was no idol, only the presence of the living God. "Well," said the headman, "I don't know what you've got over there, but since these people have been going to Dharur, something has happened to them. Why, now they're the best people in the village!"

Thought for the day: *The greatest miracle of all is a transformed life.*

John 12:20–26   NOVEMBER 17

Sir, we wish to see Jesus (v. 21).

These words were spoken by a delegation of Greeks who had come to Jerusalem for the feast of the Passover. Evidently they were proselytes to Judaism and had heard much about Jesus. Out of genuine desire for further truth, they wanted to meet and talk with the Master. So they approached Philip and said, "We would like to see Jesus." Since these persons were Greeks, or Gentiles, Philip wasn't sure how Jesus would react to the request, so he consulted Andrew. Andrew escorted them straight into the presence of Jesus.

Even today people of many nations and languages are longing to see Jesus. They have heard just enough about Him to whet their appetites. They have heard that Jesus was kind to the poor and the oppressed. They have heard the stories of the Prodigal Son and the Good Samaritan. They have heard that Jesus died on a cross—for sinners, it seems. But they want to know what all this means—who Jesus really is. And so they are saying, "We would like to see Jesus."

How is it possible for these people to see Jesus in our day? He is no longer present in the flesh. No one can actually seek Him out and talk to Him in person. The sobering truth is they will never see Jesus unless they see Him in us—in our words, our deeds, our attitudes.

A missionary visited a certain village in Africa one day. It was the first time any missionary had ever entered the place. The chief of the village met the missionary on the outskirts of town and said to him, "Missionary, we people in this village all believe in God. We know He exists. But we don't know anything about Him. We don't know what He is like. Please, you be God for us today."

Now in one way the chief was asking for the impossible, for no one can play God. But in another sense, he was right. We are to be God's representatives, so that when people look at us they see Jesus and thus see God.

Thought for the day: *Lord, may Christ be seen in me today.*

John 12:27–36   **NOVEMBER 18**

I, when I am lifted up from the earth, will draw all men to myself (v. 32).

It is clear from these words that Jesus was talking about His impending death on the cross. "All men" here refers to people of all races, nations, and cultures. Jesus was emphasizing the fact that His death was to be on behalf of the whole world, not just the Jews. Greeks and all Gentiles were to be included in the divine plan of redemption.

Jesus said that through his death on the cross He would draw all people to Himself. It is not primarily the teaching of Christ or the example of His life, but His death on the cross (in conjunction with the Resurrection) that still attracts multitudes across the world today and makes them His devoted disciples. That is why the cross is the universal symbol of the Christian faith.

A number of years ago torrential rains caused the Bhima River in south central India to overflow its banks and inundate a number of villages. Many cattle were drowned and several people lost their lives. On hearing that the Christians in the village of Saradagi were in distress, my missionary father rushed out to the village in a rescue attempt. The small band of Christians had gathered on a small knoll in the center of the village, seeking to protect themselves from rising waters which surrounded them. In order to attract their attention, my father painted a red cross on a white cloth background and held it high on a long bamboo pole. Immediately he heard faintly in the distance a shout of joy arise from the band of Christians.

When the waters subsided and the crisis was over the Christians of Saradagi said to my father, "Sir, when we saw the cross from a distance, we took hope. We knew rescue was near."

In the same way, as people across the world see the cross of Christ, they take hope, for they know that God cares and He has provided for their redemption.

Thought for the day: *The cross is still the supreme moral magnet of the world.*

John 12:37–50   NOVEMBER 19

Many even of the authorities believed in him, but for fear of the Pharisees they did not confess it (v. 42).

Among the followers of Jesus we note three distinct groups. The first group included the genuine, *committed disciples*. They were convinced that Jesus was the Messiah, the Son of God, and when Jesus called them, they immediately forsook all—home and business—and followed Him. The twelve disciples belonged to this group. They were by no means perfect and had their failures at times, but (with the exception of Judas) they were true to Christ to the end, and later became the leaders of the early church.

The second group consisted of the superficial, *bread-and-fish disciples*. They were impressed by the miracles of Jesus and enjoyed the public image of their association with such a great personality. They were excited over the possibility of Jesus' restoring to Israel their glorious kingdom of the past. But when Jesus made it clear that His was not a political kingdom, and when He laid down the heavy cost of discipleship, they gradually drifted away, unwilling to meet the demands (see John 6:66).

The third group included the *secret disciples*. They believed in Christ, but were unwilling to confess Him openly, for fear the Pharisees might excommunicate them from membership in the synagogue. As the evangelist John writes, "They loved the praise of men more than the praise of God."

The question rises, however, whether it is possible for one to be a secret disciple—at least, for long. The very term is really a contradiction in itself, for, as someone has said, "Either the secrecy kills the discipleship, or the discipleship kills the secrecy." Paul makes it clear that only those who believe in their hearts and confess with their lips that Jesus is Lord will be saved (Rom. 10:10).

Christ is not interested in *superficial* or *secret* disciples. He wants *sincere* disciples who will deny themselves, take up the cross, and follow Him, regardless of the cost, right to the end.

Thought for the day: *True discipleship requires discipline, devotion, and determination.*

He poured water into a basin, and began to wash the disciples' feet (v. 5).

Jesus came to earth not as a sovereign, but as a servant; not to be waited upon but to wait on others. All the symbols of the Christian faith are in keeping with this truth. The *manger* in Bethlehem reminds us of the divine stoop, whereby the Creator became one of the creatures; the Son of God became the son of a humble peasant woman. The *basin and towel* remind us that Christ, at whose feet all persons should kneel, was willing to wash the dirty feet of His disciples. The *cross* outside Jerusalem reminds us that Christ, in order to save others, could not save Himself; rather, He gave Himself as a ransom for all people.

The apostle Paul, in describing the extent of this divine stoop, wrote in his letter to the Philippian church: "Though [Jesus] was in the form of God, [He] did not count equality with God a thing to be grasped, but emptied himself, *taking the form of a servant*, being born in the likeness of men. And being found in human form he humbled himself and became obedient unto death, even death on a cross" (Phil. 2:6–8).

The record of Jesus washing His disciples' feet is one of the most beautiful and meaningful portraits of the servanthood of Christ. Few incidents of the gospel story reveal so clearly the character of Jesus and so perfectly show His love. We see no hint of humiliation in the incident—humility yes, but no humiliation. The word tells us that as Jesus girded Himself with a towel, poured water into a basin, and began to wash the disciples' feet, "he knew that his hour had come," and He knew "that the Father had given all things into his hands, and that he had come from God and was going to God." A certain divine dignity pervades the whole scene. Just think of it for a moment: The Son of God, voluntarily lovingly, washing the feet of sinful men, even the feet of His betrayer.

Thought for the day: *Servitude is degrading; service is dignified.*

John 13:12–20   NOVEMBER 21

I have given you an example, that you also should do as I have done to you (v. 15).

The disciples of Jesus often argued among themselves about which of them was the greatest or the most important. Again and again Jesus had to remind them that greatness is measured by service, not by status. He said to them, "He who is greatest among you shall be your servant" (Matt. 23:11). "If anyone would be first, he must be last of all and servant of all" (Mark 9:35).

But in spite of all this excellent teaching, the disciples still continued the debate. Luke tells us that even at the last supper "a dispute ... arose among them, which of them was to be regarded as the greatest" (Luke 22:24). This time Jesus gave them an object lesson of humility and service which they would never forget. He took a basin of water and a towel and washed their feet. Then He said to them, "You call me Teacher and Lord; and you are right; for so I am. If I then, your Lord and Teacher, have washed your feet, you also ought to wash one another's feet."

This sort of thing cuts right across the spirit and attitude of our age. Most people today seek position and power, riches and rank. Some politicians, instead of seeking for ways to serve the people and their country, strive for status and authority. Many Christian ministers, called to be shepherds and servants, look for bigger churches and better salaries. We all need to listen anew to the words of Jesus and walk in the footprints of His example.

I can still see the look of amazement on the faces of village people in India when my father would say to them, "For me to stay at home in my comfortable bungalow is like a *seramane* [prison], but to come to your villages and serve you is like an *aramane* [palace]." Because Dad was willing to be servant of all, the people considered him one of the greatest.

Thought for the day: *Reach for the towel rather than the top.*

John 13:21–30 NOVEMBER 22

After receiving the morsel, he immediately went out; and it was night (v. 30).

The story of the downfall of Judas is the most pitiful picture of unbelief in the Gospels.

His spiritual opportunities of knowing Christ were unsurpassed. He had received a personal call to discipleship from Jesus Himself. He had been at the side of the Master continually for three years, listening to all His teaching, watching every miracle, and observing a life that portrayed the very character of God. But he allowed sin gradually to take hold of him—the sin of avarice, unholy ambition, and, finally, unbelief and rejection.

Jesus knew what was happening in the heart and mind of Judas, but He loved him to the end. He made appeal after appeal to Judas. Clearly, from the description in this passage, Judas was seated directly on the left of Jesus, the place of highest honor kept for the most intimate friend. We can almost hear Jesus say to him, "Judas, come and sit beside me; I want to talk especially to you." When Jesus washed the feet of the disciples, he washed the feet of Judas also. And for the host to offer the guest a morsel of food taken from his own dish was a sign of special friendship.

But Judas rejected all these overtures of love, and allowed Satan to enter and take control of him. The story of Judas ends with these sad, sad words: "He immediately went out *and it was night.*" This was more than just the close of a day; it was the close of a life. The darkness in the soul of Judas was far greater than the darkness of the night.

A person is always in the dark when he or she rejects the

light of the Gospel and goes a different, selfish way. A person is always in the dark when he or she spurns the love of Christ and turns to the hatred of the world.

Thought for the day: *Sin turns the lights off, but Jesus can turn them on again.*

John 13:31–38   NOVEMBER 23

A new commandment I give to you, that you love one another; even as I have loved you, that you also love one another (v. 34).

The commandment to love one another was not new, but Jesus now adds a whole new dimension to the quality of our love. We are to love one another *as He has loved us.* That is to be the measure of our love.

How has Jesus loved us? His was a *selfless love.* He never asked what He could get out of us, but what He could do for us. He loved us in spite of our faults, our failures, and our sin. His was a *sacrificial love.* No demand was so severe, no sacrifice so great that He was unwilling to give Himself for us. Such love took Him to a cross, where He bore our sins and died in our place.

Thus, we are to love one another selflessly and sacrificially. But this is not possible in our own strength. We can love in this manner only when "God's love has been poured into our hearts by the Holy Spirit [who] has been given to us" (Rom. 5:5).

The Reverend Paul Yonggi Cho, pastor of the world's largest church (500,000 members), grew up in Korea during the Japanese occupation. He was forced to learn and speak Japanese, and he witnessed many atrocities against his people. As a result he developed a deep-seated hatred in his heart toward the Japanese. One day the inner voice said, "Go to Japan," but he didn't want to go. Finally, when he received an invitation to address a pastors' conference there, he went.

But when he saw a sea of Japanese faces, the old resentment and hatred stirred within him. He stood silent for two or three minutes, then said to his audience, "I'm sorry, but I am unable to preach to you. I'm too full of hate for the Japanese. You will have to pray for me." Speaker and congregation dropped to their knees and prayed fervently and in anguish for several minutes. Suddenly something happened. The preacher was filled with a supernatural love for his former tormentors, and he rose from his knees to address the conference with great effectiveness. He could now love Japanese as Christ loved them.

Thought for the day: *Christ's commands are His enabling acts.*

John 14:1–7   NOVEMBER 24

I am the way, and the truth, and the life; no one comes to the Father, but by me (v. 6).

Notice, Jesus did not say, "I will show you the way," or "I will teach you the truth," or "I will give you life." He said categorically, "*I am* the way; *I am* the truth; *I am* the life." He is the very embodiment, the personification of the way, the truth, and the life. Thus, when we enter into a personal relationship with Christ, we are immediately on the way. When we know Him, we are in touch with truth, with reality. When we know Him, we are alive. The Gospel is therefore based on a Person, not a set of precepts; on Christ, not a code or creed.

Again notice, Jesus said, "No one comes to the Father, but by me." He is not *a* way, but *the* way. He is not *a* savior, but the *one and only* Savior. All other ways are merely detours leading to dead ends.

Perhaps more non-Christians have been led to faith in Christ by this one verse than any other verse in the Bible. It seems to satisfy their desperate search for God.

Sugiyanto Sukarno was the leader of a popular dance

band in Indonesia. He was a staunch Muslim. One day he had a serious accident on his motorcycle, and lay unconscious in the ditch. A Christian passing that way picked him up, put him in his car, and carried him to a Christian hospital nearby. When Sukarno regained consciousness, he saw a motto on the wall: "I am the way, the truth, and the life." He asked, "Who said those words?" and was told that it was Jesus Christ. When he finally recovered from his wounds, he enrolled in the Bible school at Batu Malang in order to find out more about this Person. As a result, Sukarno was marvelously converted and came to faith in Jesus Christ. In spite of severe persecution, he kept true to his Lord, and eventually won his parents to Christ. Today he is an evangelist and uses his musical talent and testimony to lead others to the Person who is "the way, the truth, and the life."

Thought for the day: *I am in Christ; therefore, I am on the way.*

John 14:8–14 **NOVEMBER 25**

He who has seen me has seen the Father (v. 9).

Where do we start in our search for truth? If we start with God, we begin with our preconceptions of God, and these are often erroneous. If we start with people, we begin with a problem, because humankind is frail and sinful. The only true starting point is the God-man, Jesus Christ. In Him we see what humankind is and how far we have fallen; in Him we see what God is and how far we may rise.

A few days ago I quoted an old saying: "Jesus is the best photograph that God ever had taken." We now know what God is like in the person we have seen in Jesus. He is Christlike. And if He is, He is a good God and trustworthy. We can transfer every single moral quality in Jesus to God without loss or degradation to our thought of God. On the contrary, by thinking of Him in terms of Jesus, we heighten our view of

Him. All those who have tried to think of Him in other terms have lowered or impoverished our ideas of God. In Christ we see the *holiness* of God. Christ was pure in word and deed, in thought and motive. He was righteousness, justice, and goodness personified. In Christ we see the *love* of God. We see God caring intensely, yearning over men and women, loving until He bore the wounds of love upon His heart. No one would ever have dreamed of a God who, in Jesus Christ, chose the cross of our salvation. In Christ we also see the *power* of God—power to heal and make whole, power over the forces of nature, power to transform human nature, and power over death and hell.

A young lad stood gazing at a life-size portrait of his father, who had died when the boy was just a baby. So he never knew his father. The thought suddenly rushed through his mind: "If Dad would only step out of the picture and come to me, I could know him." That's exactly what God has done. He has stepped out of the picture and come to us in Jesus Christ. So if we look at Christ, we see the Father.

Thought for the day: *The highest compliment we can pay to any person is to say, "He/she is Christlike."*

John 14:15—24   **NOVEMBER 26**

[The Holy Spirit] dwells with you, and will be in you (v. 17).

Here is the promise of the permeating presence of the Holy Spirit in the life of the believer.

We must not take the prepositions "with" and "in" too literally. It doesn't mean that in conversion the Holy Spirit is merely on the outside, with the believer, and then in the experience of the fullness of the Spirit He moves within. The Holy Spirit abides in every believer but Christ is trying to emphasize a closer, more intimate relationship between the Holy Spirit and the believer. It is not enough for believers to have the Holy Spirit guide, inspire, strengthen, and comfort us. We all need the Holy Spirit to fill, rule, and overflow. The distinction is between being "born of the Spirit" and being "filled with the Spirit."

Today the Holy Spirit seems to be more *with* the average Christian than *in*. He comes now and then to illuminate in a crisis, to censure in a fall, to urge against our sloth, to point out duties undone, and to keep us going—although it is at a "poor dying rate." The average Christian lives under the lash of demand rather than under the liberty of the Spirit.

God has been constantly trying to move from the "alongside" relationship to the "abiding" relationship. In the Old Testament era religion was an *imposition*, a law. During the Incarnation stage religion was an *imitation*—trying to do what Jesus did. In the age of the Spirit, religion is an *indwelling*, a spontaneous imperative from within.

I heard a young lad in India pray this prayer: "Lord, I open the door of my heart to you. Come on in, sit down, and make yourself at home!" This is what the Holy Spirit does—makes our hearts His home. And this is exactly what it means to be a Christian. Not making a lot of resolutions or trying to live up to certain standards in our own strength, but receiving the Holy Spirit into the center of our personalities and allowing Him to cleanse and control and empower.

Thought for the day: *God first dwelt in a holy temple; then in a holy Person; now He wants to dwell in us who want to be holy.*

John 14:25–31   NOVEMBER 27

The Holy Spirit ... will teach you all things, and bring to your remembrance all that I have said to you (v. 26).

In John 14, Jesus tells us several things about the Holy Spirit. First, He tells us that the Holy Spirit is the divine

Indweller—"He dwells with you, and will be in you" (v. 17). He gets deep down into the center of our personalities, takes us over and makes us over. There, where the surgeon can't get with his knife or the psychiatrist with his probing, the Holy Spirit dwells and works. He controls our thoughts and emotions, purifies our desires and motives, and directs our wills and ambitions.

Then again, the Holy Spirit is the divine *Helper* (Comforter or Counselor). Jesus reasons with our minds; calls us to repent, obey, and follow. But it is hard for us to respond. Our hearing is dull; our understanding is darkened; our wills are weak. This is where the Holy Spirit comes in. He fans the flame within us, helps us to overcome our weakness, leads us to Jesus. He helps us to hear and understand our Lord, pleads with us to obey Him, strengthens us to follow Him. He helps Christ within us.

In the passage for today Jesus tells that the Holy Spirit is the divine *Instructor*—"he will teach you all things," for He is the Spirit of truth (v. 17). Our minds are frail; we often find it difficult to understand. But if we open our hearts and minds to the Holy Spirit, He will open the eyes of our understanding, to guide us into the truth.

Finally, the Holy Spirit is the divine *Inspirer*. Jesus told His disciples that the Holy Spirit would bring to their remembrance all that He had said to them. This is how they were able to write the four gospels and preserve all the teachings and sayings of our Lord. This is what gives authenticity to the Scriptures, so that we can rely upon them as an accurate account of all that Jesus said and did. Without the inspiring and guiding of the Holy Spirit, the writing of the Scriptures would not have been possible.

Thought for the day: *The Holy Spirit is not a substitute for an absent Lord; He is the agent of the living Christ.*

I am the vine, you are the branches ... apart from me you can do nothing (v. 5).

Earlier in John's Gospel, Jesus declared Himself to be the bread of life and the living water. That is, He alone can satisfy the hunger and quench the thirst of our souls. Now He declares that He is the vine, and we are the branches. In other words, He is the only source of our spiritual life and work.

The main idea in this analogy is that of relationship. In order for the branches to stay alive and bear fruit, they must be connected with the vine. If they are cut off from the vine, the branches will wither and die. In like manner, as long as we maintain our relationship with Christ, we will be spiritually alive and useful in His service. The moment we break the connection, we become lifeless and useless.

Christ, the true vine, is the living fountain of all our spiritual energies. He is the moral stem of humanity and the source of all goodness and virtue which are manifest in the world. Our spiritual life is a branch life. It is derivative, dependent, incomplete in itself. Apart from Christ, true life is impossible.

Christ, as the true vine is also the source of spiritual fruit in our lives. He said clearly, "Apart from me you can do nothing." Observe, He didn't merely say our work will be of inferior quality, but that it will be no work at all. It will have no lasting value. It simply won't count in the final result. Fruit is the one thing the vinedresser seeks. By fruit, is here meant some product of eternal value; some result of our life and work which will contribute to the kingdom of God. All else is really worthless.

Abiding in Christ, as the branch in the vine, we become channels for the overflow of His Spirit, and the fruits of the Spirit are wrought in us, not by any strain or effort, but as a natural product.

Thought for the day: *Apart from Christ I can do nothing; through Christ I am able for anything.*

John 15:9–11

These things I have spoken to you, that my joy may be in you, and that your joy may be full (v. 11).

We know the difference between happiness and joy. Happiness is dependent on happenings, on outer circumstances. When everything is going well—when we are physically fit, have enough money to pay our bills, and the boss is in a good mood—then we feel happy. Joy, on the other hand, is not dependent on outer circumstances. Joy is the result of inner-stances, inner well-being. A person may be in prison (like Paul in Ephesus) with hands and feet in chains and his back bleeding, yet be able to sing with joy at midnight. Things may go wrong, sickness may overtake, tragedy may strike, but still the Christian may experience joy deep within his or her heart.

The secret of joy is this: J-O-Y: Jesus, Others, Yourself. When we put Christ and others ahead of ourselves, we don't worry about self-seeking, rivalry, or enmity. The result is well-being and joy.

A certain man was given a special seed by his friend. "This is the seed of joy," explained the friend. "Plant it carefully and you will find true joy." After some time the man returned, looking very disheartened. "I planted the seed you gave me," he said to his friend, "but I did not find the joy you promised."

"Where did you plant the seed?" asked the giver.

"In my backyard," came the reply.

"Ah, that's where you went wrong," said the first. "You should have planted it in your *neighbor's* backyard!"

Thought for the day: *Joy is a gift to be received, not a reward to be sought.*

*I chose you and appointed you that you should go
and bear fruit and that your fruit should abide (v. 16).*

The only way to bear fruit in the lives of others is to show
them the fruit of the Spirit in our own lives. Jesus sends us
out—not to argue people into the Christian faith, but to attract
them into it.

When Gordon Maxwell, a missionary to India, asked a
Hindu pandit if he would teach him his language, the Hindu
replied, "No, Sahib, I will not teach you my language. You
would make me a Christian." Gordon Maxwell replied, "You
misunderstand me. I simply am asking you to teach me your
language." The Hindu replied again, "No, Sahib, I will not
teach you. No man can live with you and not become a
Christian." Can this be said of you and me?

In this chapter Jesus clearly specifies the major Christian
fruit that should be evident in our lives daily. They constitute a
glorious trio: love, obedience, and joy. Note these words of
Jesus: "Abide in my *love*. If you *keep my commandments*,
you will abide in my love. . . . These things I have spoken to
you, that my *joy* may be in you" (vv. 9–11). Love leads to
obedience, and obedience, in turn, leads to joy.

When these three qualities regulate our lives, others will
be attracted to Christ, for it is *His* love, *His* joy, and *His* will
that are manifested through us. As a result, non-Christians will
be convicted and converted; Christians will be comforted and
challenged. This is what it means for us to "bear fruit."

This fruit will *abide*, says Jesus. It will stand the test of
time. On a recent trip to India, I preached in the Methodist
Church in Bangalore. After the service an elderly man said to
me, "Twenty-five years ago when you preached in Madras I
surrendered my life to Jesus Christ. It was on the same day as
your birthday. So my spiritual birthday and your physical
birthday are the same date. I have been rejoicing and serving

the Lord ever since that day." Thank God for fruit that remains.

Thought for the day: *The only way to spread Christianity is to be Christian (William Barclay).*

John 15:18–21   DECEMBER 1

Because you are not of the world ... the world hates you (v. 19).

In yesterday's meditation we noted that the genuine Christian life acts like a magnet to attract the world to Christ and the Christian faith. It convicts people of their sins and then draws them to the Savior. But there is another side to the picture. Whereas the Christian life *attracts* some people, it *aggravates* others. They are convicted of their sins, but instead of coming to the Savior for deliverance, they get angry. Instead of responding in faith, they react with hate.

This was true in the life of Christ. His was such a beautiful, magnetic life, so full of love and compassion and service. For this reason many were attracted to Him and became His devoted disciples. They were ready to lay down their lives for Him. But then some people became angry at Him and rejected Him. They felt condemned for their hypocrisy and greed by the very presence of Christ, and they couldn't stand it. So they decided to get rid of Him, and eventually nailed Him to a cross between two thieves.

Jesus warned His disciples that "the world" would treat them the same way. A godless society would hate and persecute them just as it did Him. For the followers of Christ have two marks of their discipleship: The first is that they love one another; the second, that they are hated by the world.

As contemporary disciples of Christ, we face the same situation today. Christ's new commandment is to be the rule and law of His church. We are to love one another as He loved us. But at the same time the Christian spirit which we seek to exhibit leads to conflict in the world. Just as the world hated and persecuted the Master, because the truth which He was and taught brought condemnation to society, so it will be with us. But this truth should bring us much comfort because if we are hated for Christ's sake, it is a good sign that we are not of the world and are fruitful disciples of our Lord.

Thought for the day: *The badgering of the world is the badge of the Christian.*

John 15:22–27   DECEMBER 2

He will bear witness to me; and you also are witnesses (vv. 26, 27).

Christ is the center of the Christian faith—not a system of philosophy or theology, not a set of principles or teachings, but a Person, Christ Himself. Thus, everything in the Scriptures points to Him. I have heard that at one time the British Navy used a certain type of rope in the center of which, from beginning to end, ran a scarlet thread. If you were to cut the rope at any point, the scarlet thread would appear. In the same way, a scarlet thread runs through the whole Bible, so that if you open it at any page, the scarlet thread can be seen. It is the scarlet thread of redemption pointing to the Person of Christ.

Two important witnesses give testimony to the saviorhood and lordship of Christ: the Holy Spirit and the believer. One is the divine witness, and the other the human witness; the inner witness and the outer witness. The Holy Spirit constantly points our attention to Christ as the Son of God and the Savior of the world. He gives us the inner assurance that Christ is real, all that He claims to be. He testifies to us that Christ is the Truth, and that all He taught is the very word of God. And when we trust in Christ as Savior, the Holy Spirit witnesses with our spirits that God has forgiven our sins and has accepted us as His children.

377

The second witness to Christ is the believer, the one who has put his faith in Christ and has discovered for himself that Christ is all He claims to be, and has himself become a new person in Christ. He speaks from personal experience, from long fellowship and intimacy with Christ. He is thus able to speak with inner conviction: "This is true, *and I know it!*"

When the outer testimony of the believer is reinforced by the inner witness of the Spirit, it has a profound impact upon the unbeliever to lead him to Christ.

Thought for the day: *First-hand testimony is more effective than second-hand truth.*

John 16:1–11

When he comes, he will convince the world of sin and of righteousness and of judgment (v. 8).

The ministry of the Holy Spirit to the world is threefold. First, He convicts of *sin.* Apart from the working of the Holy Spirit in our hearts and minds, we do not really see ourselves as God sees us. The Spirit lays bare our hearts, exposes our sins, and pronounces us guilty before God. This is a disturbing experience for anyone. We may lose sleep or appetite. We certainly lose our peace of mind. But the Holy Spirit shows us our sin in order that we will seek the Savior. As Sam Shoemaker used to say, "Before the Holy Spirit can be the Comforter, He has to be the Discomforter."

Again, the Holy Spirit convicts of *righteousness.* He shows us that our own morality and good deeds are insufficient in the sight of God, and that true righteousness is found only in Jesus Christ. He teaches us that righteousness is an obtainment and not an achievement. It is the gift of God and not the product of humankind.

An immaculately dressed stranger stood at the door of my home one day. When I saw him, I looked at my pants streaked with paint and my frayed shirt, and I became embarrassed. The contrast was overwhelming. In the same way, Jesus in all His purity and perfection stood at the door of my heart one day, and when I looked at my own heart, I realized that my own goodness and morality were nothing but filthy rags in His sight. For true righteousness is not something put on but something put in.

Then again, the Holy Spirit convicts us of the *judgment.* He reveals to us that the prince of this world, Satan, has already been judged by the death of our Lord Jesus Christ, and that we too, apart from the grace of God, stand condemned before the heavenly tribunal. He reminds us that one day we will have to stand before the judgment bar of God and give an account of our deeds and words, our opportunities and privileges, our talents and possessions. We are all answerable to God.

Thought for the day: *The Holy Spirit upsets us in order to set us up.*

John 16:12–15   DECEMBER 4

He will guide you into all the truth ... He shall glorify me (vv. 13, 14).

Yesterday we noted the ministry of the Holy Spirit to the unbeliever. He convicts the individual of sin, righteousness, and the judgment. Today we observe His ministry to the believer.

Jesus said to the disciples, "When the Spirit of truth is come, he shall guide you into all the truth." The Holy Spirit had to teach them many things. For example, they did not fully understand the significance of Christ's death until after the Resurrection and the experience of Pentecost. Now they realized that Christ's suffering and death were in the plan of God from the beginning, and that the crucifixion was in effect a vicarious suffering for the sins of the world. Again, not until the Holy Spirit appeared to Peter in a vision and ordered him to go to the household of Cornelius did Peter and the rest of the disciples understand that Christ's atoning death was for all people. The Gentiles were to be included in the new covenant!

Then Jesus told the disciples, "When the Spirit is come, he will glorify me." The Holy Spirit is a self-effacing Spirit. He does not speak of Himself; He speaks only of Christ. He reveals who Christ is; He inspires faith in Christ; He makes real the living presence of Christ.

The Holy Spirit is thus the divine Ambassador, sent by both the Father and the Son (see 14:26 and 16:7). He is the Executive of the Godhead, God's Representative on earth. He delivers only the message which He is told to deliver. And when He speaks, all the authority of the Godhead is behind Him. As the divine Ambassador, the Holy Spirit is to be respected, listened to, and obeyed.

The Holy Spirit will do the same for us. He will continue to guide us into new vistas of truth about the heavenly Father, the Savior, and our mission to the world. He will continue to glorify Christ both in us and through us.

Thought for the day: *The Holy Spirit is our best Teacher in the school of life.*

John 16:16–24   DECEMBER 5

No one will take your joy from you (v. 22).

In this passage Jesus speaks of the Christian's joy. He makes three important statements:

1. "Your sorrow will turn into joy."
2. "No one will take your joy from you."
3. "Ask, and you will receive, that your joy may be full."

Christ can turn the believer's sorrow into joy. He can mend broken relationships, heal broken hearts, and remove the burden of sin and its guilt. Even when death comes into the home, Christ can wipe away all tears by hope of the future resurrection.

This joy that Jesus offers is permanent. It will stand the trials of life and the test of time. It will never be taken away by anything or anyone. This joy is independent of the circumstances and changes of the world. Even when the storms rage on the outside, inner calm and peace will abide.

The Christian's joy is not only permanent, it is also complete. Jesus grants all His gifts in abundance. He not only gives peace, but "peace that passes all understanding." He not only gives love, but "he pours it into our hearts" and fills us with His love. He not only grants joy, but "joy unspeakable and full of glory."

In the early days of the Christian faith, when Rome was severely persecuting the church, a Christian senator stood on trial before his persecutors. Then tried to persuade him to renounce his faith in Christ and bow the knee to Caesar. But he refused. "We will strip you of your name and title," threatened the officials. The Christian answered, "My name is written in the Lamb's Book of Life. You cannot erase it." "We will take your wealth and possessions," they threatened. "My treasure is laid up in heaven; you can't touch it," replied the senator. "We will take your life," shouted the persecutors angrily. The Christian answered, "My life is hid in Christ. For me to die is gain." Nothing the officials could do would rob the Christian of his joy in Christ.

Thought for the day: *Joy is the flag flown over the castle of the heart when the King is in residence (Principal Rainy).*

John 16:25–33   **DECEMBER 6**

In the world you have tribulation, but be of good cheer, I have overcome the world (v. 33).

Jesus first gives us a warning of problems to come, and then a word of promise that we shall overcome. He says, "The world will hate you because you are different, and your conduct condemns its lifestyle." But then He quickly adds,

"Be of good cheer; rejoice for I have overcome the world and you, too, shall overcome."

I have overcome temptation and trials, says Jesus, and made them stepping stones to stronger faith and character.

I have overcome the flesh with all its enticements and glitter, and built my kingdom on righteousness and truth.

I have overcome Satan and all his wiles so that you no longer need fear his onslaughts.

I have overcome suffering and pain, and turned them into redemption for all the world.

I have overcome death so that it is no longer an end but a doorway to life.

I have overcome the hate of the world through love and forgiveness.

I have overcome sin; it shall no longer have dominion over you.

Notice that Jesus spoke these words even before His death and Resurrection. He did not become Conqueror because He died and rose again. He died and rose again because He already was the Conqueror. The cross and empty tomb were merely demonstrations of His victory. And now He passes on this victory to you and me. It is a gift to be received, and not a goal to be achieved. Thus, we do not strive *toward* the victory; we work *from* the victory. Christ has already gained the victory for us.

The secret of this daily victory is the indwelling presence of the Holy Spirit. The Spirit sanctifies and empowers us so that we, like Christ, can overcome temptation, trials, suffering, persecution, hatred, death, and the Evil One.

Thought for the day: *Christ enables us to turn tribulation into triumph.*

John 17:1–3   DECEMBER 7

This is eternal life, that they may know thee, the only true God, and Jesus Christ whom thou hast sent (v. 3).

Here is the great New Testament definition of eternal life: To know the only true God and Jesus Christ whom He has sent.

The phrase *eternal life* does not refer to *duration* of life, for a life that simply goes on and on forever would not necessarily be a blessing. Eternal life is a special *quality* of life. It is actually the life of God within us. To possess eternal life means, therefore, to experience something of the glory, the joy, the peace, and the holiness which are characteristic of the life of God.

Eternal life comes from *knowing* God and His Son, Jesus Christ. A certain element of *intellectual knowledge* is implied here. We cannot know everything about God, but we need to have some concept of what God is really like before we can put our trust in Him. We must realize that He is not a hostile, capricious God who lies in wait for us at every corner. He is not a stern Judge who delights in pronouncing us guilty and punishing us. He is a compassionate God who loves us in spite of our sins, and has sent His Son into the world to redeem us from our sins.

But knowing God is more than intellectual understanding about God. It is possible to have considerable knowledge of God and yet not really know Him. To know God is to enter into intimate relationship with Him, a relationship that is just as real as that between husband and wife, or close friend with friend.

Both knowledge of God and personal relationship with God are possible only through the person of Jesus Christ. Through Jesus we know what God is like, and through Jesus we enter into the friendship of God. Through the Son we know the Father, and through the Father we receive eternal life.

Thought for the day: *Eternal life is not how long we live but how well we live.*

John 17:4–8   **DECEMBER 8**

I glorified thee on earth, having accomplished the work which thou gavest me to do (v. 4).

The supreme goal of life is to glorify God. All other objectives are secondary. Jesus, at the end of His earthly life, was able to say with all confidence, "I have glorified God. I have finished the work which He gave me to do."

Jesus Christ came to earth on a special mission. He came to reveal the nature and character of God—His wisdom and truth and His will for our lives. Above all, through His voluntary, vicarious death on the cross, followed by His glorious Resurrection, Jesus came to complete God's plan of redemption for all the peoples of the earth. By finishing this mission in total obedience to His Father, Jesus brought the highest glory to almighty God.

You and I can also bring glory to God by completing the mission He has entrusted to us. It may be a highly publicized mission, like that of a Billy Graham, or a silent mission such as that of a Brother Lawrence peeling potatoes in the kitchen. The mission may be that of the president of the United States, responsible for leading his nation under God, or the humble task of a bootblack polishing shoes for Jesus. The degree and extent of the glory may vary, but we can all bring glory to God in some way or other.

As my father approached death on a hospital bed in Vellore, South India, he kept saying over and over again, "I can't die now. I have twenty-five churches under construction that need to be completed." My brother David, who sat by his bedside, made Dad repeat several times the words of Jesus, "I have finished the work You gave me to do." "How old was Jesus when He said that?" asked David. "About thirty-three," replied Dad. Then David said to him, "Dad, if Jesus could say that at age thirty-three, surely you can say it at ninety-two!" At that, Dad relaxed and died in peace a few days later.

Thought for the day: *Am I bringing glory to God by all I say and do?*

*I do not pray that thou shouldst take them out of the
world but that thou shouldst keep them from the evil
one (v. 15).*

Here is the paradox of the Christian life. Disciples of Jesus
Christ are to be *in* the world, but not *of* the world. They are to
be separated from the *evil* of the world, but not from the
evildoers of the world; they are to be *different*, but not
detached. So Jesus prays for His followers, not that they
might be taken out of the world, but that they be kept from the
evil one. He does not pray that they might find *escape*, but
that they might find *victory*. A ship is safe in the ocean as long
as the ocean doesn't get into the ship. Likewise, Christians are
safe in the world as long as the world does not get into them.

Throughout its history the church of Jesus Christ has
been guilty of one or the other of two extreme positions. The
one is to enclose itself in a monastery or convent, in order to
protect the purity of its life and faith. In so doing, however, the
church loses contact with the world and thus becomes
impotent to change the world. The other danger is for the
church to identify itself so much with the world—in order to
maintain rapport with society—that it loses its distinctiveness
and witness. Thus, instead of the church changing the world,
the world changes the church. We have to avoid both
extremes. If the first extreme was characteristic of the early
Christian centuries, the second is prevalent in the twentieth
century.

The apostle Paul gives us the solution to this problem. In
his letter to the Colossian church, he addresses them as
"faithful brethren *in Christ in Colossae*" (1:2). Here we have
our dual citizenship as Christian disciples. We are *in Christ*
(our spiritual location) but we are also *in Chicago* or Calcutta,
Toronto or Tokyo (our geographical location). If we are in
Christ, not just in the church, we are secure. We will be like

Christ and therefore different from the world. Then we can go back into the world and, by God's grace, help to redeem it.

Thought for the day: *Contact without contamination produces change.*

John 17:16—18   DECEMBER 10

Sanctify them in the truth (v. 17).

Jesus not only prayed for our *security* ("keep them from the evil one"), but also for our *sanctity* ("sanctify them in the truth"). He knew that sanctity is actually the best guarantee of security. When we are made holy by God's grace, we will be kept from the evil of the world.

The word that is used in the Greek text is *hagiazo*, which has two complementary meanings. Its basic meaning is *separation*: separation from the sinful and unclean, and consecration unto God. Its second meaning is to *purify* or make holy. Thus, "sanctification" is an act of God, setting apart an individual for some special service, plus an act of God in which His own righteous nature is imparted to that person to equip him or her for service. Sanctification is therefore essential, not only for *security in the world*, but for *service to the world*. In order to serve God effectively, a person must have something of God's mind and character.

We can learn a lesson from the operating theater. Certain surgical instruments are necessary for a particular operation. They have been set apart, or consecrated, for a special task. But in order to be safe and effective, these instruments have to be thoroughly sterilized, that is, purified and made free from any dirt or germs. The same is true about the hands of the surgeon. They have been consecrated to the task of surgery, but they must be scrubbed and cleansed before they can go to work.

Just so, God has set us apart for a particular task in the world, but in order for us to be useful instruments in His hands, He must first sanctify us, that is, purify our hearts and deliver us from all uncleanness. We see this clearly in the lives of Christ's disciples. He had called them and set them apart for a special task, instruments. It took the sanctifying ministry of the Holy Spirit at Pentecost to prepare them for their world-wide mission.

Thought for the day: *When God enlists us, he equips us.*

John 17:20–26 DECEMBER 11

I pray ... for those who believe in me through their word, that they may all be one (vv. 20, 21).

Jesus prayed, not only for our *security* ("keep them") and our *sanctity* ("sanctify them"), but also for our *unity* ("that they may all be one"). Sanctity is necessary for our security and service in the world; unity is necessary for our witness to the world.

Unity does not necessarily mean uniformity. We all don't have to worship or sing or preach in the same way. Differences in taste and culture will always lead to variety in Christian forms. Again, unity does not necessarily mean organic union. Uniting denominations will not, merely by that act, settle our church problems. A number of already dead churches will produce only a bigger corpse. Christian unity, however, does require oneness of heart and mind. It means loyalty and obedience to one Lord, submission to the authority of one Book, and love for all the people of God. Christian unity rules out all denominational pride, competition, judgmental criticism, sheep-stealing, and exclusiveness.

A number of years ago, in a group of villages near Calcutta, a Christward movement of wide dimensions and extraordinary power took place under the ministry of a Congregational minister. Within a short while hundreds confessed their faith in Christ, and a church of great promise. was born. But suddenly Christian disunity entered the picture

Anglican missionaries came along and told the converts that the ministers serving them were not properly ordained. A little later Baptist missionaries entered with the declaration that the converts had not received the right kind of baptism and should now be immersed. Then followed the Roman Catholics contending that they were the only true church of Christ. As a result the movement Christward was completely stopped.

The world will not be convinced of the truth of the Gospel until all of us who claim to be Christians show that we love one another and demonstrate the unity of the Body of Christ.

Motto for the church: *Here we enter a fellowship; sometimes we will agree to disagree, but always we will unite to serve (E. Stanley Jones).*

John 18:1–11   DECEMBER 12

Shall I not drink the cup which the Father has given me? (v. 11)

John 18 describes the arrest and trial of Jesus. A careful study of the chapter will reveal characteristics of the death Jesus is about to experience.

In the passage of Scripture for today, we note that His death was a *voluntary death*. Jesus was God and therefore immortal. But He took upon Himself a human form and thus became mortal. He came to die; He knew He was going to die. Death was not forced upon Him; He accepted it freely. Even before His death was near, Jesus said plainly to the people, "I lay down my life for the sheep . . . No one takes it from me, but I lay it down of my own accord. I have power to lay it down, and I have power to take it again" (John 10:15, 18).

Now in the Garden of Gethsemane Jesus proved the truth of His words by His actions. The force which Judas procured to arrest Jesus is truly astonishing. He came with several "officers," that is, members of the private police force of the temple, and a "band" of Roman soldiers. The Greek word for band is *speira*, which suggests a minimum of 200 soldiers—a formidable force to send out against one unarmed, itinerant preacher!

Note the courage and authority of Jesus. He didn't try to hide or pretend. He boldly stepped forward and said to the mob, "Whom do you seek?" They answered Him, "Jesus of Nazareth." Then Jesus said, "I am he." And when Jesus spoke these words, the whole company of armed men "drew back and fell to the ground" under the sheer power of His personality. It shows that if Jesus had desired, He could have blasted His enemies with a single word. But Jesus never used for Himself the power that was His. He had come to die; He was ready to die. He voluntarily laid down His life for the sins of the world. His death was not murder; it was a sacrifice.

Thought for the day: *Jesus died, not as a martyr, but as the Savior.*

John 18:12–14, 19–24   DECEMBER 13

If I have spoken rightly, why do you strike me?
(v. 23)

In yesterday's meditation we noted that Jesus' death was *voluntary*. His life was not taken from Him; He laid it down of His own accord. Today we observe that He suffered an *unjust* death. His trial broke all the rules of justice.

According to Jewish law, a prisoner must not be asked any questions that might incriminate him. Annas violated this principle when he questioned Jesus. Our Lord reminded him of this fact when he said to Annas, "Why do you ask me? Ask those who have heard my teaching." In other words, "Gather your witnesses and examine the evidence." When Jesus said this, one of the temple officers slapped Him in the face. The fact is that Jesus was condemned before He was even tried. The chief priests had labeled Him as an "evildoer" and judged

Him worthy of death, without even calling any witnesses. Jesus never had any hope of justice.

Many testified to the innocence of Jesus. Pilate, who tried Him, testified, "I did not find this man guilty of any of [the] charges" (Luke 23:14). Pilate's wife sent word to him in the midst of the trial, saying, "Have nothing to do with that righteous man" (Matt. 27:19). Judas, who betrayed Jesus, admitted publicly, "I have sinned in betraying innocent blood" (Matt. 27:4). One of the thieves crucified with Him, gave witness, "This man has done nothing wrong" (Luke 23:41). The Roman solider who actually carried out the crucifixion, exclaimed, "Certainly this man was innocent" (Luke 23:47).

But herein lies the efficacy of Christ's death on the cross. The Just died for the unjust; the Innocent, for the guilty; the Sinless, for the sinful. One criminal cannot offer to bear the penalty of another criminal. A person condemned to die cannot offer to take the place of another person on death row. Only when an innocent person offers to take the place of a guilty person, does the offer have any meaning whatsoever. Likewise, only Christ, the sinless and innocent Son of God, could die on the cross for our sins.

Thought for the day: *Christ alone could take my place.*

John 18:15–18, 25–27   DECEMBER 14

Are not you also one of his disciples? He denied it and said, "I am not" (v. 25).

Jesus died a *voluntary* death; He suffered an *unjust* death. His was also a *lonely* death.

Loneliness is one of the most difficult emotions for human beings to deal with. People are by nature social beings. They enjoy the company of others; they need the support of others. For a person to be shut up in solitary confinement, or separated from loved ones and friends is truly a devastating experience.

To be all alone is especially difficult when a person is going through suffering or hard times. When loving, compassionate people are near, the pains of life are much easier to face. But when someone has to face tragedy and trials alone, the burden is intensified.

Jesus had to face death, an excruciating and shameful death, all alone. Most of His disciples fled the scene and went into hiding. John, it seems, did stay close by to the end, but was silent and powerless to help in any way. Peter, who had boasted of his great loyalty, who even dared to draw his sword in defense of his Master, also dared to enter the court of the high priest when Jesus was arrested. But this same Peter, in the end, denied his Lord three times before a lowly maid and a couple of servants. He was not even willing to admit that he knew the Man. This left Jesus all alone. The height of Jesus' loneliness came when He became sin for us on the cross. For a moment in time the Father had to turn His back on His Son, and Jesus was alone in the universe. At that moment Jesus experienced and knew what it meant for a sinner to be separated from God. He cried out in anguish, "My God, my God, why have you forsaken me?" It was only a brief span of time, but the intensity of the experience was more than you or I will ever be able to understand. The only fact we can understand, however, is that Jesus was taking our place and suffering for our sin.

Thought for the day: *I am never alone in the universe as long as I am at home with Christ.*

John 18:28–38   DECEMBER 15

Are you the King of the Jews? (v. 33)

Christ suffered a *voluntary* death, an *unjust* death, a *lonely* death. It was also a *majestic* death. Throughout the entire trial and crucifixion, amidst all the injustice, mockery, and shame, Jesus conducted Himself like a king. He was in command of the situation from beginning to end.

Look again at the scene in Gethsemane. A company of soldiers and policemen came with swords and spears to arrest Jesus as if he were a notorious criminal. Jesus was unarmed but unafraid. He didn't try to hide or escape. He could have called on a host of angels to defend Him, but He refused to do so. Instead He gave Himself up freely to His accusers.

Look again at the scene in the court of the high priest. What a contrast between the spotless, innocent Christ and the cunning, evil-minded Annas. Jesus stands tall and regal, like the Lion of Judah He was, while the high priest appears like a sly fox or jackal. The righteousness of Christ towers over the injustice of Annas.

Then, watch our Lord as He stands before Pilate. Pilate, representative of the greatest empire on earth at that time, recognizes that the Man who stands before Him is no ordinary person. He says to Jesus, "Are you the King of the Jews?" Jesus answers, "My kingdom is not of this world. If it were, my subjects would fight for me and deliver me from my accusers." Here the Lord of heaven stands before the earthly governor of Palestine. The Roman Empire collapsed a long time ago, but the kingdom of Christ will last forever.

When Jesus was born in Bethlehem, wise men from the East came, asking, "Where is he who is born king of the Jews?" And when they found Him, they worshiped Him. When Christ was crucified, a plaque nailed at the top of the cross read, "Jesus of Nazareth, the King of the Jews." Jesus was born a King, lived as a King, and died as a King.

Thought for the day: *The cross is not the picture of a criminal in trouble, but the portrait of a King in triumph.*

John 18:38b–40   **DECEMBER 16**

They cried out again, "Not this man, but Barabbas!" (v. 40)

Jesus died a *voluntary, unjust, lonely* and *majestic* death. Finally, His was a *vicarious* death. He died for others.

The custom in Palestine, as a gesture of good will, was for the Roman governor to release one Jewish criminal at the feast of the Passover. At that particular time, a man by the name of Barabbas was in prison. He was no ordinary prisoner but a robber, murderer, and leader of an insurrection. Pilate, finding no fault in Jesus and anxious to acquit Him, asked the mob that was storming his court, "Will you have me release for you the King of the Jews?" But to Pilate's surprise the crowd shouted, "Not this man, but Barabbas!"

Jesus, therefore, was crucified in place of Barabbas. Barabbas should have been one of three criminals who were crucified that day, but, instead, he was released and permitted to live. Possibly Barabbas, primarily out of curiosity, followed Jesus as He carried His cross to Golgotha and watched Him as He died in agony between two thieves. He probably said to himself, "I should have been carrying that cross. I should have been hanging there. He saved my life." Thus, the innocent, holy Son of God took the place of a murderer and robber.

The truth of the matter is, however, that Barabbas was only a symbol of every human being who has lived upon the face of the earth. The black spiritual asks, "Were you there when they crucified my Lord?" The answer is, "Yes, *I* was there, *you* were there, *everyone* was there." For Christ died, not only for Barabbas, but for every man, woman, boy and girl. He died for all.

We must always remember that Jesus did not die a natural death from sickness or old age, nor did He die prematurely as a martyr for a righteous cause. He died voluntarily for a purpose. "He died for our sins." That is the essence of the Gospel.

Thought for the day: *Jesus died for me. Now I shall live for Him.*

Shall I crucify your King? ... We have no king but Caesar (v. 15).

The trial of Jesus was a battle between the Roman governor, Pilate, and the chief priests of the Jews. Convinced that Jesus was innocent, Pilate tried his best to release Him, but the chief priests insisted that He was an "evil-doer." Pilate then tried to shift responsibility to the priests, so he said, "Take him yourselves and judge him by your law." But they refused, because they had decided on the death penalty for Jesus, and only the Roman governor had authority to sentence a man to die.

Pilate sought to escape responsibility once again and to engineer the release of Jesus by appealing to the custom whereby a prisoner was freed at Passover time. But to his amazement the chief priests shouted, "Not this man, but release Barabbas!" They were so inflamed with hatred for Jesus that they chose a robber and a murderer over the innocent, compassionate Jesus.

Pilate then turned to compromise as a way out of his entanglement. He ordered his soldiers brutally to scourge and humiliate Jesus, hoping that this would satisfy the hostility of His enemies. He sought to avoid the verdict of the cross by giving the verdict of scourging. But the chief priests cried out, "Crucify him, crucify him!" They would settle for nothing less than death.

Pilate then made the final appeal. He placed Jesus in the center of the court and said, "Here is your King. Shall I crucify your King?" He was appealing to the patriotism and emotions of the Jewish people. But the chief priests answered, "We have no king but Caesar." It was a blatant lie, for they hated Caesar with their whole being. But they hated Jesus even more, and were willing to choose the rule of Rome over the kingdom of God. Pilate finally made his decision and handed Jesus over to them to be crucified.

No person on earth can sidestep the responsibility of making a decision about Christ. There are only two possibilities: either crucify Him afresh or make Him Lord.

Thought for the day: *What shall I do with Jesus who is called Christ? (Matt. 27:22).*

John 19:17–22   **DECEMBER 18**

*There they crucified him, and with him two others,
one on either side, and Jesus between them (v. 18).*

What does the cross of Jesus Christ stand for? What does it reveal? First, the cross reveals *the awfulness of sin*. All around us, everyday, we find evidences of the tragedy of sin. Newspapers and newscasts are full of incidents of armed robbery, rape, gruesome murder, atrocities of terrorists, and so on. But if we really want to know the awfulness of sin, we should look at the cross. Dare anyone look at Christ hanging on the cross and then say that sin is a trifle? The cross shows us how terrible a thing sin is.

Again, the cross reveals to us *the unfathomable love of God*. If the cross shows how far sin will go in its attempts to destroy, it also shows us how far God's love will go in order to redeem. No price is so great and no suffering so severe that God would be unwilling to pay it or endure it in order to save us from our sins. His love is beyond all description.

> *Could we with ink the ocean fill,*
> *And were the skies of parchment made;*
> *Were ev'ry stalk on earth a quill,*
> *And every man a scribe by trade;*
> *To write the love of God above*
> *Would drain the ocean dry,*
> *Nor could the scroll contain the whole*
> *Though stretched from sky to sky.*
>
> F.M. Lehman

Finally, the cross stands for *the unlimited power of God*. Looking at the cross, the proud become humble, the weak become strong, the impure become pure, those in bondage are set free. Through the cross God is able to forgive all our sins, to cleanse us from all unrighteousness, and to deliver us from the evil one. God can save from the guttermost to the uttermost. He can take the devil's castaways and make monuments of grace out of them.

Thought for the day: *All my dross is buried beneath the cross.*

John 19:23–27 DECEMBER 19

Standing by the cross of Jesus were his mother, and his mother's sister, Mary the wife of Clopas, and Mary Magdalene (v. 25).

In yesterday's meditation we noted what the *cross stands for*. Today we observe what it means to *stand by the cross*.

By this time the disciples had fled the scene and were in hiding. Even Peter, who had followed Jesus as far as the court of the high priest, had disappeared. Only John, "the beloved disciple," was present at the place of the crucifixion. But standing at the foot of the cross were four remarkable women. One was Jesus' mother, Mary, who was a model of true piety, and motherhood. Her presence there was the most natural thing in the world for a mother. In the eyes of the law Jesus might be considered a criminal, but He was her son. Mary Magdalene, whom Jesus had delivered from the bondage of seven evil spirits, was also there. She could never forget what Jesus had done for her.

These women showed unusual courage when they stood by the cross of Jesus. To be an associate of a man whom the Jewish authorities considered a blasphemer and heretic, and whom the Roman government believed to be a criminal worthy of death on a cross, was a dangerous thing. But they were willing to take the risk. Their great love for Jesus gave them great courage to take their stand. "Perfect love casts out all fear" (1 John 4:18).

What does it mean for us to stand by the cross of our Lord? It means that we identify ourselves with Christ in His death, that we die to self, and accept the Father's will for our lives. It means that we are willing to take up our cross and follow our Lord. To stand by the cross signifies our willingness to bear the reproach and shame of the cross and courageously speak out for truth and right whatever the cost may be. We can take courage in the fact, however, that if we stand up for Christ, He will always stand up for us. He will never let us down.

Thought for the day: *If we take our stand for truth at the cross, we will not fall for anything else.*

John 19:28–30   **DECEMBER 20**

He said, "It is finished"; and he bowed his head and gave up his spirit (v. 30).

What was finished? Certainly it was the end of Christ's ministry. He would no more heal the sick, no longer teach and preach to the multitudes, tell no more parables, perform no more miracles. Certainly it was also the end of Christ's pain and suffering—no more abuse, no more shame, no more anguish.

But the words of Jesus meant far more than that. "It is finished" meant that the mission for which Christ had come to earth was now accomplished. God's plan of redemption was complete. All that was necessary for the salvation of the world had been provided by Christ on the cross. For those who are bound by the guilt and power of sin, nothing remains to be done but to accept Christ as the Lamb of God and believe in Him as the Savior of the world.

Jesus did not speak these words in weary defeat. This was

not the whimper of a dying man who had lost all hope. Notice that Jesus didn't say, "*I* am finished," but "*It* is finished." This was a shout of victory. All three of the other Gospel writers tell us that Christ "cried out with a loud voice" and then gave up His spirit.

During World War II, when the battle seemed to be turning against the Allied Forces in Europe, the indomitable Sir Winston Churchill kept hope alive in the hearts of the people by his famous V-sign (two fingers held up in the form of the letter V) and the slogan "V is for Victory." Then on V-Day, September 2, 1945, the news was shouted across the world, "The war is over. We have won the victory!"

The day of the crucifixion of our Lord was God's V-Day in history. On that day Jesus announced to the world: "It is finished. I have overcome the world. Redemption is complete." And the echo of that announcement has been reverberating through the corridors of time ever since.

Thought for the day: *Through His death on the cross Christ the victim became Christ the Victor.*

John 19:31–42   DECEMBER 21

One of the soldiers pierced his side with a spear, and at once there came out blood and water (v. 34).

Death by crucifixion was a lingering and excruciating death. A victim usually hung on his cross for days in the heat of the sun and cold of the night, tortured by thirst and by flies. Often men died raving mad on their crosses.

A grim method was sometimes used to hasten the death of the victims. This was crucifacture, breaking the legs below the knees with a mallet, which led to an asphyxiant death within minutes. That was done to the criminals who were crucified with Jesus, but mercifully Jesus was spared the agony. He was already dead. Instead, one of the soldiers thrust a spear into His side.

We need to make two important observations about the death of Jesus. First, it came swifter than usual for one nailed to a cross. The Gospel writer gives us the reason for this. John tells us that when Jesus realized "that all was now finished . . . he bowed his head and gave up his spirit" (vv. 28, 30). In other words, His life was not taken from Him, but He voluntarily laid it down when He knew that the plan of redemption was now complete and nothing was left undone. He chose the exact moment of His death.

Secondly, we note the fact that blood and water flowed out when a spear was thrust into Jesus' side. We cannot be sure at this point, but it is possible that Jesus literally died of a broken heart. The spiritual and emotional agony Jesus suffered was so terrible that His heart ruptured. When that happened, the blood of the heart mingled with fluid of the pericardium which surrounds the heart. The soldier's spear pierced the pericardium and mingled fluid and blood gushed forth.

But let us never forget the reason for all this. The prophet Isaiah tells us clearly "He was wounded for our transgressions, he was bruised for our iniquities . . . and with his stripes we are healed" (Isa. 53:5). Hallelujah!

Thought for the day: *Jesus died of a broken heart in order to give us a new heart.*

John 20:1–10   DECEMBER 22

Then the other disciple . . . also went in, and he saw and believed (v. 8).

In this passage we observe three facets of the resurrection of our Lord. Let us look at these briefly.

1. *The vanquished stone.* At the suggestion of Jewish authorities, Pilate commanded that the tomb of Christ be sealed with a huge stone and that a guard be posted to watch the tomb. But when Mary Magdalene came to the tomb early

on Sunday morning, she "saw that the stone had been taken away from the tomb" (v. 1). Matthew tells us that "an angel of the Lord descended from heaven and came and rolled back the stone, and *sat upon it*" (28:2). What a picture of triumph! The stone that sealed fast the tomb now became a throne for the angel from heaven.

2. *The vacant sepulchre.* When Peter and John entered the tomb, they found no body there, but only the linen cloths and napkin in which Jesus had been wrapped, folded neatly and lying in separate places (v. 7). Jesus was not there. He had risen. Thus, as Christians, we do not make a pilgrimage to Jerusalem and stand in respect at the tomb of Christ with doffed hats and folded hands. The glory of Christianity is that the tomb is empty.

3. *The victorious Savior.* By His resurrection, Jesus completely routed the forces of evil, dealt Satan a fatal blow, and robbed death of its sting. He now stands as the living, victorious Lord.

A new convert from Islam to Christianity in India was confronted by some of his Muslim friends. "Tell us, what is there in Christianity that we don't have in Islam? they asked. "Well, it's like this," replied the new Christian. "Suppose you are going down the road and suddenly the road forks and you don't know which way to go. And at the fork stand two men, one dead and one alive. Of which one would you ask directions? Mohammed lived and died and passed off the scene of human history, but Christ died and rose again. I choose to follow the living Christ."

Thought for the day: *The resurrection of Christ turned history into news.*

Jesus said to her, "Mary." She turned and said to him in Hebrew "Rabboni!" (which means Teacher) (v. 16).

Mary Magdalene came to the tomb early Sunday morning to weep over the death of Jesus. But she found the tomb empty, and suddenly came face to face with the risen Lord. She became a first-hand witness to the greatest event in all history—the resurrection of our Lord Jesus Christ.

Christ's resurrection is the Gibraltar of Christian evidences and the Waterloo of infidelity. For this reason Gulam Ahmed, the founder of the Ahmediyya sect of Islam, said to his disciples from his deathbed, "If you want to strike a deathblow to Christianity, strike directly at the Resurrection. Destroy the Christian's faith in the resurrection of Christ and he will have nothing left. Convince the Christian that Christ never rose from the dead, and the battle will be ours." The Gospel message either stands or falls with the Resurrection.

One man said to the other, "I'm going to start a new religion." His friend replied, "That's a good idea, but I can tell you the only way to start a new religion. Live a sinless life, die for humanity, and then rise from the dead."

The Resurrection is intrinsic to true religion. Humanity cries out for it, faith demands it.

The apostle Paul wrote in his letter to the Corinthian church that if there was no Resurrection, then we of all people are most miserable. If there was no Resurrection, our preaching is in vain. If there was no Resurrection, we are still in our sins and the grave is the end. Without the Resurrection we have no message, no foundation for faith, no salvation, no hope. But the moment we introduce the truth of the Resurrection, our message becomes a living force, our faith takes hold, salvation becomes a glorious possession, and our hope for the future becomes bright.

Thought for the day: *I know that Christ is alive because He has given me life.*

John 20:19–23

The doors being shut where the disciples were, for fear of the Jews, Jesus came and stood among them (v. 19).

What a difference the presence of Jesus made in this situation. Before He entered the room, the disciples were huddled together, trembling with fear. They were hiding from the Jewish leaders who had crucified Jesus. Then suddenly the risen Lord stepped into their midst, and the whole atmosphere changed.

The presence of Jesus brought *peace* to the disciples. Jesus said to them, "Peace be with you." The swift and tragic turn of events during the past few days—the sudden arrest in the garden, boisterous trial, and unjust crucifixion—had left the disciples stunned and fearful. Suddenly their hearts were at rest. It was like the calm after a great storm.

The presence of Jesus also brought *joy* to the disciples. John tells us that "the disciples were glad when they saw the Lord." The tragic end to their Master's life had overwhelmed them with crushing sorrow. Their Lord was now dead and buried. His life would be nothing more than the memory of a shattered dream. Then suddenly Jesus stood in their midst, alive and victorious. Their hearts were now filled with an indescribable joy.

Again, the presence of Jesus brought *purpose* into the lives of the disciples. He said to them, "As the Father has sent me, even so I send you." God had sent His Son into the world on a special mission—to provide salvation for the whole world. Now Jesus sends the disciples on an important mission—to proclaim to all people the news of this salvation. This gave them purpose and meaning in life. They were to be ambassadors for Christ.

Finally, the presence of Jesus bestowed *power* upon the disciples. Immediately after commissioning them, He said, "Receive the Holy Spirit." Here was the necessary spiritual equipment for the fulfillment of the commission—the fullness and power of the Holy Spirit. Without the Spirit the disciples were bound to fail; but empowered by the Spirit, nothing could stop them.

Thought for the day: *Christ's presence brings joy, peace, purpose, and power into our lives.*

John 20:24–29   **DECEMBER 25**

See my hands (v. 27).

Jesus invites us to look at His hands so that we may learn something about His character and His work. What kind of hands does Jesus have?

1. *Saving Hands.* "Jesus immediately *reached out his hand* and caught him" (Matt. 14:31). Peter tried to walk to Jesus on the sea, but he looked down and began to sink. He cried out, "Lord, save me," and the Master reached out His hand and rescued him. How many a soul, sinking in the sea of sin and despair, has cried out, "Lord save me," and the Savior has reached out in mercy and power and delivered that person from the depths? No human hands could do it, but His hands are all-sufficient.

2. *Cleansing Hands.* John the Baptist said about Jesus, "I baptize with water for repentance . . . he will baptize you with the Holy Spirit and with fire. *His winnowing fork is in his hand,* and he will clear his threshing floor and gather his wheat into the granary, but the chaff he will burn with unquenchable fire" (Matt. 3:11–12). Jesus not only rescues us from sin, but He also cleanses us from inward sin. Just as the eastern farmer sifts the grain with his winnowing fork to separate the grain from the chaff, so Christ, through the refining fire of the Holy Spirit, will burn up the chaff of our un-

403

Christlike attitudes and desires, and purify our hearts by faith. In place of pride there will be humility; in place of selfishness, kindness; in place of jealousy, thoughtfulness; in place of hatred, love.

3. *Protecting Hands.* Jesus said that He is the Good Shepherd and we are His sheep, and went on to say, "No one shall snatch them *out of my hand*" (John 10:28). What a comforting thought to realize that when we are in the hands of Jesus we are safe. The storms of life may come: temptation may surge like a flood; evil-minded men may seek to destroy; Satan may rush upon us like a roaring lion. But in the hands of Jesus we are safe! Here is the only true refuge in a day of strife and fear and insecurity. The hands of Jesus are able to rescue us from sin, cleanse us from sin, and protect us from the evil one.

Thought for the day: *Christ can defeat the devil with one hand.*

John 20:24–29

See my hands (v. 27).

We continue to look at the wonderful hands of Jesus. Yesterday we observed that He has saving hands, cleansing hands, and protecting hands. Today we see He has:

4. *Healing Hands.* "Moved with pity [Jesus] stretched out his hand and touched him . . . and he was made clean" (Mark 1:41, 42). How often does a statement similar to this appear in the Gospels! Jesus was moved with compassion, and He touched the leper, the blind, the lame, and all manner of sick people, and immediately they were healed. What hands of love! Willing to touch the filthy beggar and the repulsive leper. What hands of power! Bringing sight, strength, health and cleansing. And Jesus is still the same today. He is still the Great Physician. Many of us can testify to the healing touch of His hand upon our bodies.

5. *Wounded Hands.* "He showed them his hands and his side" (John 20:20). Look at the hands of Jesus on the cross. Hands that once rescued and set free are now bound fast with thongs. Hands that once brought comfort and health are now full of pain and suffering. Hands that once hammered nails into wood in the carpenter's shop are now fastened by nails into the wood of the cross. This was the awful price He paid for our redemption. *Our sins* bound His hands, *our self-will* drove the nails. But now in those pierced hands there is forgiveness, cleansing, and eternal life.

6. *Knocking Hands.* Jesus says, "Behold I stand at the door and knock" (Rev. 3:20). With His nail-scarred hand the Savior knocks upon the doors of our hearts and lives today. He knocks patiently in love; He calls softly in tenderness. If we open the door today, He will reach forth His hand to deliver, cleanse, heal, and protect.

Having looked at the hands of Jesus, what should we do? Exactly what Thomas did. He fell at the feet of Jesus and cried out, "My Lord and my God!" That confession changed his life and sent him forth as a missionary to India. If you and I look at the hands of Jesus and make the same confession, we will never be the same.

Thought for the day: *One look at His hands will change your heart.*

John 21:1–3 DECEMBER 27

I am going fishing . . . we will go with you (v. 3).

Jesus had already appeared to His disciples on two occasions following His resurrection. They knew by now that He was alive and victorious. However, some doubts still lingered in their minds concerning the future of their mission. Many questions were still unanswered. Why had their Master met with such a shameful and cruel death? Why did He not use His power to blast His enemies and save Himself? Why did he not restore the kingdom of Israel?

To Peter, at least, it seemed like everything was over. The memory of his denial and other failures only added to the despair of his shattered hopes. He could think of only one thing to do—go back to his former life and occupation. So he said to the six disciples who were with him, "I am going fishing." This was not a one-time fishing trip, but a return to the business of fishing. His decision influenced his colleagues so with one accord they all responded, "We will go with you." We find it difficult to understand how, after Jesus' personal resurrection appearances to them, these disciples could so quickly abandon the mission to which Christ had called them.

The third appearance of Jesus, which follows immediately in the narrative, coupled with the miraculous catch of fish, helped to reconfirm the disciples' mission to some extent. However, only the experience of the indwelling presence of the Holy Spirit in His fullness and power of the day of Pentecost put the final seal on their calling and commitment. During the interval between the Resurrection and Ascension, Jesus appeared to His disciples on and off for brief periods. Most of the time He was not with them. But the experience of Pentecost convinced them that, through the abiding presence of the Holy Spirit, Jesus was continually with them at all times to guide, comfort, and empower. His spiritual presence more than made up for the lack of His physical presence.

Thought for the day: *I have decided to follow Jesus: No turning back, no turning back.*

John 21:4–14 DECEMBER 28

Cast the net on the right side of the boat, and you will find some (v. 6).

Jesus was a master psychologist. He knew perfectly how

to use memory to prod the conscience and challenge the will. Here we have a good example of this.

Vascillating about his call, Peter decided he would go back to his original occupation. So he said to the other disciples who were with him, "I am going fishing." Immediately they responded, "We will go along with you." *But they fished all night and caught nothing.* Early in the morning Jesus appeared on the beach and called out to them, "Cast your net on the other side of the boat, and you will find some fish." At the moment they did not recognize that it was Jesus, but they followed the order. As a result their nets were filled with an abundance of large fish, 153 to be exact.

Immediately they remembered a similar incident that had taken place about three years previously. We read about it in Luke 5:1–11. Jesus met Simon Peter and a group of fishermen by the lake of Gennesaret, and He said to Simon, "Put out into the deep and let down your nets for a catch." Simon answered, "Master, *we toiled all night and took nothing!* [That sounds familiar.] But at your word I will let down the nets." When they did this, they caught so many fish their nets began to break. Then Jesus said to Simon and his two partners, James and John, "Do not be afraid; henceforth you will be catching men." That was the date of their call to be partners with Christ in His mission.

When the same miracle took place a second time, the disciples knew that the Lord was again in their midst. And they realized that He was reminding them of their original call and commitment to be His disciples. The Lord had not rescinded His call; why should they go back on it? They never again returned to their boats and fishing gear, but went on to become fishers of men and women for Christ's sake.

Thought for the day: *He who puts his hand to the plow and turns back is not fit for the kingdom of God.*

Simon, son of John, do you love me? (v. 16)

This is one of the most touching incidents in the fascinating life of Simon Peter. For three years he had been enrolled in the walking seminary of Jesus, and now his Master gave him the final examination. The test consisted of three identical questions: "Do you love me?" This was not an examination in rules and regulations but in relationships, for the Christian life is primarily a relationship between disciple and Lord. It was not a test in theology or doctrine but in character, of which one of the dominant characteristics is love.

The method of examination employed by Jesus is another classic example of the use of memory for redemptive purposes. When Peter denied His Lord on the night of Christ's arrest and trial, Peter was warming himself near a fire in the courtyard of the high priest. Three times he was asked, "Are you not one of his disciples?" And three times Peter replied, "I do not know him." So when the risen Lord met Peter on the beach that morning, he quietly built a charcoal fire to cook the fish, and in this setting He confronted Peter with His question. When, for the third time, Jesus asked him, "Do you love me?" Peter was grieved as the memory of his recent denial rushed to his mind. But that was all part of the redemptive process. Since Peter had denied his Lord three times, Jesus was now giving him an opportunity to affirm his love three times and thus wipe out the memory of his failure.

Each time Peter affirmed his love, Jesus responded with the admonition, "Feed my lambs" or "Tend my sheep." True love for Christ always involves responsibility, which, in turn, involves sacrifice. Love for God is not an emotion to enjoy; it is a motivating force that leads to action. Those who love Christ have a task to perform. Peter's ministry after Pentecost and final sacrifice in death (according to tradition he was crucified upside down) became the actual demonstration of his love for the risen Lord.

Today Christ asks each of us the same question: "Do you love me?" Are you and I able to pass the test?

Thought for the day: *Love is not just a feeling; it is an activating force.*

John 21:18–23

What is that to you? Follow me! (v. 22)

When Jesus asked Peter, "Do you love me?" Peter responded, "Lord, you know everything; you know that I love you." Jesus then went on to show Peter that love for his Lord involved responsibility, for the word *love* is not just a noun signifying emotion; it is primarily a verb calling for action. Love involves a task to be done. Peter's assignment was to feed the lambs, to tend the sheep. He was to be a shepherd of the flock. But love's responsibility goes further than that. It also involves a sacrifice, a price to be paid. So Jesus warned Peter of the death by which "he was to glorify God." Tradition tells us that Peter went to Rome to preach and there he was arrested and condemned to die on a cross. He requested his executioners to nail him to the cross head downward, for, he said, he was not worthy to die as his Lord had died.

Just as Jesus was making these things clear to Peter, Peter turned and saw John approaching. So he said to Jesus, "Lord, what about this man? What's going to happen to him?" To which Jesus replied, "If it is my will that he remain until I come, what is that to you? Follow me!" In other words, "Peter, that is no concern of yours. You just fulfill the responsibility that is yours, and be sure that you are faithful to me." Tradition tells us that John lived to be over ninety years of age, and died a natural death on the Isle of Patmos.

As disciples of Christ in this day, each of us has a task to perform and a sacrifice to make. The task is not the same for all of us. Some are called to be pastors or missionaries; others to be lawyers or teachers; some to be laborers or home-makers. But whatever our task may be, we should be witnesses for Christ and glorify Him in all we do. For each one of us also a price must be paid. A few may die as martyrs, some may have to relinquish riches and honor, but all will have to deny self, take up the cross, and follow Christ. All that He asks is that we be faithful in the place where He assigns us.

Thought for the day: *Christ does not call us to be successful, but to be faithful.*

John 20:30–31; 21:24–25   DECEMBER 31

These are written that you may believe that Jesus is the Christ, the Son of God, and that believing you may have life in his name (20:31).

Our spiritual trek through the four Gospels is now at an end. This has been an exciting adventure because we have meditated on the most exciting Person who ever lived. Christ has been the chief Actor, occupying center stage in this, the greatest drama in all human history. In His birth He became our Brother; in His life, our Teacher and Example; in His death, our Redeemer; in His resurrection, our Conqueror; and in His second coming He is our Hope. Now He is the all-sufficient One; He is all things to all people.

To the astronomer, He is the bright and morning Star.
To the architect, He is the chief Corner Stone.
To the builder, He is the sure Foundation.
To the baker, He is the living Bread.
To the banker, He is the hidden Treasure.
To the biologist, He is the Life.
To the carpenter, He is the Door.
To the doctor, He is the Great Physician.
To the florist, He is the Lily of the Valley, the Rose of Sharon.

To the geologist, He is the Rock of Ages.

To the jeweler, He is the Pearl of great price.

To the judge, He is the Judge of all nations.

To the king, He is the Lord of the universe.

To the lawyer, He is the Advocate.

To the newspaper reporter, He is the Good Tidings of great joy.

To the philosopher, He is the Truth.

To the philanthropist, He is the unspeakable Gift.

To the scientist, He is the Creator.

To the student, He is the great Teacher.

To the traveler, He is The Way.

To the sinner, He is the Lamb of God who takes away the sin of the world.

PRAISE BE TO GOD FOR THE GIFT OF HIS SON!